Life Is Short...
Compared to Eternity

Where Will You Spend Eternity?

The Choice Is Yours!

By Richard Trayler

Xulon PRESS

Dedication

This book is dedicated to Jesus Christ, the Savior and
Lord of my life,

and to

Bill and Mildred Trayler, whose unconditional and
sacrificial love for me
made it easy for me to understand that
I have a heavenly Father, whose unconditional and
sacrificial love for me
resulted in me being adopted into His family,
just as their love for me resulted in me being adopted
into the Trayler family.

Acknowledgment

I would like to publicly thank, by name, the many friends who provided encouragement and support to me while I wrote this book. However, I expect significant adverse reactions as a result of the information provided in Part 2: Competing Worldviews. Because I do not want to jeopardize them by naming them in this book, I have sincerely thanked them privately.

Table of Contents

Preface

Conversation About Islam and Christianity

It was about 12:30 a.m. when the driver and my Muslim friend and coworker (who will remain unnamed, for soon-to-be obvious reasons) picked me up at the hotel in Alexandria, Egypt. Although I was tired from conducting an international sales training meeting for the past couple of days and still feeling the effects of jet lag, I was excited about our planned activities for the coming day. My Muslim friend and I decided to take a day to go to Luxor and tour the Valley of the Kings. Since we had a very limited amount of time, we decided to leave Alexandria shortly after midnight, make the three-hour drive to Cairo, and catch the 5:00 a.m. flight from Cairo to Luxor.

As vice president of international operations and new market development for a medical equipment manufacturer, I have made many long international flights and endured frequent episodes of jet lag, so I have almost perfected the ability to nap anywhere and anytime. Consequently, I had planned to nap and get some needed rest during the drive from Alexandria to Cairo, especially since I had the back seat of the car to myself. However, after no more than 10 minutes into our journey, my plans changed quickly when my friend turned to me and said, "Rich, you know, there are many similarities between Islam and Christianity."

Although I trusted my friend and felt that we shared a respect for each other's religious beliefs, I did not know the driver, nor did I know if he understood English, nor did I know how much freedom I had to share my Christian beliefs with a Muslim, in Egypt, a Muslim country. Thoughts ran through my mind that if the driver was an "Islamic extremist," how valuable would I, as an executive in an American company, be to him and the radical Islamic extremist cause? Nevertheless, I have a great deal of confidence in the belief that no man has any power over me other than what the Lord allows. So, I decided that this time with my friend was a "divine appointment" and I should welcome this opportunity to have an open and honest discussion with my Muslim friend (and the driver) about Islam and Christianity.

Since I have a master's degree from Western Conservative Baptist Seminary, Phoenix (now Phoenix Seminary) and the topic of my master's thesis was how to share the gospel with people of different faiths, including Islam, I welcomed this opportunity to discuss and compare Islam and Christianity. So, I responded to my friend and said, "Really? For example...."

The first similarity that my friend pointed out is that both Islam and Christianity believe in Jesus. I agreed but pointed out that the similarity is very superficial. He asked what I meant by that and I told him that Islam teaches that Jesus was a prophet and Christianity teaches that Jesus was and claimed to be the Son of God, the Messiah. Additionally, Jesus claimed to be co-equal with God. (References to support these statements will be provided in Chapters 2 and 3). So I asked my friend if a prophet would lie and he said probably not.

I agreed and told him that C.S. Lewis, who was a prominent Christian apologist, pointed out that based upon Jesus' own statements, that one could only conclude that Jesus was either a liar, a lunatic, or Lord. He left no other options open. For example, if Jesus claimed to be God but knew that He was not, then He was a liar. If Jesus claimed to be God and was not but thought He was, then He was a deluded lunatic. However, if Jesus claimed to be God and was and is God, then He is who He claimed to be: Lord. [1] I told my Muslim friend that, after examining many facts, I believe that Jesus was and is Lord. In fact, I have accepted Jesus as the Savior and Lord of my life.

Another topic we discussed related to the implications of changing our religious beliefs. I told him that if I decided to abandon my Christian beliefs and convert to Islam that my Christian brothers and sisters would tell me that they thought I was making a terrible mistake, but that they would pray for me. Regardless, they would accept my decision.

When I asked my Muslim friend what would happen to him if he chose to abandon his Islamic faith and accept Christianity, he did not want to answer. However, with a little more prodding on my part, he confessed that if he abandoned his Islamic faith that his Muslim brothers were commanded to kill him. I pointed out that this represented a major difference between Islam and Christianity.

Our conversation continued throughout the early morning until we arrived at the Cairo airport. It was becoming very apparent to my Muslim friend that similarities between Islam and biblical Christianity are super-ficial, at best. Nevertheless, we respected each other and agreed that it would be okay to disagree agreeably.

Later that morning when we were having breakfast at a very nice res-taurant in Luxor, we resumed our conversation. I asked my Muslim friend if he believed that Julius Caesar lived in ancient Roman times and was the emperor of Rome. He said he did. I asked why he believed this—did he know Julius Caesar? Did he know anyone who knew him? If not, what was the foundation of his belief in Julius Caesar?

He replied that based upon reliable historical documents, he felt com-fortable believing that Julius Caesar lived and was the emperor of Rome. I agreed and confirmed that was the reason I, too, believed in Julius Caesar.

I then told my Muslim friend that if Jesus did not live, was not cruci-fied, and did not rise from the dead then my Christian faith was worthless (as I paraphrased First Corinthians 15:17, "and if Christ has not been raised, your faith is worthless; you are still in your sins"). However, I said, "If this is true, it is the foundation for my Christian beliefs."

I then asked my Muslim friend, "If Jesus lived, was crucified, and rose from the dead, what would this mean to you?"

After a long, careful consideration, he said, "Then everything I have been taught is a lie."

"Just as you can have faith and know that Julius Caesar lived and was the emperor of Rome, you can know that Jesus lived, was crucified, and rose from the dead," I said. "I can show you reliable historical documents that prove beyond a reasonable doubt that Jesus lived, was crucified, and rose from the dead. Do you want to read these?"

Again, after careful consideration, my Muslim friend said, "Yes, I do."

"Why would you want to read these?" I asked. "You have already told me that if you abandon your Islamic beliefs and convert to Christianity, you are, in effect, signing your death warrant. Why would you want to do that?"

My Muslim friend then said something very profound, "This life is short, compared to eternity. I want to get it right for eternity."

What about you, do you want to get it right for eternity?

World Cultures/Religions

For more than 12 years, I served initially as the chief operating officer and then as the vice president of international operations and new market development at CardioDynamics, a U.S. medical equipment manufacturer. During this time, I had the privilege of traveling to more than 40 countries, which gave me the opportunity to observe and experience many different cultures, religions, and worldviews. For example:

Russia and China—communism and government-enforced atheism (belief in no god);
India—Hinduism (belief in 33 million gods);
Western Europe—secular socialism;
Italy and Mexico—Roman Catholicism;
Indonesia and Egypt—Islam;
Israel—Judaism.

I was very interested to observe how the governmental systems, cultures, and religious beliefs of the people in these countries manifested themselves in a variety of areas, ranging from business practices, to morals and ethics, to the value of human life. In some countries, corruption is rampant and pervasive in business practices. In other countries, moral relativism rules business conduct (i.e., right or wrong is defined by the person or situation, rather than some absolute standard). The following two examples will illustrate these points:

I was working with one of my international distributors to close a large sale to a government in another country. As we were working through the details, I noticed that he was not particularly interested in planning for the installation of the equipment and the training of the hospital staff on the proper use of the equipment. When I asked about this, he said, "Rich, you do not understand. This is not about getting your equipment into the country. It is about getting the money out of their country." My business associate was correct, I did not understand that was his goal (but it was certainly not mine).

The second example occurred during a very enjoyable lunch. Another of my international distributors confided in me, "Rich, because you are my friend, I want to tell you something. You are a rich American and your company is a rich American company. Please do not take this personally, but I will lie to you, I will cheat, and I will steal to get what you and your company have—money." In spite of this warning, he and I remain good friends and actually had a very successful business relationship in which he exceeded the low professional standards he warned me about.

In other countries, human life has very little value because of poverty, overpopulation, or belief in reincarnation—"if he dies, so what, he is just a peasant" or "if he dies, he may come back as a better person in his next life." As I observed the effects of the various religions and worldviews, I was often reminded of the statement by an unknown author: "Man cannot rise above his view of God."

I believe that man is created in the image of God and that God has placed a "God-shaped vacuum" in each one of us. Over the centuries, man has tried to fill this vacuum with various governmental systems, cultures, man-made religions, and worldviews. However, these all fail because the only thing that will fill this vacuum is God Himself. As a Christian, it breaks my heart to know that I have seen thousands of people who will live and die without knowing the good news of Jesus Christ.

God is not interested in man-made religions or superstitions. Religions are man's attempt to reach God and superstitions are man's irrational beliefs in magic or the supernatural and both of these fail to reach or please God. He is interested in a personal, intimate relationship with you and every other person. The good news is that Jesus Christ provides the way for each of us to have a personal, intimate relationship with God.

When I accepted the position at CardioDynamics, my professional goal was to see if I could positively influence the company by incorporating biblical principles. I realized that in the U.S. business environment, particularly in a publicly traded company, there were very strict limitations on what I, as an executive and officer of the company, could say in regards to my Christian beliefs. Consequently, I decided that my ability to positively affect the company with biblical principles would have to come from my actions, rather than my words.

The two primary biblical principles that I chose to focus on were:

"Treat others the same way you want them to treat you." Luke 6:31

"Whatever you do, do your work heartily, as for the Lord rather than for men." Colossians 3:23

These verses enabled me to strive for excellence in my business activities, but also to serve as an ambassador for Jesus. As I conducted myself in the corporate office and traveled in other countries, the positive impact of these Bible verses on me and the people I worked with was very apparent. For example, the person who was the primary decision-maker regarding some of CardioDynamics' products and services in a pharmaceutical clinical trial accompanied me during the installation of the equipment at a clinical site. One morning as we were going to the hospital to complete the training sessions, he said something to the effect of, "Rich, I have been watching you for the past two days and I am amazed at how you never miss an opportunity to compliment the people. These people are drawn to you like a magnet. Why is that?"

I thanked him for the wonderful compliment and replied that it was easy for me to treat them so positively because I recognized the value and worth of each person. In fact, I was sure that I had a higher view of their worth than most or all of them had of themselves because I knew that the Savior of my life, Jesus Christ, loved them enough to die for them. Consequently, they have infinite value and I recognized that and wanted to communicate it to them through my interaction with them.

My business associate wanted to know more. Do you?

Guiding Principles for This Book

Why should I write this book, since there are many people much more qualified than I am?

I have had a very successful career in medical equipment sales, management, and business development. However, some would say that since I am not an engineer and do not know how the electronics of the medical equipment products really work that I would not be qualified to sell them. Yet I have been blessed with a very good analytical mind and have a strong academic and clinical background. Consequently, I have been able to understand and effectively communicate the features of the products, how they would benefit the prospect, and how the prospect can acquire the products and begin using them.

So, it seems to me that with the Lord's guidance, I will be able to effectively communicate the features and benefits of biblical Christianity and how you may acquire these and enjoy a personal relationship, now and forever, with someone who loved you enough to give His life for you. With this said, however, let me hasten to say that it is not my job to convince you to accept Jesus as your Savior, that is God's job. (See John 3:8;

6:44; 15:26; 16:8, 14; Acts 5:32; 1 Cor. 12:3; and 1 John 4:2.) My job is to share with you what I know and what I believe to be true.

So, just as I asked my Muslim friend, I'll ask you, "If Jesus lived, was crucified, and rose from the dead, what would this mean to you?"

The purpose of this book is to provide you with objective information that is worthy of your consideration so that you can make an informed decision about Jesus and His claims. My hope and prayer is that the information in this book will help you to decide, as I have done, to place your faith and eternal destiny in the gospel of Jesus Christ. Remember, when it comes to your eternal destiny, not making a decision about Jesus and His claims is the same as making a "no" decision. If you are already a believer, then my prayer is that the information in this book will strengthen your faith so that you know your faith in Jesus is based upon solid facts and that this will embolden you to share your faith in Jesus with others.

Before proceeding with the book, perhaps a word of warning is appropriate. As those who know me will readily affirm, I am not concerned about "political correctness." From my perspective, political correctness is an attempt not to offend anyone, particularly those in power. In America today, political correctness is typically defined by liberals, elitists, and progressives, or secular progressives, as Bill O'Reilly refers to them in his book, *Culture Warrior*[2], or as Newt Gingrich has recently named them, "secular socialists"[3]. I believe that rather than refer to these people as "progressives" or "secular progressives," that "regressives" or "secular regressives" would be a more accurate term, since I believe they are heading in the wrong direction, which has been shown in history to lead to failure. However, in Chapter 6, I'll use Mr. Gingrich's term of "secular socialists."

Nevertheless, I have no desire to try to please these people, because to me, you and your eternal destiny are too important to dilute the truth in hopes of not offending them or anyone else. You deserve truth and I will do my best to share with you what I know to be true and what I believe to be true so that you, too, can get it right for eternity.

There is one other point I would like to make. There will be a lot of biblical quotations in this book. The reason for this is very simple: you deserve to know what God says, which is infinitely more important than what I have to say. His words, as contained in the Bible, are very special and powerful. For example, Hebrews 4:12 tells us:

> "For the word of God is living and active and sharper than any two-edged sword, and piercing as far as the division of

soul and spirit, of both joints and marrow, and able to judge the thoughts and intentions of the heart."

Additionally, Isaiah confirmed the special nature of God's Word by stating:

"So will My word be which goes forth from My mouth; It will not return to Me empty, without accomplishing what I desire, and without succeeding in the matter for which I sent it." Isaiah 55:11

References:

1. Lewis, C.S. *Mere Christianity*. London, UK: Collins, 1952, p. 54-56.
2. O'Reilly, Bill. *Culture Warrior*. New York, NY: Broadway Books, 2006, p. 15.
3. Gingrich, Newt. *To Save America: A Vision to Save Our Country from Obama's Secular Socialist Machine.* Washington, D.C.: Regnery Publishing, Inc., 2010, p. 3.

PART 1

THE FOUNDATIONS
OF BIBLICAL CHRISTIANITY

The gospel of Jesus Christ is the primary foundation of biblical Christianity. In order to fully understand the gospel, you need to know about the Bible, God, and Jesus. Chapter 1 of this book provides information about the gospel of Jesus Christ, but more importantly, it clearly shows that the gospel applies to *you*. It is God's "love letter" to *you*!

How can you know that this love letter to you is real? How can you know that the God of the Bible exists and that God is who He claims to be? These questions are answered in Chapter 2: "The Bible: Is It True?"

The gospel is about one man—Jesus Christ—and what He did for you, me, and the rest of mankind. Jesus claimed to be God. Was He? Who do you say that Jesus is? This is the focus of Chapter 3.

God has some exciting things planned for *you*! So, let's explore the foundations of biblical Christianity and see how they can benefit you.

Chapter 1

The Gospel: What Does It Mean to You?

This thing we call "life" is not the final event. It is, rather, the *preliminary* event that enables us to get ready for the *final* event—eternal life. God has provided the "rules of the game" for the "game of life." The good news is that God's rules indicate that each person gets to choose where he or she will live for eternity. There are two options: heaven or hell. At the end of your life, God honors the choice you have made regarding where you will spend eternity, whether in heaven in fellowship with God, or in hell in separation from God.

Most of us want to win when we play a game. Knowing the rules increases the possibility of winning. The good news about the game of life is that God has provided the rules of the game in the Bible. Even better news is that He wants us to win. How do we know? Because God told us just that in John 3:16 when Jesus said,

> "For God so loved the world, that He gave His only begotten Son, that whoever believes in Him shall not perish, but have eternal life." John 3:16

Is this the first time you have read this Bible verse? Whether it is the first or hundredth time you have read it, take some time to carefully consider and ask yourself, "What does this mean to *me*?"

Your first thoughts may be, "I am not convinced that there is a God. I do not know if the Bible is even relevant to me." If so, that is understandable. The next chapter addresses these topics. So, for now, just assume that there is a God and He guided the writers of the Bible to include the right rules of the game so that you could win the game of life.

With this temporary assumption in mind, this might lead to questions like: Who is the God of the Bible? Why would He love the world? What does it mean that He gave His only Son? What is eternal life and where will it be?

Before we begin considering answers to these and other questions, I will define some very important words.

Definition of Terms

Gospel: This word is used to summarize God's plan for salvation.

> "For I am not ashamed of the gospel, for it is the power of God for salvation to everyone who believes, to the Jew first and also to the Greek." Romans 1:16

According to this verse, "the gospel" is an extremely important part of the rules of the game of life. Therefore, it is important to understand exactly what is meant by the term "the gospel." Fortunately, the Bible provides a clear definition:

> "For I delivered to you as of first importance what I also received, that Christ died for our sins according to the Scriptures, and that He was buried, and that He was raised on the third day according to the Scriptures," 1 Corinthians 15:3-4.

The gospel, then, is that Jesus Christ lived, died to pay the penalty of our sins, and rose from the dead—historical events that were all predicted (i.e., prophesied) in the Bible hundreds of years before Jesus' birth. Let's take a moment to consider some of the specifics of the gospel as defined in this passage from First Corinthians.

Christ: In his *Systematic Theology: An Introduction to Bible Doctrine*, theologian Wayne Grudem says this about Jesus: "Jesus Christ was fully God and fully man in one person, and will be so forever." [1] Chapter 3 provides additional information about Jesus and why it was necessary that he live, die, and rise from the dead.

Sin: Grudem defines sin as *"any failure to conform to the moral law of God in act, attitude, or nature."* He also states, "Sin is defined in relation to God and his moral law. Sin includes not only individual acts such as stealing or lying or committing murder, but also attitudes that are contrary to the attitudes God requires of us." [2]

The Bible clearly teaches that each one of us has sinned:

> "for all have sinned and fall short of the glory of God," Romans 3:23.

Scriptures: This term refers to the Bible, which consists of 66 books, of which 39 are in the Old Testament and 27 are in the New Testament. The books of the Old Testament were written before the birth of Jesus and the books of the New Testament were written after the death of Jesus. All 66 books of the Bible were written by men inspired (guided) by God.

> "All Scripture is inspired by God and profitable for teaching, for reproof, for correction, for training in righteousness; so that the man of God may be adequate, equipped for every good work." 2 Timothy 3:16

In other words, the Bible provides God's "rules of the game of life."

Faith: The words *faith* and *belief* are often used interchangeably. Faith that leads to salvation (eternal life in heaven) has been defined as "a reliance on the truth of the Gospel as revealed in the Word of God." [3] This kind of faith has three components: intellectual, emotional, and volitional. *Intellectual* faith is the acknowledgment of the historical truth of the gospel. *Emotional* faith acknowledges that believing in the gospel would provide positive personal benefits. Finally, *volitional* faith is the willingness to personally rely on and accept the benefits of the gospel.

To illustrate how these three components of faith are sometimes required to help us achieve a goal, let's say that you need to fly from Phoenix, Arizona to Dallas, Texas. If you have *intellectual* faith, you believe that planes can fly, that you could be a passenger on a plane, and that there are flights from Phoenix to Dallas. However, just having this intellectual faith will not get you from Phoenix to Dallas. So, intellectual faith by itself is not enough.

Let's add *emotional* faith to the illustration. If you have emotional faith, you know that it would be much faster and easier to fly, rather than to drive, take a bus, or walk. But emotional faith still doesn't transport you from Phoenix to Dallas. What's missing? *Volitional* faith.

Volitional faith enables you to personally commit to flying from Phoenix to Dallas by buying a ticket and getting on a flight bound from Phoenix to Dallas. It is only by *combining* intellectual, emotional, and volitional faith that you have taken the necessary steps that will result in you achieving the goal, which is to be transported from Phoenix to Dallas on an airplane. With these three different kinds of faith in mind, let's consider a summary of God's rules of the game of life, as they relate to eternity.

Rules of the Game

The majority of my professional career focused on medical equipment sales. As such, my responsibilities included identifying prospective customers for my medical equipment, determining their wants and needs, deciding which of my products would best meet or exceed their wants and/or needs, presenting the relevant features and benefits of my products, and then closing the sale, i.e., helping customers take the necessary steps to obtain ownership of the product. Over the years, I have noticed that many salespeople think that when they have closed the sale, that their job is finished. I have a different perspective: the sale is only the beginning of a long-term, mutually beneficial relationship.

When the sale is closed, I have the privilege of conducting the training to ensure that my customer fully understands how to use the product effectively so that they enjoy the benefits that my product provides. Although I am good at teaching my customers how to use the equipment they buy from me, I still refer them to the operator's manual. Why? Because I know the manual contains additional information provided by the manufacturer that I might not cover during training. Interestingly, the vast majority of my customers do not take time to read the operator's manual, even though they have invested thousands of dollars to buy the medical equipment.

Just as medical equipment manufacturers provide operator's and service manuals, so has the "manufacturer" of the human race provided a manual. God is the "manufacturer" and He has provided the Bible. Unfortunately, most people don't take the time to read God's operator's and service manual. If they did, they would realize that it provides guiding principles that help us to not only live life to the fullest, but also how to repair "broken" lives. The New Testament is particularly helpful in these areas.

Furthermore, the Bible teaches us how we can have a personal and intimate relationship with God, how to relate to family members and other people, and how to conduct ourselves in business. Jesus summarized all the guidelines very well when asked which of God's laws was the most important. This is what He said:

> "'YOU SHALL LOVE THE LORD YOUR GOD WITH ALL YOUR HEART, AND WITH ALL YOUR SOUL, AND WITH ALL YOUR MIND.'" This is the great and foremost commandment. The second is like it, 'YOU SHALL LOVE YOUR NEIGHBOR AS YOURSELF.' Matthew 22:37-39

Take time to reflect on Jesus' words. Wouldn't it be a wonderful world if everyone followed these two rules? People would be more focused on pleasing God than themselves. They would trust one another because, they know that everyone loves and respects one another. You might say that this would be heaven on earth! However, as you know, people don't follow these two rules. The result? We don't have heaven on earth.

The purpose of this book is to share the information you need to win life's ultimate prize—eternal life in heaven. So, let's consult God's operator's manual, the Bible, to learn God's plan for your salvation.

The Bible begins with the words,

> "In the beginning God created the heavens and the earth." Genesis 1:1

As you consider the earth, the sun, the moon, the stars, and the universe, do you think they came into existence by random chance? Do you see logic and order in things such as gravity, the rotation of the moon around the earth, and the earth around the sun? Doesn't this logic and order suggest an intelligent design? The Bible says that God created everything in the universe. In fact, His fingerprints are visible to each of us:

> "For since the creation of the world His invisible attributes, His eternal power and divine nature, have been clearly seen,

being understood through what has been made, so that they are without excuse." Romans 1:20

Knowledge of God through the creation is known as the *general revelation* of God. In other words, God reveals Himself through the vastness of the universe and through its logic and order. But God didn't stop the revelation of Himself with *general* revelation. He has also provided *special revelation* in the Bible so that we could know even more about Him and His plans for us.

1. "God created man in His own image, in the image of God He created him; male and female He created them." Genesis 1:27

God created humans in His image. This means that we are blessed with intellect, emotion, and volition. We have the ability to think, reason, and know. We have feelings and can express them. We have the ability to make decisions and act upon them. Furthermore, God has granted us the freedom to exercise our intellect, emotion, and volition in any way we choose.

Take some time to consider the implications of this compared to what you may have been taught about evolution. Are you the product of mindless chance? Did you evolve from lower forms of life? Is there no purpose to life? No, No, and No! God created you, and you are very special, and God has specific plans for you. As you consider this, you may begin to understand why David, a king of ancient Israel, could write:

> "For You formed my inward parts; You wove me in my mother's womb. I will give thanks to You, for I am fearfully and wonderfully made; Wonderful are Your works, and My soul knows it very well.... Your eyes have seen my unformed substance; And in Your book were all written the days that were ordained for me, when as yet there was not one of them." Psalm 139:13-14, 16

God created us, He knows us, and wants to have a personal relationship with each of us. However, there is a problem—He is holy and we are not, and He cannot have a relationship with an unholy person. Because He created the universe and everything in it, He has the right and authority to establish the rules of the game of life in any way He desires.

Fortunately for us, His rules provide a way that we can have a relationship with Him—but the choice is yours and mine.

2. "for all have sinned and fall short of the glory of God." Romans 3:23

As indicated above, God gave us freedom to utilize our intellect, emotion, and volition in any way that we choose. Unfortunately, as recorded in Genesis chapter 3, mankind chose to disobey God and this is sin. Even more unfortunate, each of us inherited this sinful nature and all of us have committed many sins (refer to definition of sin above). In other words, you and I are sinners and our sins separate us from God. Furthermore, no amount of good works or religious activities on our part can bridge the gap between us and God.

> "For all us have become like one who is unclean, and all our righteous deeds are like a filthy garment; and all of us wither like a leaf, and our iniquities, like the wind, take us away." Isaiah 64:6

3. "For the wages of sin is death, but the free gift of God is eternal life in Christ Jesus our Lord." Romans 6:23

Because of our sins, we deserve death (eternal separation from God). In spite of our sins, God still loves us and desires to have an intimate relationship with each one of us.

4. "But God demonstrates His own love toward us, in that while we were yet sinners, Christ died for us." Romans 5:8

God is holy and righteous, and consequently, He must judge and punish sins. In the Old Testament, in order to demonstrate the seriousness of sin, God instituted a sacrificial system that required animals to be sacrificed and the blood of the sacrificed animal was used in a ritual to symbolize payment for the penalty of the people's sins (see Leviticus 16:3-28 for details of the sacrificial system.) However, over time, this system became a routine ritual and the people became insensitive to the seriousness of sin.

Because of His love for us and the necessity of God to judge and punish sin, He set forth a New Covenant (explained in the New Testament) with mankind. He sent His Son, Jesus, to live on this earth as a man. Jesus lived a perfect and sinless life and willingly sacrificed His life as a "blood offering" to pay the penalty of our sins. In other words, God has judged our sins, Jesus paid the penalty of our sins with His death, and we now have the opportunity to enter into a personal, intimate relationship with God.

> "For God so loved the world, that He gave His only begotten Son, that whoever believes in Him shall not perish, but have eternal life." John 3:16

God loves you enough to sacrifice His Son—Jesus—so that He, as a holy and righteous God, could have a personal, intimate relationship with you! What does that say about your worth? How does that affect your opinion of yourself and your self-esteem? What is your worth? From God's perspective, you are worth the life of His Son, which means you are incredibly valuable to God!

5. Jesus said to him, "I am the way, and the truth, and the life; no one comes to the Father but through Me." John 14:6

This is a very bold statement. Just in case you think Jesus may have misspoken, consider the following statements by Jesus:

> "Truly, truly, I say to you, he who hears My word, and believes Him who sent Me, has eternal life, and does not come into judgment, but has passed out of death into life." John 5:24

> "For this is the will of My Father, that everyone who beholds the Son and believes in Him will have eternal life, and I Myself will raise him up on the last day." John 6:40

> "Jesus said to her, "I am the resurrection and the life; he who believes in Me will live even if he dies." John 11:25

There can be no misinterpretation or misunderstanding of Jesus' statements. He provides the only way to obtain eternal life.

Jesus' claim was reinforced by Peter, one of Jesus' disciples. After Peter witnessed the crucifixion and death of Jesus and then saw the resurrected Jesus, he stated:

> "And there is salvation in no one else; for there is no other name under heaven that has been given among men by which we must be saved." Acts 4:12

Peter's statement is even more remarkable when you consider the following facts:

(a) Prior to Jesus' crucifixion, Jesus went through a series of both Jewish and Roman trials. During one of the trials, Peter was accused of being a disciple of Jesus, but Peter denied even knowing Jesus not once, not twice, but three times.

(b) However, following Jesus' resurrection, Peter's life and commitment to Jesus was so complete that he died a martyr's death because he would not recant or deny the fact that Jesus rose from the dead. Peter realized that Jesus' resurrection confirmed His claim to be the promised Messiah.

Similarly, the apostle Paul, who persecuted Jesus' followers prior to seeing the resurrected Jesus, subsequently made the statements that are listed below in rules 6-8. Paul also willingly died a martyr's death because of his faith in Jesus.

The following two chapters provide evidence that you can evaluate to see if you, as Peter, Paul, and millions of other people, have concluded that belief in Jesus is the only way to obtain eternal life.

6. "For I am not ashamed of the gospel, for it is the power of God for salvation to everyone who believes, to the Jew first and also to the Greek." Romans 1:16

The gospel or "good news" about Jesus is that everyone who places their faith in Jesus will spend eternity in heaven. No more and no less is required to obtain salvation.

You may wonder about the phrase, "to the Jew first and also to the Greek." Jesus was a Jew and fulfilled the messianic prophecies related to the role of Savior that God had promised to the Jewish people. It is important to note that the prophecies about the Messiah indicated that

He would serve as Savior, Priest, and Lord, and rule forever. [4,5] The Jewish people expected all three roles to be fulfilled simultaneously by a political figure, who would return them to the position of political power that they had enjoyed during previous times, e.g., during the rule of kings David and Solomon. (For details about these kingdoms, see the books in the Old Testament of 2 Samuel, 1 Kings, 1 Chronicles 10-30, and 2 Chronicles 1-9). However, these messianic prophecies did not indicate that all three roles would be fulfilled simultaneously. In fact, God's plan was that the Messiah, Jesus, would:

(a) first come as Savior (which He did almost 2,000 years ago, see John 3:16);
(b) then after His death and resurrection Jesus would serve as a 'priest' for believers (which He is currently doing, see 1 John 2:1-2), and finally,
(c) Jesus would return to the earth as Lord (which He will do during His second coming, see Revelation 19:11-20:15).

The good news of Jesus Christ as Savior was first presented to the Jews; however, because they rejected Him, the gospel now applies to all people (Jews and Gentiles).

7. "For I delivered to you as of first importance what I also received, that Christ died for our sins according to the Scriptures, and that He was buried, and that He was raised on the third day according to the Scriptures." 1 Corinthians 15:3-4

This is "the gospel." Thousands of years before Jesus was born, God had told people that the Savior must die and would be raised from the dead. Additionally, Jesus predicted His death and resurrection. Jesus fulfilled these prophecies and was (and is) the promised Messiah.

Chapter 3 will provide more information about Jesus, His death, and resurrection.

8. "For by grace you have been saved through faith; and that not of yourselves, it is the gift of God; not as a result of works, so that no one may boast." Ephesians 2:8-9

What is required for you to receive the gift of eternal life? That you place your faith (intellectual, emotional, and volitional faith) in the fact that Jesus lived, died, and was raised from the dead, according to the Scriptures. No more and no less is required.*

[*Note: Some Christians believe that faith alone is not enough to secure salvation. They may say that faith plus repentance, baptism, or even living a good life is required. Others (e.g., Catholics) would say that membership in a particular church is required. Still others would claim that subsequent revelations were given by God to prophets and that these provide the final requirements for salvation (e.g., Muhammad and Islam, Joseph Smith and Mormonism, Charles Russell and Jehovah's Witnesses.) Interestingly, as diverse as these groups are, all, to one degree or another, recognize the Bible as being inspired by God and the Bible forms the foundation of their belief/religion. So, let's consider each of these claims in light of the Gospel of John.

As Charles Ryrie points out, "This [the Gospel of John] is the most theological of the Four Gospels. It deals with the nature and person of Christ and the meaning of faith in Him." [6] John's primary purpose in writing his Gospel was to present Jesus as the "Word of God" and clearly states the purpose of his Gospel:

"Therefore many other signs Jesus also performed in the presence of the disciples, which are not written in this book; but these have been written so that you may believe that Jesus is the Christ, the Son of God; and believing you may have life in His name." John 20:30-31

This statement of purpose by John certainly lends credibility to the assertion that faith alone is required for salvation. However, let's carefully examine John's Gospel for additional information.

To my brothers and sisters in Christ, who believe that things such as repentance, baptism, or living a good life are additional requirements for salvation, consider that In the Gospel of John, the words "believe, believes, believed" occur in 85 verses. Of these, 20 are in the context of eternal life and are the sole requirement for salvation or eternal life. These are: 1:7, 1:12; 3:15; 3:16; 3:18; 3:36; 5:24; 6:35; 6:40; 6:47; 7:38; 8:24; 10:26; 11:25; 11:26; 11:40; 12:46; 13:19; 20:29; and 20:31. Of these 20 verses, 17 are direct quotes from Jesus (3:15; 3:16; 3:18; 3:36; 5:24; 6:35; 6:40; 6:47; 7:38; 8:24; 10:26; 11:25; 11:26; 11:40; 12:46; 13:19; and 20:29).

31

"Baptism" or "baptize" is found in 11 verses in John, but none of them refer to baptism being a condition for salvation (1:25; 1:26 1:28; 1:31; 1:33: 3:22; 3:23; 3:26; 4:1; 4:2; and 10:40). "Repent" is not used by John. Therefore, based upon both Jesus' own words and the apostle John's words, we can confidently conclude that belief or faith in Jesus (the gospel) is the only requirement for salvation and eternal life.

To the members of the Catholic Church, some of whom are my brothers and sisters in Christ, there is no doubt that the central teachings of the Catholic Church are consistent with biblical teaching. For example, belief in God, the virgin birth of Jesus, His sinless life, His death for our sins, His resurrection and ascension to heaven, and the coming judgments for believers and non-believers, are all biblical. Additionally, many of you have accepted Jesus as your personal Savior and I commend you on this.

However, there are good reasons why Martin Luther nailed his 95 theses on the door of the Catholic Church at the University of Wittenberg. As you may know, Luther protested, among other things, a deal made in 1517 between Pope Leo and Archbishop Albert of Mainz to raise money by selling indulgences for the forgiveness of sins, changing vows, and less time in purgatory. [7] In other words, holding man-made traditions, such as praying to Mary, worshiping Mary, and confessions to priests, as equal to the Bible is not scriptural. This led Martin Luther to break away from the Catholic Church and begin the Protestant Reformation. I would encourage you to carefully consider the effect that the man-made traditions and non-scriptural teachings of the Catholic Church have on your relationship with Jesus Christ.

To the members of Islam, Mormonism, and Jehovah's Witnesses, do you see any evidence in the Bible that God would be motivated to withhold vital salvational information from the Bible? Do you have any evidence that Jesus was not the perfect and only sacrifice that was sufficient to pay the penalty of mankind's sins? If you believe that God withheld salvation doctrine from the Bible and that Jesus did not pay the full penalty of man's sins, then the God and Jesus that you worship is not the God and Jesus of the Bible. Are you aware that God specifically prohibited additions to the Bible (Revelation 22:18)? I encourage you to please read the rest of this book and carefully consider the information supporting biblical integrity and how biblical truth will impact your life now and in eternity.

I have one additional comment for your consideration. If my words seem harsh and offensive, please review Jesus' scathing comments to the scribes and Pharisees, who were misleading people by their erroneous teaching (Matthew 23:13-29). My desire and purpose is to share biblical truth with you, so that you may know the truth and be set free from erroneous teaching (John 8:32).]

There is nothing that we can do on our own to work our way into heaven. It is only by the grace of God that we can have hope in eternal life. Perhaps the following acronym for "grace" will put this in perspective for you: GRACE is <u>G</u>od's <u>R</u>iches <u>A</u>t <u>C</u>hrist's <u>E</u>xpense. What is your response to this? Perhaps "Thank you, Lord" would be a good start!

When you place your faith in the gospel, you are immediately transformed from being a *creation* of God to being a *child* of God. You are sanctified or set apart by God to be used by Him. The best way to learn what God has in mind for you is to read, study, and apply biblical truths to your life:

"All Scripture is inspired by God and profitable for teaching, for reproof, for correction, for training in righteousness; so that the man of God may be adequate, equipped for every good work." 2 Timothy 3:16

9. "These things I have written to you who believe in the name of the Son of God, so that you may know that you have eternal life." 1 John 5:13

One of the wonderful things about the gift of salvation is that you can *know* that it is true and that your eternal destiny is secure. The words quoted above were written by the apostle John, who was an eyewitness to Jesus' life, death, and resurrection. When you read John's writings, it will be very obvious that he had no doubts that Jesus was the Messiah and Savior. You, too, can have that confidence and knowledge.

These are the rules of the game of life as they relate to God's plan for your salvation.

Don't Like the Rules of the Game?

Some people may not like these rules. They may say that all religions are basically the same and there are many roads that lead to heaven. If you believe this, then that is why the rest of this book was written—to provide you with objective evidence that the rules of the game, as presented above, are true.

For now, however, consider the following sports analogy. Let's say that you want to play the game of basketball. In basketball, a free throw is worth one point, a field goal is worth two points, and a field goal behind the three-point line is worth three points when made. If you decide to play the game and try to compete against professional basketball players, you might soon decide that you do not have a fair chance to win. So, to make it fair you propose that the rules be changed so that each of your made shots count 4X their normal value, e.g., your made free throws are worth four points, field goals are eight points, and three pointers are 12 points. Absurd, isn't it? Realistically, when we choose to play a game, we agree to abide by the rules of the game.

The same should be true of the game of life. God created it and specified the rules of the game. If you want to win the game of life, then understand the rules and play by them.

> "'For My thoughts are not your thoughts,
> Neither are your ways My ways,' declares the Lord.
> 'For as the heavens are higher than the earth,
> So are My ways higher than your ways,
> And My thoughts than your thoughts.
> For as the rain and the snow come down from heaven,
> And do not return there without watering the earth,
> And making it bear and sprout,
> And furnishing seed to the sower and bread to the eater;
> So shall My word be which goes forth from My mouth;
> It shall not return to Me empty,
> Without accomplishing what I desire,
> And without succeeding in the matter for which I sent it.'"
> Isaiah 58:8-11

The Gospel Is Exclusionary

Some people may object to the gospel because it is exclusionary, i.e., it claims that belief in Jesus is the *only* way to obtain eternal life. Yes, that is true. However, as O.S. Hawkins pointed out, all absolute truth is exclusionary. [8] For example:

> Mathematical truth: 2 + 2 = 4, not 5
> Scientific truth: water freezes at 32 degrees F, not 40 degrees
> Historical truth: George Washington was the first president of the U.S., not Abraham Lincoln
> Geographical truth: Phoenix is the capitol of Arizona, not Tucson

We readily accept and affirm the absolute nature of mathematical, scientific, historical, and geographical truth. Why should religious truth be any different? Jesus declared that biblical truth is also absolute:

> Jesus said to him, "I am the way, and the truth, and the life; no one comes to the Father but through Me." John 14:6

What Is Your Response?

Based upon this information, are you ready to place your faith and eternal destiny in the truth of the gospel? Do you need more information?

Accept

If you are ready to place your faith and eternal destiny in the truth of the gospel, you may do so by praying the following prayer:

> "God, I believe that Jesus lived, died to pay the penalty of my sins, and that He rose from the dead, according to the Scriptures. I want to have a personal relationship with you now and forever. I place my faith, my life, and my eternal destiny in Jesus. Thank you, God, for hearing and accepting my prayer. In Jesus' name I pray."

If you prayed this prayer and were sincere about it, welcome to the family of God! Although you may not feel any different now than before you prayed, you have been transformed from a *creation* of God to a *child* of God.

There are some things that you can do to help your faith grow and to help you mature as a believer in Jesus. These will be explained in detail in Chapter 6. However, for now, read the rest of this book so that you may better understand that your faith is based upon solid facts and not upon feelings.

> "And the testimony is this, that God has given us eternal life, and this life is in His Son. He who has the Son has the life; he who does not have the Son of God does not have the life. These things I have written to you who believe in the name of the Son of God, so that you may know that you have eternal life." 1 John 5:11-13

Need More Information?

If you are not ready to place your faith in the gospel or if you want to know more, please continue reading. The purpose of the rest of this book is to provide you with objective data and facts so that you can make an informed decision.

References:

1. Grudem, Wayne. *Systematic Theology: An Introduction to Bible Doctrine*. (Electronic version, Copyright 1997, 2004 Wayne Grudem and John Hughes; published by Bits & Bytes, Inc., Whitefish, MT. Print version: Leicester, Great Britain: Inter-Varsity Press and Grand Rapids, MI: Zondervan Publishing House, 1994, p. 27.
2. _____. p. 489.
3. Ryrie, Charles C. *Basic Theology*. Wheaton, IL: Victor Books, 1988, p. 377.
4. _____. pp. 105, 292.
5. Grudem, Wayne. *Systematic Theology: An Introduction to Bible Doctrine*. (see reference 1 for complete bibliographical information), p. 627.
6. Ryrie, Charles C. *Ryrie Study Bible Expanded Edition, New American Standard Version*, 1995 update. Chicago, IL: Moody Press, 1995, p. 1675.
7. McDowell, Josh. *Josh McDowell's Handbook on Apologetics*. Nashville, TN: Thomas Nelson, Inc. 1997, Part 4, Chapter 9, Page 1. (Libronix Digital Library System version.)
8. O.S. Hawkins. "The Question of Our Time (Matthew 16:13-16)". A sermon presented at Scottsdale Bible Church, Scottsdale, AZ on March 22, 2009.

Chapter 2

The Bible: Is It True?

Uniqueness of the Bible

Compared to all of the books that have been and will be written, the Bible is truly unique. It consists of 66 books, 39 in the Old Testament and 27 in the New Testament. These books were written by more than 40 authors over a 1,500 year time period.

The authors included men from diverse backgrounds. For example:

Moses—a Jewish political leader, educated in ancient Egypt;
David and Solomon—kings of Israel;
Isaiah—a prophet of God;
Amos—a herdsman;
Matthew—a tax collector, before becoming a disciple of Jesus;
Peter—a fisherman, before becoming a disciple of Jesus;
Luke—a physician; and
Paul—a Jewish rabbi, who persecuted Christians before becoming a follower of Jesus.

The first book was written approximately 1500 BC and the last book of the Bible was written in AD 95 or 96. The complete version of the Bible has been translated into more than 459 languages and portions of the Bible have been translated into more than 2,508 languages. [1] Greater than 80% of the world's population has access to at least a portion of the Bible in their language. The members of the United Bible Society have distributed more than 29 million Bibles. [1]

The principal characters in the Bible are God and mankind. The Bible begins with the book of Genesis, which can be summarized by saying that paradise was created by God, given to man, and lost by man. The Bible ends with the book of Revelation in which paradise is recreated, given to Jesus, and is eternal. In between Genesis and Revelation is the story of mankind, created by and in the image of God, exercising free will to most often pursue its own will, rather than God's will. Fortunately, God demonstrates His love for mankind and His desire to have a personal, intimate relationship with each person by implementing His plan of salvation that, when accepted personally, transforms each believing person from a *creation* of God to a *child* of God.

The Old Testament is primarily a history of the Jewish people, God's chosen people. It can be summarized by saying that the principal concepts for us to learn from Jewish history is that disobedience to God's will brings discipline, but obedience to God's will brings blessings. The Old Testament highlights important promises or covenants that God made to the Jewish people: the Abrahamic and Davidic covenants. The Abrahamic covenant was:

> "Now the Lord said to Abram,
> Go forth from your country,
> And from your relatives
> And from your father's house,
> To the land which I will show you;
> And I will make you a great nation, And I will bless you,
> And make your name great;
> And so you shall be a blessing;
> And I will bless those who bless you,
> And the one who curses you I will curse.
> And in you all the families of the earth will be blessed."
> Genesis 12:1-3

This covenant was made with Abram around 2000 BC. As indicated above, God promised land (present location of Israel), offspring that would become a great nation, and that Abram's name would be great. Considering that Abram was 75 years old and that his wife, Sarai, was 65 years old and that they had no children, this was a remarkable promise by God! However, when God makes a promise He fulfills it—on His time schedule and not necessarily on our time schedule—and our responsibility is to trust and obey.

Both Abram and Sarai believed that God would fulfill His promise, but thought that they should probably help God and take matters into their own hands. So, Sarai told Abram that because she was too old to have children that Abram should have sexual relations with her servant, Hagar. He did and the son that was born to Hagar was Ishmael. The Arabic people come from Ishmael. However, this was not what God had in mind when He made the covenant with Abram....

> "Now when Abram was ninety-nine years old, the LORD appeared to Abram and said to him, 'I am God Almighty; Walk before Me, and be blameless, I will establish My covenant between Me and you, and I will multiply you exceedingly.' Abram fell on his face, and God talked with him, saying, 'As for Me, behold, My covenant is with you, and you will be the father of a multitude of nations. No longer shall your name be called Abram, but your name shall be Abraham; For I will make you the father of a multitude of nations." Genesis 17:1-5

It is interesting to note the name change from Abram, which means "exalted father" to Abraham, which means "father of a multitude." The following year, as promised, Sarai, his wife (whose name was changed to Sarah), bore a son—Isaac. This was the beginning of the Jewish nation. The promises of land, a great nation, and blessings to all people were (and are being) fulfilled through Isaac's offspring. It is also interesting to note that God's promise to make Abram's name great has been fulfilled in that three of the world's principal religions recognize Abraham as their forefather—Judaism and Christianity through Isaac, and Islam, through Ishmael. When God makes a promise, He keeps it!

The covenant that God made with David was recorded in Second Samuel 7:8-17 and includes the following:

> "Your house and your kingdom shall endure before Me forever; your throne shall be established forever." 2 Samuel 7:16

"Your house" refers to the Jewish people and "your kingdom" and "your throne" refer to the future rule of Jesus, which begins at the second coming of Jesus (i.e., return of Jesus to this earth as "King"). [2]

The New Testament was written after Jesus' resurrection and represents God's New Covenant with believers. The New Testament provides details about the life, death, and resurrection of Jesus and the significance of these events to us and how we should respond appropriately to these. The key verse of the New Testament is:

> "For God so loved the world, that He gave His only begotten Son, that whoever believes in Him shall not perish, but have eternal life." John 3:16

Just as the Old Testament included key concepts, so also does the New Testament. For example, in the Old Testament, disobedience brought forth discipline; in the New Testament, unbelief brings forth condemnation. Conversely, in the Old Testament, obedience brought forth blessings; in the New Testament, faith brings salvation. There is consistency of God's Word between the Old and New Testament.

The Bible makes some very unusual claims about itself. For example, it claims to be divinely inspired:

> "All Scripture is inspired by God and profitable for teaching, for reproof, for correction, for training in righteousness; so that the man of God may be adequate, equipped for every good work." 2 Timothy 3:16-17

The Bible claims that its writers were moved by the Holy Spirit:

> "for no prophesy was ever made by an act of human will, but men moved by the Holy Spirit spoke from God." 2 Peter 1:21

It claims to be living and active:

> "For the word of God is living and active and sharper than any two-edged sword, and piercing as far as the division of soul and spirit, both joints and marrow, and able to judge the thoughts and intentions of the heart." Hebrews 4:12

Finally, it claims to be eternal:

> "Heaven and earth will pass away, but My words will not pass away." Matthew 24:35; Mark 13:31; Luke 21:33

Remarkable claims, aren't they? The real question, however, is, "Are these claims true?" This chapter will provide evidence for you to consider so that you can determine if the Bible's claims are true.

Books of the Bible

There are 66 books in the Bible. Thirty-nine of these are in the Old Testament and these were written from 425 to 1,450 years before Jesus' birth. Twenty-seven of these are in the New Testament and these were written from 20 to 65 years after Jesus' death. The Old Testament books consist of "five books of Law, twelve books of History, five books of Poetry, and seventeen books of Prophesy" [3] and are shown below:

Table 2-1. Books of the Old Testament, grouped by category (adapted from Geisler & Nix [3])

The Law	Poetry	History	Prophets	
			Major	**Minor**
1. Genesis	1. Job	1. Joshua	1. Isaiah	1. Hosea
2. Exodus	2. Psalms	2. Judges	2. Jeremiah	2. Joel
3. Leviticus	3. Proverbs	3. Ruth	3. Lamentations	3. Amos
4. Numbers	4. Ecclesiastes	4. 1 Samuel	4. Ezekiel	4. Obadiah
5. Deuteronomy	5. Song of Solomon	5. 2 Samuel	5. Daniel	5. Jonah
		6. 1 Kings		6. Micah
		7. 2 Kings		7. Nahum
		8. 1 Chronicles		8. Habakkuk
		9. 2 Chronicles		9. Zephaniah
		10. Ezra		10. Haggai
		11. Nehemiah		11. Zechariah
		12. Esther		12. Malachi

The books of the Law were written by Moses between 1445 and 1405 BC. [4] and provide details about the creation, fall of man (Adam and Eve's sin), and God's selection of and provision for the Jewish people as His chosen people. The poetical books do not advance the story of the Jewish people, but provide insight into God, pain, wisdom, life, and love. [5] The historical books record the history of the Jewish people from 1405 to 420 BC.[6] The prophets were men who were divinely chosen to receive and relay God's messages to the Jewish nation. These prophetic messages had four major themes:

1. "The prophets exposed the sinful practices of the people."
2. "The prophets called the people back to the moral, civil, and ceremonial law of God."
3. "They warned the people of coming judgment."
4. "The prophets anticipated the coming Messiah." [7]

The Jewish or Hebrew Scriptures, which form the Old Testament in the Bible, were completed and finalized by the fourth century BC. [8]

The books of the New Testament can be divided into the following categories: four books on the life of Jesus (Gospels); one book on history; 21 books that are letters; and one book on prophecy. These are listed in the table below:

Table 2-2. Books of the New Testament, arranged by category (Adapted from Geisler & Nix [9])

Gospels	History	Letters		Prophecy
1. Matthew	1. Acts	Written by Paul	General	1. Revelation
2. Mark		1. Romans	1. Hebrews	
3. Luke		2. 1 Corinthians	2. James	
4. John		3. 2 Corinthians	3. 1 Peter	
		4. Galatians	4. 2 Peter	
		5. Ephesians	5. 1 John	
		6. Philippians	6. 2 John	
		7. Colossians	7. 3 John	
		8. 1 Thessalonians	8. Jude	
		9. 2 Thessalonians		
		10. 1 Timothy		
		11. 2 Timothy		
		12. Titus		
		13. Philemon		

The Gospels present the life of Jesus from four different perspectives:

"Matthew—The first Gospel presents Jesus as the Christ, *Israel's messianic King*."

"Mark—The second Gospel presents Jesus as the *Servant* who came to 'give His life a ransom for many'."

"Luke—The third Gospel presents Jesus as the *perfect Son of Man* whose mission was 'to seek and to save that which was lost'."

"John—The fourth Gospel presents Jesus as the *eternal Son of God* who offered eternal life to all who would believe in Him." [10]

Luke, a physician, historian, and traveling companion of the apostle Paul, wrote both the Gospel of Luke and the Acts of the Apostles. Acts documents the activities of the leaders of the Christian faith. The primary purposes of the 21 letters were to (a) provide explanation on the significance of the life, death, and resurrection of Jesus; (b) to prove guidance to believers on how to live their lives in manners that would be pleasing to God; and (c) to answer questions that had arisen among the new believers.

As shown above, the apostle Paul wrote 13 books (letters) of the New Testament. Paul was a Jewish rabbi (teacher) who was extremely passionate about his Jewish faith. After Jesus' death, he aggressively pursued and participated in the persecution, which often lead to the death, of Jesus' believers. However, after the resurrected Jesus appeared to Paul, he converted from his Jewish faith to the Christian faith. He, himself, underwent many trials and persecutions for his belief that Jesus was the Messiah. Paul sealed his testimony about Jesus being his Savior and Lord with his martyrdom in AD 67 or 68. [11]

Peter was one of the 12 men that Jesus chose as His disciples. As one of the disciples, Peter spent approximately three years traveling with Jesus, during Jesus' public ministry. It is interesting to note that during the trials of Jesus (prior to Jesus' crucifixion) he denied on three separate occasions that he even knew Jesus. However, after Peter saw the resurrected Jesus, his faith became so strong that he became a leader of the early Christian believers, testified boldly about his faith in Jesus as the Messiah and risen Lord, wrote the books of First and Second Peter, and sealed his testimony with his own crucifixion in AD 68. [12]

John was also a disciple of Jesus and he wrote the Gospel of John, First, Second, and Third John, and Revelation. Revelation records the prophetic vision that John received from Jesus, which predicts many events that will be fulfilled in the future. These predictions reassure believers in the ultimate triumph of Jesus Christ and provide insight into eternal life. [13] (The details of the prophetic events will be provided in Chapter 5.) It is interesting to note that John is the only disciple that is mentioned as being present at Jesus' crucifixion and he is the only disciple (other than Judas, who betrayed Jesus and committed suicide) who did not die a martyr's death.

The New Testament books were written by apostles (disciples) of Jesus (e.g., Matthew, John, Peter, and Paul) or had apostolic approval (e.g., Mark, Luke, James, and Jude). [14] All 27 books that make up our modern New Testament were recognized by early church leaders as early as the second century AD. General recognition of all of the books in the Bible was accomplished by the Councils of Hippo (AD 393) and Carthage (AD 397). [15] (An excellent overview of each book of the Bible is provided by Bruce Wilkinson and Kenneth Boa in *Talk Thru the Bible* (Thomas Nelson Publishers: Nashville, TN. 1980).

As you consider the list of the Old and New Testament books shown in the tables above, you might wonder, "How did men decide which books should be included in the Bible, from all of the ancient writings?" That is a great question, but in reality, men did not decide—God decided and men discovered the books that God specified. [16] In other words, God determined what to reveal to man, directed specific men to write His words, and enabled men to "discover" which books were from God.

How did man discover the books that are in the Bible? Geisler and Nix, in the book, *A General Introduction to the Bible*, answer this question by stating,

> "How men *discovered* what God had *determined* was by looking for the "earmarks of Inspiration." It was asked whether the book (1) was written by a man of God, (2) who was confirmed by an act of God, (3) told the truth about God, man, and so on, (4) came with the power of God, and (5) was accepted by the people of God." [17]

Geisler and Nix also point out that in addition to these factors, men responsible for making the decisions about the appropriate books to include in the Bible were also providentially guided by God. [18]

The statement, that God determined which books should be in the Bible, may lead you to ask, "Who is God?" and "What gives Him the authority to dictate which books are sacred?" Now would be an appropriate time to take a detour from the facts about the Bible and to learn more about the God of the Bible.

God of the Bible

The existence of God cannot be proven, nor can it be disproven. Nevertheless, we can examine relevant evidence and determine the likelihood that the God of the Bible exists. God has chosen to reveal Himself through creation (general revelation) and also through the Bible (special revelation). The Bible provides insight into the general revelation of God in several passages, including:

> "For since the creation of the world His invisible attributes, His eternal power and divine nature have been clearly seen, being understood through what has been made, so that they are without excuse." Romans 1:20

> "The heavens are telling of the glory of God;
> And their expanse is declaring the work of His hands."
> Psalm 19:1

Most people will admit that when they see a beautiful sunset, look at the millions of stars in the night sky, or consider the awesomeness of the universe that they think that there must be a god who created it. Fortunately, the God of the Bible has provided much more specific information about Himself through His special revelation.

So what does the special revelation tell us about God? The good news is that it tells us a lot; the bad news is that it soon becomes apparent that our finite minds have difficulty comprehending God, who is an infinite being. For example the Bible teaches that God is eternal, omniscient (all-knowing), omnipresent (all-present), and omnipotent (all-powerful):

> Eternal: "Before the mountains were born; Or You gave birth to the earth and the world, Even from everlasting to everlasting, You are God" Psalm 90:2

> Omniscient: "... God ... knows all things." 1 John 3:20

Omnipresent: "Can a man hide himself in secret places so that I cannot see him? Declares the LORD. Do I not fill heaven and earth? Declares the LORD." Jeremiah 23:24

Omnipotent: "Ah, Lord God! Behold, You have made the heavens and the earth by Your great power and by Your outstretched arm! Nothing is too difficult for You." Jeremiah 32:17

As humans, we cannot fully understand these characteristics or how one being can be all of these things. Fortunately, the Bible also tells us things about God that we can better understand. These are the attributes of God.

Table 2-3. The Attributes of God (Adapted from Grudem [19])*

Incommunicable Attributes: How God Is Different From Us		
Attribute	Definition	Reference
1. Independence	God does not need us or the rest of creation for anything, yet we and the rest of creation can glorify Him and bring Him joy.	"The God who made the world and all things in it, since He is Lord of heaven and earth, does not dwell in temples made with hands; nor is He served by human hands, as though He needed anything, since He himself gives to all people life and breath and all things;" Acts 17:24-25. Also Job 41:11; Psalm 50:10-12.

2. Unchangeableness	God is unchanging in His being, perfections, purposes, and promises, yet God does act and feel emotions and He acts and feels differently in response to different situations.	"Of old you laid the foundation of the earth, and the heavens are the work of your hands. They will perish, but you will remain;... but you are the same and your years have no end." Psalm 102:25-27. Also Malachi 3:6; James 1:17.
3. Eternity	God has no beginning, end, or succession of moments in His own being and He sees all time equally vividly, yet God sees events in time and acts in time.	"Before the mountains were brought forth, or ever you had formed the earth and the world, from everlasting to everlasting, you are God." Psalm 90:2. Also Revelation 1:8; 4:8.
4. Omnipresence	God does not have size or spatial dimensions and is present at every point of space with His whole being, yet God acts differently in different places.	"Can a man hide himself in secret places so that I cannot see him? Declares the lord. Do I not fill heaven and earth? Declares the LORD." Jeremiah 23:24. Also Psalm 139:7-10; 1 Kings 8:27; Isaiah 66:1-2; Acts 7:48.

5. Unity	God is not divided into parts, yet we see different attributes of God emphasized at different times.	"...And there is no other God besides Me, a righteous God and a Savior; There is none except Me. Turn to Me and be saved, all the ends of the earth; For I am God, and there is no other." Isaiah 45:21-22. "Go therefore and make disciples of all the nations, baptizing them in the name of the Father and the Son and the Holy Spirit." Matthew 28:18.

Communicable Attributes: How God Is Like Us in Being, Mental, and Moral Attributes		
A. Attributes Describing God's Being		
1. Spirituality	God's spirituality means that God exists as a being that is not made of any matter, has no parts or dimensions, is unable to be perceived by our bodily senses, and is more excellent than any other kind of existence.	"God is spirit..." John 4:24; Psalm 139:7-10; 1 Kings 8:27.

2. Invisibility	God's invisibility means that God's total essence, all of His spiritual being, will never be able to be seen by us, yet God still shows Himself to us through visible, created things.	"To the King of ages, immortal, invisible, the only God, be honor and glory forever and ever. Amen." 1 Timothy 1:17. Also John 1:18; 6:46.
B. Mental Attributes		
3. Knowledge	God fully knows Himself and all things actual and possible in one simple and eternal act.	"… God is greater than our heart, and he knows everything." 1 John 3:20. Also Job 37:16; 1 Corinthians 2:10-11; Hebrews 4:13; Isaiah 46:9-10; Psalm 139:1-2, 4, 16.
4. Wisdom	God always chooses the best goals and the best means to those goals.	"O LORD, how manifold are your works! In wisdom have you made them all; the earth is full of your creatures." Psalm 104:24. Also Romans 16:27; Job 9:4; 12:13.
5. Truthfulness (and Faithfulness)	God's truthfulness means that He is the true God, and that all His knowledge and words are both true and the final standard of truth.	"And this is eternal life, that they may know you the only true God, and Jesus Christ whom you have sent." John 17:3. Also Jeremiah 10:10; Job 37:16; Deuteronomy 32:4.

C. Moral Attributes		
6. Goodness	The goodness of God means that God is the final standard of good, and that all that God is and does is worthy of approval.	"For the LORD is good; his steadfast love endures forever, and his faithfulness to all generations." Psalm 100:5. Also Luke 18:19; Psalm 106:1-7; 119:68; Romans 12:2.
7. Love	God's love means that God eternally gives of Himself to others.	"Anyone who does not love does not know God, because God is love. In this the love of God was made manifest among us, that God sent his only Son into the world, so that we might live through him." 1 John 4:8-9. Also John 3:16, 35; 14:31; 17:24; Romans 5:8.
8. Mercy (Grace, Patience)	God's mercy means God's goodness toward those in misery and distress; grace means God's goodness toward those who deserve only punishment; patience means God's goodness in withholding of punishment toward those who sin over a period of time.	"The LORD is merciful and gracious, slow to anger and abounding in steadfast love." Psalm 103:8. Also Exodus 34:6; Numbers 14:18; 2 Samuel 24:14; Matthew 9:27; Romans 2:4; 3:23-24; 2 Corinthians 1:3; 1 Timothy 1:16; Hebrews 4:16; James 1:19.

9. Holiness	God's holiness means that He is separated from sin and devoted to seeking His own honor.	"...Holy, holy, holy is the LORD of hosts; the whole earth is full of his glory!" Isaiah 6:3. Also Psalm 3:5; 22:3; 99:9.
10. Peace (or Order)	God's peace means that in God's being and in His actions He is separate from all confusion and disorder, yet He is continually active in innumerable well-ordered, fully controlled, simultaneous actions.	"For God is not a God of confusion but of peace." 1 Corinthians 14:33. Also Romans 15:33; 16:20; Philippians 4:9; 1 Thessalonians 5:23; Hebrews 13:20.
11. Righteousness (or Justice)	God's righteousness means that God always acts in accordance with what is right and is Himself the final standard of what is right.	"...His work is perfect, For all His ways are just; A god of faithfulness and without injustice, Righteous and upright is He." Deuteronomy 32:4. Also Genesis 18:25; Isaiah 45:19; Psalm 19:8.
12. Jealousy	God's jealousy means that God continually seeks to protect His own honor.	"You shall not worship them or serve them; for I, the LORD your God, am a jealous God ..." Deuteronomy 5:9. Also Exodus 34:14; Deuteronomy 4:24; Isaiah 48:11.

13. Wrath	God's wrath means that He intensely hates all sin.	"For the wrath of God is revealed from heaven against all ungodliness and unrighteousness of men, who by their unrighteousness suppress the truth." Romans 1:18. Also Exodus 32:9-10; Deuteronomy 9:7-8; John 3:36; 1 Thessalonians 1:10; 2:16, 5:9; Revelation 6:16-17; 19:15
D. Attributes of Purpose		
14. Will	God's will is that attribute of God whereby He approves and determines to bring about every action necessary for the existence and activity of Himself and all creation.	"In him, we have obtained an inheritance, having been predestined according to the purpose of him who works all things according to the counsel of his will." Ephesians 1:11. Also Colossians 1:16-17; Romans 11:36; 1 Corinthians 8:6; 15:27-28; Revelation 4:11.
15. Freedom	God's freedom is that attribute of God whereby He does whatever He pleases.	"Our God is in the heavens; he does all that he pleases." Psalm 115:3. Also Daniel 4:35; Proverbs 21:1.

16. Omnipotence (or Power, and Sovereignty)	God's omnipotence means that God is able to do all His holy will.	"Ah, Lord God! It is you who have made the heavens and the earth by your great power and by your outstretched arm! Nothing is too hard for you." Jeremiah 32:17. Also Genesis 18:14; Psalm 24:8; Matthew 19:26; Luke 1:37; Ephesians 3:20.
E. Summary Attributes		
17. Perfection	God's perfection means that God completely possesses all excellent qualities and lacks no part of any qualities that would be desirable for Him.	"You there must be perfect, as your heavenly Father is perfect." Matthew 5:48. Also Deuteronomy 32:4; Psalm 18:30.
18. Blessedness	God's blessedness means that God delights fully in Himself and in all that reflects His character.	"And God saw everything that he had made, and behold, it was very good...." Genesis 1:31. Also Isaiah 62:5; Proverbs 8:30-31; Zephaniah 3:17.

19. Beauty	God's beauty is that attribute of God whereby He is the sum of all desirable qualities.	"One thing have I asked of the LORD, that will I seek after: that I may dwell in the house of the LORD all the days of my life, to gaze upon the beauty of the LORD and to inquire in his temple." Psalm 27:4. Also Psalm 73:25; Rev. 22:4.
20. Glory	God's glory is the created brightness that surrounds God's revelation of Himself.	"And an angel of the Lord appeared to them, and the glory of the Lord shone around them, and they were filled with fear." Luke 2:9. Also Psalm 24:10; 104:1-2; Matthew 17:2; Revelation 21:23.

* In fairness to you and to God, the Bible teaches much more about God than can be presented in this overview. For more complete discussion on God, I highly recommend that you read Wayne Grudem's excellent text, *Systematic Theology: An Introduction to Bible Doctrine.* Inter-Varsity Press and Zondervan Publishing House. 2000.

Are you suffering from brain strain now? I am! However, there is even more. Have you heard of the Trinity? This means that God exists as three beings, but is one. Although the word *trinity* is not found in the Bible, the concept is clearly taught and can be summarized as follows:

1. God is three persons: the Father, the Son, and the Holy Spirit

"After being baptized, Jesus came up immediately from the water; and behold, the heavens were opened, and he saw the Spirit of God descending as a dove and lighting on Him, and behold, a voice out of the heavens said, 'This is My beloved

Son, in whom I am well-pleased'." Matthew 3:16-17 (God the Father is speaking from heaven, God the Son, Jesus, has been baptized, and God the Holy Spirit descends upon Jesus.) [20]

"Go therefore and make disciples of all the nations, baptizing them in the name of the Father and the Son and the Holy Spirit." Matthew 28:19

2. Each person is fully God

God, the Father: "In the beginning God created the heavens and the earth." Genesis 1:1

God, the Son: "In the beginning was the Word [Jesus], and the Word was with God, and the Word was God." John 1:1

God, the Holy Spirit: "But Peter said, 'Ananias, why has Satan filled your heart to lie to the Holy Spirit ... You have not lied to men but to God." Acts 5:3-4

3. There is one God

"Hear, O Israel! The LORD is our God, the LORD is one!" Deuteronomy 6:4

"For there is one God, and one mediator also between God and men, the man Christ Jesus." 1 Timothy 2:5

Each person of the Trinity has always existed and is equal in all attributes. However, each exercises different functions or roles in how each relates to the world and the human race. For example, during creation:

God, the Father, spoke the words to begin the creation process.

"Then God said, "let there be light"; and there was light."" Genesis 1:2

God, the Son, carried out the Father's directive and actually created light.

> "He was in the beginning with God. All things came into being through Him, and apart from Him nothing came into being that has come into being." John 1:2-3

God, the Holy Spirit, acted to sustain and to "represent" God in the creation:

> "The earth was formless and void, and darkness was over the surface of the deep, and the Spirit of God was moving over the surface of the waters." Genesis 1:2

Their different roles in the redemption of man can be summarized as follows:

God, the Father, developed the plan of redemption and sent God, the Son, Jesus, to implement the plan in the world. God, the Holy Spirit, was sent by both the Father and Son to continue the redemptive plan in the lives of believers. For example,

God, the Father:

> "For God so loved the world, that He gave His only begotten Son, that whoever believes in Him shall not perish, but have eternal life." John 3:16

God, the Son

> "For I have come down from heaven, not to do My own will, but the will of Him who sent me." John 6:38

> "but [Jesus] emptied Himself, taking the form of a bond-servant, and being made in the likeness of men. Being found in appearance as a man, He humbled Himself by becoming obedient to the point of death, even death on a cross." Philippians 2:7-8

God, the Holy Spirit:

> "But the Helper, the Holy Spirit, whom the Father will send in My name, He will teach you all things, and bring to your remembrance all that I said to you." John 14:26

> "But I tell you the truth, it is to your advantage that I go away; for if I do not go away, the Helper will not come to you; but if I go, I will send Him to you." John 16:7

From their activities in creation and redemption, it can be said that, in general, the primary roles can be summarized as follows:

God, the Father, plans and authorizes;
God, the Son, obediently carries out the directives of the Father; and
God, the Holy Spirit, supports and completes the work planned by God the Father and begun by God the Son. [21]
In other words, each person of the Trinity possess equally all attributes of God, listed above, and works together in perfect harmony to bring about God's will.

Perhaps the following illustration will help you visualize and understand the concept of the Trinity:

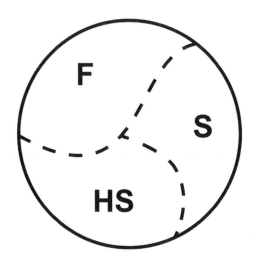

There are three persons of the Trinity, the Father (F), the Son (S), and the Holy Spirit (HS), and each has different primary areas of responsibility as shown by the areas separated by the dashed lines, but are one God, as represented by the circle. Each person of the Trinity is "fully and wholly God." [22]

[Note: As you read the information about the attributes of God and the fact that God is three persons (the Trinity), you may have noticed that all of the quotations were from Wayne Grudem's book, *Systematic Theology: An Introduction to Biblical Doctrine*. Although many other references could have been cited, my purpose on solely quoting from Grudem was to summarize biblical teaching about a very complex subject—God—in a clear and concise manner. I think Grudem has done this exceptionally well in *Systematic Theology*, which is why his text was referenced extensively in this section. For an even more complete understanding of God, I strongly recommend his book to you.]

Chapter 3 will provide additional information about God the Son, Jesus. Chapter 6 will provide additional information about God, the Holy Spirit. The rest of this chapter will continue to examine the evidence that the Bible is God's special revelation.

Validity

This section will present information that supports the assertion that the Bible is the inspired Word of God. You might think this is a little premature, since the previous section did not prove the existence of God, but rather provided an overview of His attributes and His triune nature, if He exists as indicated in the Bible. If so, you are correct. So, please have patience because information supporting the existence of the God of the Bible will be presented incrementally. By the time you have finished reading through Chapter 5, you will have ample evidence to make an informed decision about the existence of the God of the Bible.

If the God of the Bible exists and if He directed men to write the Bible, we can examine the claims of the Bible to see if they are consistent with things we know to be true. Let's consider the following four categories of evidence: Historical Documents/Archeology, Scientific, Prophetic, and Jesus' view of Old Testament and New Testament.

Historical Documents/Archeology

The earliest books of the Bible were written in approximately 1450 BC and the last book, Revelation, was written in AD 95 or 96. The writers of the books of the Bible frequently referenced people, places, and things that were present during this 1,500+ year period. So, we can consult other historical documents and archeological findings to see if the biblical accounts of people, places, and things are consistent with these sources.

People

Adam and Eve The Bible claims that God created the first humans: Adam and Eve.

> "Then God said, "Let Us make man in Our image...."
> Genesis 1:26

> "Then the LORD God formed man of dust from the ground and breathed into his nostrils the breath of life; and man [Adam] became a living being." Genesis 2:7

> "So the LORD God caused a deep sleep to fall upon the man, and he slept; then He took one of his ribs and closed up the flesh at that place. The LORD God fashioned into a woman the rib which He had taken from the man, and brought her to the man." Genesis 2:21-22

There are no other written records or archeological findings to confirm or deny the biblical account. However, Geisler presents the following 10 reasons for believing that Adam and Eve were historical persons. [23]

1. Chapters 2-5 of Genesis refer to them as actual persons and narrate important events in their lives.

> "Then to Adam He said, "Because you have listened to the voice of your wife, and have eaten from the tree about which I commanded you, saying, 'You shall not eat from it'; Cursed is the ground because of you; In toil you will eat of it All the days of your life. Both thorns and thistles it shall grow for you; And you will eat the plants of the field; By the sweat of your face you will eat bread, till you return to the ground, because from it you were taken; for you are dust, and to dust you shall return." Genesis 3:17-19

2. They gave birth to children who also gave birth to literal children according to Genesis 4-5.

"Now the man [Adam] had relations with his wife Eve, and she conceived and gave birth to Cain, and she said, "I have gotten a manchild with the help of the LORD." Genesis 4:1

"Cain had relations with his wife and she conceived, and gave birth to Enoch; and he built a city, and called the city Enoch, after the name of his son." Genesis 4:17

3. The phrase, "this is the history of" (this phrase is translated as "the account of" and "the records of" in the New American Standard Bible") is used to record other historical accounts in Genesis (e.g., 6:9, 10:1, 11:10, 11:27; 25:12; 25:19; 36:1, 36:9; 37:2) and also in other Old Testament books: Numbers 3:1; 2 Chronicles 9:29; 12:15; 33:18; 33:19; Judges 7:15; 1 Kings 9:15 and 1 Chronicles 27:24).

"This is the account of the heavens and the earth when they were created, in the day that the LORD God made earth and heaven." Genesis 2:4

"These are the records of the generations of Noah. Noah was a righteous man, blameless in this time; Noah walked with God." Genesis 6:9

"Now these are the records of the generations of Shem, Ham, and Japheth, the sons of Noah; and sons were born to them after the flood." Genesis 10:1

"Now these are the records of the generations of Isaac, Abraham's son: Abraham became the father of Isaac." Genesis 25:19

4. Old Testament chronologies indicate Adam was the first man.

"This is the book of the generations of Adam..." Genesis 5:1

Genealogy from Adam: "Adam, Seth, Enosh, ..." 1 Chronicles 1:1

5. Luke indicates that Adam is the first of Jesus' literal ancestors.

"When He began His ministry, Jesus Himself was about thirty years of age, being, as was supposed, the Son of Joseph, the son of Eli, ... the son of Enosh, the son of Seth, the son of Adam, the son of God." Luke 3:23-38

6. Jesus referred to Adam and Eve as the first man and woman and said that their union established the basis for marriage.

"And He answered and said, "Have you not read that He who created them from the beginning MADE THEM MALE AND FEMALE, and said, 'FOR THIS REASON A MAN SHALL LEAVE HIS FATHER AND MOTHER AND BE JOINED TO HIS WIFE, AND THE TWO SHALL BECOME ONE FLESH'?" Matthew 19:4

7. The apostle Paul declared that physical death was the result of one man: Adam.

"Therefore, just as through one man [Adam] sin entered into the world, and death through sin, and so death spread to all men, because all sinned." Romans 5:12

8. Paul made direct comparisons between the man, Adam, and the man, Jesus.

"So also it is written, 'The first MAN, Adam, BECAME A LIVING SOUL." The last Adam [Jesus] became a life-giving spirit." 1 Corinthians 15:45

"For as in Adam all die, so also in Christ all will be made alive." 1 Corinthians 15:22

"But the free gift is not like the transgression. For if by the transgression of the one [Adam] the many died, much more did the grace of God and the gift by the grace of the one Man, Jesus Christ, abound to the many." Romans 5:15

9. Paul spoke of Adam and Eve as real persons.

"For it was Adam who was first created, and then Eve." 1 Timothy 2:13

10. A literal first male and first female had to exist to begin the human race. "Scripture pictures the first man and woman, Adam and Eve, as possessing highly developed linguistic, moral, and spiritual abilities from the moment they were created." [24] Furthermore, according to the Bible, all humans descended from Adam and Eve.

Saul, the first king of Israel (1050 BC). [25] His fortress at Gibeah has been excavated and a significant finding was numerous slingshots, which were reportedly primary weapons of his soldiers. [26] This is consistent with the biblical account that there were expert "slingers" in Saul's army.

"Out of all these people 700 choice men were left-handed; each one could sling a stone at a hair and not miss." Judges 20:16

Additionally, the Philistine Temple of Ashtaroth has been excavated. The historical significance of this temple is that the Bible says that when the Philistines defeated Saul and his army, they took his armor and put them in the Temple of Ashtaroth. [27]

"They put his weapons in the temple of Ashtaroth,..." 1 Samuel 31:10

David, the second king of Israel, began his reign at the age of 30 [28] in 1010 BC. [29] God told the prophet Samuel that He had selected the person who would succeed Saul as king of Israel and instructed Samuel to anoint the selected person.

"Now the LORD said to Samuel, ...I will send you to Jesse the Bethlehemite, for I have selected a king for Myself among his sons. ... Now he was ruddy, with beautiful eyes and a handsome appearance. And the LORD said, "Arise, anoint him; for this is he." Then Samuel took the horn of oil and anointed him in the midst of his brothers; and the Spirit of the Lord came mightily upon David from that day forward...." 1 Samuel 16:1, 12-13

An inscription from the ninth century BC refers both to David and the House of David as rulers over Israel. This inscription is thought to be the oldest non-biblical reference to the Jewish nation of Israel. [30]

During the first seven-and-one-half years of David's reign, his capital city was Hebron. However, he decided to relocate to Jerusalem, which was controlled by the Jebusites. Because Jerusalem was well fortified, it would have been difficult for David's army to invade. The Bible states that his men found an unguarded entrance into the city through a water tunnel. They entered through the water tunnel and captured the city of Jerusalem. This water tunnel was excavated in the 1960s. [31]

"David said on that day, "Whoever would strike the Jebusites, let him reach [the city]... through the water tunnel... So, David lived in the stronghold and called it the City of David [Jerusalem]..." 2 Samuel 5:8-9

Jesus The first chapter of this book presented Jesus as the promised Messiah and Savior. The section about God in this chapter presented Jesus as God, the Son. Chapter 3 provides more detailed information about Jesus' birth, life, death, resurrection, ascension, and second coming. Since all of this information comes from the Bible, you may wonder if there is any evidence, outside of the Bible, that supports the fact that the Jesus of the Bible actually existed. The answer is "Yes, there is."

The first century Roman historian, Tacitus, wrote:

"Consequently, to get rid of the report, Nero fastened the guild and inflicted the most exquisite tortures on a class hated for their abominations, called Christians by the populace. Christus, from whom the name had its origin, suffered the extreme penalty during the reign of Tiberius at the hands of one of our procurators, Pontius Pilatus... " [32]

"Christus" refers to Jesus Christ and "Christians" are the believers in the resurrected Jesus. This provides evidence that Jesus lived in the first century, was crucified, and His followers claimed that He rose from the dead.

Flavius Josephus was a Jewish historian who lived from AD 37 or 38 to AD 97. In his writings, *Antiquities*, he wrote:

> "Now there was about this time Jesus, a wise man, if it be lawful to call him a man. For he was one who wrought surprising feats. ... He was (the) Christ ... he appeared to them alive and again the third day, as the divine prophets had foretold these and then thousand other wonderful things concerning him." [33]

There is some debate among scholars whether or not all of these words were written. Since Josephus was a Jew and not thought to be a believer, it appears unlikely that he would refer to Jesus as the Christ. An Arabic translation of Josephus' *Antiquities* includes a similar account of Jesus, which seems more likely to be consistent with a first century Jewish historian's view of Jesus:

> "At this time there was a wise man who was called Jesus. His conduct was good and (he) was known to be virtuous. And many people from among the Jews and the other nations became his disciples. Pilate condemned him to be crucified and to die. But those who had become his disciples did not abandon his discipleship. They reported that he had appeared to them three days after his crucifixion, and that he was alive; accordingly he was perhaps the Messiah, concerning whom the prophets have recounted wonders." [34]

An interesting reference to Jesus appears in the Talmud, a Jewish religious document:

> "On the eve of the Passover Yeshu [Jesus] was hanged.... Because he has practiced sorcery and enticed Israel to apostasy..." [35]

The significance of these and other non-Christian writings has been summarized by Dr. Norman Geisler:

> "The primary sources for the life of Christ are the four Gospels. However, there are considerable reports from non-Christian sources that supplement and confirm the Gospel accounts. These come largely from Greek,

Roman, Jewish, and Samaritan sources of the first century. In brief they inform us that:

(1) Jesus was from Nazareth;
(2) He lived a wise and virtuous life;
(3) He was crucified in Palestine under Pontius Pilate during the reign of Tiberius Caesar at Passover time, being considered the Jewish King;
(4) He was believed by His disciples to have been raised from the dead three days later;
(5) His enemies acknowledged that He performed unusual feats they called "sorcery";
(6) His small band of disciples multiplied rapidly, spreading even as far as Rome;
(7) His disciples denied polytheism, lived moral lives, and worshiped Christ as divine.
     This picture confirms the view of Christ presented in the New Testament Gospels" [36]

Pontius Pilate The Bible tells us that Pontius Pilate was governor of the province of Judea at the time of Jesus, that he conducted one of the trials of Jesus, and that he condemned Jesus to be crucified.

"Now in the fifteenth year of the reign of Tiberius Caesar, when Pontius Pilate was governor of Judea,..." Luke 3:1

"Then the whole body of them [Jewish religious authorities] got up and brought Him before Pilate." Luke 23:1

"But they [Jewish religious authorities] were insistent, with loud voices asking that He be crucified. And their voices began to prevail. And Pilate pronounced sentence that their demand be granted." Luke 23:23-24

Roman historians, Tacitus and Josephus, confirm that Pilate was governor of Judea at the time of Jesus' death. Additionally, coins minted in AD 30-31 to honor Pilate have been discovered and an inscription with his name was discovered at Caesarea. [37]

Places

Babylon A city mentioned often in the Bible that still exists today. Additionally, historical records document that one of the kings of Babylon was Nebuchadnezzar.

> "In his days Nebuchadnezzar king of Babylon came up, and Jehoiakim became his servant for three years; …" 2 Kings 24:1

Jerusalem Another city that was mentioned many times in both the Old and New Testaments that still exists.

> "At Hebron he [David] reigned over Judah seven years and six months, and in Jerusalem he reigned thirty-three years over all Israel and Judah." 2 Samuel 5:5

> "Now after Jesus was born in Bethlehem of Judea in the days of Herod the king, magi from the east arrived in Jerusalem.…" Matthew 2:1

Cities Listed by Luke in the New Testament. Luke has proven himself to be a reliable historian even in the details. William Ramsay spent 20 years of research in the area Luke wrote about. His conclusion was that in references to 32 countries, 54 cities, and nine islands Luke made no mistakes! That is a record to be envied by historians of any era. [38]

Things

Genesis Flood The Bible states that there was a worldwide flood that destroyed all of the people, except Noah and his family, and all of the animals, except two of each kind, which were on an ark with Noah and his family.

> "Then the LORD saw that the wickedness of man was great on the earth, and that every intent of the thoughts of his heart was only evil continually." Genesis 6:5

> "But Noah found favor in the eyes of the LORD…Noah was a righteous man, blameless in his time; Noah walked with God." Genesis 6:8-9

"Then God said to Noah, 'The end of all flesh has come before Me; for the earth is filled with violence because of them; and behold, I am about to destroy them with the earth. Make for yourself an ark of gopher wood; you shall make the ark with rooms, and shall cover it inside and out with pitch. This is how you shall make it: the length of the ark three hundred cubits, its breadth fifty cubits, and its height thirty cubits. You shall make a window for the ark in the side of it; you shall make it with lower, second, and third decks.'" Genesis 6:13-16

"Behold, I, even I am bringing the flood of water upon the earth, to destroy all flesh in which is the breath of life, from under heaven; everything that is on the earth shall perish. But I will establish My covenant with you; and you shall enter the ark—you and your sons and your wife, and your son's wives with you. And of every living thing of all flesh, you shall bring two of every kind into the ark, to keep them alive with you; they shall be male and female." Genesis 6:17-19

"Noah did according to all that the LORD commanded him." Genesis 7:5

"Then the flood came upon the earth...The water prevailed and increased greatly upon the earth and the ark floated on the surface of the water. The water prevailed more and more upon the earth, so that all the high mountains everywhere under the heavens were covered....All flesh that moved on the earth perished...." Genesis 7:17-21

"But God remembered Noah and all the beasts and all the cattle that were with him in the ark; and God caused a wind to pass over the earth, and the water subsided....In the seventh month, on the seventeenth day of the month, the ark rested upon the mountains of Ararat." Genesis 8:1, 4

"And God blessed Noah and his sons and said to them, "Be fruitful and multiply, and fill the earth.... Then God spoke to

Noah and to his sons with him, saying...'I establish My covenant with you; and all flesh shall never again be cut off by the water of the flood, neither shall there again be a flood to destroy the earth. God said, 'This is the sign of the covenant which I am making between Me and you and every living creature that is with you, for all successive generations; I set My bow [rainbow] in the cloud, and it shall be a sign of a covenant between Me and the earth....Never again shall the water become a flood to destroy all flesh" Genesis 9:1, 8, 11-13, 15

We can examine several of the details provided in this account to determine if they are reasonable. First, is there evidence that a worldwide flood actually occurred? McDowell [39] states that there are stories and folklore from every continent of a great flood. These range from the Kamaar tribe in Kashmir, the Karens in Thailand, Vietnamese, Chinese, Japanese, Australian aborigines, Natives of Fiji, Alaskans, Arizona Indians, ancient Druids and Greeks, to Egyptian priests. He summarizes by saying,

"The parallels between the many stories are amazing. They generally agree that (1) there was some provision made (an ark, barge, etc.); (2) living things were destroyed by water; (3) only a few were saved through divine intervention; (4) the flood was judgment against the man's wickedness; (5) animals are often saved with the few humans, and birds are often used by the humans to report the end of the flood; (6) the vessel comes to rest on a mountaintop, or the people are saved on a mountaintop." [40]

Realistically, these stories and folklore, even though they appear to be pervasive, do not prove that there was a worldwide flood. However, these are consistent with the Genesis flood account. Additionally, if the Genesis flood occurred, then all families of the earth descended from Noah's family. Even as they dispersed over the world, they carried the story of the flood with them as they populated the earth after the flood.

Since the dimensions of the ark are given, let's consider various aspects of this. A cubit equals approximately 18 inches. Therefore, the dimensions of 300 cubits long x 50 cubits wide x 30 cubits high would be approximately 450 x 75 x 45 feet or 150 x 25 x 15 yards (l × w × h). This resulted in a structure with more than 1.5 million cubic feet, which is the same capacity as 569 railroad box cars. [41] Since there were three decks in the ark, there would have been sufficient space for Noah and his family, two animals of each kind, and food to sustain them for the 150 days that they were in the ark (Genesis 7:24). Additionally, modern-day testing has determined that the structure of the ark was very stable and could have withstood up to 200 foot waves and could tip as much as 90 degrees and still right itself. [41] (See http://www.pbase.com/paulthedane/ image/78108249 for photos of a replica of Noah's ark.[42])

Census at the Time of Jesus' Birth Luke wrote the Gospel of Luke and Acts of the Apostles. He has earned a reputation as an excellent historian. He reported the following:

> "Many have undertaken to draw up an account of the things that have been fulfilled among us, just as they were handed down to us by those who from the first were eye-witnesses and servants of the word. Therefore, since I myself have carefully investigated everything from the beginning, it seemed good also to me to write an orderly account for you, most excellent Theophilus, so that you may know the certainty of the things you have been taught." Luke 1:1-4

> "Now in those days a decree went out from Caesar Augustus, that a census be taken of all the inhabited earth. This was the first census taken while Quirinius was governor of Syria. And everyone was on his way to register for the census, each to his own city. Joseph also went up from Galilee, from the city of Nazareth, to Judea, to the city of David which is called Bethlehem, because he was of the house and family of David, in order to register along with Mary, who was engaged to him and was with child." Luke 2:1-5

Archeology has confirmed the following facts: Augustus was emperor of Rome from 23 BC to AD 14; Quirinius as governor of Syria from 10 to 4 BC and also was made governor of Syria for a second term in AD 6. Census taking and taxation in the Roman Empire, and in Judea (Israel), was common and people were required to return to their hometowns for the census. [43]

Crucifixion, a Method of Capital Punishment by the Romans In 1968 an archaeological investigation, led by Vasilius Tzaferis, uncovered an ancient burial site about one mile north of the Old Damascus Gate in Jerusalem. In the burial site, they found the remains of 35 bodies, which were examined by Dr. N. Haas, a pathologist from Hebrew University. One of these bodies was the remains of a man named Yohanan Ben Ha'galgol, who died sometime around AD 70 as a result of crucifixion. Habermas described the crucifixion evidence as:

> "Still piercing his feet was a large nail about seven inches long that had been driven sideways through his heel bones, which indicates the direction in which the feet and legs were twisted in order to be attached to the cross. The nail pierced an acacia beam on the cross, which was anchored in the ground. Small pieces of wood still attached to the spike indicated that the beam itself was olive wood. The end of the nail was bent backwards toward the head due either to a knot in the wood or to purposeful bending.
>
> An examination disclosed the fact that nails had also been driven between the radius and ulna bones in the lower arm. The radius bone was both scratched and actually worn smooth. This latter result was apparently due to repeated friction caused by the crucifixion victim pulling himself upward in order to breathe, followed by sinking back down again. As the weight of the body was repeatedly moved in order to free the pectoral and intercostals muscles, which inhibit breathing in the "down" position, the radius was worn.
> Additionally, Haas discovered that Yohanan's lower leg bones were broken. The left tibia and fibula bones and the right tibia bone were apparently crushed by a common blow, with the legs being sawed off at a later time. This is quite consistent with the dreaded Roman crucifragium spoken of in John 19:31-32." [44]

The Empty Tomb of Jesus There is no doubt that the tomb of Jesus was empty on that first Easter Sunday morning. Even the Jewish authorities, who demanded Jesus' crucifixion, admitted this fact. In an attempt to discredit the resurrection of Jesus, the Jewish authorities claimed that the body was stolen.

> "... some of the guard came into the city and reported to the chief priests all that had happened. And when they had assembled with the elders and consulted together, they gave a large sum of money to the soldiers, and said, "You are to

say, 'His disciples came by night and stole Him away while we were asleep.' And if this should come to the governor's ears, we will win him over and keep you out of trouble." And they took the money and did as they had been instructed; and this story was widely spread among the Jews, and is to this day." Matthew 28:11-15

In 1878 a slab of stone was found in Nazareth with a decree from the Roman Emperor Claudius, who reigned from AD 41 to 54. The English translation of the Greek inscription is:

"Ordinance of Caesar. It is my pleasure that graves and tombs remain perpetually undisturbed for those who have made them for the cult of their ancestors or children or members of their house. If, however, anyone charges that another has either demolished them, or has in any other way extracted the buried, or has maliciously transferred them to other places in order to wrong them, or has displaced the sealing on other stones, against such a one I order that a trial be instituted, as in respect of the gods, so in regard to the cult of mortals. For it shall be much more obligatory to honor the buried. Let it be absolutely forbidden for anyone to disturb them. In case of violation I desire that the offender be sentenced to capital punishment on charge of violation of sepulcher." [45]

Although the reason for this decree is not known, it is interesting to note that Claudius ruled shortly after the death of Jesus. It is certainly possible that this decree is a reaction to the Christian teaching that Jesus rose from the dead and the Jewish authorities claiming that the body of Jesus had been stolen from the tomb.

Additional evidence supporting the New Testament comes from early non-Christian writers. Josh McDowell, in his book, *The New Evidence that Demands a Verdict*, cites several quotations from early non-Christian writers. These are summarized in Table 2-4 below:

Table 2-4. Early Non-Christian Writers and Their Confirmation of the New Testament (Adapted From McDowell [46])

Author	Topic
Tacitus: "first century Roman ... historian"	Indicates that the Roman Emperor, Nero, blamed the great fire of Rome on Christians.
Suetonius: "chief secretary to Emperor Hadrian (reigned the Roman Empire from AD 117 to 138)"	Reported that Emperor Claudius commanded all Christians to leave Rome, in AD 49. This confirms Acts 18:2 "...because Claudius had commanded all the Jews to leave Rome..."
Josephus: "a Pharisee of the priestly line and Jewish historian (AD 37 to 100)"	Confirmed that the Jewish Scriptures are the same as the 39 books of the Old Testament; confirmed that James, the half-brother of Jesus, was stoned to death for his belief that Jesus rose from the dead and was the Messiah; confirmed the life and death of John the Baptist; confirmed that Jesus lived, was a virtuous and wise man, that he was crucified, reportedly rose from the dead, and that His followers believed He was the Messiah.
Thallus: "wrote around AD 52"	Wrote about the darkness that occurred immediately following Jesus' death, confirming the report in Luke 23:44-45. "It was now about the sixth hour, and darkness fell over the whole land until the ninth hour, because the sun was obscured; and the veil of the temple was torn in two."

Pliny the Younger: "a Roman author and administrator"	Wrote a letter to Emperor Trajan describing early Christian worship practices.
Emperor Trajan: "Emperor of Rome"	Responded to Pliny's letter proclaiming that Christians must be punished for their faith unless they repented and worshiped the Roman gods.
Talmudic writings: "official Jewish documents, written between AD 70 and 200"	Declared "On the eve of Passover Yeshu (Jesus) was hanged."
Lucian of Samosata "a second century Greek writer"	His writings indicated that, among other things, Jesus lived and taught new principles; Jesus was crucified because of His teachings; Jesus' followers worshipped Jesus and thought that they were immortal, which lead many of them to martyrdom.
Valentinus: "lived AD 135 to 160"	Jesus lived, was crucified, and rose from the dead.

Additionally, McDowell summarizes archeological evidence supporting the accuracy of the New Testament, including the items listed in Table 2-5:

Table 2-5. Archeological Finds That Support the Accuracy of the New Testament [47]

Item	Significance
Tower of Antonia	This was the Roman military headquarters during Jesus' time and would have been the location of Pontius Pilate's court, where Jesus was tried and convicted. This was buried when Jerusalem was destroyed in AD 70 and was discovered recently.
Pool of Bethesda	This is the site of one of Jesus' miracles and was discovered in 1888.
Additional Writings Found With the Dead Sea Scrolls	In addition to confirming the Old Testament, as described above, additional writings found in the Qumran caves show similar styles of writing and imagery as found in the Gospel of John and the other New Testament writers, confirming that they were written before the end of the first century.
The Nazareth Decree by Emperor Claudius	This made grave robbery a capital offense and may have been in response to Jesus' empty tomb.
Yohanan Crucifixion	This indicated that crucifixion was a method of capital punishment used by the Romans at the time of Jesus.

Pilate Inscription	In 1961, Antonio Frova, an Italian archeologist, discovered a stone slab with Pontius Pilate's name and title, indicating that he was a Roman governor during the time of Jesus' life.
Erastus Inscription	An inscription on a limestone slab in the city of Corinth mentions the name of Erastus, a city authority. This is consistent with Paul's statement in Romans 16:23, "... Erastus, the city treasurer greets you ..."
New Testament Coins: 1. "Tribute Penny" (denarius) 2. "Thirty Pieces of Silver" 3. "Widow's Mite" (two small coins, worth only a fraction of a penny)	1. A small silver coin with the image of Caesar on one side. Jesus referred to this coin: "Show Me a denarius. Whose likeness and inscription does it have?" They said, "Caesar's."" Luke 20:24 2. Judas betrayed Jesus for 30 pieces of silver and said, "'What are you willing to give me to betray Him to you?' And they weighed out thirty pieces of silver to him." Matthew 26:14 3. Jesus commented on a widow donating this amount: "And He saw a poor widow putting in two small copper coins." Luke 21:2

Based upon the examination of these and other historical documents and archeological findings, the vast majority of scholars agree that the Bible can be trusted as historically valid.

Scientific:

The Bible is not a scientific text. However, if it was inspired by the Creator of the universe, when it refers to scientific topics, it should be compatible with what we know about science (assuming what we "know" about science is correct and true).

In his excellent book, *Examine the Evidence: Exploring the Case for Christianity*, Ralph O. Muncaster highlighted a number of areas in which biblical reference to nature or scientific facts preceded scientific discovery or understanding by thousands of years. Some of these are summarized below: [48]

1. The Earth Hangs in Empty Space
Science: Copernicus - 1543
Bible: 3000 BC:

> "He stretches out the north over empty space and hangs the earth on nothing." Job 26:7

2. The Earth Is a Sphere
Science: Copernicus - 1543
Bible: 700 BC:

> "It is He who sits above the circle of the earth...." Isaiah 40:22 (the broader definition of the Hebrew word *khug* translated as "circle" implies a sphere

3. Air Has Weight
Science: Torricelli discovered barometric pressure in 1643
Bible: 3000 BC:

> "When He imparted weight to the wind, and meted out the waters by measure." Job 28:25

4. Hydrological Cycle
Science: Perrault and Marriotte described this process in the 1700s
Bible: Job - 3000 BC and Solomon - 935 BC:

"For He draws up the drops of water, they distill rain from the mist, which the clouds pour down, they drip upon man abundantly." Job 36:27-28

"All the rivers flow into the sea, yet the sea is not full. To the place where the rivers flow, There they flow again." Ecclesiastes 1:7

5. Circumcision on the Eighth Day
Science: Newborn infants are particularly susceptible to hemorrhaging from the second to fifth day after birth. Vitamin K, which is required in the blood clotting process, is not sufficiently present until days five to seven and it increases to 110% of normal on day eight - 1947
Bible: 1450 BC:

"And every male among you who is eight days old shall be circumcised...." Genesis 17:9

6. Proper Waste Disposal
Science: 1500s
Bible: 1450 BC:

"You shall also have a place outside the camp and go out there, and you shall have a spade among your tools, and it shall be when you sit down outside, you shall dig with it and shall turn to cover up your excrement." Deuteronomy 23:12-14

7. The First Law of Thermodynamics
Science: Joule and Mayer proposed that matter and energy can neither be created nor destroyed (but can be converted) - 1842
Bible: 1450 BC

"By the seventh day God completed His work...." Genesis 2:2

8. The Second Law of Thermodynamics

Science: Commonly known as entropy, this law states that all things progress from a state of order to a state of disorder (within a closed system) without a purposeful input of energy - 1850

Bible: 1000 BC:

> "Of old You founded the earth, and the heavens are the work of Your hands. Even they will perish, but You endure; All of them will wear out like a garment." Psalm 102:25-26

9. The Universe Is Expanding

Science: Albert Einstein proposed the theory of general relativity - 1916

Bible: 3000 BC:

> "Who alone stretches out the heavens...." Job 9:8

10. Time, Space, and Matter Had a Beginning - "The Big Bang Theory"

Science: Albert Einstein proposed the theory of general relativity - 1916

Bible: 1450 BC:

> "In the beginning, God created the heavens and the earth." Genesis 1:1

As indicated above, Albert Einstein's theory of general relativity provided the foundation for the Big Bang Theory, which indicates that the universe and everything in it had a definite beginning. This was supported by research by Penzias and Wilson in 1964 and 1965 with the discovery of background radiation. On April 24, 1992, the COBE (Cosmic Background Explorer) research team provided more proof of the Big Bang Theory when they reported that they had "discovered the edge of the universe" through confirming background radiation and mapping the universe. [49]

To support the importance of the scientific confirmation that the universe had a beginning, Muncaster provides the following:

"Stephen Hawking, Cambridge University's Lucasian professor of mathematics, said, "It's the discovery of the century, if not of all time." Michael Turner, astrophysicist at Fermilab and the University of Chicago, indicated that the discovery was "unbelievably important....The significance of this cannot be overstated. They have found the Holy Grail of cosmology." Project leader Smoot exclaimed, "What we have found is evidence for the birth of the universe." He added, "It's like looking at God." [49]

Since the Big Bang Theory is so important in science, it may be helpful to consider some additional information about the Genesis creation account. Among some Christians there is considerable debate about the creation account in Genesis as it relates to the age of the earth. The debate centers around the word *day* and the fact that Genesis says that God created the universe and everything in it in six days and rested on the seventh day.

If the word *day* means a 24-hour period of time, then this supports the view of a "young" earth, which states that the earth is no more than 10,000 to 20,000 years old. Certainly, the literal reading of the creation account, which states there was "evening and morning" of each of the six days of creation supports this view. Additionally, there are other verses in the Bible in which "day" refers to a 24-hour period of time. These include Genesis 7:4, 11, 24; 8:6; 17:12; and Exodus 20:8-11.

If, however, the word *day* can be used to refer to an extended period of time, i.e., more than 24 hours, then the six days of creation could refer to six periods of an indeterminate and unspecified time that could literally include millions of years. If so, then this view would indicate that the earth and universe could be billions of years old, which would be consistent with current scientific consensus that the earth is 4.5 billion years old and the universe is 13.5 billion years old. [50,51] In fact, there are numerous examples in the Bible where the word *day* refers to a period of time longer than a 24-hour period of time. Interestingly, a strong case can be made that one of these verses is actually included in the Genesis account of the seventh day.

"Thus the heavens and earth were completed, and all their hosts. By the seventh day God completed His work which He had done, and He rested on the seventh day from all His work which he had done." Genesis 2:1-2

This implies that since God is no longer creating anything in the universe, that He is still resting and this could indicate that the seventh day is still continuing, thousands or millions of years after the "day" of rest began. Other verses in which day is used to refer to a period of time more than 24 hours include Genesis 2:4, Job 20:28, Psalm 20:1, Proverbs 11:4, Ecclesiastes 7:14, and Isaiah 2:12.

As you can see, both the "young earth" and "old earth" views can find support in the Genesis account. So, why did God not make the Genesis creation account more precise so that we could know the age of the universe and earth and also how He created everything? Several answers to this question come to mind immediately:

(1) The Bible is not and was not intended to be a scientific textbook; however, when it touches on scientific topics, it is accurate;

(2) God's intent was not to communicate "how" and "when" He created, but more importantly "why" He created, i.e., to demonstrate His power and majesty and His desire to have a loving relationship with each created man and woman;

(3) From a practical perspective, the ancient Hebrew language was very limited in that it only had about 2,000 words compared to the modern English language which has more than 200,000 words. Realistically, the word that we translate as "day" comes from the ancient Hebrew word *yom*. The ancient Hebrew language did not have a word for era, age, or epoch so the word *yom* was used for these words. [52] So, if the ancient Hebrew language did not have enough word power to distinguish between a 24-hour day and a longer time period of an age, era, or epoch, how could God have communicated the infinitely more complex "how's" and "when's" of creation to His finite creation with an extremely limited language?

Many people find the "young earth" versus "old earth" debate and the creation account versus current scientific theories about the origins of the universe to be very interesting. For an excellent overview of these topics, refer to Grudem's *Systematic Theology* textbook [19] Additional information supporting a "young earth" can be viewed at www.icr.org (Institute for Creation Research) and information supporting an "old earth" can be viewed at www.reasons.org (Reasons to Believe). [53]

The good news is that the age of the universe has nothing to do with your eternal destiny. When we encounter a different opinion on the age of the universe, then this is a topic on which we should agree it is okay to disagree.

There are certainly areas of compatibility between the scientific view that the universe began with a Big Bang and the Bible's creation account in Genesis. More importantly, however, is that the biblical creation account provides objective evidence of the creative power, infinite intelligence, and eternal majesty of God, who created us in His image and demonstrated His desire to have an intimate, personal relationship with each person. How does it feel to know that the Creator of the universe created you and wants you to have a personal relationship with Him?

To summarize, "we can approach both scientific and biblical study with the confidence that when all the facts are correctly understood, and when we have understood Scripture rightly, our findings will never be in conflict with each other: there will be 'no final conflict.' This is because God, who speaks in Scripture, knows all facts, and He has not spoken in a way that would contradict any true fact in the universe." [54]

Prophetic (Non-messianic):

In my opinion, fulfilled prophecy represents one of the strongest proofs that the God of the Bible exists and that the Bible represents His inspired Word. The accurate foretelling or prophesying of specific events that are fulfilled exactly as predicted hundreds or thousands of years later, certainly supports the assertion that the omniscient and omnipotent God of the Bible exists and has used prophecy to demonstrate His existence and control over human events and history.

This section will provide some examples of non-messianic prophecies and their fulfillment. Chapter 3 will provide some of the prophecies concerning the coming Messiah and how Jesus fulfilled these. Chapter 5 presents prophecies that have been made that will be fulfilled in the future.

Prophecy is an extremely important aspect of the Bible. Approximately 25% of the Bible was prophetic when it was written. [55] As you have seen, the Old Testament writings include 17 books written by prophets. God told the people of Israel that He would provide prophets to them and that they would know that they were His prophets because of the accuracy of their predictions:

> "The LORD your God will raise up for you a prophet like me from among you, from your countrymen, you shall listen to him....I will put My words in his mouth, and he shall speak to them all that I command him....You may say in your heart, 'How will we know the word which the LORD has not spoken?' "When a prophet speaks in the name of the LORD, if the thing does not come about or come true, that is

the thing which the LORD has not spoken. The prophet has spoken it presumptuously; you shall not be afraid of him. But the prophet who speaks a word presumptuously in My name which I have not commanded him to speak, or which he speaks in the name of other gods, that prophet shall die." Deuteronomy 18:15, 18, 20-22

Examples of the Old Testament prophecies that were fulfilled exactly are the prophecies concerning David becoming the king of Israel, and Solomon, his son, becoming king of Israel and building the temple.

"Now the LORD said to Samuel....I will send you to Jesse the Bethlehemite, for I have selected a king for Myself among his sons....Now he was ruddy, with beautiful eyes and a handsome appearance. And the LORD said, "Arise, anoint him; for this is he." Then Samuel took the horn of oil and anointed him in the midst of his brothers; and the Spirit of the Lord came mightily upon David from that day forward...." 1 Samuel 16:1, 12-13

"Surely as I vowed to you by the LORD the God of Israel, saying 'Your son Solomon shall be king after me, and he shall sit on my throne in my place'; I will indeed do so this day." 1 Kings 1:30

"And Solomon sat on the throne of David his father, and his kingdom was firmly established." 1 Kings 2:10

"Behold, I intend to build a house for the name of the LORD my God, as the LORD spoke to David my father, saying, 'Your son, whom I will set on your throne in your place, he will build the house for My name." 1 Kings 5:1

The facts that David and Solomon were kings of ancient Israel and that Solomon built the first temple for the Lord are firmly established historical facts. These are just three of many prophecies in the Old Testament. In fact, Muncaster summarizes Old Testament prophecies by stating, "Taking only 118 verifiable Old Testament prophecies and applying an extremely conservative probability of 10 percent chance for each still indicates only 1 chance in 10^{118} that they could, taken together, be fulfilled without God. [56] To put this probability in perspective, the likelihood of all these prophecies being fulfilled, just by chance, is:

"1. It would be like winning 17 state lotteries in a row with a single ticket for each.
2. It would be like dividing all time since the beginning of the universe (an estimated 15 billion years) into seconds, randomly "marking" 7 of these seconds, then correctly guessing by chance every one of the 7 designated seconds.
3. It would be like being struck by lightning 24 times in one year." [57]

There are a couple of factors related to these probabilities that should be considered. Firstly, the probability that any of these prophetic events would occur by chance alone is much less than 1 in 10 (or 10%), so if more realistic probability estimates were used, the cumulative estimate would be actually much smaller than 1 in 10^{118} (i.e., there would be many more zeros following 10 than 118). Secondly, from a skeptical perspective, one might argue that these prophecies were stated in the Bible and then the Bible was used as evidence to indicate that the prophecies were fulfilled exactly as predicted in the Bible. Objectively, a single source (the Bible) cannot be used as both the source of the prediction and the only source documenting fulfillment of the prediction.

Muncaster has effectively addressed this valid criticism by stating, "Another way to analyze such prophecies is to select only the prophecies whose fulfillment occurred centuries later and which were confirmed by history outside the Bible, then to assign them reasonable odds and calculate the probabilities." He lists 10 of these prophecies, cites the biblical reference, and then assigns reasonable odds of each occurring by chance (i.e., without providential guidance). These are shown in Table 2-6.

Table 2-6. Estimation of the Probability of Old Testament Prophecies Being Fulfilled by Chance (adapted from Muncaster) [58]

Prophecy	Scripture Reference	Probability estimate
1. Isaiah's naming of Cyrus nearly two centuries in advance.	Isaiah 44:28-45:3	1/10,000

2. Daniel's 400 years of precisely predicted history.	Daniel 8	1/1,000,000
3. Prophecies by five prophets of the total destruction of Ammon, Edom, and Moab.	Isaiah 11:14; Jeremiah 49:1; Ezekiel 25:1-14; Amos 1:13; Zephaniah 2:9	1/10,000,000
4. Detailed prophecy of the destruction of Tyre, hundreds of years in advance.	Ezekiel 26	1/100,000
5. Prophecy of the destruction of Nineveh more than 100 years in advance.	Isaiah 10:5-34	1/1,000,000
6. Destruction of the Amelekites predicted 450 years in advance.	Exodus 17:14	1/10,000
7. Jerusalem to be rebuilt from the "Tower of Hanenel to the Corner Gate."	Jeremiah 31:38-40	1/1,000
8. Detailed prophecies of the first Jewish exile by seven prophets, some more than a century in advance.		1/100,000
9. The Jews' ultimate survival of their dispersion and their return to their homeland in 1948.	Isaiah 11:12; Ezekiel 37:21-22	1/100,000
10. Israel's survival since 1948 despite being heavily outnumbered during many conflicts.	Amos 9:14-15	1/1,000,000

The cumulative probability of these occurring is 1 in 10^{53}, which is 1 followed by 53 zeros! Scientists consider events with statistical probability less than 1 in 10^{50} as being **impossible** to occur simply due to random chance. [59] Consequently, when these events are fulfilled exactly as predicted in the Bible, then this is very strong evidence that they were providentially guided, as God claimed that they would be.

Jesus also made many prophecies, some of which were fulfilled during or shortly after His death and others will be fulfilled in the future (see Chapter 5: Prophecy). It is interesting to note that Jesus was aware of His forthcoming death and wanted to prepare His disciples for this potentially devastating event. For example,

> "As Jesus was about to go up to Jerusalem, He took the twelve disciples aside by themselves, and on the way He said to them, "Behold, we are going up to Jerusalem; and the Son of Man [Jesus] will be delivered to the chief priests and scribes, and they will condemn Him to death, and will hand Him over to the Gentiles to mock and scourge and crucify Him, and on the third day He will be raised up." Matthew 20:17-19

In fact, it was so important to Jesus that the disciples clearly understood that He would die and rise from the dead that He prophesied His death and resurrection on numerous times, with 18 references recorded in the New Testament: Matthew 12:40, 16:21, 17:22-23, 20:17-19, 26:61, 27:40, 27:63; Mark 8:31, 9:30-32, 10:32-34; 14:58, 15:29-30; Luke 9:21-22, 44-45; 18:31-34; and John 2:13-22; 3:14-16, 12:32-34.

There are several things about Jesus' prophecy concerning His death that are very interesting. These will be more evident in the next chapter when some of the details of the Jewish and Roman legal systems are presented. For now, however, consider that although Jesus lived a sinless life (according to the Bible), the Jewish chief priests and scribes (Jewish religious authorities) were jealous of His popularity and were infuriated that He accused them of being hypocrites and of leading the people astray (Matthew 23:13-29). Since Jesus claimed to be God, the Jewish authorities could say that this claim represented blasphemy and the penalty for blasphemy was death. However, because the Jews were under Roman authority, they could not put anyone to death.

Consequently, they would have to convince the Roman governor, Pontius Pilate, that Jesus deserved to be put to death. However, the Romans did not place any value on the Jewish law or traditions, so it was very unlikely that they could convince Pilate to condemn Jesus to be scourged and crucified. Objectively, it seems unlikely that Jesus would be crucified, but that is what He predicted. Even more remarkable was that He predicted He would rise from the dead, three days after His crucifixion!

The events of Jesus' death and resurrection occurred exactly as Jesus predicted. Are you a betting person? If you had to place a bet on these events occurring just as Jesus predicted as being due to chance or by divine providence, which would you choose? I suspect that most people who read this about Jesus predicting His own death and resurrection are now ready to place their bet on divine providence. If, however, you are not ready to do so, that's okay because additional evidence will be presented in the rest of this chapter and also in Chapters 3, 4, and 5.

Jesus' View:

So far, we have examined the historical/archeological, scientific, and prophetic facts that support the assertion that the Bible is what it claims to be—the inspired Word of God. Before leaving the topic of the validity of the Bible, let's consider what Jesus said about the Old Testament, as well as the New Testament.

It is very apparent Jesus believed that the Hebrew Scriptures—which are the same as the books of the Old Testament—were inspired by God. Jesus affirmed the following Old Testament teachings: [60]

Creation and Adam and Eve:

> "But from the beginning of creation, God MADE THEM MALE AND FEMALE." Mark 10:6

Noah and the Flood:

> "For the coming of the Son of Man will be just like the days of Noah. For as in those days before the flood they were eating and drinking, marrying and giving in marriage, until the day that Noah entered the ark, and they did not understand until the flood came and took them all away; so will the coming of the Son of Man be." Matthew 24:37-39

Moses Wrote the Law (first five books of the Old Testament):

"Did not Moses give you the Law, and yet none of you carries out the Law? Why do you seek to kill Me?" John 7:19

Jonah and the Great Fish:

"But He answered and said to them, An evil and adulterous generation craves for a sign; and yet no sign will be given to it but the sign of Jonah the prophet; for just as JONAH WAS THREE DAYS AND THREE NIGHTS IN THE BELLY OF THE SEA MONSTER, so will the Son of Man be three days and three nights in the heart of the earth." Matthew 12:39-40

Abraham, Isaac, and Jacob Were Real Persons:

"I AM THE GOD OF ABRAHAM, AND THE GOD OF ISAAC, AND THE GOD OF JACOB..." Matthew 22:32

David (king of Israel) Lived and Wrote the Book of Psalms:

"For David himself says in the book of Psalms, 'THE LORD SAID TO MY LORD, SIT AT MY RIGHT HAND, UNTIL I MAKE YOUR ENEMIES A FOOTSTOOL FOR YOUR FEET." Luke 20:42-43

Solomon (king of Israel) Lived:

"Consider the lilies, how they grow: they neither toil nor spin; but I tell you, not even Solomon in all his glory clothed himself like one of these." Luke 12:27

Sodom (a sinful city) Existed:

"I say to you, it will be more tolerable in that day for Sodom than for that city." Luke 10:12

Isaiah Was a Prophet of God:

"This was to fulfill the word of Isaiah the prophet..." John 12:38

Old Testament Law and Prophets' Writings:

"In everything, therefore, treat people the same way you want them to treat you, for this is the Law and the Prophets." Matthew 7:12

Geisler has summarized Jesus' teachings about the Old Testament, as follows: [61]

1. *Divine Authority*—Matthew 4:4, 7, 10

" But He answered and said, "It is written, 'MAN SHALL NOT LIVE ON BREAD ALONE, BUT ON EVERY WORD THAT PROCEEDS OUT OF THE MOUNT OF GOD.'" Matthew 4:4

2. *Indestructibility*—Matthew 5:17-18

"Do not think that I came to abolish the Law or the Prophets; I did not come to abolish but to fulfill. For truly I say to you, until heaven and earth pass away, not the smallest letter or stroke shall pass from the Law until all is accomplished." Matthew 5:17-18

3. *Infallibility or Unbreakability*—John 10:35

"...and the Scripture cannot be broken" John 10:35

4. *Ultimate Supremacy*—Matthew 15:3, 6

"And He answered and said to them, "Why do you yourselves transgress the commandment of God for the sake of your tradition?" Matthew 15:3

5. *Factual Inerrancy*—Matthew 22:29; John 17:17

"Sanctify them in the truth; Your word is truth." John 17:17

6. *Historical Reliability*—Matthew 12:40; 24:37-38

"For the coming of the Son of Man will be just like the days of Noah. For as in those days before the flood they were eating and drinking, marrying and giving in marriage, until the day that Noah entered the ark, and they did not understand until the flood came and took them all away; so will the coming of the Son of Man be." Matthew 24:37-39

7. *Scientific Accuracy*—Matthew 19:4-5; John 3:12

"And He answered and said, "Have you not read that He who created them from the beginning MADE THEM MALE AND FEMALE?" Matthew 19:4

It is also important to remember that the Scripture that Jesus used is the same as our current day Old Testament. [62] Furthermore, Jesus "pre-approved" the New Testament when He said:

"These things I have spoken to you while abiding with you. But the Helper, the Holy Spirit, whom the Father will send in My name, He will teach you all things, and bring to your remembrance all that I said to you." John 14:25-26

"But when He, the Spirit of truth, comes, He will guide you into all the truth; for He will not speak on His own initiative, but whatever He hears, He will speak; and He will disclose to you what is to come." John 16:13

To conclude, historical documents, archeological findings, scientific evidence, fulfilled prophecy, and Jesus' statements all support the validity of the statement that:

"the Bible is the inspired word of God. It logically follows then that "if the Bible is the Word of God and God can only speak truth, then there is no way to avoid the conclusion that the Bible contains no errors. Inspiration guarantees inerrancy." [63]

The concept of "inerrancy" has been defined by Grudem as, "The inerrancy of Scripture means that Scripture in the original manuscripts does not affirm anything that is contrary to fact." [64] Certainly this would be true for the original writings, but is our modern day Bible the same as the original writings? The next section examines the assertion that the Bible we have today is virtually identical to the original writings.

Reliability and Accuracy

Now that we have examined some of the evidence that indicates the Bible does represent God's words, how do we know what we have today is the same as was originally written?

Old Testament:

In March 1947, a young Bedouin shepherd boy was searching for a lost goat around the hills of Qumran (in the area of ancient Judea (Israel). When he came to a cave, he tossed a rock inside and heard the sound of breaking pottery. When he entered and explored the cave, he discovered several clay pottery jars that contained leather scrolls wrapped in linen cloth. Subsequent exploration of this and nearby caves resulted in finding several hundred scrolls and several thousands of fragments.

These scrolls are referred to as the "Dead Sea Scrolls." As shown in the table below, the Dead Sea Scrolls represent every book of the Old Testament (with the exception of Esther) either in part or in entirety. [65] Most significantly, these scrolls were written around 150 BC, which pre-dates one of the earliest versions of the Old Testament (Masoretic Hebrew Text, which was written in AD 916) by more than 1,000 years.

Table 2-7. Books of the Bible Found in Scroll Form in the Caves at Qumran (Dead Sea Scrolls). (adapted from Muncaster) [65]

Book	Number of Copies
Genesis	18 + 3?
Exodus	8
Leviticus	17
Numbers	12
Deuteronomy	31 + 3?

Joshua	2
Judges	3
Ruth	4
1 & 2 Samuel	4
1 & 2 Kings	3
1 & 2 Chronicles	1
Ezra & Nehemiah	1
Esther	0
Job	4
Psalms	39 + 2?
Proverbs	2
Ecclesiastes	3
Song of Solomon	4
Isaiah	22
Jeremiah	6
Lamentations	4
Ezekiel	7
Daniel	8 + 1?
Minor Prophets	10 + 1?

"?" = possible fragment.

Comparing the Dead Sea Scrolls with today's Old Testament provides an incredible opportunity to objectively evaluate the reliability of today's text versus texts more than 1,000 years older to determine if our version has been corrupted over the centuries. According to detailed analysis there is greater than 99% agreement between the words of the Dead Sea Scrolls and the Old Testament. [66]

Since the Dead Sea Scrolls contain many prophecies about the Messiah that were written hundreds of years before Jesus' birth, this proves that these prophecies were not written after Jesus' life to ensure that He fulfilled them. Because these prophecies were written before Jesus' birth and because He precisely fulfilled these, we can confidently state that Jesus is the Messiah promised in the Old Testament. To help you place more confidence in this statement, the section on prophecy will provide statistical probability that one man could fulfill these prophecies simply by chance.

When you think about the fact that there is greater than 99% agreement in the texts of the earliest version of the Old Testament and the Dead Sea Scrolls, with more than 1,000 years separating them, this is remarkable. How could this be?

The reverence that the Jewish scribes had and have for Scripture is remarkable. The copying procedure followed by the scribes provides some insight into their reverence for Scripture. The procedure followed by the scribes as they copied Scripture is summarized below:

"A synagogue roll must be written on the skins of clean animals,
Prepared for the particular use of the synagogue by a Jew.
These must be fastened together with strings taken from clean animals.
Every skin must contain a certain number of columns, equal throughout the entire codex.
The length of each column must not extend over less than 48 nor more than 60 lines; and the breadth must consist of 30 letters.
The whole copy must be first-lined; and if three words should be written without a line, it is worthless.
The ink should be black, neither red, green, nor any other color, and be prepared according to a definite recipe.
An authentic copy must be the exemplar, from which the transcriber ought not in the least deviate.
No word or letter, not even a *yod*, must be written from memory, the scribe not having looked at the codes before him...
Between every consonant the space of a hair or thread must intervene;
Between every new *parashah*, or section, the breadth of nine consonants;
Between every book, three lines.
The fifth book of Moses must terminate exactly with a line; but the rest need not do so.
Besides this, the copyist must sit in full Jewish dress,
Wash his whole body,
Not begin to write the name of God with a pen newly dipped in ink
And should a king address him while writing the name he must take no notice of him."[67]

In addition to these rules, to verify the accuracy of every scroll that was copied, the scribes "counted every letter and compared to the master scroll. They counted the number of words. And as a final crosscheck, they would count through each scroll to the halfway point and compare the letter with the "halfway letter" of the master scroll."[68]

Because of the Jewish scribes' reverence for Scripture and their meticulous attention to detail in the copying process, we can confidently conclude that our modern-day Old Testament is virtually identical to the wording of the original writings.

New Testament:

As with the Old Testament, the New Testament original manuscripts no longer exist. The following chart will provide some comparisons of the New Testament with other works of antiquity:

Table 2-8. Comparison of Ancient Writings (Adapted from Geisler and Nix). [69]

Author/ Book	Date Written	Earliest Copies	Time Gap	# of Copies	% Accuracy
Hindu/ *Mahabharata*	13th century BC				90
Homer/*Iliad*	800 BC			643	95
Herodotus/ *History*	480-425 BC	c.* AD 900	c. 1,350 yrs	8	?
Thucydides/ *History*	460-400 BC	c. AD 900	c. 1,300 yrs	8	?
Plato	400 BC	c. AD 900	c. 1,300 yrs	7	?
Demosthenes	300 BC	c. AD 1100	c. 1,400 yrs	200	?
Caesar/ *Gallic Wars*	100-44 BC	c. AD 900	c. 1,000 yrs	10	?
Livy/*History of Rome*	59 BC– AD 17	4th cent. (partial) mostly 10th cent.	c. 400 yrs c. 1,000 yrs	1 partial 19	?
Tacitus/*Annals*	AD 100	c. AD 1100	c. 1,000 yrs	20	?
Pliny Secundus/ *Natural History*	AD 61-113	c. AD 850	c. 750	7	?
New Testament	AD 50-100	c. AD 114 - fragment c. AD 200 - books c. AD 250 - most of NT c. AD 325 - complete	± 50 years 100 years 150 years 225 years	5,366	99+

"c" in the table above is an abbreviation for "circa," which means "about" or "approximately."

Josh McDowell indicates that the number of early manuscript copies of the New Testament in Greek and other languages is more than 24,970 copies. [70] These are shown in Table 2-9 below:

Table 2-9. Early New Testament Manuscripts. [70]

Greek Manuscripts	Number
Uncials	307
Minuscules	2,860
Lectionaries	2,410
Papyri	109
SUBTOTAL	**5,686**
Manuscripts in Other Languages	**Number**
Latin Vulgate	10,000+
Ethiopic	2,000+
Slavic	4,101
Armenian	2,587
Syriac Pashetta	350+
Bohairic	100
Arabic	75
Old Latin	50
Anglo Saxon	7
Gothic	6
Sogdian	3
Old Syriac	2
Persian	2
Frankish	1
SUBTOTAL	**19,284+**
TOTAL OF ALL MANUSCRIPTS	**24,970+**

Certainly the number of early manuscripts of the New Testament books is impressive and far exceeds any other ancient writing. Additionally, the fact that there are so many early manuscripts in different languages allows scholars to compare the different translations to ensure that the current version of the New Testament is as close as possible to the original writings.

It is fair to conclude, as numerous biblical scholars have, that the superiority of the New Testament in terms of number of copies, closeness of these copies to the original writings, and the accuracy of the copies is clearly superior to any other ancient writing.

Commenting on the reliability of the New Testament, Sir Frederick Kenyon, the British scholar, author, and director of the British Museum, concluded:

> "The interval then between the dates of original composition and the earliest extant evidence becomes so small as to be in fact negligible, and the last foundation for any doubt that the Scriptures have come down to us substantially as they were written has now been removed. Both the authenticity and the general integrity of the books of the New Testament may be regarded as finally established."[71]

Similarly, he concluded, "The Christian can take the whole Bible in his hand and say without fear or hesitation that he holds in it the true word of God, handed down without essential loss from generation to generation throughout the centuries."[72]

Summary

This chapter has provided an overview of the Bible and demonstrated its uniqueness among the world's literature. Since it claims to be the inspired Word of God, information about God was presented. Finally, information supporting the validity and reliability of the Bible was presented. Based upon this information, I think we can agree with Grudem:

> "For most practical purposes, then, the current published scholarly texts of the Hebrew Old Testament and Greek New Testament are the same as the original manuscripts. Thus, when we say that the original manuscripts were inerrant, we are also implying that over 99 percent of the words in our present manuscripts are also inerrant, for they are exact copies of the originals."[66]

I believe that the Bible is the inspired Word of God. Do you?

References:

1. United Bible Societies website. http://www.biblesociety.org/index.php?id=22; and http://www.biblesociety.org/index.php?id=21.
2. Ryrie, Charles C. *Basic Theology*. Wheaton, IL: Victor Books, 1988, pp. 458-460.
3. Geisler, Norman L. and William E. Nix. *A General Introduction to the Bible*. Chicago, IL: Moody Press, 1986, p. 25.
4. Wilkinson, Bruce and Kenneth Boa. *Talk Thru the Bible*. Nashville, TN: Thomas Nelson Publishers, 1983, pp. 13,21.
5. _____. p. 139.
6. _____. pp. 47-49.
7. _____. p. 186.
8. Geisler, Norman L. and William E. Nix. *A General Introduction to the Bible*. Chicago, IL: Moody Press, 1986, p. 237.
9. _____. pp. 25-26.
10. Wilkinson, Bruce and Kenneth Boa. *Talk Thru the Bible*. Nashville, TN: Thomas Nelson Publishers, 1983, p. 305.
11. _____. p. 369.
12. _____. p. 471.
13. _____. p. 513.
14. Geisler, Norman L. and William E. Nix. *A General Introduction to the Bible*. Chicago, IL: Moody Press, 1986, p. 283.
15. _____. p. 293.
16. _____. p. 221.
17. _____. p. 234.
18. _____. p. 233.
19. Grudem, Wayne. *Systematic Theology: An Introduction to Bible Doctrine*. (Electronic version, Copyright 1997, 2004 Wayne Grudem and John Hughes; published by Bits & Bytes, Inc., Whitefish, MT. Print version: Leicester, Great Britain: Inter-Varsity Press and Grand Rapids, MI: Zondervan Publishing House, 1994, pp. 155-225.
20. _____. p. 230.
21. _____. p. 249.
22. _____. p. 254.
23. Geisler, Norman L. *Baker Encyclopedia of Christian Apologetics*. Grand Rapids, MI: Baker Book House, 1999, p. 8. (Libronix Digital Library System version.)
24. Grudem, Wayne. *Systematic Theology: An Introduction to Bible Doctrine*. (see reference 19 for complete bibliographical information). p. 278.
25. Ryrie, C.C. *Ryrie Study Bible: New American Standard Bible*, 1995 update. Chicago, IL: Moody Press, 1995, p. 478. (Libronix Digital Library System version.)

26. McDowell, Josh. *The New Evidence That Demands a Verdict*. Nashville, TN: Thomas Nelson Publishers, 1999, p. 95.
27. _____. p. 95.
28. Walvoord, J.F., R.B. Zuck, and Dallas Theological Seminary. *The Bible Knowledge Commentary: An Exposition of the Scriptures*. Wheaton, IL: Victor Books, 1985, p. 1:461. (Libronix Digital Library System version.)
29. Ryrie, C.C. *Ryrie Study Bible: New American Standard Bible*, 1995 update. Chicago, IL: Moody Press, 1995, p. 478. (Libronix Digital Library System version.)
30. McDowell, Josh. *The New Evidence That Demands a Verdict*. Nashville, TN: Thomas Nelson Publishers, 1999, p 97.
31. _____. p. 96.
32. Tacitus. *Annals* 15.44, as quoted by Gary Habermas. *The Historical Jesus: Ancient Evidence for the Life of Christ*. Joplin, MO: College Press Publishing Company, 1996, 6th printing 2003, p. 188.
33. Josephus. *Antiquities* 18:3, as quoted by Gary Habermas. *The Historical Jesus: Ancient Evidence for the Life of Christ*. Joplin, MO: College Press Publishing Company, 1996, 6th printing 2003, p. 192.
34. Charlesworth. *Jesus Within Judaism*, page 95 as quoted by Gary Habermas. *The Historical Jesus: Ancient Evidence for the Life of Christ*. Joplin, MO: College Press Publishing Company, 1996, 6th printing 2003, pp. 193-194.
35. *Babylonian Talmud*, translated by I. Epstein (London: Soncino, 1935, vol. III, Sanhedrin 43a, P. 281, as quoted by Gary Habermas. *The Historical Jesus: Ancient Evidence for the Life of Christ*. Joplin, MO: College Press Publishing Company, 1996, 6th printing 2003, p. 203.
36. Geisler, Norman L. *Baker Encyclopedia of Christian Apologetics*. Grand Rapids, MI: Baker Book House, 1999, p. 384. (Libronix Digital Library System version.)
37. Habermas, Gary. *The Historical Jesus: Ancient Evidence for the Life of Christ*. Joplin, MO: College Press Publishing Company, 1996, 6th printing 2003, pp. 184, 188.
38. Geisler, Norman L. *Baker Encyclopedia of Christian Apologetics*. Grand Rapids, MI: Baker Book House, 1999, p. 431. (Libronix Digital Library System version.)
39. Josh McDowell. *Josh McDowell's Handbook on Apologetics*. Nashville, TN: Thomas Nelson, 1997. Article entitled "Noah's Ark." (Libronix Digital Library System version.)
40. _____. Article entitled "Noah's Ark." (Libronix Digital Library System version.)
41. Geisler, Norman L. *Baker Encyclopedia of Christian Apologetics*. Grand Rapids, MI: Baker Book House, 1999, p. 258. (Libronix Digital Library System version.)
42. Noah's Ark Replica Schagen Netherlands website. http://www.pbase.com/paulthedane/image/78108249.

43. Habermas, Gary. *The Historical Jesus: Ancient Evidence for the Life of Christ.* Joplin, MO: College Press Publishing Company, 1996, 6th printing 2003, pp. 172-173.
44. _____. pp. 174-175.
45. Maier, P, *First Easter*, P. 119, as quoted by Gary Habermas. *The Historical Jesus: Ancient Evidence for the Life of Christ.* Joplin, MO: College Press Publishing Company, 1996, 6th printing 2003, p. 176.
46. McDowell, Josh. *The New Evidence That Demands a Verdict.* Nashville, TN: Thomas Nelson Publishers, 1999, pp. 55-59.
47. _____. pp. 66-68.
48. Muncaster, Ralph O. *Examine the Evidence: Exploring the Case for Christianity.* Eugene, OR: Harvest House Publishers, 2004, pp. 160-167.
49. _____. pp. 82-85.
50. Grudem, Wayne. *Systematic Theology: An Introduction to Bible Doctrine.* (see reference 19 for complete bibliographical information). p. 278.
51. Lennox, John C. *God's Undertaker: Has Science Buried God?* Oxford, England: Lion Book, 2009, p. 164.
52. Muncaster, Ralph O. *Examine the Evidence: Exploring the Case for Christianity.* Eugene, OR: Harvest House Publishers, 2004, p. 63.
53. _____. p. 64.
54. Grudem, Wayne. *Systematic Theology: An Introduction to Bible Doctrine.* (see reference 19 for complete bibliographical information). p. 274.
55. Walvoord, John F. *The Prophecy Knowledge Handbook.* Wheaton, IL: Victor Books, 1990, p. 9. (Libronix Digital Library System version.)
56. Muncaster, Ralph O. *Examine the Evidence: Exploring the Case for Christianity.* Eugene, OR: Harvest House Publishers, 2004, p. 322.
57. _____. p. 321.
58. _____. pp. 322-323.
59. _____. p. 302.
60. Geisler, Norman L. and Ron Brooks. *When Skeptics Ask: A Handbook on Christian Evidences.* Wheaton, IL: Victor Books, 1990, p. 149.
61. Geisler, Norman L. *Baker Encyclopedia of Christian Apologetics.* Grand Rapids, MI: Baker Book House, 1999, p. 93. (Libronix Digital Library System version.)
62. Muncaster, Ralph O. *Examine the Evidence: Exploring the Case for Christianity.* Eugene, OR: Harvest House Publishers, 2004, pp. 191-192.
63. Geisler, Norman L. and Ron Brooks. *When Skeptics Ask: A Handbook on Christian Evidences.* Wheaton, IL: Victor Books, 1990, p. 151.
64. Grudem, Wayne. *Systematic Theology: An Introduction to Bible Doctrine.* (see reference 19 for complete bibliographical information). p. 90.
65. Muncaster, Ralph O. *Examine the Evidence: Exploring the Case for Christianity.* Eugene, OR: Harvest House Publishers, 2004, pp. 188.
66. Grudem, Wayne. *Systematic Theology: An Introduction to Bible Doctrine.* (see reference 19 for complete bibliographical information). p. 96.

67. Davidson, Samuel, *The Hebrew Text of the Old Testament* (London: 1856), p. 89 as quoted by Norman L. Geisler and William E. Nix. *A General Introduction to the Bible*. Chicago, IL: Moody Press, 1986, p. 237.

68. Muncaster, Ralph O. *Examine the Evidence: Exploring the Case for Christianity*. Eugene, OR: Harvest House Publishers, 2004, p. 157.

69. Geisler, Norman L. and William E. Nix. *A General Introduction to the Bible*. Chicago, IL: Moody Press, 1986, p. 408.

70. McDowell, Josh. *The New Evidence That Demands a Verdict*. Nashville, TN: Thomas Nelson Publishers, 1999, p. 34.

71. Kenyon, Fredrick. *The Bible and Archeology*, Page 288ff, as quoted by Norman L. Geisler and William E. Nix. *A General Introduction to the Bible*. Chicago, IL: Moody Press, 1986, p. 405.

72. Kenyon, Fredrick. *The Bible and Archeology*, Page 55, as quoted by Norman L. Geisler and William E. Nix. *A General Introduction to the Bible*. Chicago, IL: Moody Press, 1986, p. 382.

Chapter 3

Jesus: "Who Do You Say I Am?"

Is Jesus someone that you can know, someone that you can trust, and someone that you can love? This chapter will introduce the Jesus of the Bible to you. Then you can objectively decide if you want to place your faith and eternal destiny in Him.

Occasionally, I'll hear a sermon that is so good that my response afterward is "Wow! That was special." Such was the case on March 22, 2009, when O.S. Hawkins was a visiting pastor at Scottsdale Bible Church and gave a sermon entitled "The Question of Our Time." I was impressed not only by Dr. Hawkins' presentation, but more importantly by his skillful and insightful application of the Word of God. [1]

The text for Dr. Hawkins' sermon was Matthew 16:13-16:

> "Now when Jesus came into the district of Caesarea Philippi, He was asking His disciples, "Who do people say that the Son of Man is?"
>
> And they said, "Some say John the Baptist; and others, Elijah; but still others, Jeremiah, or one of the prophets."
>
> He said to them, "But who do you say that I am?"
>
> Simon Peter answered, "You are the Christ, the Son of the living God."

Why did Simon Peter answer this way? Why was he so sure? When Jesus began His ministry around age 30 He selected 12 men as His disciples and Simon Peter was one of these disciples. They lived and traveled with Jesus. They watched Him, learned from Him, and saw Him perform miracles. They knew Him, just as you would know someone you lived with for a couple of years. So, it was easy for Simon Peter to confess Jesus as the Christ.

What about you and me? We have not seen Jesus or know anyone who has. So, how can we know or know about Jesus? Certainly the Bible, particularly the New Testament, provides the best and most complete source of information about Jesus, but there are other non-biblical sources as well. These will be presented in this chapter to facilitate your examination of them. After considering this information, you will have sufficient objective evidence to answer Jesus' question, "Who do you say that I am?"

My answer to Jesus' question of "Who do you say that I am?" is "Jesus, you are the Savior and Lord of my life." There will come a time when you, along with every person who has ever lived, also will acknowledge Jesus as Lord.

> "so that at the name of Jesus EVERY KNEE WILL BOW, of those who are in heaven and on earth and under the earth, and that every tongue will confess that Jesus Christ is Lord, to the glory of God the Father." Philippians 2:10

That will happen and I did not write this book to tell you that. The reason I wrote this book is so that you can join me, and millions of other people, who can also say, "Jesus is *my* personal Savior."

In Chapter 1 I wrote that salvational faith consists of three components: intellectual, emotional, and volitional. This chapter provides information to address each of these components. The sections on prophecies about the coming Messiah and the death and resurrection of Jesus will provide the facts to satisfy your *intellectual* curiosity. As you study the words and works of Jesus, you will come to know *emotionally* that Jesus is not only worthy, but also that He desires to become your Savior and BEST FRIEND. And as you learn how Jesus' resurrection transformed the lives of many of the people of His time and about Jesus' present and future roles, you can decide *volitionally* if you want to place your faith and your eternal destiny in Him.

As you consider the information in this chapter, please understand that, as Dr. Hawkins pointed out in his sermon, Jesus is not asking you who do *others* say that I am? That is a question of *consensus* and is illustrated below:

Here is a man who was born in an obscure village, the child of a peasant woman. He grew up in another obscure village, where he worked in a carpenter's shop until he was thirty. Then for three years he was an itinerant preacher.

He never wrote a book. He never held an office. He never had a family or owned a home. He never set foot inside a big city. He never traveled two hundred miles from the place he was born. He did none of the things that usually accompany greatness.

While He was still a young man, the tide of popular opinion turned against him. His friends deserted him. He was turned over to his enemies, and went through the mockery of a trial. He was nailed to a cross between two thieves. While he was dying, his executioners gambled for the only piece of property he had—his coat.

When he was dead, he was taken down and laid in a borrowed grave.

Nineteen centuries have come and gone, and today he is the central figure for much of the human race. All the armies that ever marched, and all the navies that ever sailed, and all the parliaments that ever sat, and all the kings that ever reigned, put together, have not affected the life of people on this earth as powerfully as this "One Solitary Life." Anonymous

Although this description of Jesus is true, it is a description of consensus—what others say about Jesus. That is not the question Jesus is asking you. Jesus is asking, "Who do *you* say that I am?" This is a question of *personal conviction* and that is the question that Jesus is asking *you* today.

If your answer is currently that you cannot affirm as I and millions of other people have that Jesus is your personal Savior, then perhaps that is because you do not *know* enough to say yes. So, to help you "know" enough to accept Jesus as your Savior, this chapter will present evidence on the following topics: Prophecies Concerning the Messiah and Jesus' Words, Works, Death, Resurrection, Ascension, Present Role, and Future Role.

If your answer to Jesus' question is that He is your personal Savior, then perhaps this material will provide you with additional facts to strengthen your faith so that you can share your faith as confidently as Peter did that Jesus is the Christ and our Savior. Peter's encouragement for us today is:

> "but sanctify Christ as Lord in your hearts, always being ready to make a defense to everyone who asks you to give an account for the hope that is in you, yet with gentleness and reverence." 1 Peter 3:15

Prophecies Concerning the Messiah

As you recall, God created us in His image and wants to have a personal relationship with each one of us. However, our sin prevents Him from having a personal relationship with us. Consequently, He developed and implemented a plan of redemption, i.e., a way to judge and remove our sin from us so that He could remain true to His attributes of holiness and righteousness and have a personal relationship with us. His plan included sending Jesus to earth as Messiah, one who would pay the penalty of our sins. The Messiah would come not only as our Savior, but would also serve as our High Priest and Lord.

God did not want there to be any misunderstanding about who was the Messiah (His Son and our Savior and Lord). So, He provided nearly 300 prophecies in the Old Testament about the coming Messiah. [2] Perhaps you are wondering that if God provided almost 300 prophecies in the Old Testament to identify the Messiah, then why didn't the Jewish religious leaders and Jewish people recognize Jesus as the Messiah, both then and now?

This is a very good question. The answer is that the prophecies indicated that the Messiah would serve as Savior, Priest, and Lord. [3] The Jewish people of Jesus' time were under an oppressive Roman rule. Consequently, they wanted and expected the Messiah to save or rescue them from the Roman rule and take his rightful role as an earthly ruler and king. In other words, they wanted (and the Jews of today want) the Messiah to return the Jewish nation to the position as the world's pre-eminent power, as it was during the reigns of King David and King Solomon.

As often is the case, God's plan is different than man's plan. Isaiah summarizes this fact very well by saying,

"For My thoughts are not your thoughts, nor are your ways My ways," declares the Lord. For as the heavens are higher than the earth, so are My ways higher than your ways and My thoughts than your thoughts." Isaiah 55:8-9

The Jews of Jesus' time and afterward were correct that the Messiah would fulfill all three roles of Savior, Priest, and Lord. However, their assumption and hope that all three roles would be fulfilled simultaneously was wrong. From our perspective, 2,000 years later, we can easily see that the messianic prophecies will be fulfilled incrementally by Jesus. His first coming was to fulfill the role of Savior. He is currently serving as the High Priest for believers. Jesus will come back to earth in the future as Lord. Each of these three roles of the Messiah will be discussed in this chapter, beginning with the role of Savior.

Let's consider some of the prophecies concerning the Savior and see how these were completely fulfilled by Jesus. One of the first prophecies about the Messiah was that he would be born of a woman (Genesis 3:15). You might think that this is not a particularly impressive prophecy since every person (with the exception of Adam and Eve) has been born of a woman. However, it is important to know that the Messiah would be a human. He would live among and directly communicate with people. He would experience life's joys, sorrows, blessings, and temptations. He would personally experience the things that each of us experience so we would know that He could identify perfectly with us.

The next prophecy we will consider is much more impressive or unique. The Messiah would be born of a virgin!

"Therefore the Lord Himself will give you a sign: Behold, a virgin will be with child and bear a son, and she will call His name Immanuel." Isaiah 7:14

How is that for a challenge for God? How many people do you know that were born of a virgin? None, because that is not the way humans reproduce. But, Jesus was born of a virgin.

"Now the birth of Jesus Christ was as follows: when His mother Mary had been betrothed to Joseph, before they came together she was found to be with child by the Holy Spirit. And Joseph her husband, being a righteous man and not wanting to disgrace her, planned to send her away secretly.

But when he had considered this, behold, an angel of the Lord appeared to him in a dream, saying, "Joseph, son of David, do not be afraid to take Mary as your wife; for the child who has been conceived in her is of the Holy Spirit. She will bear a Son; and you shall call His name Jesus, for He will save His people from their sins. Now all this took place to fulfill what was spoken by the Lord through the prophet: 'BEHOLD, THE VIRGIN SHALL BE WITH CHILD AND SHALL BEAR A SON, AND THEY SHALL CALL HIS NAME IMMANUEL,' which translated means, 'GOD WITH US.' And Joseph awoke from his sleep and did as the angel of the Lord commanded him, and took Mary as his wife, but kept her a virgin until she gave birth to a Son; and he called His name Jesus." Matthew 1:18-25

There are many things that are very interesting about this account. For example, since Jesus did not have a human father, God had to provide new input into the laws of nature to accomplish something unusual or out of the ordinary, that is, perform a miracle that resulted in the virgin birth of Jesus. This is unique and demonstrates the power of the Holy Spirit. He has the power and ability to interact with the laws of nature to produce an unexpected or miraculous outcome.

It is also important to note that God sent an angel to Joseph to explain God's plan and to comfort him. How do you think Joseph felt when Mary, his finance, told him that she was going to have a baby, even though she and Joseph had not had sexual relations and she said that she had not had sexual relations with any other man? Joseph's emotions probably ranged from shock to disbelief to anger to disappointment. However, the angel of the Lord convinced him that Mary was still a virgin and that her baby was the promised Messiah.

This reminds me of a saying that I heard recently: "No matter what challenges or problems are in front of you, they are not as strong as the power behind you (the Holy Spirit)." You will appreciate the meaning and significance of this statement as you read more of Jesus' words in a following section.

Back to Matthew's account of the announcement of the virgin birth to Joseph. Did you notice that the angel referred to Joseph as a "son of David"? Do you remember in the previous chapter that I mentioned the Davidic Covenant, which indicated that David's kingdom and throne would be established forever? (See 2 Samuel 7:8-16.) This is a messianic prophecy that the Jewish leaders wanted and expected to be fulfilled by the Messiah during their time. Remember, however, that the prophecies did not specify that the Messiah would fulfill this prophecy during His first coming. (Jesus will fulfill this prophecy during His second coming, when He returns as Lord.)

Do you remember in the previous chapter that I also mentioned the Abrahamic Covenant, which promised that through Abraham all the families of the earth would be blessed? This is also a messianic prophecy that is in the process of being fulfilled now, as people place their faith in Jesus.

So, if Jesus is or will fulfill both the covenants that God made with David and Abraham, was Jesus related to them? Matthew provides the genealogy of Jesus through Joseph.

> "The record of the genealogy of Jesus the Messiah, the son of David, the son of Abraham: Abraham was the father of Isaac....Jesse was the father of David the king.... Jacob was the father of Joseph the husband of Mary, by whom Jesus was born, who is called the Messiah." Matthew 1:1-16

As you think about this, you may realize that Joseph was not the biological father of Jesus. Consequently, his relationship to David and Abraham would not apply to Jesus. From a biological perspective that is true. However, from a Jewish legal perspective, Joseph was recognized as Jesus' father. So, his genealogy would legally apply to Jesus.

It is very interesting to note that Luke also provides the genealogy of Jesus. However, upon close inspection, it is apparent that this genealogy differs in some ways from that provided by Matthew. Why is this? Does the Bible make a mistake? No, the Bible did not make a mistake concerning Jesus' genealogy. Remember that Matthew's Gospel was written to demonstrate that Jesus was the Jewish Messiah, so he traced Jesus lineage through Joseph, Jesus' legal father. Luke's intent was to show that Jesus was the perfect Son of Man, so he traced Jesus' lineage through Jesus' biological mother, Mary, through David through Abraham through Adam to God.

> "When He began His ministry, Jesus himself was about thirty years of age, being, as was supposed [legally] the son of Joseph, [but biologically, the son of Mary] ... the son of David,

… the son of Abraham … the son of Adam, the son of God."
Luke 3:23-38

So, Jesus was legally and biologically a descendant of both David and Abraham, qualifying him to fulfill both the covenants God made to David and Abraham. Another prophecy that Jesus fulfilled was that the Messiah would be born in Bethlehem.

"But as for you, Bethlehem Ephrathah, Too little to be among the clans of Judah, From you One will go forth for Me to be the ruler in Israel. His goings forth are from long ago, from the days of eternity." Micah 5:2

This is interesting, because Luke tells us that Joseph and Mary lived in Nazareth, not Bethlehem. So, was Jesus born in Bethlehem? Yes. How did that happen?

In the previous chapter, the census of Quirinius was included in the section on historical documents/archeology. The census required all citizens to travel back to their ancestral home. Since Joseph was an ancestor of David, he and Mary traveled back to Bethlehem, the ancestral home of David.

"Now in those days a decree went out from Caesar Augustus, that a census be taken of all the inhabited earth. This was the first census taken while Quirinius was governor of Syria. And everyone was on his way to register for the census, each to his own city. Joseph also went up from Galilee, from the city of Nazareth, to Judea, to the city of David which is called Bethlehem, because he was of the house and family of David, in order to register along with Mary, who was engaged to him, and was with child. While they were, the days were completed for her to give birth. And she gave birth to her first born son...." Luke 2:1-7

Isn't this just an amazing "coincidence" that Joseph and Mary traveled to Bethlehem and that she delivered her baby there? In reality, this was not a "coincidence," it was part of the divine plan of God.

Muncaster has analyzed just 30 (there are many more) of the other messianic prophecies that Jesus fulfilled during His first coming. He assigned reasonable probabilities to them to determine the scientific likelihood that these could have been coincidences, that is, that they were filled by Jesus simply by chance. These are listed below:

Table 3-1. Thirty Messianic Prophecies and the Estimated Probability of Being Fulfilled by One Person [4]

Messianic Prophecy	Bible Reference	An Estimate of Odds
Shem an ancestor	Genesis 9-10	1/3
Abraham an ancestor	Genesis 22:18	1/1,000
Isaac an ancestor	Genesis 26:4	1/10,000
Jacob an ancestor	Genesis 28:14	1/100,000
Judah an ancestor	Genesis 49:10	1/1,000,000
Jesse an ancestor	Isaiah 11:1-5	1/10,000,000
King David an ancestor	2 Samuel 7:11-16	1/100,000,000
Bethlehem Ephrathah as birthplace	Micah 5:2	1/100,000
Star connected with birth	Numbers 24:17	1/100,000
Called "God with us"	Isaiah 7:14	1/100,000
Calming the sea	Psalm 107:29	1/10,000,000
"Special" miracles	Isaiah 35:4-6	1/100,000,000
Names given	Isaiah 9:6	1/10,000
Use of parables	Psalm 78:2	1/10
Ultimate king over all	Isaiah 45:2-3; Psalm 22	1/10
Sin offering and Passover lamb	Isaiah 53	1/100
Will die with "wicked men"	Isaiah 53:3-9	1/10
Will be buried with a rich man	Isaiah 53:3-9	1/10
Timing of entry into Jerusalem	Daniel 9:20-27	1/10,000,000

Entering Jerusalem as a king on a donkey	Zechariah 9:9	1/100
Betrayed by a friend for 30 pieces of silver	Zechariah 11:12-13	1/1,000
Rejection by Israel and will say nothing at trial	Isaiah 8:10; 53	1/10,000
Hands and feet pierced	Psalm 22	1/10,000
Identifying the place of crucifixion	Genesis 22	1/1,000,000
Will thirst while being put to death	Psalm 69:20-22	1/10
No bones broken	Psalm 22	1/10
Identification of words at the beginning and end of execution	Psalm 22	1/1,000
Lots cast for clothing	Psalm 22	1/1,000
Will be given gall and wine	Psalm 69:20-22	1/10
Will be "pierced"	Isaiah 53:5; Zechariah 12:10	1/100

Muncaster puts these in perspective by saying:

"The cumulative probability of all these prophecies randomly coming true in one person would be 1 chance in 10^{110}. This would be like winning 16 lotteries in a row. Even if a skeptic were to substantially reduce some of the above estimates, the result would still be deemed impossible. For example, let's very conservatively assume the above estimates are off by a factor of a trillion trillion! This would still result in the "impossible odds" of all prophecies coming true in one man—Jesus—of one chance in 10^{86}! How remote are these odds? They would still be like taking all of the matter in the entire universe (that is, one billion billion stars and solar systems) and breaking it all down into subatomic particles, and randomly selecting one marked electron! Truly the prophecies made about Jesus in the Old Testament alone verify his divinity because they verify the Bible's claims about him, and his claims about himself." [5]

Later in this chapter, we will also consider prophecies that predicted the Messiah would suffer, die, and rise from the dead. As you consider the prophecies above and the ones to follow, I think you will agree that from both historical and statistical perspectives, the evidence that Jesus fulfilled many of the messianic prophecies concerning the role of Savior is very compelling.

Jesus' Words

Now that we have seen what God said about the Messiah, Jesus, let's examine Jesus' sayings and see what we can learn about Him through His words. Who was Jesus? What did He do? Was He the kind of person you would like to know and have as a friend? The Bible answers these questions very effectively.

The New Testament books of Matthew, Mark, Luke, and John represent about 40% of the New Testament. These books provide detailed description of the birth, life, death, and resurrection of Jesus. Of all the words in these four books, almost half are direct quotes from Jesus. [6] You will probably be relieved to know that I am not going to quote all of Jesus' words in this book! However, I have selected some of them that I think are particularly worthy of your consideration, given the evangelistic nature of this book. I think these words will help you not only know more *about* Jesus, but more importantly, in a sense help you *know* Jesus.

You have read about the messianic prophecies and the fact that Jesus fulfilled many of these in His first coming to the earth. Did Jesus know He was the promised Messiah? Did Jesus know He was God? Yes, Jesus clearly knew He was the Messiah and also that He was God:

> "The woman said to Him, 'I know that Messiah is coming (He who is called Christ); when that One comes He will declare all things to us.' Jesus said to her, 'I who speak to you am He.'" John 4:25-26

> "Truly, truly, I say to you, before Abraham was born, I am." John 8:58

> "I and the Father are one." John 10:30

"...Again the high priest was questioning Him, and saying to Him, "Are You the Christ, the Son of the Blessed One? And Jesus said, "I am...." Mark 14:61-62

Jesus knew that He was the Messiah and was co-equal with God. The quote from Mark 14:61-62 is of considerable significance because Jesus said this during His trial before the Jewish high priest. Jesus knew that when He answered, "I am," that the high priest would use this statement as proof that Jesus was guilty of blasphemy (i.e., claiming to be God) and that He would be condemned to death. Jesus, in effect, stated that He was willing to seal His testimony with His death, which He did.

Prior to His trial, Jesus said many other things about Himself. John recorded seven "I am" statements in which Jesus provided more insight into who He was and the purpose of His first coming to earth. These and their significance or meaning are summarized in Table 3-2 below:

Table 3-2. Jesus' "I Am" Statements [7]

"I AM..."	Reference	Significance/Meaning
The way, the truth, and the life	"Jesus said to him, "I am the way, and the truth, and the life; no one comes to the Father but through Me." John 14:6	Jesus provides the only way to eternal life with God.
The gate	"I am the door; if anyone enters through Me, he will be saved...." John 10:9	Jesus provides the entrance into eternal life.

The good shepherd	"I am the good shepherd; the good shepherd lays down His life for the sheep....and I know My own and My own know Me, even as the Father knows Me and I know the Father; and I lay down My life for the sheep." John 10:11, 14-15	Since the Jewish people of Jesus' time viewed a shepherd as any kind of leader, spiritual or political, Jesus compared Himself to a good shepherd. [7] In fact, He was willing to die to protect 'His sheep' (people who place their faith in Him). He also said that He knows each believer and promised that someday we will know Him completely, as He knows God, the Father!
The resurrection and the life	"Jesus said to her, "I am the resurrection and the life; he who believes in Me will live even if he dies." John 11:25	Jesus promises that anyone who believes in Him will receive the gift of eternal life in heaven.
The bread of life	"Jesus said to them, "I am the bread of life; he who comes to Me will not hunger, and he who believes in Me will never thirst." John 6:35	Just as we need food to sustain our physical lives, we need 'food' to sustain our spiritual lives. Jesus provides 'bread' to sustain and nourish our spiritual life so that we may become a productive, mature follower of Jesus.

The light of the world	"Then Jesus again spoke to them, saying, "I am the Light of the world; he who follows Me will not walk in the darkness, but will have the Light of Life." John 8:12	Just as the sun provides light to the world, Jesus provides spiritual light to the world. He promises that His spiritual light will guide believers, as they walk with Him.
The true vine	"I am the vine, you are the branches; he who abides in Me and I in him, he bears much fruit, for apart from Me you can do nothing." John 15:1, 5	Jesus provides life to believers, as the vine provides life to the branches. As a result of the spiritual life He gives us, we are able to produce good works (fruit) to bring glory to Him.

These statements clearly show that Jesus was focused on fulfilling the messianic role of Savior in His first coming. He knew that He was God's only provision for salvation of the human race and that each person must place his or her faith in Him to receive the gift of eternal life with God.

Jesus' interaction with the Jewish religious leaders was very interesting. Many of Jesus' teachings and actions exposed the fact that the religious leaders were more interested in promoting their personal welfare than in accurately teaching the Scriptures. Consequently, they felt threatened by Jesus and wanted to find ways to discredit Him, as demonstrated by the following interaction with Jesus:

"Then the Pharisees went and plotted together how they might trap Him in what He said. And they sent their disciples to Him, along with the Herodians, saying, 'Teacher, we know that You are truthful and teach the way of God in truth, and defer to no one; for You are not partial to any. Tell us then, what do You think? Is it lawful to give a poll-tax to Caesar, or not? But Jesus perceived their malice, and said, "Why are you testing Me, you hypocrites? Show me the coin used for the poll-tax." And they brought Him a denarius. And He said to them, "Whose likeness and inscription is this?" They said to Him, "Caesar's." Then He said to them, "Then render to Caesar the things that are Caesar's; and to God the things that are God's." And hearing this, they were amazed, and leaving Him, they went away." Matthew 22:15-22

As Ravi Zacharias, one of the great Christian apologists of our time, often points out, if these men were really serious about knowing truth, after Jesus told them to render to Caesar what is Caesar's, they would have asked in whose image they were made. Jesus would have answered that they were created in the image of God and that they should render themselves to God. [8]

People often think of Jesus as a meek and mild man who just taught us to love one another so that we could all go to heaven and live happily ever after. Although it is true that He told us to love one another and to forgive those who sin against us, He was not meek and mild when He encountered people in positions of authority who were leading people astray. Consider His words to the scribes and Pharisees, the Jewish religious leaders:

"But woe to you, scribes and Pharisees, hypocrites, because you shut off the kingdom of heaven from people; for you do not enter in yourselves, nor do you allow those who are entering to go in. [Woe to you, scribes and Pharisees, hypocrites, because you devour widows' houses, and for a pretense you make long prayers; therefore you will receive greater condemnation.] Woe to you, scribes and Pharisees, hypocrites, because you travel around on sea and land to make one proselyte; and when he becomes one, you make him twice as much a son of hell as yourselves. Woe to you, blind guides, who say, "Whoever swears by the temple, that is nothing; but whoever swears by the gold of the temple is obligated. You fools and blind men! Which is more important, the gold or the temple that sanctified the gold? And 'Whoever swears by the altar, that is nothing, but whoever swears by the offering on it, he is obligated. You blind men, which is more important, the offering, or the altar that sanctifies the offering? Therefore, whoever swears by the altar, swears both by the altar and by everything on it. And whoever swears by the temple, swears both by the temple and by Him who dwells within it. And whoever swears by heaven, swears both by the throne of God and by Him who sits upon it. Woe to you scribes and Pharisees, hypocrites! For you tithe mint and dill and cummin, and have neglected the weightier provisions of the law: justice and mercy and faithfulness; but these are the things you should have done without neglecting the others. You blind guides, who strain out a gnat and swallow a camel! Woe to you, scribes and Pharisees, hypocrites! For you clean the outside of the cup and of the dish, but inside they are full of robbery and self-indulgence. You blind Pharisee, first clean the inside of the cup and of the dish, so that the outside of it may become clean also. Woe to you, scribes and Pharisees, hypocrites! For you are like whitewashed tombs which on the outside appear beautiful, but inside they are full of dead men's bones and all uncleanness. So you, too, outwardly appear righteous to me, but inwardly you are full of hypocrisy and lawlessness. Woe to you scribes and Pharisees, hypocrites! For you build the tombs of the prophets and adorn the monuments of the righteous, and say, 'If we had been living in the days of our fathers, we would not have been partners with them in shedding the blood of the prophets.' So you testify against your selves, that you are the sons of those who murdered the prophets. Fill up, then, the measure of guilt from your fathers. You serpents, you brood of vipers, how will you escape the sentence of hell? Therefore, behold, I am sending you prophets and wise men and scribes; some of then you will kill and crucify, and some of them you will scourge in your synagogues, and persecute from city to city, so that upon you may fall the guilt of all righteous blood shed on earth, from the blood of righteous Abel to the blood of Zechariah, the son of Berechiah, whom you murdered between the temple and the altar. "Truly I say to you, all these things will come upon this generation." Matthew 23:13-36

On another occasion, He said this to another group of Pharisees:

"Now when He had spoken, a Pharisee asked Him to have lunch with him; and He went in, and reclined at the table. When the Pharisee saw it, he was surprised that He had not first ceremonially washed before the meal. But the Lord said to him, "Now, you Pharisees clean the outside of the cup and of the platter; but inside of you, you are full of robbery and wickedness. You foolish ones, did not He who made the outside make the inside also? But give that which is within as charity, and then all things are clean for you. But woe to you Pharisees! For you pay tithe of mint and rue and every kind of garden herb, and yet disregard justice and the love of God; but these are the things you should have done without neglecting the others. Woe to you Pharisees! For you love the chief seats in the synagogues and the respectful greetings in the market places. Woe to you! For you are like concealed tombs, and the people who walk over them are unaware of it." Luke 11:37-44

Jesus had similar words of condemnation to a group of attorneys:

"One of the lawyers said to Him in reply, "Teacher, when You say this, You insult us too." But He said, "Woe to you lawyers as well! For you weigh men down with burdens hard to bear, while you yourselves will not even touch the burdens with one of your fingers. Woe to you! For you build the tombs of the prophets, and it was your fathers who killed them. So you are witnesses and approve the deeds of your fathers; because it was they who killed them, and you build their tombs. For this reason also the wisdom of God said, 'I will send to them prophets and apostles, and some of them they will kill and some they will persecute, so that the blood of all the prophets, shed since the foundation of the world, may be charged against this generation, from the blood of Abel to the blood of Zechariah, who was killed between the altar and the house of God; yes, I tell you, it shall be charged against this generation. Woe to you lawyers! For you have taken away the key of knowledge; you yourselves did not enter, and you have hindered those who were entering." Luke 11: 45-52

Does this sound like a meek and mild Jesus who just went around telling people to love one another? No, it doesn't. Directly and publicly, Jesus called the religious and legal authorities of His time the following: "hypocrites, son of hell, blind guides, fools, blind men, full of robbery and self-indulgence, full of hypocrisy and lawlessness, serpents, brood of vipers, guilty of murdering the prophets, full of robbery and wickedness, foolish ones, and like concealed tombs." With words like these, it is fair to say that Jesus was not interested in being "politically correct" or in following the rules of *"How to Win Friends and Influence People"* [9]

Why do you think that Jesus said these things about the religious and legal authorities? The answer to this can be found in reviewing the attributes of God (Chapter 2). Do you remember that the attributes of God included holiness, righteousness, and wrath? These combine to mean that God intensely hates sin, which is anything that separates us from God, and that He will deal with the sinful acts of people directly and righteously.

The attitudes, words, and actions of these religious and legal authorities were leading people away from God and were preventing them from knowing the truth about God. These were sinful acts that adversely affected the eternal destiny of not only themselves, but also of others. These acts were completely in opposition to Jesus' primary purpose in coming to the earth as a man to provide "the way, the truth, and the life."

With these factors in mind, re-read Jesus' "I Am" statements in Table 3-2 above and see how these are very consistent with His holiness, righteous, and wrath toward the hypocritical leaders of His day. In essence, these attributes demanded that He expose the true attitudes and actions of these people and their sinful nature.

Before you get too comfortable in thinking that because you are not a scribe, Pharisee, or lawyer that Jesus did not have any scathing words that apply to you, consider the following:

"But woe to you who are rich, for you are receiving your comfort in full. Woe to you who are well-fed now, for you shall be hungry. Woe to you who laugh now, for you shall mourn and weep. Woe to you when all men speak well of you, for their fathers used to treat the false prophets in the same way." Luke 6:20-26

Jesus condemned those who take pleasures in the material things of this world and ignore the spiritual things. Do you fall into this category? Jesus' condemnation of those who lead people astray or kept them from knowing the truth of the Scriptures is very evident from His words cited above. Consequently, I think it is important to warn you of other major worldviews that are currently and aggressively leading people away from and/or keeping them from knowing the truth of the gospel. Three of these will be exposed in the following chapter.

As you have seen, God's attributes of holiness, righteousness, and wrath demonstrate His hatred of sin. Now let's consider the equally strong attributes of God that demonstrate His love for each one of us: love, mercy, and wisdom. God created you and me in His image and gave us the freedom to live our lives according to our own will. Unfortunately, we all fall short of God's standards, that is we sin. God loves us, but hates our sin. His mercy and wisdom have combined to provide a way that the penalty of our sins can be paid by the ultimate sacrifice of His Son, Jesus, so that we can have a personal, eternal relationship with Him, even though we do not deserve it. This is exactly what Jesus meant when He said:

> "For God so loved the world, that He gave His only begotten son, that whoever believes in Him shall not perish, but have eternal life." John 3:16

> "...I came that they may have life, and have it abundantly." John 10:10

> "Greater love has no one than this, that one lay down his life for his friends." John 15:13

God demonstrated His love, mercy, and wisdom by sending the Messiah, Jesus, to fulfill the role of Savior. Jesus willingly came to earth as a man to give us abundant life, now and in the future. He then demonstrated His supreme love for each of us by laying down His life. But His love for us did not end with His resurrection:

"For this is the will of My Father, that everyone who beholds the Son and believes in Him will have eternal life, and I Myself will raise him up on the last day." John 6:40

"I will ask the Father, and He will give you another Helper, that He may be with you forever; that is the Spirit of truth, whom the world cannot receive, because it does not see Him or know Him, but you know Him because He abides with you and will be in you." John 14:16-17

"In My Father's house are many dwelling places; if it were not so, I would have told you; for I go to prepare a place for you. If I go and prepare a place for you, I will come again and receive you to Myself, that where I am there you may be also." John 14:2-3

With these statements, Jesus confirms that those of us who believe in Him will be raised up to eternal life. As further proof of His love for us, He has asked the Holy Spirit to abide and live within us to help us in this life. Additionally, Jesus has prepared a place for us in heaven so that we may be with Him forever! Does this help put the love of God the Father, God the Son, and God the Holy Spirit for you in better perspective? God loves you!

Jesus' Works

It has been said that "actions speak louder than words." So, let's consider some of Jesus' actions. If Jesus was the Messiah, as the previous sections indicated, and if He was equal with God, as He claimed to be, how could He demonstrate or prove His divinity? Well, He could do things that only God could do. So, among other things, Jesus demonstrated His deity by performing miracles.

What is a miracle? The *Merriam-Webster's Collegiate Dictionary* defines it as "an extraordinary event manifesting divine intervention in human affairs." [10] Grudem refines this definition by writing: "A miracle is a less common kind of God's activity in which he arouses people's awe and wonder and bears witness to himself." [11]

Jesus performed many miracles prior to His death. Thirty-five of these are recorded in Matthew, Mark, Luke, and John. In doing these, He demonstrated His power over nature, demons, physical ailments/needs, and death. The table below summarizes these by showing the probable chronological order, the description of the miracle, the references for these, and the place that each miracle was performed.

Table 3-3. The Miracles of Jesus, Grouped by Activity (Adapted from Pentecost [12] and Ryrie [13]).

#	Description	Reference	Place
Power Over Nature			
1	Turning Water Into Wine	Mk 1:16-20; Lk 5:1-11; Jn 2:1-11	Cana
3	Draught of Fishes	Mt 4:18-22	Sea of Galilee
12	Stilling the Storm	Mt 8:18-27; Mk 4:35-41; Lk 8:22-25	Sea of Galilee
19	Walking on Water	Mt 14:24-33; Mk 6:47-52; Jn 6:16-21	Sea of Galilee
25	Money in Fish's Mouth	Mt 17:24-27	Capernaum
33	Cursing the Fig Tree	Mt 21:12-19; Mk 11:12-18; Lk 19:45-48	Jerusalem
35	Second Draught of Fishes	Jn 21:1-25	Sea of Galilee
Power Over Demons			
4	Demoniac in Synagogue	Mk 1:21-28; Lk 4:31-37	Capernaum
13	Demoniac of Gadara	Mt 8:28-34; Mk 5:1-20; Lk 8:26-39	Gadara
17	Casting out Dumb Spirit	Mt 9:27-34	Capernaum
27	Casting out Blind & Dumb Spirit	Lk 11:14-36	Galilee
Power Over Physical Ailments/Needs			
2	Healing the Nobleman's Son	Jn 4:46-54	Capernaum
5	Healing Peter's Wife's Mom	Mt 8:14-17; Mk 1:29-34; Lk 4:38-41	Capernaum

6	Cleansing of the Leper	Mt 8:2-4; Mk 1:40-45; Lk 5:12-16	Galilee
7	Healing the Paralytic	Mt 9:1-8; Mk 2:1-12; Lk 5:17-26	Capernaum
8	Healing the Cripple	Jn 5:1-47	Jerusalem
9	Healing a Withered Hand	Mt 12:9-14; Mk 3:1-6; Lk 6:6-11	Galilee
10	Healing the Centurion's Servant	Mt 8:5-13; Lk 7:1-10	Capernaum
14	Healing of the Woman	Mt 9:20-22; Mk 5:25-34; Lk 8:43-48	Capernaum
16	Healing Two Blind Men	Mt 9:27-34	Capernaum
18	Feeding of the 5,000	Mt 14:13-21; Mk 6:30-49; Lk 9:10-17; Jn 6:1-13	Near Bethsaida
20	Healing Daughter	Mt 15:21-28; Mk 7:24-30	Phoenicia
21	Healing Deaf Man	Mk 7:31-37	Decapolis
22	Feeding of the 4,000	Mt 15:29-38; Mk 8:1-9	Decapolis
23	Healing the Blind Man	Mt 16:5-12; Mk 8:13-26	Bethsaida
24	Healing the Epileptic Boy	Mt 17:14-21; Mk 9:14-29; Lk 9:37-43	Mt. Herman
26	Healing the Man Born Blind	Jn 9:1-41	Jerusalem
28	Healing the Woman	Lk 13:10-17	Perea
29	Healing the Man with Dropsy	Lk 14:1-6	Perea
31	Cleansing 10 Lepers	Lk 17:11-19	Samaria
32	Healing Bartimaeus	Mt 20:29-34; Mk 10:46-52; Lk 18:35-43	Jericho
34	Restoring Malcus' Ear	Lk 22:49-51; Jn 18:10-11	Gethsemane

Power Over Death			
11	Raising Widow's Son	Lk 7:11-17	Nain
15	Raising Jairus's Daughter	Mt 9:18-26; Mk 5:21-43; Lk 8:40-56	Capernaum
30	Raising Lazarus	Jn 11:1-46	Bethany

Although each of these miracles deserve our serious consideration and contemplation on the significance and purpose, I have chosen one from each category above for comment:

Power Over Nature: #12 Stilling the Storm

> "On that day, when evening came, He said to them, "Let us go over to the other side. Leaving the crowd, they took Him along with them in the boat....And there arose a fierce gale of wind, and the waves were breaking over the boat so much that the boat was already filling up. Jesus Himself was in the stern, asleep on the cushion; and they woke Him and said to Him, 'Teacher, do You not care that we are perishing? And He got up and rebuked the wind and said to the sea, 'Hush, be still.' And the wind died down and it became perfectly calm. And He said to them, 'Why are you afraid? How is it that you have no faith?' They became very much afraid and said to one another, 'Who then is this, that even the wind and the sea obey Him?'" Mark 4:35-41

When you consider that several of the disciples, e.g., Simon, Andrew, James, and John, were professional fishermen and that they thought they were going to perish in the storm, then this must have been a very severe storm. When Jesus rebuked the storm, the wind and sea immediately calmed. Even with this display of power and the fact that many of the disciples in the boat with Jesus had seen Him perform other miracles, they still did not understand that He had the power of God.

Power Over Demons: #4 Demoniac in Synagogue

> "And He came down to Capernaum, a city of Galilee, and He was teaching them on the Sabbath; and they were amazed

at His teaching, for His message was with authority. In the synagogue there was a man possessed by the spirit of an unclean demon, and he cried out with a loud voice, 'Let us alone! What business do we have with each other, Jesus of Nazareth? Have You come to destroy us? I know who You are—the Holy One of God!' But Jesus rebuked him, saying, 'Be quiet and come out of him!' And when the demon had thrown him down in the midst of the people, he came out of him without doing him any harm. And amazement came upon them all, and they began talking with one another saying, 'What is this message? For with authority and power He commands the unclean spirits and they come out.'" Luke 4:31

This passage documents several facts about demons: (1) they exist, (2) they can exhibit power over people, (3) they know that Jesus is God, the Son, and (4) they must obey Jesus. Additionally, this demonstrates why "intellectual" faith is not sufficient to obtain salvation. Even the demons know and acknowledge that Jesus is the Son of God; however, their intellectual admission of the deity of Jesus does not result in their salvation (spending eternity in heaven).

Perhaps it would be helpful to take a quick detour and consider what the Bible says about Satan, demons, and hell. Satan was created by God, as the head of the cherubim, the highest order of angels. [14] The Bible does not indicate when Satan and the other angels were created, but it was prior to creation of man, since Satan was the one who tempted Eve. [15] Although Satan was the highest created being of God, he wanted more. He wanted to be worshiped as God, which is a direct challenge to the power and authority of God and is sin. [16]

In attempting to gain this power, he convinced some of the other angels to support him and to rebel against God. Satan and the angels who were loyal to him, who are now referred to as demons, were cast out of heaven. Satan and the demons are active in this world in by presenting a counterfeit kingdom and programs designed to deceive people and keep them separated from God, now and for eternity. [17] Grudem summarizes the present activities of Satan and demons as:

"Just as Satan tempted Eve to sin against God (Gen 3:1-6), so he tried to get Jesus to sin and thus fail in his mission as Messiah (Matt. 4:1-11). The tactics of Satan and his demons are to use lies (John 8:44), deception (Rev. 12:9), murder (Ps. 106:37; John 8:44), and every other kind of destructive activity to attempt to cause people to turn away from God and destroy themselves (John 10:10). Demons will try every tactic to blind people to the gospel (2 Cor. 4:4) and keep them in bondage to things that hinder them from coming to God (Gal. 4:8). They will also try to use temptation, doubt, guilt, fear, confusion, sickness, envy, pride, slander or any other means possible to hinder a Christian's witness and usefulness." [18]

Ryrie adds,

"In relation to unbelievers Satan blinds their minds so that they will not accept the Gospel (2 Cor. 4:4). He often does this by making them think that any way to heaven is as acceptable as the only way. Again, a counterfeit....In other words, Satan will use any aspect of the world system [including counterfeit religions] ... to keep people from thinking about or doing that which will bring them into the kingdom of God. (See Col. 1:13; 1 John 2:15-17)." [19]

The counterfeit kingdom and programs promoted by Satan and his demons lead to a place called hell. "Hell is a place of eternal conscious punishment for the wicked." [20] It was created by God and is the final destination of Satan, demons, and all who reject the gospel of Jesus. Inhabitants of hell will be eternally separated from God. [21]

Many people have difficulty in understanding or believing that hell exists and that a loving God would condemn unbelievers to hell. Certainly this is understandable from our sin-warped perspective, especially when we think about God's attributes of love and mercy. However, when we consider His attributes of holiness, righteousness, and wrath (His hatred of sin), then we can begin to understand the necessity of hell. When we consider that God created us in His image, which includes freedom of choice, then we can begin to understand that some people (and angels) have chosen and will choose to ignore God and His love for them. From my perspective, it is not accurate to say that God sends Satan, demons, and unbelievers to hell. Rather, He honors the decision that they have made not to have a relationship with Him, either now or in eternity, and allows them to go to hell. To do anything else would be un-God like. This topic will be covered in more detail in Chapter 5.

Power Over Physical Ailments: #7 Healing the Paralytic

> "And they brought to Him a paralytic lying on a bed. Seeing their faith, Jesus said to the paralytic, 'Take courage, son; your sins are forgiven.' And some of the scribes said to themselves, 'This fellow blasphemes.' And Jesus knowing their thoughts said, 'Why are you thinking evil in your hearts? Which is easier to say, 'Your sins are forgiven,' or to say, 'Get up, and walk'? But so that you may know that the Son of Man has authority on earth to forgive sins,' then He said to the paralytic, 'Get up, pick up your bed and go home.' And he got up and went home. But when the crowds saw this, they were awestruck, and glorified God, who had given such authority to men." Matthew 9:1-8

The miracle certainly demonstrates Jesus' power over physical ailments. Equally important, however, is the fact that Jesus preceded His demonstration of miraculous power by claiming to do something that only God can do: forgive sins. He then substantiated His claim that He has the authority to forgive sins by performing the healing miracle.

Power Over Death: #30 Raising Lazarus

> "Now a certain man was sick, Lazarus of Bethany, the village of Mary and her sister Martha. It was the Mary who anointed the Lord with ointment, and wiped His feet with her hair, whose brother Lazarus was sick. So the sisters sent word to Him, saying, 'Lord, behold, he whom You love is sick.' But when Jesus heard this, He said, 'This sickness is not to end in death, but for the glory of God, so that the Son of God may be glorified by it.'... So when Jesus came, He found that he had already been in the tomb for four days... Therefore, when Mary came where Jesus was, she saw Him and fell at His feet, saying to Him, 'Lord, if You had been here, my brother would not have died.' When Jesus therefore saw her weeping, and the Jews who came with her also weeping, He was deeply moved in spirit and was troubled, and said, 'Where have you laid him?' They said 'Lord, come

and see.' Jesus wept. So the Jews were saying, 'See how He loved him!' ... So, Jesus, again being deeply moved within, came to the tomb. Now it was a cave, and a stone was lying against it. Jesus said, 'Remove the stone.' Martha, the sister of the deceased, said to Him, 'Lord, by this time there will be a stench, for he has been dead four days. Jesus said to her, 'Did I not say to you that if you believe, you will see the glory of God?'... When He had said these things, He cried out with a loud voice, 'Lazarus, come forth.' The man who had died came forth, bound hand and foot with wrappings, and his face was wrapped around with a cloth. Jesus said to them, 'Unbind him, and let him go.' Therefore many of the Jews who came to Mary, and saw what He had done, believed in Him." John 11:1-45

As indicated in the table above, Jesus raised two other people from the dead. However, the resurrection of Lazarus certainly was the most dramatic, because Lazarus was not only dead, but had been buried for four days! It also provides considerable insight into both Jesus' humanly nature and His divine nature. Jesus was a personal friend of Lazarus, and his sisters, Mary and Martha. Jesus understood the grief and loss that Mary and Martha felt due to the death of their brother. Jesus was also deeply moved and displayed His emotional grief by weeping. All of these things are consistent with His humanity. However, Jesus knew that Lazarus would die, but his death and subsequent resurrection would be used by God to bring glory to Himself and Jesus. Jesus knew that He had power over death and demonstrated His power by commanding Lazarus to rise from the dead. All of these things are consistent with His deity.

The miracles listed above, which were witnessed by many people, (one of which, #18, was witnessed by more than 5,000 people), clearly demonstrated Jesus' divinity. However, it is important to realize that Jesus was more than just a miracle worker.

In addition to learning about Jesus through the miracles He performed, we can learn about Him through some of the titles that were given to Him. For example, if you know that in my professional career some of the titles I have had include research assistant, cardiac exercise physiologist, director, sales representative, regional sales manager, divisional sales manager, vice president international operations and new market development, chief operating officer, and president, then you would know more about me.

You might conclude that I have some advanced academic, scientific, and medical training (research assistant, cardiac exercise physiologist), as well as business experience (sales representative, regional and divisional sales manager), and corporate executive experience (vice president, chief operating officer, and president). Likewise, by considering the titles given to Jesus by those who knew Him, as well as those given to Him by Himself, you can gain some additional insight into the person of Jesus. Some of these are summarized below:

Table 3-4. Titles for Jesus

Title	Reference	Significance
Son of God	Mt 27:43; Mk 3:11; Lk 1:35; Jn 1:34	The second person of the Trinity
Christ/Messiah	Mt 23:10; Mk 8:29; Lk 4:41; Jn 4:25	"Christ" is the Greek translation of the Hebrew word "Messiah." [22]
Son of Man	Mt 8:20; Mk 8:31; Lk 6:22; Jn 1:51	The title was first used by the prophet Daniel, referring to someone of divine origin who was given eternal rule over the world. This title was used 84 times in the NT and always by Jesus to refer to Himself and strongly affirms His equality with God the Father. [23]
Teacher	Mt 26:18; Jn 13:13-14	Jesus' ability to explain the Scriptures with power and authority was unsurpassed.
Master	Lk 5:5; 8:24-25; 17:13	A title of respect

| Lord | Mk 5:19; Jn 20:28 | "This is the name of the Creator and Sustainer of the universe, the omnipotent God." [24] |
| Savior | Lk 2:11; Jn 4:42 | The announcement by the angel at Jesus' birth that He would be the Savior of His people. |

The miracles performed by Jesus, as well as other actions and words, as indicated by the titles bestowed upon Jesus, led many who personally knew and observed Him to believe that He was, in fact, the promised Messiah.

Jesus' Trials, Conviction, and Death

If you knew that you had only one week to live, what would you do? If you knew that God's plan for your last week included a triumphal entry into the capital city of your country and that you would be proclaimed as the Messiah, the King, but the week would end with illegal trials that condemned you to be mocked, tortured, and crucified, would you obediently follow God's plan? Jesus did. Why? There are many reasons, one of which is *because He loves you*!

The most significant events of the final week of Jesus' earthly life are summarized in the table below:

Table 3-5. Traditional Chronology of the Events of the Final Week of Jesus' Earthly Life. [25-28]

Day	Event	Scripture Reference
Sunday ("Palm Sunday")*	1. Triumphal entry into Jerusalem—presentation of Jesus to Israel as Messiah 2. Brief visit to the temple, rejection by religious leaders, which fulfilled Daniel's prophecy (Daniel 9:24-26)	1. Mt 21:4-11; Mark 11:7-11; Luke 19:36-44; John 12:12-19 (see below for combined narrative) 2. Mt 21:14-17

Monday	Cleansing the temple	Mt 21:12-13; Mk 11:15-18; Lk 19:45-46
Tuesday	1. Debates with religious leaders, 2. Teaching, 3. Judas agrees to betray Jesus	1. Mt 21:23-39; Mk 11:27-12:40; Luke 20:1-47 2. Mt 24:1-25, 46; Mk 13:1-37; Lk 21:5-36 3. Mt 26:14-16; Mk 14:10-11; Lk 22:3-6
Wednesday	No recorded events	
Thursday/ Friday	1. The Last Supper 2. Teaching Disciples 3. Garden of Gethsemane	1. Mt. 26:17-29; Mk 14:12-25; Lk 22:7-20 2. Jn 13:2-14:31; 15:1-18 3. Mt 26:30-46; Mk 14:26-42; Lk 22:39-46
Friday	1. Betrayal and arrest of Jesus 2. Trials of Jesus (see following section for details) 3. Crucifixion and burial of Jesus	1. Mt 26:47-56; Mk 14:43-52; Lk 22:47-53; Jn 18:2-12 2. See following section for references 3. See following section for references
Saturday	1. Women visit tomb 2. Roman guard is placed at tomb	1. Mt 27:61; Mk 15:47; Lk 23:55-57 2. Mt 27:62-66
Sunday	1. Women return and find empty tomb 2. Peter and John see empty tomb 3.Resurrected Jesus makes appearances (see Jesus' Resurrection section below for details)	1. Mt 28:1-8; Mk 16:1-8; Lk 24:1-12; Jn 20:1-10 2. Jn 20:3-8 3. See following section for references

* Note: Mills presents a compelling argument that Jesus' triumphal entry into Jerusalem actually occurred on Monday (not Sunday) on March 30, 33 A.D. [29]

Certainly, this was an event-filled, emotional week for Jesus. A few of these events are highlighted and explained below:

Triumphal Entry The Old Testament prophets, Daniel (9:24-26) and Zechariah (9:9), had predicted that the Messiah would enter Jerusalem and be rejected by the Jewish religious leaders. Jesus' entry into Jerusalem on this day fulfilled this prophecy.

The writers of the Gospels (Matthew, Mark, Luke, and John) narrate Jesus' life from their unique perspective. Cheney has combined the words of all four Gospel accounts into one chronological order in the book, *The Life of Christ in Stereo*. [30] His book provides the following four-dimensional narrative of Jesus' triumphal entry into Jerusalem:

> "Now as he proceeded, they began to spread their garments on the road; and as he was already drawing near, at the descent of the Mount of Olives, the whole multitude of the disciples began to rejoice and praise God with a loud voice for all the mighty works which they had seen, saying, *'Blessed is the King who is coming in the name of the Lord!'* ... *'Peace in heaven, and glory in the highest!'* "And a great throng who had come to the feast, when they heard that Jesus was coming into Jerusalem, cut branches from the palm trees and went out to meet him, and strewed them on the road. And the crowds who went before him, and those who followed kept crying out, *'Hosanna!'... Hosanna to the Son of David!'* ... *'Blessed is He who is coming in the name of the Lord, the king of Israel?'* ... *'Blessed is the name of the Lord – the King of Israel!'... 'Blessed is the kingdom of our father David!'* ... *'Hosanna in the highest!'"* [30]

The great throng of people witnessing Jesus' entry into Jerusalem included both common men and the religious leaders. Mills summarizes the situation very well:

> "However, the nation's leaders, too, were in the crowd—the Gospels mention them three times (Luke 19:39; John 12:19; Matt. 14:15); their presence is both sinister and negative. John 12:19; Luke 19:39; Matt 21:15-16 together present the confusion which reigned among them; it seemed to them that their worst fears about Jesus were materializing before their very eyes. The common people, on the other hand, though happy to welcome their King, still focused on the physical benefits of the Messiah's reign, and not on the spiritual Kingdom that Jesus offered (Luke 19:37 supplements John 12:17-18 in indicating that the crowd's acclaim was because of Jesus' spectacular works, not because of His spiritual message. This combination

held not hope: with the hierarchy's antagonism added to the populace's interest only in His physical provision, Jesus would not force His spiritual Kingdom on them." [31]

Cleansing the Temple This was the second time that Jesus went into the temple and drove out the people who were buying and selling things. This certainly did not please the religious authorities whom were making a profit on the items being bought and sold.

> "Then they came to Jerusalem. And He entered the temple and began to drive out those who were buying and selling in the temple, and overturned the tables of the moneychangers and the seats of those who were selling doves; and He would not permit anyone to carry merchandise through the temple. And He began to teach and say to them, 'Is it not written, 'MY HOUSE SHALL BE CALLED A HOUSE OF PRAYER FOR ALL THE NATIONS?' But you have made it a ROBBERS' DEN.'" The chief priests and the scribes heard this, and began seeking how to destroy Him; for they were afraid of Him, for the whole crowd was astonished at His teaching." Mark 11:15-18

Notice the statement above that indicates the chief priests and scribes began seeking how to destroy Him. This led to their questioning Him about the legality of paying a poll-tax to Caesar and to Jesus pronouncing the "woes" on the scribes, Pharisees, and lawyers, as quoted in the section on Jesus' Words.

The Trials of Jesus After Jesus was betrayed by Judas, one of His disciples, He went through six trials—three in the Jewish legal system and three in the Roman legal systems. Although these were two of the most sophisticated legal systems that have ever been designed to protect an innocent person, the final verdict was that Jesus, the most innocent of all men, was condemned to be crucified. How could this have happened? Why did this happen?

Answers to these questions are that Jesus' crucifixion and death were:

Ordained by God,
Embraced by Jesus,

Demanded by the Jews,
Executed by the Romans, and
Required because of my and your sins.

This was a divinely appointed event that was part of God's plan of redemption (salvation). God used the sinfulness of the Jewish religious leaders and people, the Romans, and all mankind, including you and me, to accomplish His purpose. In other words, God can and does use the evil actions of man to bring about His righteous will.

The six trials are summarized below, with the illegalities of these trials noted below the table.

Table 3-6. The Trials of Jesus. [32, 33]

Judge	Accusation	Verdict	Reference
Jewish Religious Trials			
Annas, father-in-law of Caiaphas and previous High Priest (a)	Jesus was making false teachings	Guilty (but not substantiated by the facts)	Jn 18:12-14, 19-24
Caiaphas, High Priest (b)	Blasphemy	Guilty (but not substantiated by the facts)	Mt 26:57-68; Mk 14:53-65; Lk 22:54, 63-65; Jn 18:24
Sanhedrin (c)	Blasphemy	Guilty (but not substantiated by the facts)	Matt 27:1-2; Mk 15:1; Lk 22:66-71. "And they all said, 'Are You the Son of God, then?' And He said to them, 'Yes, I am.' Luke 22:70
Roman Civil Trials			
Pontius Pilate (d)	'Evil doer'; He claimed to be a King; inciting people to rebellion	Not Guilty (Innocent)	Mt 27:2, 11-14; Mk 15:1-5; Lk 23:1-5; Jn 18:28-38 "Then Pilate said to the chief priests and the crowds, 'I find no guilt in this man.'" Luke 23:4

Herod (e)	He claimed to be a King; inciting people to rebellion	Not Guilty (Innocent)	Lk 23:6-12 "Herod ... sent Him back to Pilate." Luke 6:11 (no verdict meant 'not guilty')
Pontius Pilate (f)	Treason against Rome	Not Guilty (Innocent), but sentenced to scourging and crucifixion	Mt 27:15-26; Mk 15:6-15; Lk 23:13-25; Jn 18:39-19:6 "Pilate summoned the chief priests and the rulers and the people, and said to them, 'You brought this man to me as one who incites the people to rebellion, and behold, having examined Him before you, I have found no guilt in this man regarding the charges which you make against Him. No, nor has Herod ..."Luke 23:13-15

The Illegalities of these trials included:

(a) The trial at Anna's house (or apartment in the high priest's palace) was illegal because it was held at night and not in the temple. [34]

(b) The trial at Anna's house (or apartment in the high priest's palace) and meeting of the Sanhedrin was illegal because it was held at night and not in the temple. Additionally, it was illegal to force the accused to testify against himself and to use that testimony as the basis of the verdict. Finally, it was forbidden for a high priest to tear his clothes, which Caiaphas did. [35]

(c) It was illegal to use the testimony of the accused to reach a verdict requiring death of the accused. The law specified that a unanimous verdict was not accepted and that one day must separate the verdict from the sentence. Each of these laws was broken by the Sanhedrin. [36]

(d) When Pilate announced that he found no guilt in Jesus, the case should have been dismissed and Jesus set free. He was not.

(e) When Herod found no guilt in Jesus, the case should have been dismissed and Jesus set free. He was not.

(f) This was Pilate's second pronouncement of the innocence of Jesus, the case should have been dismissed and Jesus set free. He was not. Pilate made two additional statements of Jesus' innocence: after Jesus had been scourged (John 19:4) and after Jesus was brought out so that the Jewish leaders could see that He had been scourged (John 19:6).

"When Pilate saw that he was accomplishing nothing, but rather that a riot was starting, he took water and washed his hands in front of the crowd, saying, 'I am innocent of this Man's blood; see to that yourselves....he handed Him over to be crucified." Matthew 27:24-26

The most amazing display of disregard for the rule of law and of hypocrisy throughout the trials of Jesus was demonstrated by the Jewish religious authorities when they refused to enter Pilate's Praetorium, because it would defile them and they could not eat the Passover feast later that evening. These men had clearly broken several of their own religious laws, lied to Pilate about Jesus, demanded Jesus' crucifixion, and threatened to tell the Emperor of Rome that Pilate did not uphold the laws of Rome by condemning someone claiming to be a King (John 19:12); yet these same men were concerned about entering the Roman Praetorium *because it would defile them*! This is what happens when men become more interested in protecting their own power and position through man-made religion and political power than in following God's will.

The Crucifixion of Jesus It is fair to say that crucifixion is one of the most gruesome, horrible, and inhumane methods that men have devised to torture and kill another man. Perhaps this is the reason that neither Matthew, Mark, Luke, nor John provided any details about the procedure. [37] They simply stated, "they crucified him" (Mark 15:24, Luke 23:3, John 19:18) or "when they had crucified him" (Matthew 27:35). The procedure can be described as one of the most gruesome, inhumane methods of torture and death ever devised by man.

In an article in the *Journal of the American Medical Association*, entitled, "On the Physical Death of Jesus" Edwards, et al, [38] describe the medical aspects of this evil process in great detail:

"The scourging prior to crucifixion served to weaken the condemned man and, if blood loss was considerable, to produce orthostatic hypotension and even hypovolemic shock. When the victim was thrown to the ground on his back, in preparation for transfixion of the hands, his scourging wounds most likely would become torn open again and contaminated with dirt. Furthermore, with each respiration, the painful scourging wounds would be scraped against the rough wood of the stipes. As a result, blood loss from the back probably would continue throughout the crucifixion ordeal.

With arms outstretched but not taut, the wrists were nailed to the patibulum. It has been shown that the ligaments and bones of the wrist can support the weight of a body hanging from them, but the palms cannot. Accordingly, the iron spikes probably were driven between the radius and the carpals or between the two rows of carpal bones, either proximal to or through the strong bandlike flexor retinaculum and various intercarpal ligaments. Although a nail in either location in the wrist might pass between the bony elements and thereby produce no fractures, the likelihood of painful periosteal injury would seem great. Furthermore, the driven nail would crush or sever the rather large sensorimotor median nerve. The stimulated nerve would produce excruciating bolts of fiery pain in both arms.

Most commonly, the feet were fixed to the front of the stipes by means of an iron spike driven through the first or second intermetatarsal space, just distal to the tarsometatarsal joint. It is likely that the deep peroneal nerve and branches of the medial and lateral plantar nerves would have been injured by the nails....

The major pathophysiologic effect of crucifixion, beyond the excruciating pain, was a marked interference with normal respiration, particularly exhalation. The weight of the body, pulling down on the outstretched arms and shoulders, would tend to fix the intercostals muscles in an inhalation state and thereby hinder passive exhalation. Accordingly, exhalation was primarily diaphragmatic, and breathing was shallow. It is likely that this form of respiration would not suffice and that hypercarbia would soon result. The onset of muscle cramps or titanic contractions, due to fatigue and hypercarbia, would hinder respiration even further.

Adequate exhalation required lifting the body by pushing up on the feet and by flexing the elbows and adducting the shoulders. [see figure 1] However, this maneuver would place the entire weight of the body on the tarsals and would produce searing pain. Furthermore, flexion of the elbows would cause rotation of the wrists about the iron nails and cause fiery pain along the damaged median nerves. Lifting of the body would also painfully scrape the scourged back against the rough wooden stipes. Muscle cramps and paresthesias of the outstretched and uplifted arms would add to the discomfort. As a result, each respiratory effort would become agonizing and tiring and lead eventually to asphyxia." [39]

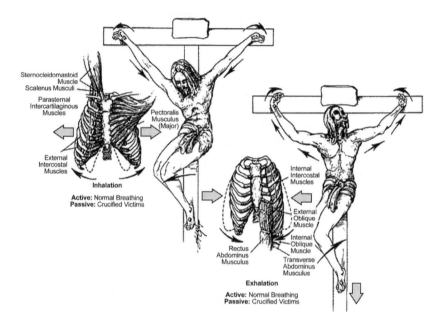

Figure 3-1. "Respirations During Crucifixion. Left, inhalation. With elbows extended and shoulders abducted, respiratory muscles of inhalation are passively stretched and thorax is expanded. Right, Exhalation. With elbows flexed and shoulders adducted and with weight of body on nailed feet, exhalation is accomplished as active, rather than passive, process...." [40]

Edwards, et al, concluded by stating, "Death by crucifixion was, in every sense of the word, excruciating." [40] Edersheim, a respected historian, provided the following insight: "The punishment was invented to make death as painful and as lingering as the power of human endurance." [41]

The crucifixion of Jesus was a public event, which was witnessed by many people, including Jesus' mother, her sister, Mary Magdalene, John (the disciple) (John 19:26-27), the Jewish chief priests, scribes, and elders (Matt. 27:41, Mark 15:31, and Luke 23:35). Additionally, the crucifixion of Jesus was also reported in non-biblical accounts by Josephus, Tacitus, Lucian, Mara Bar, Serapion, and the Jewish Talmud. [42]

Death of Jesus Jesus' crucifixion began at 9:00 a.m. (Mark 15:25). Jesus died at 3:00 p.m. (Matthew 27:45; Mark 15:33; Luke 23:44) Historically, there is no doubt that Jesus was crucified (not an imposter, as claimed by the Qur'an) and died.

Edwards, et al, conclude their medical assessment of the physical death of Jesus:

"Jesus' death may have been hastened simply by his state of exhaustion and by the severity of the scourging, with its resultant blood loss and pre-shock state....The actual cause of Jesus' death, like that of other crucified victims, may have been multifactorial and related primarily to hypovolemic shock, exhaustion asphyxia, and perhaps acute heart failure. A fatal cardiac arrhythmia may have accounted for the apparent catastrophic terminal event....Clearly the weight of historical and medical evidence indicates that Jesus was dead before the wound to his side was inflicted and supports the traditional view that the spear, thrust between his right ribs, probably perforated not only the right lung but also the pericardium and heart and thereby ensured his death." [43]

Luke, the first century physician and historian, documented Jesus' death by writing:

"And Jesus, crying out with a loud voice, said, 'Father, INTO YOUR HANDS I COMMIT MY SPIRIT.' Having said this, He breathed His last." Luke 34:46

John, an eyewitness to the crucifixion, recorded Jesus' death by writing:

"...He said, 'It is finished!' And He bowed His head and gave up His spirit." John 19:37

It is difficult for us to really comprehend the agony, pain, and suffering that Jesus experienced during the trials, flogging, and crucifixion. Mel Gibson's movie, *The Passion of the Christ* [44] provides a powerful and an unforgettable perspective of the evil of mankind and the torture and suffering that Jesus willingly submitted Himself to in order to pay the penalty for our sins and to demonstrate His love for us. At least once a year, usually before Easter, I watch this movie on DVD to remind me of the seriousness of my sins and the price that Jesus paid so that my sins could be forgiven. Although I have seen the movie many times, each time I watch it I weep, even though I know that God was in complete control and that the story has an incredibly happy ending.

Jesus' Resurrection

Certainly, the resurrection of Jesus, if it happened, would be one of the most important events in all of human history. But is there any evidence that Jesus actually rose from the dead? Three categories of evidence will be provided in this section:

(1) the empty tomb;
(2) resurrection appearances;
(3) transformed lives.

The Empty Tomb Matthew, Mark, Luke, and John provided details about Jesus' burial. Matthew's narrative is quoted below:

> "When it was evening, there came a rich man from Arimathea, named Joseph, who himself had also become a disciple of Jesus. This man went to Pilate and asked for the body of Jesus. Then Pilate ordered it to be given to him. And Joseph took the body and wrapped it in a clean linen cloth, and laid it in his own new tomb, which he had hewn out in the rock; and he rolled a large stone against the entrance of the tomb and went away." Matthew 27:57-60

Matthew's narrative continues with the actions taken by the chief priests and Pharisees:

"Now on the next day, the day after the preparation, the chief priests and the Pharisees gathered together with Pilate, and said, 'Sir, we remember that when He was alive that deceiver said, "after three days I am to rise again." 'Therefore, give orders for the grave to be made secure until the third day, otherwise His disciples may come and steal Him away and say to the people, 'He has risen from the dead,' and the last deception will be worse than the first.' Pilate said to them, 'You have a guard; go, make it as secure as you know how.' And they went and made the grave secure, and along with the guard they set a seal on the stone." Matthew 27:62-66

The guard that was provided by Pilate was a Roman guard, which typically consisted of four soldiers. When such a guard was assigned a duty, if they failed or were even found sleeping while on duty, their penalty would have been death by burning. [45] These were highly motivated men, unlikely to fail in their assignment to guard the tomb of Jesus. Additionally, breaking the Roman seal that was placed on the tomb carried the death penalty. Consequently, the tomb was well guarded, at least from human intervention. [45]

It is very interesting that on the first "Easter Sunday" that women were the first to discover the empty tomb. Since women were not regarded as equal to men in these times, their testimony would not be as convincing as the testimony of men. So, if the resurrection story were fabricated by Jesus' believers, it is extremely unlikely that they would have written the story with women being the first to discover the empty tomb. [46]

"Now after the Sabbath, as it began to dawn toward the first day of the week, Mary Magdalene and the other Mary came to look at the grave. And behold, a severe earthquake had occurred, for an angel of the Lord descended from heaven and came and rolled away the stone and sat upon it. And his appearance was like lightning, and his clothing as white as snow. The guards shook for fear of him and became like dead men. The angel said to the women, 'Do not be afraid; for I know that you are looking for Jesus who has been crucified. 'He is not here, for He has risen, just as He said. Come, see the place where He was lying. Go quickly and tell His disciples that He has risen from the dead...." Matthew 28:1-7

When Mary Magdalene reported the empty tomb to the disciples, Peter and John ran to the tomb to see if her story was true.

> "So Peter and the other disciple [John] went forth and they were going to the tomb. The two were running together; and the other disciple ran ahead faster than Peter and came to the tomb first; and stooping and looking in, he saw the linen wrappings lying there; but he did not go in. And so Simon Peter also came, following him, and entered the tomb; and he saw the linen wrappings lying there, and the face-cloth which had been on His head, not lying with the linen wrappings, but rolled up in a place by itself. So the other disciple who had first come to the tomb then also entered, and he saw and believed." John 20:1-8

What about the guards? They were assigned to secure and guard the tomb. Matthew provides the story that Jews devised then and now still hold.

> "the guard came into the city and reported to the chief priests all that had happened. And when they had assembled with the elders and consulted together, they gave a large sum of money to the soldiers, and said, 'You are to say, 'His disciples came by night and stole Him away while we were asleep. And if this should come to the governor's ears, we will win him over and keep you out of trouble.' And they took the money and did as they had been instructed; and this story was widely spread among the Jews, and is to this day." Matthew 28:11-15

Following Jesus' death the disciples were discouraged and defeated. They did not know what to do because their leader had been scourged, crucified, and died. If the disciples didn't have enough courage to admit they knew Jesus at His trial, would they have had enough courage to risk their own crucifixion for stealing the body of their dead leader?

Additionally, these were not violent men and would not have even considered trying to overpower the Roman guard. Even if they had, what would have been the purpose, how would they overcome the Roman guard, and what would they do with the dead body of Jesus? Finally, did you notice that the Jewish authorities told the Roman guard to say that the disciples stole Jesus' body when they were asleep? Since the penalty for sleeping while on guard was death, it is extremely unlikely that the Roman guards were asleep during their assignment. Consequently, the story fabricated by the Jewish authorities is not plausible. [47]

There is no doubt that the tomb of Jesus was empty on that first Easter Sunday morning. Furthermore, since the Jewish authorities had every motivation to produce the dead body of Jesus, but did not (and could not); this provides solid evidence that the tomb of Jesus was empty and supports the assertion that Jesus bodily rose from the dead.

Resurrection Appearances There are numerous eyewitness accounts by people who saw the resurrected Jesus. These are summarized below in order of Jesus' appearances:

Table 3-7. Post Resurrection Appearances by Jesus. [48]

Appearance to:	Scripture Reference
1. Mary Magdalene	John 20:11-17
2. Other women as they were returning to the tomb	Matthew 28:9-10
3. Peter	Luke 24:34; 1 Corinthians 15:5
4. To the disciples on the road to Emmaus	Mark 16:12-13
5. To the 10 disciples	Mark 16:14
6. To the 11 disciples, a week after His resurrection, Thomas was present	John 20:26-29
7. To the seven disciples by the Sea of Galilee	John 21:1-23
8. To 500 people as reported by Paul	1 Corinthians 15:6
9. To James, the Lord's brother	1 Corinthians 15:7
10. To the 11 disciples on a mountain in Galilee	Matthew 28:16-20

11. At the time of His ascension from the Mount of Olives	Luke 24:44-53
12. To Stephen at the time of his martyrdom	Acts 7:55-56
13. To Paul on the road to Damascus	Acts 9:3-6
14. To Paul in Arabia	Galatians 1:12, 17
15. To Paul in the temple	Acts 22:17-21
16. To Paul in the prison in Caesarea	Acts 23:11
17. The final appearance of Christ was to the apostle John at the beginning of the revelation given to him	Revelation 1:12-20

Although each of these deserve comment and provide valuable information about the risen Lord, three of these are of particular interest: numbers 6, 12, and 13.

Appearance #6: Have you ever heard the phrase "doubting Thomas"? It originated after Jesus' resurrection with one of Jesus' original disciples:

> "But Thomas, one of the twelve, called Didymus, was not with them when Jesus came. So the other disciples were saying to him, 'We have seen the Lord!' But he said to them, 'Unless I see in His hands the imprint of the nails, and put my finger into the place of the nails, and put my hand into His side, I will not believe.' After eight days His disciples were again inside, and Thomas with them. Jesus came to the doors having seen shut, and stood in their midst and said, 'Peace be with you.' Then He said to Thomas, 'Reach here with your finger, and see My hands; and reach here your hand and put it into My side; and do not be unbelieving, but believing.' Thomas answered and said to Him, 'My Lord and My God!' Jesus said to him, 'Because you have seen Me, have you believed? Blessed are they who did not see, and yet believed.' John 20:23

Do you have doubts about Jesus and the fact that He rose from the dead? If so, if you honestly seek the truth, Jesus will provide evidence so that you can believe. In fact, that is the specific purpose of this book—to provide evidence so that you can believe in the truth of the gospel of Jesus.

Appearance #12: The first recorded martyrdom of a Christian was Stephen. The account is summarized below:

> "And Stephen, full of grace and power, was performing great wonders and signs among the people. But some men from what was called the Synagogue of the Freedmen...rose up and argued with Stephen. But they were unable to cope with the wisdom and the Spirit with which he was speaking. Then they secretly induced men to say, 'We have heard him speak blasphemous words against Moses and against God.' And they stirred up the people, the elders and the scribes, and they came up to him and dragged him away and brought him before the Council. They put forward false witnesses who said, 'This man incessantly speaks against this holy place and the Law; for we have heard him say that this Nazarene, Jesus, will destroy this place and alter the customs which Moses handed down to us.'... The high priest said, 'Are these things so?' Acts 6:8-14; 7:1
>
> And he said, 'Hear me, brethren, and fathers!... You men who are stiff-necked and uncircumcised in heart and ears are always resisting the Holy Spirit; you are doing just as your fathers did. Which one of the prophets did your fathers not persecute? They killed those who had previously announced the coming of the Righteous One, whose betrayers and murderers you have now become; you who received the law as ordained by angels, and yet did not keep it.' Acts 7:2, 51-53
>
> Now when they heard this, they were cut to the quick, and they began gnashing their teeth at him. But being full of the Holy Spirit, he gazed intently into heaven and saw the glory of God, and Jesus standing at the right hand of God; and he said, 'Behold, I see the heavens opened up and the Son of Man standing at the right hand of God.' But they cried out

143

with a loud voice, and covered their ears and rushed at him with one impulse. When they had driven him out of the city, they began stoning him; and the witnesses laid aside their robes at the feet of a young man named Saul. Acts 7:54-58

Saul was in hearty agreement with putting him to death. And on that day a great persecution began against the church in Jerusalem, and they were all scattered throughout the regions of Judea and Samarian, except the apostles.... But Saul began ravaging the church, entering house after house, and dragging off men and women, he would put them in prison. Acts 8:1, 3

The Jewish religious leaders had heard, and possibly some of them had even seen, the resurrected Jesus (appearances #8 and #11), and were very worried that Jesus and/or His followers, which were growing rapidly, would destroy their position of power and authority over the Jewish people. Therefore, they sought to destroy the Christian movement by trying and then stoning Stephen to death. As often is the case, persecution of these first Christians did not dissuade them from proclaiming the truth of the resurrection of Jesus, but it caused them to scatter from Jerusalem to other regions and spread the good news of Jesus outside the city of Jerusalem.

Appearance #13: Notice that a young man by the name of Saul observed and fully supported the stoning of Stephen. Saul was a Pharisee and was extremely zealous about his Jewish faith (See Galatians 1:14; Philippians 3:5-6). Furthermore, Saul aggressively pursued believers in Jesus for their faith (considered blasphemy) and put them in prison for their teachings (1 Corinthians 15:9; Galatians 1:13; Philippians 3:6). Little did he know that God had other plans for him:

"Now Saul, still breathing threats and murder against the disciples of the Lord, went to the high priest, and asked for letters from him to the synagogues at Damascus, so that if he found any belonging to the Way [Christians], both men and women, he might bring them bound to Jerusalem. As he was traveling, it happened that he was approaching Damascus, and suddenly a light from heaven flashed around him; and he fell to the ground and heard a voice saying to him, 'Saul, Saul, why are you persecuting Me?' And he said, 'Who are You, Lord?" And He said, 'I am Jesus whom you are persecuting, but get up and enter the city, and it will be told you what you must do.' The men who traveled with him stood speechless, hearing the voice but seeing no one. Saul got up from the ground, and though his eyes were open, he could see nothing; and leading him by the hand, they brought him into Damascus. And he was three days without sight, and neither ate nor drank.

Now there was a disciple at Damascus named Ananias; and the Lord said to him in a vision, 'Ananias.' And he said, 'Here I am, Lord.' And the Lord said to him, 'Get up and go to the street called Straight, and inquire at the house of Judas for a man from Tarsus named Saul, for he is praying and he has seen in a vision a man named Ananias come in and lay his hands on him, so that he might regain his sight.' But Ananias answered, 'Lord, I have heard from many about this man, how much harm he did to Your saints at Jerusalem; and here he has authority from the chief priests to bind all who call upon Your name. But the Lord said to him, 'Go, for he is a chosen instrument of Mine, to bear My name before the Gentiles and kings and the sons of Israel; for I will show him how much he must suffer for My name's sake.' So Ananias departed and entered the house, and after laying hands on him, said, 'Brother Saul, the Lord Jesus, who appeared to you on the road by which you were coming, has sent me so that you may regain your sight and be filled with the Holy Spirit.' And immediately there fell from his eyes something like scales, and he regained his sight, and he got up and was baptized; and he took food and was strengthened.

Now for several days he was with the disciples who were at Damascus, and immediately he began to proclaim Jesus in the synagogues, saying, 'He is the Son of God.' All those hearing him continued to be amazed, and were saying, 'Is this not he who in Jerusalem destroyed those who called on this name, and who had come here for the purpose of bringing them bound before the chief priests?' But Saul kept increasing in strength and confounding the Jews who lived at Damascus by proving that this Jesus is the Christ." Acts 9:1-22

This is an amazing conversion story. There are several key points in the account of Saul becoming a believer in Jesus for your consideration. These include the following:

(a) The resurrected Jesus communicated directly with people—audibly and visually with Saul and audibly with Saul's traveling companions and Ananias;
(b) When Jesus communicates directly with someone, He expects obedience—Saul went to Damascus and asked the Lord for further guidance, Ananias went to meet with Saul;
(c) Jesus will provide strength and protection for us to follow His will—Ananias was afraid to go to Saul because of his previous persecution of believers and the purpose of his trip to Damascus to capture believers and take them back to Jerusalem; and
(d) Even though Saul had aggressively persecuted and supported capital punishment of believers, Jesus could change him and could use him to bring the good news of the gospel to other people. The same applies today to you and me—no matter what we have done in the past, Jesus can forgive us of our sins and use us to fulfill His desired purpose for our lives.

As you read these three accounts of people who saw the resurrected Jesus, you can conclude that these accounts support the assertion that there were many people who claimed they had seen the resurrected Jesus and proclaimed that He was alive. What about you? Do you also believe?

Transformed Lives Following the trials and crucifixion of Jesus, the disciples were a discouraged, confused group of men. In fact, Peter had actually denied even knowing Jesus three times during Jesus' trials. However, after these men saw the resurrected Jesus, their lives were radically transformed. They boldly proclaimed that Jesus was the Messiah and that He had risen from the dead, as He prophesied. So convinced were they that Jesus rose from the dead that 10 of the 11 original disciples sealed their testimony with their own death. [49]

Peter: crucified upside down,

Thomas: speared to death,

James: was beheaded,

Bartholomew: beaten and crucified,

Matthew: pierced by a halberd,

Andrew: crucified,

Philip: crucified,

Simon: crucified,

Jude: crucified,

Matthias: stoned to death,

James (Jesus' 1/2 brother): beaten to death, and

Paul: beheaded.

> "From references in Paul's letters, we know that he was whipped five different times by the Jews, thirty-nine lashes each time (a triple-thonged whip was used to deliver twenty-six lashes to the back and thirteen to the chest. The Romans whipped him on three occasions. Once he was stoned (according to Luke he was left for dead; Acts 14:19). He was in constant danger during his travels. Three times he was shipwrecked, and once he was afloat in the water for twenty-four hours. Robbers were always a threat, as were both Jewish and pagan adversaries, who sought to kill him. He experienced great hardship, often going without sleep and sometimes without food.... Without a doubt, Paul, whose letters make up much of what we

call the New Testament, was one of the most remarkable men who ever lived. And it all began because
outside Damascus in A.D. 33 he had an experience
that absolutely shattered his former life and outlook
and turned him to an unquenchable faith in Jesus....
And Paul tells us the reason for that change: he had
seen Jesus the Lord." [50]

Would you die for something that you knew to be a lie? Neither did
these men. They died for what they knew and experienced...Jesus as
Savior and Lord.

The transformed lives of these men resulted in founding the Christian
faith. [51, 52] The gospel of Jesus has transformed the lives of millions of
people since the resurrection of Jesus. It has the power to transform your
life also, which is the primary topic of Chapter 6.

Jesus' Present and Future Roles

For 40 days after Jesus' resurrection, He remained on earth. He used
this time to teach His disciples about the kingdom of God and to prepare
them to proclaim the gospel of Jesus.

> "To these He also presented Himself alive after His suf-
> fering, by many convincing proofs, appearing to them over
> a period of forty days and speaking of the things concerning
> the kingdom of God." Acts 1:3

> "Now He said to them, 'These are My words which I spoke
> to you while I was still with you, that all things which are
> written about Me in the Law of Moses and the Prophets and
> the Psalms must be fulfilled.' Then He opened their minds
> to understand the Scriptures, and he said to them, 'Thus it
> is written, that the Christ would suffer and rise again from
> the dead the third day, and that repentance for forgiveness
> of sins would be proclaimed in His name to all the nations,
> beginning from Jerusalem....'" Luke 24:40-47

> "Go therefore and make disciples of all the nations, bap-
> tizing them in the Name of the Father and the Son and the

Holy Spirit, teaching them to observe all that I commanded you; and lo, I am with you always, even to the end of the age." Matthew 28:19-20

After Jesus said these things, He ascended into heaven:

"And after He had said these things, He was lifted up while they were looking on, and a cloud received Him out of their sight. And as they were gazing intently into the sky while He was going, behold, two men in white clothing stood beside them. They also said, 'Men of Galilee, why do you stand looking into the sky? This Jesus, who has been taken up from you into heaven, will come in just the same way as you have watched Him go into heaven." Acts 1:9-11

These verses claim that Jesus is now in heaven, but He will return to the earth. This leads to several questions: "What is Jesus doing in heaven now? When will He return to the earth and Why?" The answer to the second question: "When will Jesus return to the earth?" was provided by Jesus prior to His ascension to heaven:

"He said to them, 'It is not for you to know times or epochs which the Father has fixed by His own authority." Acts 1:7

The answer to the first and last of these questions is that Jesus is and will in the future fulfill the two remaining roles of the Messiah. Recall that the roles of the Messiah are: (1) Savior, (2) Priest, and (3) Lord. Through His birth, life, death, and resurrection He fulfilled the role of Savior. He is currently filling the role of Priest and will return to the earth in the future to fulfill the final role of Messiah: Lord.

Priest: In the Old Testament, priests were appointed by God to offer sacrifices and praises to God on behalf of the people. Jesus has now become our High Priest in that (a) He offered the perfect sacrifice for our sins, Himself; (b) He provides access for us to God; and (c) He continually prays for us. [53]

"Therefore, since we have a great high priest who has passed through the heavens, Jesus the Son of God, let us hold fast to our confession. For we do not have a high priest who cannot sympathize with our weaknesses, but One who has been tempted in all things as we are, yet without sin. Therefore, let us draw near with confidence to the throne of grace, so that we may receive mercy and find grace to help in time of need." Hebrews 4:14-16

"By this will we have been sanctified through the offering of the body of Jesus Christ once for all. Every priest stands daily ministering and offering time after time the same sacrifices, which can never take away sins; but He, having offered one sacrifice for sins for all time, SAT DOWN AT THE RIGHT HAND...For by one offering he has perfected for all time those who are sanctified." Hebrews 10:10-12, 14

"Christ Jesus is He who died, yes, rather who was raised, who is at the right hand of God, who also intercedes for us." Romans 8:34

Did you know that if you have placed your faith in Jesus He is praying for you? That is an incredible thought: the Creator of the universe is praying for you! To put this in perspective, consider this:

"It is a consoling thought that Christ is praying for us, even when we are negligent in our prayer life; that He is presenting to the Father those spiritual needs which were not present to our minds and which we often neglect to include in our prayers; and that He prays for our protection against the dangers of which we are not even conscious, and against the enemies which threaten us, though we do not notice it. He is praying that our faith may not cease, and that we may come out victoriously in the end." [54]

Lord: Jesus will return to the earth as Lord. In fact, when He does, He will be acknowledged as the King of Kings and the Lord of Lords and everyone will confess Him as Lord.

"And I saw heaven opened, and behold, a white horse, and He who sat on it is called Faithful and True, [Jesus]...And on His robe and on His thigh He has a name written, "KING OF KINGS AND LORD OF LORDS." Revelation 19:11,16

"so that at the name of Jesus EVERY KNEE WILL BOW, of those who are in heaven and on earth and under the earth, and that every tongue will confess that Jesus Christ is Lord, to the glory of God the Father." Philippians 2:10-11

As discussed earlier, God did not want there to be any mistake about who was the Messiah. So, He provided dozens of prophecies about the Messiah. Jesus fulfilled these that relate to Savior and is now fulfilling those that relate to Priest. However, there are many unfulfilled prophecies concerning the final role of the Messiah: Lord. These will be examined in Chapter 5, Biblical Prophecy: What is Coming?

Summary

Was Jesus the promised Messiah? Since Jesus fulfilled the messianic prophecies relating to the role of Savior in His first coming and the Bible indicates He is currently filling the prophecies of Priest now, and will fulfill prophecies of Lord in His second coming, the evidence strongly supports the conclusion that Jesus was, is, and will be, the promised Messiah.

Did Jesus provide evidence that He is God, the Son? His words and works demonstrated that He could do things that only God could do.

Was Jesus crucified, did He die, and did He rise from the dead? Historical evidence as well as millions of transformed lives of believers support the answer of "Yes" to the questions of His crucifixion, death, and resurrection.

Your Response?

So, what is your answer to Jesus' question, "Who do you say that I am"?

Do you want to be a child of God or continue as a creation of God? Will you be able to say that Jesus is your Savior and Lord or just Lord? It is your choice and God will honor your decision.

My hope and prayer is that you have decided to place your faith in the gospel of Jesus. If now is the first time you have made that decision, then you may pray the following prayer to indicate that you have placed your faith in Jesus:

"God, I believe that Jesus lived, died to pay the penalty of my sins, and that He rose from the dead. I want to have a personal relationship with you now and forever and I place my faith, my life, and my eternal destiny in Jesus. Thank you, God, for hearing and accepting my prayer. In Jesus' name I pray."

If you prayed this prayer and were sincere about it, welcome to the family of God! Although you may not feel any different now than before you prayed, you have been transformed from a *creation* of God to a *child* of God. There are some things that you can do to help your faith grow and to help you mature as a believer in Jesus. These will be explained in detail in Chapter 6.

References:

1. Hawkins, O.S. "The Question of Our Time (Matthew 16:13-16)." A sermon presented at Scottsdale Bible Church, Scottsdale, AZ on March 22, 2009. http://scottsdalebible.com/tag/sunday-am/page/2.
2. McDowell, Josh. *The New Evidence That Demands a Verdict*. Nashville, TN: Thomas Nelson Publishers, 1999, p. 164.
3. Ryrie, Charles C. *Basic Theology*. Wheaton, IL: Victor Books, 1988, pp. 105, 292.
4. Muncaster, Ralph O. *Examine the Evidence: Exploring the Case for Christianity*. Eugene, OR: Harvest House Publishers, 2004, pp. 353-355.
5. _____. P. 355.
6. Ryrie, C.C. *Ryrie Study Bible: New American Standard Bible*, 1995 update. Chicago, IL: Moody Press, 1995, p. 1504. (Libronix Digital Library System version.)
7. Wiersbe, W.W. *The Bible Exposition Commentary: An Exposition of the New Testament*. Wheaton, IL: Victor Books, 1996, John 10:1. (Libronix Digital Library System version.)
8. Zacharias, Ravi. "Is Christianity Unique Amongst World Religions?" A sermon presented in Oxford, England, Town Hall Meeting #2, February 7, 2007. Ravi Zacharias International Ministries, Norcross, Georgia. (http://www.rzim.org/)

9. Carnegie, Dale. *How to Win Friends and Influence People*. New York, NY: Simon and Schuster, 1937.

10. Merrian-Webster. *Merrian-Webster's Collegiate Dictionary*. Springfield, Mass.: Merrian-Webster, 1996, miracle.

11. Grudem, Wayne. *Systematic Theology: An Introduction to Bible Doctrine*. (Electronic version, Copyright 1997, 2004 Wayne Grudem and John Hughes; published by Bits & Bytes, Inc., Whitefish, MT. Print version: Leicester, Great Britain: Inter-Varsity Press and Grand Rapids, MI: Zondervan Publishing House, 1994, p. 354. (Libronix Digital Library System version.)

12. Pentecost, J. Dwight. *The Words and Works of Jesus Christ*. Grand Rapids, MI: Zondervan Publishing House, 1981, pp. 588-589.

13. Ryrie, C.C. *Ryrie Study Bible: New American Standard Bible*, 1995 update. Chicago, IL: Moody Press, 1995, p. 1502.

14. Ryrie, Charles C. *Basic Theology*. Wheaton, IL: Victor Books, 1988, p. 158.

15. _____. p. 161

16. _____. p. 165.

17. _____. p. 168.

18. Grudem, Wayne. *Systematic Theology: An Introduction to Bible Doctrine*. (see reference 11 for complete bibliographical information.) p. 415.

19. Ryrie, Charles C. *Basic Theology*. Wheaton, IL: Victor Books, 1988, p. 168.

20. Grudem, Wayne. *Systematic Theology: An Introduction to Bible Doctrine*. (see reference 11 for complete bibliographical information.) p. 1148.

21. _____. p. 1152.

22. _____. p. 543.

23. _____. pp. 546-547.

24. _____. p. 543.

25. Ryrie, C.C. *Ryrie Study Bible: New American Standard Bible*, 1995 update. Chicago, IL: Moody Press, 1995, p. 1599.

26. Richards, L. and L.O. Richards. *The Teacher's Commentary*. Wheaton, IL: Victor Books, 1987, p. 636. (Libronix Digital Library System version.)

27. Wiersbe, W.W. *The Bible Exposition Commentary: An Exposition of the New Testament*. Wheaton, IL: Victor Books, 1996, p. 76. (Libronix Digital Library System version.)

28. Mills, M.S. *The Life of Christ: A Study Guide to the Gospel Record*. Dallas, TX: 3E ministries, 1999, Sections 207-285. (Libronix Digital Library System version.)

29. _____. Section 207.

30. Cheney, Johnston M. *The Life of Christ in Stereo*. Portland, OR: Multnomah Press, 1969, p. 149.

31. Mills, M.S. *The Life of Christ: A Study Guide to the Gospel Record*. Dallas, TX: 3E ministries, 1999, Sections 207. (Libronix Digital Library System version.)

32. Pentecost, J. Dwight. *The Words and Works of Jesus Christ*. Grand Rapids, MI: Zondervan Publishing House, 1981, pp. 459-476.

33. Stott, John R.W. *The Cross of Christ*. Downers Grove, IL: InterVarsity Press, 1986, pp. 49-54.
34. Pentecost, J. Dwight. *The Words and Works of Jesus Christ*. Grand Rapids, MI: Zondervan Publishing House, 1981, pp. 461.
35. _____. pp. 462.
36. _____. p. 463.
37. Stott, John R.W. *The Cross of Christ*. Downers Grove, IL: InterVarsity Press, 1986, p. 49.
38. Edwards, William D., Wesley J. Gabel, Floyd E. Hosmer. "On the Physical Death of Jesus Christ." *Journal of the American Medical Association*. March 21, 1986; Vol. 255, No. 11, pp. 1455-1463.
39. _____. pp. 1460-1461.
40. _____. p. 1461.
41. Edersheim, Alfred. The *Life and Times of Jesus the Messiah*. Grand Rapids, MI: Wm. B. Eerdmans Publishing Co., 1987 (reprinted) Vol. 2. p. 589.
42. Habermas, Gary R. and Michael R. Licona. *The Case for the Resurrection of Jesus*. Grand Rapids, MI: Kregel Publications, 2004, p. 50.
43. Edwards, William D., Wesley J. Gabel, Floyd E. Hosmer. "On the Physical Death of Jesus Christ." *Journal of the American Medical Association*. March 21, 1986; Vol. 255, No. 11, p. 1463.
44. Gibson, Mel. "The Passion of the Christ" (a movie by Mel Gibson). Icon Productions, 2004.
45. McDowell, Josh. *The New Evidence That Demands a Verdict*. Nashville, TN: Thomas Nelson Publishers, 1999, pp. 236-249.
46. Craig, William Lane. *The Son Rises: The Historical Evidence for the Resurrection of Jesus*. Eugene, OR: Wipf and Stock Publishers, 2000, pp. 60-61.
47. _____. pp. 83-84.
48. Walvoord, John. *The Prophecy Knowledge Handbook*. Wheaton, IL: Victor Books, 1990, p. 435.
49. Darryl DelHousaye. "The Easter Factor." A sermon given at Scottsdale Bible Church, Scottsdale, AZ. DD-32-03, 03-30-86 AM.
50. Craig, William Lane. *The Son Rises: The Historical Evidence for the Resurrection of Jesus*. Eugene, OR: Wipf and Stock Publishers, 2000, pp. 60-61.
51. _____. pp. 127-134.
52. Walvoord, John F. *Jesus Christ Our Lord*. Chicago, IL: Moody Press, 1969, p. 200.
53. Grudem, Wayne. *Systematic Theology: An Introduction to Bible Doctrine*. (see reference 11 for complete bibliographical information.) pp. 626-628.

PART 2

THREE COMPETING WORLDVIEWS

There are three religions or worldviews that represent very significant threats to biblical Christianity. Each of these is becoming bolder and more aggressive in their attempts to discredit and destroy biblical Christianity. These are:

Islam, which states that God exists, but He is the God of the Qur'an and not the God of the Bible;

Atheism, which states that God does not exist, and certainly not the God of the Bible; and

Secular Socialism, which states it doesn't care whether or not God exists, government can solve all of man's problems; if, however, you must believe in God, then keep him very personal and out of public view.

The following sections provide information on each of these so that you can evaluate their claims and also decide which worldview provides you the greatest hope and security—one of these three religions/worldviews or biblical Christianity. As you are considering these religions/worldviews, ask yourself, "Why are these antagonistic to biblical Christianity?"

I suggest that you keep in mind the information provided in the previous chapter about how Satan uses counterfeit religions and governments to keep people from knowing and serving the God of the Bible. Also recall that religious truth, just as mathematical, scientific, historical, and geographical truth, is exclusionary. Then ask yourself, "Are any of these three religions or worldviews from God or are they from Satan?"

Chapter 4

Islam: What Does It Teach?

Certainly, there are some similarities between Islam and Christianity. For example, both are monotheistic, i.e., each teaches that there is only one God. Both consider the Bible, in its original writings, inspired by God. Both teach that Moses, Abraham, and Jesus were men, used mightily by God. Additionally, both share similar views on creation, angels, heaven, hell, and resurrection (after death) of all people. [1] However, as you will soon see, the similarities are very superficial and both Islam and biblical Christianity cannot be true.

There are five basic doctrines of Islam:

1. There is one and only one God.
2. There have been many prophets, including Noah, Abraham, Moses, Jesus, and Muhammad.
3. God created angels (jinn), some of which are good and others evil.
4. The *Qur'an* is God's full and final revelation.
5. A final day of judgment is coming, followed by heaven for the faithful and hell for the lost. [2]

In addition to these five basic doctrines in Islam, there are five basic pillars of Islamic practice:

1. All that is necessary to become a Muslim is to confess the *shahadah*: "There is no God but Allah, and Muhammad is his messenger."
2. One must pray the *salat*, usually five times a day.
3. One keeps an annual fast (*sawn*) through the ninth lunar month of *Ramadan*.

4. One gives alms (*sakat*) to the needy, one-fortieth of one's income.
5. Every able Muslim must make one pilgrimage during life to Mecca. [2]

Two of the common misconceptions about Islam are that the word *Islam* means "peace" and that it is a peaceful religion. This is not true, etymologically, theologically, or historically. Islam is an Arabic word that means "submission," with the implicit understanding that this is submission to the will of God [Allah]. "It is the religious faith of Muslims that includes the belief that Allah is the sole God and Muhammad is his prophet." [3] Caner and Caner, both former Muslims, provide additional insight:

"This assessment [that Islam means peace] overlooks some important details of the word *Islam*. First, the word is not rooted in the word peace (*salam*) but in the infinitive word *Salama*, which can be translated as either "the stinging of a snake" or "the tanning of the leather." The root word, from which *peace (salam)* also comes is then modified. This changes the meaning emphatically. Hence, the term *Islam* has been translated as "submission, surrender, and resignation."

Second, there is no historical evidence that Islam ever had the connotation of "peace." This explains why Muslim apologists have never substantiated their argument that Islam means peace. On the other hand, Muhammad himself clearly explained his intention by the word. When the founder of Islam sent letters to Arabian tribal leaders asking them to become Muslims and surrender to God, he would sign the letters, *Aslem, Taslam*, "Surrender and you will be safe." Therefore Muhammad's use of the word meant surrender within the context of military conquest, not spiritual submission to Allah." [4]

It is accurate to say that Islam is more than just a religion. "Islam is a religious, social, economic, educational, health, political, and philosophical way of life. In fact, Islam is an all-embracing socio-politico-religious utopian ideology that encompasses every field of human endeavor." [5]

The holy book of Islam is the Qur'an (or Koran). Muslims believe that Allah (God) gave the words of the Qur'an to the Prophet Muhammad (AD 570 to 632) through the angel Gabriel over a period of 23 years. [6] Muslims believe that Muhammad subsequently dictated these and that they were accurately recorded and that these are the final revelation of Allah. [7,8]

The Qur'an consists of 114 chapters (suras). Eighty-six of these were revealed to Muhammad when he was in Mecca and the last 28, when he resided in Medina. The chapters contain from as few as three to as many as 286 verses (ayats) and the 114 chapters are arranged according to length—from the longest in the front to the shortest in the back. [9] In other words, they are not arranged in chronological order and Muslim scholars believe it is impossible to place the books and verses in chronological order because they were given to the Prophet in piecemeal fashion (i.e., verses in one book were given at the same time as verses in another book). [6]

It is claimed that the Qur'an is unique among all other religious books:

"Among all the religious books of the world, the Holy Qur'an is the only Book which enjoys the distinction of having a pure text. Every word and letter of the Holy book, as we have it today, is as it left the lips of the Holy Prophet Muhammad to whom the Book was revealed." [10]

Additionally, it is claimed that the transforming power of the Qur'an is evident from its effect on the Arabs:

"In fact, the transformation wrought by the Holy Qur'an is unparalleled in the history of the world. No other reformer brought about such an entire change in the lives of a whole nation in his lifetime. The Qur'an found the Arabs worshippers of idols, stones, trees, heaps of sand, and yet, within less than a quarter of a century, the worship of the One God ruled the whole country, idolatry being wiped out from one end to the other. It swept away all superstitions and gave in their place the most rational religion that the world could imagine. … the Qur'an welded together a nation, a united nation full of life and vigour, before whose onward march the greatest kingdoms of the world crumbled as if they were but toys before the reality of the new faith. No faith ever imparted such a new life to its votaries on such a wide scale—a life affecting all branches of human activity; a transformation of the individual, of the family, of the society, of the nation, of the country; an awakening material as well as moral, intellectual as well as spiritual. The Qur'an effected a transformation of humanity from the lowest depths of degradation to the highest pinnacle of civilization within an incredibly short time where centuries of reformation work had proved fruitless. [11]

This section will provide information that will enable you to compare and contrast Islam versus biblical Christianity in five areas: (1) Comparison of the Qur'an and Bible; (2) Allah of the Qur'an and God of the Bible; (3) Muhammad and Jesus; (4) Worth of Women; and (5) Violence. The primary support for statements in this section will be direct quotes from the Qur'an and the Bible. It should be noted that all references to Islam and Muslims are based upon the Qur'an and not some form of radical teachings by "fanatical Muslim extremists". All quotations from the Qur'an are from the Online Quran Project. (http://al-quran.info/?x=y#&&sura=1&a ya=1&trans=en-marmaduke_pickthall&show=trans&ver=2.00. The 1930 English translation by Muhammad Marmaduke Pickthall (1876-1936). "The permission for use of this work has been verified and archived in the Wikimedia OTRS system....*This file has been (or is hereby) released into the **public domain** by its author, **Online Quran Project**. This applies worldwide.... Online Quran Project grants anyone the right to use this work for any purpose, without any conditions, unless such conditions are required by law."*)

Comparison of the Qur'an and the Bible

Validation through fulfilled prophecy: As you have already seen, there are many historical examples of fulfilled biblical prophecy that supports its claim of being the inspired Word of God. This is not true for the Qur'an.

Table 4-1. Prophetic Verses in the Qur'an and Bible.

Qur'an	Bible
Chapters (Suras): 114 Verses (Ayiahs): 6,237 (or 6,350 if common opening verse is included Prophetic Verses: 22 claimed by Muslim scholars [8]	Books: 66 (39 in Old Testament and 27 in New Testament [12] Chapters: 1,189 (929 in Old Testament, 260 in New Testament [12] Verses: 31,173 (23,214 in Old Testament, 7,959 in New Testament [13] 25% were prophetic when written [14]

Commenting on the prophetic verses in the Qur'an, Muncaster states:

"Islamic leaders say there are 22 predictive prophecies in the Qur'an (Sura 2:23-24; 3:10, 106, 107, 144; 5:70; 8:7; 9:14;15:9, 96; 24:55; 28:85; 30:2-4; 41:42; 48:16-21, 27-28;54:44-48; 56:1-56; 110:1-2).

However, of those listed, Sura 2:23-24, 88-89; Sura 3:10, 106, 107, 144; Sura 8:7; Sura 9:14; Sura 28:85; Sura 48:16-21, 27-28; Sura 54:44-48; and Sura 56:1-56 all deal with end-time prophecy and can't be tested (just like the biblical prophecy that was excluded.) Sura 5:70; 15:9; 41:42; and 15:96 are not prophecies, but generalities and warnings. Sura 24:55 is a promise of a blessing of land and wealth to believers in Islam. However, it does not specify what land, as in the case of Israel. Sura 54:44-48 prophesies military action against enemies of the religion—but this doesn't say much, as it is what people tend to do anyway. And Sura 110:1-2 promises help from Allah (Islam's God) in time of war. Again, this isn't specific, as in a claim to victory in a specific battle or war.

Sura 30:2-4 is the only potential historical prophecy, although it has problems. It essentially says, "The Roman Empire has been defeated in a land close by; but they, (even) after (this) defeat of theirs, will soon be victorious within a few years. With Allah is the Decision, in the past and in the Future: on that Day shall the Believers rejoice." In history, the Persians were victorious over the Eastern Roman Empire in AD 615, and then the Romans returned to defeat the Persians 13 years later in 628. According to Muhammad, "a few" years in this prophecy was meant to mean three to nine years, with 13 falling outside of this range. Even so, the prophecy would not be particularly surprising since there was an ongoing war in this region, and it was not uncommon for territory to be recaptured." [8]

Sura 30:2-4 is quoted below, for your consideration:

30:2. The Romans have been defeated 3. In the nearer land, and they, after their defeat will be victorious 4. Within ten years — Allah's is the command in the former case and in the latter — and in that day believers will rejoice.

Muncaster concludes, "It [Islam] cannot prove its inspiration from God using prophecy." [8]

As you have read in the preceding chapters, many of the biblical prophecies have already been fulfilled in history. In addition, there are many biblical prophecies that relate to the future and these will be presented and discussed in the next chapter.

Claims that the Bible has been corrupted: Muslims claim that the Bible has been corrupted, but this is not consistent with the Qur'an's teachings. [15, 16]

Table 4-2. Support of the Divine Inspiration of the Bible. [15]

Qur'an:	Bible:
Directs Muslims to refer to Bible: 10.94; 21.7; 29.46; 4.136; 5.46, 47, 68. Consequently, Bible could not have been corrupted prior to writing of Qur'an because Allah would not have directed Muslins to consult a corrupted text. Warns against considering non-scriptural texts equal to scriptural texts: 2.78; 2.79.	10,000 Latin vulgate manuscripts 5,300 Greek manuscripts 9,000 others for total of more than 24,000 manuscripts of New Testament More than 230 predate the sixth century Entire NT from fourth century is in a London museum 19,000 translations in 11 languages pre-date Muhammad. If our Bible/NT is corrupt, all of these would have had to been corrupted/changed after Muhammad, because the Koran tells Muslims to go back to the Bible and the Gospels (10.94, 21.7, 29.46, 4.136, 5.46,47,68)

Objectively, the Bible could not have been corrupted prior to the life of Muhammad and his dictation of the Qur'an because the Qur'an directs Muslims to the Bible: [15]

10:94.   And if thou (Muhammad) art in doubt concerning that which We reveal unto thee, then question those who read the Scripture (that was) before thee [the Bible]. Verily the Truth from thy Lord hath come unto thee. So be not thou of the waverers.

29:46.   And argue not with the People of the Scripture [the Jews] unless it be in (a way) that is better, save with such of them as do wrong; and say: We believe in that which hath been revealed unto us and revealed unto you; our Allah and your Allah is One, and unto Him we surrender.

Since Allah and Muhammad referred people to the Bible, it seems highly unlikely that they would have referred them to a corrupted text. Additionally, there are so many copies of the Old and New Testament that both pre- and post-date Muhammad, it is easy to see that there have not been any changes in the Bible before or after Muhammad's life. Consequently, the claim that the Bible has been corrupted is without merit.

Contradictions between the Qur'an and Bible: There are many contradictions between the teachings of the Qur'an and the Bible. There are also contradictions in some of the same historical accounts in these two books.

Table 4-3. Contradictions in Historical Accounts Between the Qur'an and the Bible: [15]

Qur'an:	Bible:
5:31-32 Cain kills and buries Abel (same as second century story by Talmud of John Ben Aliazer and not in the Bible)	Genesis 4:8 Cain and Abel
21:57-70 Abraham destroys idols and is thrown into a fiery pit (from Talmud of Rabba, a second century apocryphal account, and not in the Bible)	Genesis 16:1-21:21 Abraham, Sarah, and Isaac
27:17-44 Solomon and Sheba (same as in Targum of Esther, written in second century, and not in the Bible)	First Kings 10:1-13 Solomon and Queen of Sheba
These are examples of 2:79...Do not take non-scriptural writings and call them Scripture.	

Due to the length of these accounts, they will not be reproduced here. Nevertheless, as summarized in the table above, the accounts in the Qur'an of Cain, Abraham, and Solomon are not from the Bible. In fact, these are examples of the warning in the Qur'an of taking non-scriptural writings and calling it Scripture.

2:79.   Therefore woe be unto those who write the Scripture with their hands and then say, "This is from Allah," that they may purchase a small gain therewith. Woe unto them for that their hands have written, and woe unto them for that they earn thereby.

There is no historical evidence to support Muslim claims that the Bible has been corrupted. [17] There are, however, questions concerning the Qur'an. [15, 18, 19] Caner and Caner state:

"…since both internal and external evidence shows inconsistencies and inaccuracies in the Qur'an. First, although Muslims claim that there has only been one version of the Qur'an, facts do not support that assertion. Historically, the Qur'an of today is a redacted work completed under the third Muslim Caliph, Uthman ibn Affan, who came to power in 644. Only after Muhammad's death was the Qur'an compiled by order of his successor, Abu Bakr. Soon Medina, Mecca, Basra, Kufa, Damascus, and other population centers had developed their individual versions of the writings of Muhammad. These versions evidently varied dramatically. In his monumental work, *Materials for the History of the Text of the Qur'an*, archeologist Arthur Jeffery argues that Uthman canonized the Median Codes. More important, he ordered that all copies of every other version should be destroyed. This is why only one version is extant.

Even the Qur'an in Muhammad's day was not guarded from corruption, as shown in the long-standing controversy over the popular passage known as the "Satanic Verses" (sura 53:21-23). In this text, Muhammad publicly pronounced that three idols (al-Hat, al-Uzza, and al-Manat) could intercede on behalf of Muslims. Quickly realizing the impropriety of such a view, Muhammad revised the section, canceling any intercession of idols. He explained his lapse by stating that Satan had interjected this text in the divine communication to accommodate surrounding paganism. Allah had prevailed and replaced the "Satanic Verses" with his own (sura 22:52-53)." [19]

These verses are quoted below:

53:21.   Are yours the males and His the females? 22.   That indeed were an unfair division! 23.   They are but names which ye have named, ye and your fathers, for which Allah hath revealed no warrant. They follow but a guess and that which (they) themselves desire. And now the guidance from their Lord hath come unto them.

22:52.   Never sent We a messenger or a prophet before thee but when He recited (the message) Satan proposed (opposition) in respect of that which he recited thereof. But Allah abolisheth that which Satan proposeth. Then Allah establisheth His revelations. Allah is Knower, Wise. 53.   That He may make that which the devil proposeth a temptation for those in whose hearts is a disease, and those whose hearts are hardened — Lo! the evil-doers are in open schism.

Allah of the Qur'an and God of the Bible

Allah of the Qur'an and God of the Bible are not the same being. "Islam repudiates the Christian concepts of God as triune and personal, as it repudiates Christianity itself." [20]

Sura 112 provides a summary of Allah:

112:1.   Say: He is Allah, the One! 2.   Allah, the eternally Besought of all! 3.   He begetteth not nor was begotten. 4.   And there is none comparable unto Him.

Caner and Caner summarize the attributes of Allah by stating,

"In all of the descriptions of Allah in the Qur'an, in all of Allah's reported ninety-nine names, in all of his dealings with humankind, the glaring omission is immanence or divine-human intimacy. Allah is never described as personal. A Muslim does not have a 'personal relationship with Allah,' in the sense that a Christian speaks of having a personal relationship with God. The attributes of Allah ascribed in the Qur'an present him as transcendent Judge, but never as close Friend." [21]

Absolute Attributes of Allah:

1.   Unity. "Islam denies any partner or companionship with Allah, but rather His complete unity and uniqueness."
2.   Sovereignty. "Allah is self-existent and can sustain all by Himself." (2:255)

2:255.   Allah! There is no deity save Him, the Alive, the Eternal. Neither slumber nor sleep overtaketh Him. Unto Him belongeth whatsoever is in the heavens and whatsoever is in the earth. Who is he that intercedeth with Him save by His leave? He knoweth that which is in front of them and that which is behind them, while they encompass nothing of His knowledge save what He will. His throne includeth the heavens and the earth, and He is never weary of preserving them. He is the Sublime, the Tremendous.

3. Equity. "Sura al-Imran (3:9) speaks of Allah's precise judgment, which is part of his holiness."

3:9. Our Lord! Lo! it is Thou Who gatherest mankind together to a Day of which there is no doubt. Lo! Allah faileth not to keep the tryst.

4. Mercy. This "speaks of Allah's wiliness to forgive if the Muslim does right."
5. Volitionality. "Many terms and descriptions in the Qur'an depict Allah as ordering existence and all about him.
6. Inscrutability. Allah "is ultimately beyond human comprehension in any meaningful way." [22]

When one compares this summary of Allah's attributes with the attributes of the God of the Bible, the conclusion is that the Allah of the Qur'an is not the same deity as the God of the Bible. Furthermore, the Qur'an's teaching about Allah are incompatible with God's love for His creation, and His statement,

> "For God so loved the world, that He gave His only begotten Son, that whoever believes in Him shall not perish, but have eternal life." (John 3:16)

Muhammad and Jesus
Jesus of the Qur'an and Jesus of the Bible
Islam supports the following statements about Jesus: Jesus was born of a virgin, lived, performed miracles, was a servant of the eternally existing one true God. [23] However, Islam does not support the divinity of Jesus or His crucifixion, death, and resurrection.

4:157. And because of their saying: We slew the Messiah, Jesus son of Mary, Allah's messenger — they slew him not nor crucified him, but it appeared so unto them; and lo! those who disagree concerning it are in doubt thereof; they have no knowledge thereof save pursuit of a conjecture; they slew him not for certain. 158.   But Allah took him up unto Himself. Allah was ever Mighty, Wise.

Additionally, the Qur'an indicates that Jesus claimed not to be God: [15]

5:116.   And when Allah saith: O Jesus, son of Mary! Didst thou say unto mankind: Take me and my mother for two gods beside Allah? he saith: Be glorified! It was not mine to utter that to which I had no right. If I used to say it, then Thou knewest it. Thou knowest what is in my mind, and I know not what is in Thy Mind. Lo! Thou, only Thou, art the Knower of Things Hidden!

Consequently, "The Islamic Jesus (Isa) is not the Christ of the biblical record, but He is accorded respect as a human prophet in whom Allah has done great things." [23]

Muhammad
There are five areas that Islamic apologists typically use to support the assertion that Muhammad is the greatest and final prophet of God. [24] Let's consider each of these areas, examine the evidence, and then form our conclusions.

1. *Claim: The Old and New Testaments prophesied Muhammad.*
The biblical verses that are frequently cited to support this claim are listed below. The analysis of each of these verses will utilize standard biblical interpretive principles [25] and common sense.

"The LORD your God will raise up for you a prophet like me from among you, from your countrymen, you shall listen to him...." Deuteronomy 18:15-18

The phrase "from your countrymen," as used here and various other places always refers to members of the Jewish nation, not an Arab. The Qur'an even states that the prophetic line comes from Isaac (a Jew).

29:27.   And We bestowed on him Isaac and Jacob, and We established the prophethood and the Scripture among his seed, and We gave him his reward in the world, and lo! in the Hereafter he verily is among the righteous.

This eliminates Muhammad, who was an Arab and a descendant of Ishmael. This prophecy was fulfilled by Jesus, not Muhammad. [26, 27]

"He said, The LORD came from Sinai, and dawned on them from Seir; He shone forth from Mount Paran, and He came from the midst of ten thousand holy ones; at His right hand there was flashing lightning for them." Deuteronomy 33:2

This verse is referring to when God spoke to Moses on Mount Sinai and gave him the Ten Commandments. "There is no basis in this text for the Muslim contention that it is a prediction of Muhammad." [26]

"Since that time no prophet has risen in Israel like Moses, whom the LORD knew face to face." Deuteronomy 34:10

"...this could not refer to Muhammad, since the prophet to come was like Moses who did 'all the signs and wonders which the Lord sent' (Deuteronomy 34:11). Muhammad by his own confession did not perform signs and wonders like Moses and Jesus did." [28] Also, Muhammad never claimed to speak to God, but received his revelations through an angel. Jesus fulfilled this prophecy.

"God comes from Teman and the Holy One from Mount Paran. His splendor covers the heavens, and the earth is full of His praise." Habakkuk 3:3

This verse refers to God ("God" and "the Holy One") and not a man. Additionally, Mount Paran is hundreds of miles from Mecca, where Muhammad resided. Finally, even Muhammad and Muslims agree that "praise" should be directed to God and not a man, even if he is a prophet. [26]

"Gird Your sword on Your thigh, O Mighty One, In Your splendor and Your majesty! And In Your majesty ride on victoriously, for the cause of truth and meekness and righteousness; Let Your right hand teach You awesome things. Your arrows are sharp; the peoples fall under You; Your arrows are in the heart of the King's enemies." Psalm 45:3-5

Although Jesus did not come with a sword in His first coming, He will when He returns to the earth as Lord. The next verse in this passage indicates that the verses above refer to God, which Jesus claimed to be, and Muhammad repeatedly denied being God, saying He was only a human prophet. [29, 30]

"When he sees riders, horsemen in pairs, a train of donkeys, a train of camels, let him pay close attention, very close attention." Isaiah 21:7

"Again, there is absolutely nothing here about the prophet Muhammad." [29]

"As for me, I baptize you with water for repentance, but He who is coming after me is mightier than I, and I am not fit to remove His sandals; He will baptize you with the Holy Spirit and fire." Matthew 3:11

This verse refers to Jesus, which is confirmed in the following verses. [29, 31]

"After being baptized, Jesus came up immediately from the water; and behold, the heavens were opened, and he saw the Spirit of God descending as a dove and lighting on Him, and behold, a voice out of the heavens said, 'This is My beloved Son, in whom I am well pleased." Matthew 3:16-17

"I will ask the Father, and He will give you another Helper, that He may be with you forever." John 14:16

Jesus clearly identifies "another Helper" in verse 26:

"But the Helper, the Holy Spirit, whom the Father will send in My name, He will teach you all things, and bring to your remembrance all that I said to you." John 14:26

Additionally, Jesus indicated that the "Helper" would be with them forever, but Muhammad would not be born for more than five centuries and now has been dead for more than 13 centuries! [32]

After examining each of these verses and Muslim claims, do you agree with Geisler and Saleeb and others who have concluded, "the claim that Muhammad is predicted in Scripture is found to be completely groundless"? [32]

2. Claim: The nature of Muhammad's call was miraculous.

The Qur'an claims that Muhammad received revelation from Allah through the angel Gabriel.

2:97.   Say (O Muhammad, to mankind): Who is an enemy to Gabriel! For he it is who hath revealed (this Scripture) to thy heart by Allah's leave, confirming that which was (revealed) before it, and a guidance and glad tidings to believers;

In various passages, Gabriel was also referred to as "Faithful Spirit" (26:193) and Holy Spirit (16:102). Some of Muhammad's contemporaries accused him of receiving his ideas from foreigners in the city (16:103, 25:4f) [33] It is interesting to note that Muhammad initially thought the source of the revelations he received were from Satan and described his first encounter with an angel as:

"He choked me with the cloth until I believed that I should die. Then he released me and said 'Recite!' (Iqra)." [33]

Apparently, the angel choked Muhammad two additional times during their initial encounter. [33] On the nature of the "angelic encounter" Geisler comments:

"This seems to many an unusual form of coercion; unlike a gracious and merciful God Muslims claim Allah to be, as well as contrary to the free choice they claim he has granted his creatures.

Muhammad himself questioned the divine origin of the experience. At first he thought he was being deceived by a *jinn* or evil spirit. In fact, Muhammad was at first deathly afraid of the source of his newly found revelation, but he was encouraged by his wife Khadija and her cousin Waraqah to believe that the revelation was the same as that of Moses, and that he, too, would be a prophet of his nation. One of the most widely respected modern Muslim biographers, M.H. Haykal, speaks vividly of Muhammad's plaguing fear that he was demon-possessed: [33]

'Stricken with panic, Muhammad arose and asked himself, "What did I see? Did Possession of the devil which I feared all along come to pass? Muhammad looked to his right and his left but saw nothing. For a while he stood there trembling with fear and stricken with awe. He feared the cave might be haunted and that he might run away still unable to explain what he say.' [34]

It is interesting to consider the Bible's warning about Satan and his demons:

"No wonder, for even Satan disguises himself as an angel of light. Therefore, it is not surprising if his servants also disguise themselves as servants of righteousness, whose end will be according to their deeds." 1 Corinthians 11:13

"Be of sober spirit, be on the alert. Your adversary, the devil, prowls around like a roaring lion, seeking some to devour." 1 Peter 5:8

Certainly the Bible confirms that God can and has spoken to men and women in the past through angels (e.g., Hagar (Muhammad was a descendant of Abraham and Hagar), Genesis 16:7-11; Abraham, Genesis 22:11; Moses, Exodus 3:2; and Mary, Luke 1:30-38). However, as quoted above, the Bible also states that Satan and his demons can also communicate with men. Consequently, it seems reasonable to consider one other verse from the Bible to gain more insight into the likely source of revelation received by Muhammad:

"By this the children of God and the children of the devil are obvious: anyone who does not practice righteousness is not of God, nor the one who does not love his brother. For this is the message which you have heard from the beginning, that we should love one another." 1 John 3:10-11

As you think about the words and works of Muhammad, ask yourself if these promoted love for one another. If not, then, according to the Bible, Muhammad's revelation was not from God.

3. *Claim: The language and teaching of the Qur'an are without parallel and this proves the claims of Muhammad.*

As has been previously pointed out, fulfilled prophecy cannot be used to substantiate the divine inspiration of the Qur'an. Literary style and elegance are often cited as proof of its divine origin, yet even if you do agree and are in awe of the style and elegance of the Qur'an (which is doubtful), this would not prove divine inspiration. Additionally, as pointed out in the section "The Qur'an and the Bible," the internal and external inconsistencies within the Qur'an and the lack of fulfilled prophecies do not support claims that the Qur'an is divinely inspired.

4. *Claim: Muhammad performed miracles to prove he was a prophet.*

Although Muhammad was asked on several occasions to prove that he was a prophet of Allah by performing miracles (3:181-184; 4:153; 6:8-9), Muhammad's reply was that the language and teaching in the Qur'an were sufficient proof that he was a prophet. The Qur'an, however, does list miracles performed by other prophets of God (e.g., Moses, 7:106-119 and Jesus, 5:112-115), which confirmed their claims that they were true prophets of God. [35]

The Qur'an does not record any miracles over nature that were performed by Muhammad. Although other Muslim writings claim that Muhammad performed miracles, these writings, as admitted by Muslim scholars, are not divinely inspired and therefore are open to question regarding their validity.

5. *Claim: Muhammad's life and character prove that he was the greatest of the prophets.* [26]

Consider the following facts regarding Muhammad's character and morals:

(a) Character: Muhammad apparently participated in raiding commercial caravans, sanctioned a follower to lie to an enemy and kill him, and authorized assassinations of political enemies. [36] Additionally, according the Qur'an, Muhammad committed sins.

40:55. Then have patience (O Muhammad). Lo! the promise of Allah is true. And ask forgiveness of thy sin, and hymn the praise of thy Lord at fall of night and in the early hours.

47:19. So know (O Muhammad) that there is no Allah save Allah, and ask forgiveness for thy sin and for believing men and believing women. Allah knoweth (both) your place of turmoil and your place of rest.

48:2. That Allah may forgive thee of thy sin that which is past and that which is to come, and may perfect His favour unto thee, and may guide thee on a right path,

(b) Morals: The Qur'an specifically states that Muslim men may have up to four wives (4:3). However, Muhammad married 15 women, the youngest of which, Aisha, was six years old when he married her and was nine when the marriage was consummated (with sexual relations, when he was 51 years old). [37] Muhammad justified having 15 wives by claiming he had received the following revelation:

33:50. O Prophet! Lo! We have made lawful unto thee thy wives unto whom thou hast paid their dowries, and those whom thy right hand possesseth of those whom Allah hath given thee as spoils of war, and the daughters of thine uncle on the father's side and the daughters of thine aunts on the father's side, and the daughters of thine uncle on the mother's side and the daughters of thine aunts on the mother's side who emigrated with thee, and a believing woman if she give herself unto the Prophet and the Prophet desire to ask her in marriage - a privilege for thee only, not for the (rest of) believers - We are Aware of that which We enjoined upon them concerning their wives and those whom their right hands possess - that thou mayst be free from blame, for Allah is ever Forgiving, Merciful. 51. Thou canst defer whom thou wilt of them and receive unto thee whom thou wilt, and whomsoever thou desirest of those whom thou hast set aside (temporarily), it is no sin for thee (to receive her again); that is better; that they may be comforted and not grieve, and may all be pleased with what thou givest them. Allah knoweth what is in your hearts (O men), and Allah is ever Forgiving, Clement. 52. It is not allowed thee to take (other) women henceforth, nor that thou shouldst change them for other wives even though their beauty pleased thee, save those whom thy right hand possesseth. And Allah is ever Watcher over all things.

Without a doubt, Muhammad had some character flaws and moral issues (as all of us do). Additionally, with the exception of Jesus, who was sinless, sinful men have been utilized as prophets by God in the past (e.g., Abraham lied, Moses murdered, David committed adultery). Nevertheless, from an objective perspective, Muhammad's life and character do not support the assertion that he was the greatest and final prophet. Similarly, none of the other reported proofs meet objective standards to support the assertion that Muhammad was divinely inspired and was the greatest and final prophet.

Additionally, Jay Smith summarized some other interesting differences between Muhammad and Jesus:

> Muhammad was not born of a virgin; Jesus was.
> Muhammad did not perform any miracles; Jesus healed the sick, gave sight to the blind, raised people from the dead, and exercised control over nature.
> Muhammad did not live a sinless life; Jesus did. [15]
> An objective consideration of these facts would lead one to conclude that Muhammad was not a prophet of the God of the Bible.

Women

There are major differences in the worth of women presented in the Qur'an and the Bible. These are summarized in Table 4-4.

174

Table 4-4. Worth of Women [15, 38]

Qur'an	Bible
A man can have up to four wives 4:3	Jesus placed great value on women (Luke 10:39)
A man can have countless concubines 4:24	After Jesus' resurrection, he appeared first to women (John 20:11; Matthew 28:9)
A woman gets half the inheritance as a man 4:11	Women are equal to men (Galatians 3:28)
A husband can beat his wife 4:34	A husband is to be willing to die for his wife, as Jesus died for the church (Ephesians 5:21-33)
A woman's testimony in court has half the value as a man's testimony 2:282	A husband is commanded to love his wife (Ephesians 5:25; Colossians 3:19)
A woman may be sexually assaulted any time by her husband 2:223	

Each of the Qur'an verses cited above are shown below:

A man can have up to four wives:

4:3.   And if ye fear that ye will not deal fairly by the orphans, marry of the women, who seem good to you, two or three or four; and if ye fear that ye cannot do justice (to so many) then one (only) or (the captives) that your right hands possess. Thus it is more likely that ye will not do injustice.

A man can have as many concubines (prisoners of war) as he wants and children from these concubines are legitimate children (same as children from his wives):

4:24.   And all married women (are forbidden unto you) save those (captives) whom your right hands possess. It is a decree of Allah for you. Lawful unto you are all beyond those mentioned, so that ye seek them with your wealth in honest wedlock, not debauchery. And those of whom ye seek content (by marrying them), give unto them their portions as a duty. And there is no sin for you in what ye do by mutual agreement after the duty (hath been done). Lo! Allah is ever Knower, Wise.

A woman has half the inheritance as a man:

4:11.   Allah chargeth you concerning (the provision for) your children: to the male the equivalent of the portion of two females, and if there be women more than two, then theirs is two-thirds of the inheritance, and if there be one (only) then the half. And to each of his parents a sixth of the inheritance, if he have a son; and if he have no son and his parents are his heirs, then to his mother appertaineth the third; and if he have brethren, then to his mother appertaineth the sixth, after any legacy he may have bequeathed, or debt (hath been paid). Your parents and your children: Ye know not which of them is nearer unto you in usefulness. It is an injunction from Allah. Lo! Allah is Knower, Wise.

A woman is protected by her husband but can be admonished, thrown from the bed, and beaten (chastised) ("lightly" has been inserted in modern texts, but the Arabic word actually means "scourge"):

4:34.   Men are in charge of women, because Allah hath made the one of them to excel the other, and because they spend of their property (for the support of women). So good women are the obedient, guarding in secret that which Allah hath guarded. As for those from whom ye fear rebellion, admonish them and banish them to beds apart, and scourge them. Then if they obey you, seek not a way against them. Lo! Allah is ever High, Exalted, Great.

A woman has half the testimony in court as a man because women are less intelligent and less obedient than men.

2:282.   O ye who believe! When ye contract a debt for a fixed term, record it in writing. Let a scribe record it in writing between you in (terms of) equity. No scribe should refuse to write as Allah hath taught him, so let him write, and let him who incurreth the debt dictate, and let him observe his duty to Allah his Lord, and diminish naught thereof. But if he who oweth the debt is of low understanding, or weak, or unable himself to dictate, then let the guardian of his interests dictate in (terms of) equity. And call to witness, from among your men, two witnesses. And if two men be not (at hand) then a man and two women, of such as ye approve as witnesses, so that if the one erreth (through forgetfulness) the other will remember. And the witnesses must not refuse when they are summoned. Be not averse to writing down (the contract) whether it be small or great, with (record of) the term thereof. That is more equitable in the sight of Allah and more sure for testimony, and the best way of avoiding doubt between you; save only in the case when it is actual merchandise which ye transfer among yourselves from hand to hand. In that case it is no sin for you if ye write it not. And have witnesses when ye sell one to another, and let no harm be done to scribe or witness. If ye do (harm to them) lo! it is a sin in you. Observe your duty to Allah. Allah is teaching you. And Allah is knower of all things.

A woman may be sexually assaulted at any time by her husband; the woman has no right over her body.

2:223.   Your women are a tilth for you (to cultivate) so go to your tilth as ye will, and send (good deeds) before you for your souls, and fear Allah, and know that ye will (one day) meet Him. Give glad tidings to believers, (O Muhammad).

Compare these verses from the Qur'an to verses from the Bible regarding women and wives:

> "There is neither Jew nor Greek, there is neither slave nor free, there is no male and female, for you are all one in Christ Jesus." Galatians 3:28

> "Husbands, love your wives, as Christ loved the church and gave himself up for her, that he might sanctify her, that he might present the church to himself in splendor, without spot or wrinkle or any such thing, that she might be holy and without blemish. In the same way husbands should love their wives as their own bodies. He who loves his wife loves himself. For no one ever hated his own flesh, but nourishes

and cherishes it, just as Christ does the church, because we are members of his body. 'Therefore a man shall leave his father and mother and hold fast to his wife, and the two shall become one flesh.' This mystery is profound, and I am saying that it refers to Christ and the church. However, let each one of you love his wife as himself, and let the wife see that she respects her husband." Ephesians 5:25-31

As you can see, there are major differences in the views of women and wives taught by the Qur'an and the Bible.

Violence and Peace

It is often said that Islam is a religion of peace and it is falsely claimed that the word Islam means peace. Frequently, the following verse is used to support the claim that Islam is a peaceful religion:

2:256.   There is no compulsion in religion. The right direction is henceforth distinct from error. And he who rejecteth false deities and believeth in Allah hath grasped a firm handhold which will never break. Allah is Hearer, Knower.

Unfortunately, there are many verses that directly contradict this tolerant view of other religions. Geisler and Saleeb highlight some of these verses:

"Laying aside the question of whether war is ever justified, Muhammad believed in holy wars (the *jihad*). Muhammad, by divine revelation, commands his followers: "fight in the cause Of God" (2:244). He adds, "fight and slay The Pagans wherever ye find them" (9:5). And "when ye meet The Unbelievers (in fight) Smite at their necks" (47:4). In general, they were to "Fight those who believe not In God nor the Last Day" (9:29). Indeed, Paradise is promised for those who fight for God: "Those who have left their homes ... Or fought or been slain, Verily, I will blot out From them their iniquities, And admit them into Gardens With rivers flowing beneath; A reward from the Presence Of God, and from His Presence Is the best of rewards" (3:195; cf. 2:244; 4:95 cf. 8:12). These "holy wars" were carried out "in the cause Of God" (2:244) against "unbelievers." In 5:36–38, we read: "the punishment of those Who wage war against God [i.e., unbelievers] And His

Apostle, and strive With might and main For mischief through the land Is: execution, or crucifixion, Or the cutting off of hands And feet from opposite sides, Or exile from the land." Acknowledging that these are appropriate punishments, depending on "the circumstances," Ali offers little consolation when he notes that the more cruel forms of Arabian treatment of enemies, such as, "piercing of eyes and leaving the unfortunate victim exposed to a tropical sun," were abolished! Such war on and persecution of enemies on religious grounds—by whatever means—is seen by most critics as a clear example of religious intolerance. [39]

So how do Muslims explain the obvious discrepancies between "there is no compulsion in religion" and "fight those who believe not in God"? Various explanations may be given, but the two most frequent are that the verses that show Islam in an unfavorable light are taken out of context, or if necessary, that these represent Allah's progressive revelation. The latter supports the "law of abrogation," which basically states that if there is a conflict between two or more verses that the one(s) written later in time supersedes and replaces the one(s) written earlier. This is an effective (convenient?) way of dealing with the many internal consistencies found in the Qur'an, especially those relating to peace and violence. The law of abrogation is stated in Sura 2:106 and 16:101 [15]:

2:106. Nothing of our revelation (even a single verse) do we abrogate or cause be forgotten, but we bring (in place) one better or the like thereof. Knowest thou not that Allah is Able to do all things?

16:101. And when We put a revelation in place of (another) revelation, and Allah knoweth best what He revealeth they say: Lo! thou art but inventing. Most of them know not.

Although, as stated earlier, Muslin scholars claim that it is impossible to place the chapters (sura) and verses (ayats) in chronological order. Consequently, it is sometimes difficult to determine which verses abrogate or replace conflicting verses. In the case of the verses under consideration now, scholars (both Muslim and non-Muslim) agree that 2:256, "no compulsion in religion" (i.e., Islam is a religion of peace), was one of the early revelations received by Muhammad.

Historically, when Muhammad initially began promoting the new religion of Islam (when he resided in Mecca), he found that there were a significant number of people who rejected his message as being from God (especially since he did not or could not justify his claim to be a prophet by performing miracles as most other prophets had done). As a result of growing hostilities in Mecca against him, in 622, Muhammad fled to Medina, where he became a head of state and military leader. Since he found that he was unable to convert many people to Islam using peaceful means, he turned to violent methods. There is no question about the fact that the latter days of Muhammad's life and teaching were filled with violence; thus invalidating the peaceful and tolerant verses related to other religions. [40]

So fast forward in time from 622-632, when Muhammad moved to Medina (where he died), to today. What do we see happening in the world relative to Islam—peace or violence? Spencer provides a summary of the early years following Muhammad's death:

"Before the Prophet had been dead ten years, Muslim armies had taken Syria, Egypt, and Persia. Muslim armies conquered Damascus in 635, only three years after Muhammad's death; substantial portions of Iraq in 636; Jerusalem in 638; Caesarea in 641; and Armenia in 643.... By 709 they had complete control of North Africa; by 711 they had subdued Spain and were moving into France. Muslim forces first besieged "Caesar's city" of Muhammad's promise, Constantinople, for a full year starting in August 716; but despite repeated subsequent attempts, it would not fall to them for another 700 years. Meanwhile, Sicily fell in 827. By 846 Rome was in danger of being captured by Muslim invaders; repulsed, they "sacked the cathedrals of St. Peter beside the Vatican and of St. Paul outside the walls, and desecrated the graves of the pontiffs."... These were not defensive wars.... Nor were they Arab wars; after the conquests, the victors constructed a society based on Muslim, not Arab, hegemony.... The Muslim armies considered themselves to be advancing in the spirit dictated by Muhammad: accept Islam or face war." [41]

In more recent times, consider the following acts by Muslims claiming to be acting in the name of Islam, as cited in Wikipedia:

Table 4-5. Examples of [Muslim] Attacks: [42]

- 26 February 1993—World Trade Center bombing, New York City. 6 killed.
- 13 March 1993—Bombay bombings. Mumbai, India. 250 dead, 700 injured.
- 28 July 1994—Buenos Aires, Argentina. Vehicle suicide bombing attack against AMIA building, the local Jewish community representation. 85 dead, more than 300 injured.
- 24 December 1994—Air France Flight 8969 hijacking in Algiers by 3 members of Armed Islamic Group of Algeria and another terrorist. 7 killed, including 4 hijackers.
- 25 June 1996—Khobar Towers bombing. 20 killed, 372 wounded.
- 17 November 1997—Luxor attack, 6 armed Islamic terrorists attack tourists at Egypt's famous Luxor Ruins. 68 foreign tourists killed.
- 14 February 1998—Bombing in Coimbatore, Tamil Nadu, India. 13 bombs explode within a 12 km radius. 46 killed and over 200 injured.
- 7 August 1998—United States embassy bombings in Tanzania and Kenya. 224 dead. 4000+ injured.
- 4 September 1999—A series of bombing attacks in several cities of Russia, nearly 300 killed.
- 12 October 2000—Attack on the USS Cole in the Yemeni port of Aden.
- 11 September 2001—4 planes hijacked and crashed into World Trade Center and the Pentagon by 19 hijackers. Nearly 3000 dead.
- 13 December 2001—Suicide attack on Indian parliament in New Delhi by Pakistan-based Islamist terrorist organizations, Jaish-E-Mohammad and Lashkar-e-Toiba. Aimed at eliminating the top leadership of India and causing anarchy in the country. 7 dead, 12 injured.
- 27 March 2002—Suicide bomb attack on a Passover Seder in a Hotel in Netanya, Israel. 30 dead, 133 injured.
- 30 March 2002 and 24 November 2002—Attacks on the Hindu Raghunath temple, India. 25 dead.
- 7 May 2002—Bombing in al-Arbaa, Algeria. 49 dead, 117 injured.
- 24 September 2002—Machine gun attack on Hindu temple in Ahmadabad, India. 31 dead, 86 injured.
- 12 October 2002—Bombing in Bali nightclub. 202 killed, 300 injured.
- 16 May 2003—Casablanca attacks. 4 simultaneous attacks in Casablanca killing 33 civilians (mostly Moroccans) carried out by Salafia Jihadia.
- 11 March 2004—Multiple bombings on trains near Madrid, Spain. 191 killed, 1,460 injured (alleged link to Al-Qaeda).
- 1 September 2004—Beslan school hostage crisis. About 344 civilians, including 186 children, killed.http://en.wikipedia.org/wiki/Islamic_ terrorism - cite_note-last_casualty-161

- 2 November 2004—Ritual murder of Theo van Gogh (film director) by Amsterdam-born jihadist Mohammed Bouyeri.
- 4 February 2005—Muslim terrorists attacked the Christian community in Demsa, Nigeria, killing 36 people, destroying property and displacing an additional 3,000 people.
- 5 July 2005—Attack at the Hindu Ram temple at Ayodhya, India; one of the most holy sites of Hinduism. 6 dead.
- 7 July 2005—Multiple bombings in London Underground. 53 killed by 4 suicide bombers. Nearly 700 injured.
- 23 July 2005—Bomb attacks at Sharm el-Sheikh, an Egyptian resort city. At least 64 people killed.
- 29 October 2005—Delhi bombings, India. Over 60 killed and over 180 injured in a series of three attacks in crowded markets and a bus, just 2 days before the Diwali festival.
- 9 November 2005—Amman bombings. A series of coordinated suicide attacks on hotels in Amman, Jordan. Over 60 killed and 115 injured. Four attackers, including a husband and wife team, were involved.
- 7 March 2006—Varanasi bombings, India. A series of attacks in the Sankath Mochan Hanuman temple and Cantonment Railway Station in the Hindu holy city of Varanasi. 28 killed and over 100 injured.
- 11 July 2006—Mumbai train bombings, Mumbai, India; a series of 7 bomb blasts that took place over a period of 11 minutes on the Suburban Railway in Mumbai. 209 killed and over 700 injured.
- 14 August 2007—Qahtaniya bombings: Four suicide vehicle bombers massacred nearly 800 members of northern Iraq's Yazidi sect in the Iraq war's deadliest attack to date.
- 26 July 2008—Ahmedabad bombings, India. Islamic terrorists detonate at least 21 explosive devices in the heart of this industrial capital, leaving at least 56 dead and 200 injured. A Muslim group calling itself the Indian Mujahideen claims responsibility. Indian authorities believe that extremists with ties to Pakistan and/or Bangladesh are likely responsible and are intent on inciting communal violence. Investigation by Indian police led to the eventual arrest of a number of terrorists suspected of carrying out the blasts, most of whom belong to a well-known terrorist group, The Students Islamic Movement of India.
- 13 September 2008—Bombing series in Delhi, India. Pakistani extremist groups plant bombs at several places including India Gate, out of which the ones at Karol Bagh, Connaught Place and Greater Kailash explode leaving around 30 people dead and 130 injured, followed by another attack two weeks later at the congested Mehrauli area, leaving 3 people dead.
- 26 November 2008—Muslim extremists kill at least 174 people and wound numerous others in a series of coordinated attacks on India's largest city and financial capital, Mumbai. A group calling itself the

Deccan Mujaheddin claims responsibility; however, the government of India suspects Islamic terrorists based in Pakistan are responsible. Ajmal Kasab, one of the terrorists, was caught alive.

- 25 October 2009—Baghdad, Iraq. During a terrorist attack, two bomber vehicles detonated in the Green Zone, killing at least 155 people and injuring 520.
- 28 October 2009—Peshawar, Pakistan. A car bomb is detonated in a woman-exclusive shopping district. Over 110 killed and over 200 injured.
- 5 November 2009—Fort Hood shooting, Texas, USA. U.S. Army Major Nidal Malik Hasan, an American Muslim of Palestinian descent, shot and killed 13 people and wounded 30 others at a U.S. Army base.
- 3 December 2009—Mogadishu, Somalia. A male suicide bomber disguised as a woman detonates in a hotel meeting hall. The hotel was hosting a graduation ceremony for local medical students when the blast went off, killing 4 government ministers as well as other civilians.
- 1 January 2010—Lakki Marwat, Pakistan. A suicide car bomber drove his explosive-laden vehicle into a volleyball pitch as people gathered to watch a match, killing more than 100 people.
- 1 May 2010—New York, New York, USA. Faisal Shahzad, an Islamic Pakistani American who received U.S. citizenship in December 2009, attempted to detonate a car bomb in Times Square working with the Pakistani Taliban or Tehrik-i-Taliban Pakistan.

As you can see in the list above, these attacks frequently target non-military people, including women and children. Do Muslims purposely attack non-military people including women and children? Yes. Why? Osama Bin Ladin has stated, "Muslim scholars have issued a fatwa [a religious order] against any American who pays taxes to his government. He is our target because he is helping the American war machine against the Muslim nation." In another interview Bin Ladin also stated, "We don't differentiate between those dressed in military uniforms and civilians. They are all targets in this fatwa." [43]

What is the explanation for all of these acts of violence? The answer is that all of these were inspired by, or are in accordance with, teachings of violence against non-Muslims. There are more than 100 verses in the Qur'an that support or command violence against non-Muslims (and abrogate all peaceful verses). [15, 44] Consider the following examples (with key phrases underlined by me for emphasis):

1. 9:29. Fight against such of those who have been given the Scripture as believe not in Allah nor the Last Day, and forbid not that which Allah hath forbidden by His messenger, and follow

not the Religion of Truth, until they pay the tribute readily, being brought low. 30.   And the Jews say: Ezra is the son of Allah, and the Christians say: The Messiah is the son of Allah. That is their saying with their mouths. They imitate the saying of those who disbelieved of old. Allah (Himself) fighteth against them. How perverse are they! 31.   They have taken as lords beside Allah their rabbis and their monks and the Messiah son of Mary, <u>when they were bidden to worship only One Allah</u>. There is no Allah save Him. Be He Glorified from all that they ascribe as partner (unto Him)! 32.   Fain would they put out the light of Allah with their mouths, but Allah disdaineth (aught) save that He shall perfect His light, however much the disbelievers are averse. 33.   He it is Who hath sent His messenger with the guidance and the Religion of Truth, <u>that He may cause it to prevail over all religion</u>, however much the idolaters may be averse. (Underlining was added by me for emphasis. These verses present three choices to non-Muslims: convert to Islam; submit to Islam with second-class status under Islamic rule, or death. [45])

2.   2:191.   <u>And slay them wherever ye find them</u>, and drive them out of the places whence they drove you out, for persecution is worse than slaughter. And fight not with them at the Inviolable Place of Worship until they first attack you there, but if they attack you (there) then slay them. Such is the reward of disbelievers.

3.   2:193.   And <u>fight them until persecution is no more, and religion is for Allah</u>. But if they desist, then let there be no hostility except against wrong-doers.

4.   4:89.   They long that ye should disbelieve even as they disbelieve, that ye may be upon a level (with them). So <u>choose not friends from them</u> till they forsake their homes in the way of Allah; if they turn back (to enmity) then take them and <u>kill them wherever ye find them</u>, and choose no friend nor helper from among them,

5.   4:91.   Ye will find others who desire that they should have security from you, and security from their own folk. So often as they are returned to hostility they are plunged therein. If they keep not aloof from you nor offer you peace nor hold their hands, then take them and <u>kill them wherever ye find them</u>. Against such We have given you clear warrant.

6.   5:33.   The only reward of those who make war upon Allah and His messenger and strive after corruption in the land will be that <u>they will be killed or crucified, or have their hands and feet on</u>

alternate sides cut off, or will be expelled out of the land. Such will be their degradation in the world, and in the Hereafter theirs will be an awful doom;

7. 8:39.   And fight them until persecution is no more, and religion is all for Allah. But if they cease, then lo! Allah is Seer of what they do.

8. 9:123.   O ye who believe! Fight those of the disbelievers who are near to you, and let them find harshness in you, and know that Allah is with those who keep their duty (unto Him).

9. 48:16.   Say unto those of the wandering Arabs who were left behind: Ye will be called against a folk of mighty prowess, to fight them until they surrender; and if ye obey, Allah will give you a fair reward; but if ye turn away as ye did turn away before, He will punish you with a painful doom.

10. 66:9.   O Prophet! Strive against the disbelievers and the hypocrites, and be stern with them. Hell will be their home, a hapless journey's end.

Have you read enough to know that Islam cannot be considered a peaceful religion, according to the Qur'an? Did you know that in the last eight years of Muhammad's life, he was involved in 29 battle campaigns, planned 39 more, and assassinated 25 people because they did not believe in him? [15] Do you have any doubts that the ultimate mission of Islam is to conquer the world so that it is in complete submission to Allah? [46] If you are not yet convinced that Islam promotes the use of violence to achieve control of all nations and peoples in the world to be in submission to Allah, then here are some additional verses and an online Qur'an to facilitate your additional study: 2:178; 2:179; 2:190; 2:216; 2:244; 3:121; 3:157; 3:158; 3:168; 4:71; 4:74; 4:76; 4:77; 4:84; 8:12; 8:16; 8:17; 8:65; 8:67; 9:5; 9:12; 9:14; 47:4; 56:25; and 61:4 [44]

Did you know that the Qur'an promises entry into paradise for all Muslims who die fighting in jihad, the holy war?

9:111.   Lo! Allah hath bought from the believers their lives and their wealth because the Garden will be theirs: they shall fight in the way of Allah and shall slay and be slain. It is a promise which is binding on Him in the Torah and the Gospel and the Qur'an. Who fulfilleth His covenant better than Allah? Rejoice then in your bargain that ye have made, for that is the supreme triumph.

47:4. Now when ye meet in battle those who disbelieve, then it is smiting of the necks until, when ye have routed them, then making fast of bonds; and afterward either grace or ransom till the war lay down its burdens. That (is the ordinance). And if Allah willed He could have punished them (without you) but (thus it is ordained) that He may try some of you by means of others. And those who are slain in the way of Allah, He rendereth not their actions vain. 5. He will guide them and improve their state, 6. And bring them in unto the Garden which He hath made known to them.

The combination of commands to kill the infidels (non-Muslims), commands of Islam to seek world domination, and promises of entry into paradise for those who die while in jihad (fighting the holy war) produces the deadly scenario that is active in the world today. The hope that we can negotiate for peace, particularly in the Middle East, or achieve peace through sanctions against Islamic extremists is unrealistic and certainly contrary to Islamic teachings and history. As Dick Morris, a Fox News contributor, stated so accurately, "If the Muslims would lay down their weapons, there would be peace with Israel. If the Israelis laid down their weapons, there would be no Israel." [47]

Isn't it interesting that much of the deadly scenario we are witnessing in the world today is focused in the Middle East, and particularly in the little country of Israel? Would you be surprised to know that a section of the Bible, written almost 3,500 years ago, provides the explanation of the beginnings of the hostilities between the Jewish people and the Arab people who would later become Muslims? Some might say that this is merely a coincidence, but I believe it is further evidence of the divine inspiration of the Bible.

As pointed out in Chapter 2 of this book, God made a covenant with Abram (later named Abraham) in which He promised to give Abraham and his descendants land (including present-day Israel), bless him, make him the father of a great nation, and bless those who bless Abraham. As you recall, since Sarai (later named Sarah), Abraham's wife, was too old to have a child according to the laws of nature, she convinced her maidservant, Hagar, and Abraham to have sexual relations so that Abraham could have children to fulfill God's promise that Abraham would be the father of a great nation. Although Sarai's plan was in accordance with the legal custom of the day, it was not God's plan:

"After Abram had lived ten years in the land of Canaan, Abram's wife Sarai took Hagar the Egyptian, her maid, and gave her to her husband Abram as his wife. He went in to Hagar, and she conceived; and when she saw that she had conceived, her mistress was despised in her sight." Genesis 16:3-4

As might be expected, bad feelings arose between Sarai and Hagar. Perhaps Hagar, the former servant, became prideful and arrogant because she thought that her offspring would fulfill the Abrahamic covenant and consequently despised Sarai. Perhaps Sarai was jealous that Hagar was able to give Abram the son that she could not. Nevertheless, Sarai treated Hagar harshly and blamed Abram for the awkward situation. This placed Abram in a very unenviable position—between two fighting women! So, Abram told Sarai to do whatever she wanted to do with Hagar. Sarai treated Hagar harshly, causing Hagar to flee.

"And Sarai said to Abram, 'May the wrong done me be upon you. I gave my maid into your arms, but when she saw that she had conceived, I was despised in her sight. May the LORD judge between you and me.' But Abram said to Sarai, 'Behold, your maid is in your power; do to her what is good in your sight. So Sarai treated her harshly, and she fled from her presence." Genesis 16:5-6

However, an angel appeared to Hagar and told her to return to Sarai and Abram and submit to them. He also confirmed that she would bear a son, Ishmael, and that the Lord would multiply her descendents through Ishmael.

"Then the angel of the LORD said to her, 'Return to your mistress, and submit yourself to her authority.' Moreover the angel of the LORD said to her, 'I will greatly multiply your descendants so that they will be too many to count.' The angel of the LORD said to her further, 'Behold, you are with child, and you will bear a son; and you shall call his name Ishmael, because the LORD has given heed to your affliction. He will be a wild donkey of a man, his hand will be against everyone, and everyone's hand will be against him; and he will live to the east of all his brothers.' So Hagar bore Abram a son; and Abram called the name of his son, whom Hagar bore, Ishmael." Genesis 16:10-12, 15 (underlining was added by me for emphasis.)

Later, the story continues...

"And Abraham said to God, 'Oh that Ishmael might live before You!' But God said, 'No, but Sarah your wife will bear you a son, and you shall call his name Isaac; and I will establish My covenant with him for an everlasting covenant for his descendants after him. As for Ishmael, I have heard you; behold, I will bless him and will make him fruitful and will multiply him exceedingly. He shall become the father of twelve princes, and I will make him a great nation. But my covenant I will establish with Isaac, whom Sarah will bear to you at this season next year." Genesis 17:18-21 (underlining was added by me for emphasis)

"So Sarah conceived and bore a son to Abraham in his old age, at the appointed time of which God had spoken to him. Abraham called the name of his son who was born to him, whom Sarah bore to him, Isaac." Genesis 21:2-3

God performed a miracle so that His covenant would be fulfilled, as promised, through Abraham and Sarah. The Jewish nation descended from Abraham through Isaac. It is interesting to note that the biblical account of Ishmael and his 12 sons continued later in Genesis with the following comment: [48]

"They [sons of Ishmael] settled from Havilah to Shur which is east of Egypt as one goes toward Assyria; he (Ishmael) settled in defiance of all his relatives." Genesis 25:18

Ishmael and his descendants lived in hostility toward all their brothers. This fulfilled God's word to Hagar and is supported by the statement "he (Ishmael) settled in defiance of all his relatives." [48]

Why do you think that Ishmael lived in hostility toward all his brothers? The Bible does not say, so we cannot be sure. We can speculate that because he was the first and only son of Abram for the first 12 years of his life he thought he was the fulfillment of God's covenant with Abram. The custom of the time was that the first-born son would receive his father's blessing and perhaps he wanted and expected this blessing. It seems reasonable to think that even though God promised that he would be the father of a multitude (the Arab people) that he wanted more.

He may have been jealous or angry that God's and Abraham's blessing was bestowed on Isaac (father of the Jewish nation). It is also reasonable to speculate that perhaps he and his mother were treated harshly by Sarah before and after the birth of Isaac. Since the Bible does not say, we do not know whether jealousy, anger, harsh treatment, or some other factors contributed to the hostility of Ishmael and his descendants toward Isaac and the Jewish nation. We do know, however, that as God indicated, the hostility between the Arabs and Muslims toward the Jews continues to this day. [48]

With this background on the Muslim/Jewish conflicts, you might wonder if there is any way to resolve this conflict and achieve peace in the Middle East, as well as throughout the world. As a matter of fact, yes, there is a solution that would result in peace.

Ravi Zacharias, an internationally renowned Christian apologist, tells about a meeting he and several other prominent Christian leaders had with an unnamed Muslim leader in Palestine. During their conversation, Ravi reminded the Muslim leader about when God tested Abraham's faith by asking him to sacrifice his son (Genesis 22:1-19). He pointed out that Muslims believe that Ishmael was the son that was involved in this test and that Jews and Christians believe that Isaac was the son that that was involved in the test.

To avoid debate, Ravi pointed out that for the purposes of his point it did not matter which son God used to test Abraham's faith. He reminded the Muslim leader that just before Abraham sacrificed his son, God told Abraham to stop and that He would provide an appropriate sacrifice, which He did. Ravi then said, "On a hill, not far from where we sit, God provided the ultimate sacrifice—His son, Jesus Christ." He then said something very profound: "Until you and I accept God's sacrifice, we will continue sacrificing our sons and daughters on the battlefield of war." [49]

Ravi Zacharias is exactly right. The only solution to the hostility, battles, destruction, and death that are present in this world is the solution that God provided through the life, crucifixion, death, and resurrection of His Son, Jesus Christ. Man's attempts to resolve the hostility between the Muslims and Jews, although noble, will continue to fail.

The hostility, hatred, and history between the Muslims and Jews is so engrained in these people that only a miracle from God can provide lasting peace. That miracle is the gospel of Jesus Christ. Will you help spread the good news of the gospel? The Bible does have some bad news and some good news about how the story ends. The next chapter on biblical prophecy will provide insight into what the Bible says is coming.

Let There Be No Misunderstanding

I am certainly aware of the fact that some people will call me a religious bigot and say that my writing this book in general, and this section on Islam in particular, is narrow-minded and motivated by hatred. So, let me address this accusation. Frankly, my motivation is not motivated by hatred, but rather by love.

I have some very good friends that are Muslims. I feel sorry for them because I think they are trapped by a man-made religion that demands their death if they decide to leave Islam. I certainly do not question their intelligence and their ability to make an informed decision when they have sufficient facts regarding Islam and biblical Christianity. Because they have not had the freedom to question Islam or obtain facts about other religions, they do not have sufficient information to make an informed decision about biblical Christianity.

However, I do question their courage to leave Islam, which would require them to turn away from many of their family members and friends, to be ostracized in the communities in which they live, and to face the probability of being murdered by their former "Muslim brothers." Consequently, they, and all other Muslims, deserve my best effort at providing objective information so that they can decide whether or not to confidently and courageously place their faith in the gospel of Jesus Christ.

So, with this in mind, who is guilty of hatred? Me for sharing what I know and what I believe to be true so that my friends and others trapped by Islam may be set free, or those who would demand the death of any who leave Islam and accept Jesus as their personal savior and would also demand my death for sharing the truth of the gospel and exposing the truth about Islam?

References:

All Qur'an quotes are from: Online Quran Project. http://al-quran.info/?x= y#&&sura=1&aya=1&trans=en-marmaduke_pickthall&show=trans& ver=2.00. The 1930 English translation by Muhammad Marmaduke Pickthall (1876-1936) was used for all quotations above. "The permission for use of this work has been verified and archived in the Wikimedia OTRS system.... *This file has been (or is hereby) released into the public domain by its author, Online Quran Project. This applies worldwide....Online Quran Project grants anyone the right to use this work for any purpose, without any conditions, unless such conditions are required by law."* (http://en.wikipedia.org/wiki/File:Online_Quran_Project_Screenshot. png)

1. Geisler, N. L. *Baker Encyclopedia of Christian Apologetics.* Baker reference library (368). Grand Rapids, MI.: Baker Books. (1999), p. 368. (Libronix Digital Library System version.)
2. _____. p. 369.
3. Merrian-Webster. *Merriam-Webster's Collegiate Dictionary.* Springfield, MA: Merriam Webster, 1996.
4. Caner, Emir Fethi and Ergun Mehmet Caner. *More than a Prophet: An Insider's Response to Muslim Beliefs about Jesus and Christianity.* Grand Rapids, MI: Kregel Publications, 2003, pp. 192-193.
5. _____. p. 161.
6. English Introduction to the Holy Qur'an. Part 1. (http://www.muslim.org/ english-quran/quran-intro.htm)
7. Muncaster, Ralph O. *Examine the Evidence: Exploring the Case for Christianity.* Eugene, OR: Harvest House Publishers, 2004, p. 521.
8. _____. pp. 362-363.
9. McDowell, Josh. *A Ready Defense: The Best of Josh McDowell.* San Bernardino, CA: Here's Life Publisher's Inc. 1990, pp. 307-308.
10. English Introduction to the Holy Qur'an. Part 7. (http://www.muslim.org/ english-quran/quran-intro.htm)
11. _____. Part 2.
12. "All About God." (http://www.allaboutgod.com/bible-facts.htm)
13. *New American Standard Bible: The Open Bible Edition. Nashville, TN*: Thomas Nelson Publishers, 1979, p. 1227.

14. Walvoord, J. F. *The Prophecy Knowledge Handbook*. Wheaton, Ill.: Victor Books, 1990, p. 86.
15. Smith, Jay. "Engaging Islam Part II" Presented at the Seeking 7 Conference, Birmingham, AL, January 15, 2010. (http://www.seeking7.org/; Co-sponsored by Fixed Point Foundation and Ravi Zacharias International Ministry. A CD of this presentation may be ordered at: http://www.fixed-point.org/index.php/onlinestore?page=shop.browse&category_id=23.
16. Geisler, Norman L. *Baker Encyclopedia of Christian Apologetics*. Grand Rapids, MI: Baker Book House, 1999, p. 368.
17. McDowell, Josh. *A Ready Defense: The Best of Josh McDowell*. San Bernardino, CA: Here's Life Publisher's Inc. 1990, p. 313.
18. Spencer, Robert. *The Complete Infidel's Guide to the Koran*. Washington, DC: Regnery Publishing, Inc. 2009, p. 37.
19. Caner, Emir Fethi and Ergun Mehmet Caner. *More than a Prophet: An Insider's Response to Muslim Beliefs About Jesus and Christianity*. Grand Rapids, MI: Kregel Publications, 2003, p. 70.
20. _____. p. 29.
21. _____. p. 30.
22. _____.p. 32,33.
23. _____.p. 49.
24. Geisler, Norman L. and Abdul Saleeb. *Answering Islam: The Crescent in Light of the Cross*. Grand Rapids, MI: Baker Book House, 2002, p. 152.
25. McQuilkin, J. Robertson. *Understanding and Applying the Bible: An Introduction to Hermeneutics*. Chicago, IL: Moody Press.1983.
26. Geisler, Norman L. and Abdul Saleeb. p. 152-153.
27. Walvoord, J. F., Zuck, R. B., & Dallas Theological Seminary. (1983-c1985). *The Bible Knowledge Commentary: An Exposition of the Scriptures* (1:296). Wheaton, IL: Victor Books. (Libronix Digital Library System version.)
28. Geisler, Norman L. and Abdul Saleeb. p. 154.
29. _____. p. 155.
30. Walvoord, J. F. *The Prophecy Knowledge Handbook*. Wheaton, Ill.: Victor Books, 1990, p. 86.
31. Walvoord, J. F., Zuck, R. B., & Dallas Theological Seminary. (1983-1985). *The Bible Knowledge Commentary: An Exposition of the Scriptures* (2:25). Wheaton, IL: Victor Books.
32. Geisler, Norman L. and Abdul Saleeb. p. 158.
33. _____. p. 159.
34. Haykal, Muhammad Husayan. *The Life of Muhammad*. Indianapolis: North American Trust Publications, 1976, p. 74, as quoted by Geisler, Normal L. and Abdul Saleeb. p. 159.
35. Geisler, Norman L. and Abdul Saleeb. pp. 162-173.
36. _____. pp. 178-180.
37. Caner, Emir Fethi and Ergun Mehmet Caner. p. 261.

38. Schmidt, Alvin J. *The Great Divide: The Failure of Islam and the Triumph of the West*. Boston, MA: Regina Orthodox Press, Inc., 2004, p. 66-69.

39. Geisler, Norman L. and Abdul Saleeb. p. 178.

40. Spencer, Robert. *Onward Muslim Soldiers*. Washington, DC: Regnery Publishing Inc., 2003, pp.134-135.

41. _____. pp. 168-169.

42. "Islamic Terrorism." http://en.wikipedia.org/wiki/Islamic_terrorism.

43. Silas. "Muhammad, Islam, and Terrorism." http://www.answering-islam. org/Silas/terrorism.htm.

44. Schmidt, Alvin. p. 259.

45. Spencer, Robert. p. 35.

46. Caner, Emir Fethi and Ergun Mehmet Caner. p. 217.

47. Morris, Dick. Quote from an interview on *The O'Reilly Factor*, Fox News Channel, June 2, 2010.

48. Moore, Beth. "The Patriarchs: Eyes on Isaac (Session 4)" A Bible Study CD. http://www.lproof.org/

49. Zacharias, Ravi. *Is Christianity Unique Amongst World Religions*? a CD presentation given at Town Hall Meeting # 2, Oxford, England, February 7, 2007. http://www.rzim.org/default.aspx

Chapter 5

Atheism: How Firm Are Its Foundations?

A theism is the belief that God does not exist. As stated in Chapter 2, no one can prove that God exists. Likewise, no one can prove that God does not exist. So, why is atheism included as a competing religion/ worldview that is antagonistic to biblical Christianity?

It seems to me there are two factors that justify including atheism as being significant threats to biblical Christianity: (1) more aggressive promotion of an anti-God perspective and what might be considered intellectual bullying by some prominent atheists and (2) an unholy alliance with secular socialists, particularly in the promotion of the theory of evolution. The theory of evolution is proposed by both atheists [1] and secular socialists as proof that God does not and never did exist.

Richard Dawkins is one of the most ardent proponents of atheism and aggressive attackers of all religions, including Christianity. He writes and speaks extensively on the merits of science and the worthlessness of religion. The mission statement of his foundation openly links religion to superstition, intolerance, and human suffering:

> "The mission of the Richard Dawkins Foundation for Reason and Science is to support scientific education, critical thinking and evidence-based understanding of the natural world in <u>the quest to overcome religious fundamentalism, superstition, intolerance and human suffering</u>." [2] (underlining was added by me for emphasis)

Similarly, the promotion of one of his recent books, *The Greatest Show on Earth*, states the following:

> "Evolution is accepted as scientific fact by all reputable scientists and indeed theologians, yet millions of people continue to question its veracity. In *The Greatest Show on Earth*, Richard Dawkins takes on creationists, including followers of "Intelligent Design" and all those who question the fact of evolution through natural selection. Like a detective arriving on the scene of a crime, he sifts through fascinating layers of scientific facts and disciplines to build a cast-iron case: from the living examples of natural selection in birds and insects; the "time clocks" of trees and radioactive dating that calibrate a timescale for evolution; the fossil record and the traces of our earliest ancestors; to confirmation from molecular biology and genetics. All of this, and much more, bears witness to the truth of evolution. *The Greatest Show on Earth* comes at a critical time: systematic opposition to the fact of evolution is now flourishing as never before, especially in America. In Britain and elsewhere in the world, teachers witness insidious attempts to undermine the status of science in their classrooms. Richard Dawkins provides unequivocal evidence that boldly and comprehensively rebuts such nonsense. ... it is ... totally convincing." [3] (underlining was added by me for emphasis)

In case you have any doubts about the fervor with which Dr. Dawkins attacks religion and those who believe, consider the following promotion of the "Out Campaign," also on his website:

> "It is time to let our voices be heard regarding the intrusion of religion in our schools and politics. Atheists along with millions of others are tired of being bullied by those who would force their own religious agenda down the throats of our children and our respective governments. We need to KEEP OUT the supernatural from our moral principles and public policies." [4] (underlining was added by me for emphasis)

As you read these quotes, did you note that evolution is presented as a "scientific fact" and that any questioning of this is seen as an insidious attempt to undermine reason and force religious superstition upon our children and our governments? As you will see in the next section, secular socialists are very happy to join forces with atheists like Dawkins to achieve their goals, which include excluding God from public life.

This section will examine four fundamental doctrines of atheism: (1) God does not exist; (2) all living things evolved from a common ancestor (evolution); (3) there are no moral absolutes (moral relativism); and (4) man's destiny is death. Since evolution is embraced by both atheism and secular socialism, it will be examined extensively.

God Does Not Exist

As has already been stated, the existence of God can neither be proven nor disproven. However, I trust that you have seen the evidence supporting the existence of the God of the Bible is at least compelling, and hopefully, convincing. An interesting "scientific" perspective on the existence of God is provided below:

"Let me explain the problem science has with God." The atheist professor of philosophy pauses before his class and then asks one of his new students to stand.

"You're a Christian, aren't you, son?"

"Yes sir," the student says.

"So you believe in God?"

"Absolutely."

"Is God good?"

"Sure God's good."

"Is God all-powerful? Can God do anything?"

"Yes."

"Are you good or evil?"

"The Bible says I'm evil."

The professor grins knowingly. "Aha! The Bible!" He considers for a moment.

"Here's one for you. Let's say there's a sick person over hear and you can cure him. You can do it. Would you help him? Would you try?"

"Yes sir, I would."

"So you're good...!"

"I wouldn't say that."

"But why not say that? You'd help a sick and maimed person if you could. Most of us would if we could. But God doesn't."

The student does not answer, so the professor continues. "He doesn't, does he? My brother was a Christian who died of cancer, even though he prayed to God to heal him. How is this God good? Hmmm? Can you answer than one?"

The student remains silent.

"No, you can't, can you?" The professor takes a sip of water from a glass on his desk to give the student time to relax. "Let's start again, young fellow, "Is God good?"

"Er...yes," the student says.

"Is Satan good?"

The student doesn't hesitate on this one. "No."

"Then where does Satan come from?"

The student: "From God..."

"That's right. God made Satan, didn't he? Tell me, son, Is there evil in this world?"

"Yes, sir."

"Evil's everywhere, isn't it? And God did make everything, correct?"

"Yes."

"So, who created evil?" The professor continued, "if God created every-thing, then God created evil, since evil exists and according to the principle that our works define who we are, then God is evil."

Without allowing the student to answer, the professor continues: "Is there sickness? Immorality? Hatred? Ugliness? All these terrible things, do they exist in this world?"

The student: "Yes."

"So who created them?"

The student dos not answer again, so the professor repeats his ques-tion. "Who created them?" There is still no answer. Suddenly the lecturer breaks away to pace in front of the classroom. The class is mesmerized.

"Tell me, "He continues onto another student." Do you believe in Jesus Christ, son?"

The student's voice is confident: "Yes, professor, I do."

The old man stops pacing. "Science says you have five senses you use to identify and observe the world around you. Have you ever seen God?"

"No sir, I have not."

"Have you ever actually felt your Jesus, tasted your God or smelt your God? Have you ever had any sensory perception of God?"

"No, sir, I'm afraid I haven't."

"Yet you still believe in him?"

"Yes."

"According to the rules of empirical, testable, demonstrable protocol, science says your God doesn't exist. What do you say to that, son?"

"Nothing." The student replies. "I only have my faith."

"Yes, faith," the professor repeats. "And that is the problem science has with God. There is no evidence, only faith."

The student stands quietly for a moment, before asking a question of his own. "Professor is there such a thing as heat?"

"Yes," the professor replies. "There's heat."

"And is there such a thing as cold?"

"Yes, son, there's cold, too."

"No sir, there isn't."

The professor turns to face the student, obviously interested. The room suddenly becomes very quiet. The student begins to explain.

"You can have lots of heat, even more heat, super heat, mega heat, unlimited heat, white heat, a little heat or no heat, but we don't have anything called 'Cold.'" We can hit up to 458 degrees below zero, which is no heat but we can't go any further after that. There is no such thing as cold; otherwise we would be able to go colder than the lowest -458 degrees. Every body or object is susceptible to study when it has or transmits energy, and heat is way makes a body or matter have or transmit energy. Absolute zero (-458 F) is the total absence of heat. You see, sir, cold is only a word we use to describe the absence of heat. We cannot measure cold. Heat we can measure in thermal units because heat is energy. Cold is not the opposite of heat, sir, just the absence of it."

Silence across the room. A pen drops somewhere in the classroom, sounding like a hammer.

"What about darkness, professor. Is there such a thing as darkness?"

"Yes," the professor replies without hesitation. "What is night if it isn't darkness?"

"You're wrong again, sir. Darkness is not something; it is the absence of something. You can have low light, normal light, bright light, flashing light, but if you have no light constantly, you have nothing and it is called darkness, isn't it? That's the meaning we use to define the word. In reality, darkness isn't. If it were, you would be able to make darkness darker, wouldn't you?"

The professor begins to smile at the student in front of him. This will be a good semester. "So what point are you making young man?"

"Yes, professor. My point is your philosophical premise is flawed to start and so your conclusion must also be flawed."

The professor's face cannot hide his surprise this time. "Flawed? Can you explain how?"

"You are working on the premise of duality," the student explains. "You argue that there is life and then there's death; a good God and a bad God. You are viewing the concept of God as something finite, something we can measure. Sir, science can't even explain a thought. It uses electricity and magnetism, but has never seen, much less fully understood either one. To view death as the opposite of life is to be ignorant of the fact that death cannot exist as a substantive thing. Death is not the opposite of life, just the absence of it."

"Now tell me professor, do you teach your students that they evolved from a monkey?"

"If you are referring to the natural evolutionary process, young man, yes, of course I do."

"Have you ever observed evolution with your own eyes, sir?"

The professor begins to shake his head, still smiling, as he realizes where the argument is going. This will be a very good semester, indeed.

"Since no one has ever observed the process of evolution at work and cannot even prove that this process is an on-going endeavor, are you not teaching your opinion, sir? Are you now not a scientist, but a preacher?"

The class is in uproar. The student remains silent until the commotion has subsided.

"To continue the point you were making earlier to the other student, let me give you an example of what I mean."

The student looks around the room. "Is there anyone in this class who has ever seen the professor's brain?" The class breaks out into laughter.

"Is there anyone here who has ever heard the professor's brain, felt the professor's brain, touched or smelled the professor's brain? No one appears to have done so. So, according to the established rules of empirical, stable, demonstrable protocol, science says that you have no brain, with all due respect, sir. So if science says you have no brain, how can we trust your lectures, sir?"

Now the room is silent. The professor just stares at the student, his face unreadable.

Finally, after what seems an eternity, the old man answers. "I guess you'll have to take them on faith."

"Now, you accept that there is faith, and, in fact, faith exists with life," the student continues. "Sir, is there such a thing as evil?"

Now uncertain, the professor responds, "Of course, there is. We see it every day. It is in the daily example of man's inhumanity to man. It is in the multitude of crime and violence everywhere in the world. These manifestations are nothing else but evil."

To this the student replied, "Evil does not exist sir, or at least it does not exist unto itself. Evil is simply the absence of God. It is just like darkness and cold, a word that man has created to describe the absence of God. God did not create evil. Evil is the result of what happens when man does not have God's love present in his heart. It's like the cold that comes when there is no heat or the darkness that comes when there is no light.

The professor sits down." (Author unknown)

I don't know whether or not this is a true story. Nevertheless, it does provide some interesting perspectives on the limitations of the scientific method, the existence and nature of God, the nature of evil, and the importance of faith, even in science. From my biased perspective, it appears that the student presented some very compelling points. What do you think?

John Lennox, the holder of Ph.D., D.Phi., and D.Sci. degrees, professor of mathematics at the University of Oxford, and a fellow in mathematics and the philosophy of science at Green Templeton College, certainly qualifies as a scientist. He concludes his interesting and thought-provoking book, *God's Undertaker: Has Science Buried God?* with the following:

"In conclusion, I submit that, far from science having buried God, not only do the results of science point towards his existence, but the scientific enter-prise itself is validated by his existence.

Inevitably, of course, not only those of us who do science, but all of us, have to choose the presupposition with which we start. There are not many options—essentially just two. Either human intelligence ultimately owes its origin to mindless matter; or there is a Creator. It is strange that some people claim that it is their intelligence that leads them to prefer the first to the second." [5]

The following sections of this chapter will provide some of the back-ground information that supports Dr. Lennox's conclusion and will enable you to make a more informed decision about atheism.

Evolution

The theory of evolution was popularized by Charles Darwin (1809-1882) through his book, *On the Origin of Species*, published in 1859. The theory states that natural selection (evolution) accounts for the simi-larities as well as the adaptations that are seen within species (micro-evolution) and that genetic mutations account for the different species (macro-evolution). Examples of micro-evolution (adaptations within a species) are well-documented and include such things as Darwin noticing different lengths of beaks of finches in the Galapagos islands and he the-orized that this adaptation provided survival advantages to the finches with longer, stronger beaks during periods of drought. [6] If the theory of evolution stopped with micro-evolution, there would be no controversy or disagreement. But, it does not stop with micro-evolution and, as you will see, there is considerable, legitimate controversy and disagreement.

The theory of evolution also teaches that all life evolved from a common ancestor or gene pool. In other words, over millions or billions of years, as a result of countless genetic mutations from the first microbe or single cell organism, all other living creatures have evolved, with man at the pinnacle of the evolutionary process. Macro-evolution is respon-sible for all of the complexity and diversity of life that we see on the earth. [7] (For the purposes of this chapter, when the term *evolution* is used, it will refer to macro-evolution or one species changing into another, distinctly different species (e.g., a fish to a mammal).

As mentioned earlier, one of the most outspoken proponents of both atheism and the theory of evolution is Richard Dawkins. He is the author of many books and journal articles promoting atheism and evolution, including *The God Delusion*, *The Blind Watchmaker*, and *The Greatest Show on Earth*. He has a D. Phil. degree and is the former Charles Simonyi Professor of the Public Understanding of Science at Oxford University. He certainly has a very impressive curriculum vitae and I'll readily admit that Dawkins is much more learned and smarter than I am. So, does that mean you should believe everything he says and nothing I say? I don't think so.

In my opinion, I think a case can be made that Dawkins and other atheists often resort to "intellectual bullying" or "intellectual intimidation" to try to convince people that belief in God is incompatible with higher learning and refined intellectual capacity. Consequently, I think it is appropriate to tell you a couple of true stories and then to give you a test to help put things in proper perspective, before considering some of the fundamental teachings of atheism.

I earned a Master's of Science degree at the University of Washington, with a specialty in exercise physiology. During the course of my studies, I further specialized into the area of exercise cardiology and had the privilege of having Dr. Robert Bruce, considered to be the father of modern day exercise stress testing, as a member of my Master's thesis committee. Additionally, I was employed as one of Dr. Bruce's research assistants. Having the opportunity to study and learn from one of the world's foremost authorities in the field of exercise cardiology was an incredible opportunity for me and I cherished the time that I spent one-on-one with Dr. Bruce.

After one of our lunch meetings, I analyzed our time together and realized that it had been a very enjoyable question and answer period. Although I was able to ask more than my fair share of questions of "the master," he also asked me a lot of questions. As might be expected, some of his questions were to evaluate my knowledge to make sure I was learning and meeting his expectations. However, a surprising number of his questions were to find out my answers to things that he thought I knew that he did not know. Then it hit me, I know some things that the world-famous Dr. Bruce does not know. WOW! That was a revolutionary and confidence-building thought for me.

The same is true for you. You have a lot of knowledge that no one else has. Additionally, each of us has the ability to learn, reason, and think for ourselves. So, I encourage you to use your mind to carefully consider the principles and assumptions associated with atheism/Darwinism and biblical Christianity.

Let me tell you one other story that has some relevance to this topic. Several years ago, one of my friends, for whom I have a tremendous amount of respect, and I were having a discussion and disagreement. He jokingly told me that my brain was like a 256K processor, while his brain was like a Pentium processor—newer and faster. I readily admitted that his "Pentium brain" was newer and faster than my "256K brain."

However, I then good naturedly pointed out that although my brain might be slower at processing data and information, nevertheless, when it finished, it produced the right answers. Conversely, his Pentium processor brain was so new that it still had bugs in the hardware and although it would produce answers faster than mine, his answers were often wrong! Yes, in spite of numerous exchanges like this one, we remain very good friends and have strong respect for one another (and the processing power of the other's brain).

So, what is the point of this story? I submit for your consideration that if incorrect presuppositions are forced on your thought processes, no matter how intelligent you are, there is a strong probability that you will arrive at the wrong answers. Perhaps this is the case with Richard Dawkins and other atheists. They conclude there is no God, because they don't want there to be a God. [8] So, use your brain and its "processing power" to carefully consider the facts and opinions presented to you and make informed decisions.

Now, for the test that I mentioned earlier: Let's say that the circle below contains all known and all unknown data, information, and knowledge in the universe. Now, draw a circle inside the first circle to represent all the data, information, and knowledge that you think Richard Dawkins has and another circle to represent all of the data, information, and knowledge that you think I have and a third circle to represent all of the data, information, and knowledge that you have. Realistically, to put this in proper perspective, the amount of data, knowledge, and information any human possesses would be best represented by a microscopic dot; however, for this exercise, it is okay to use circles.

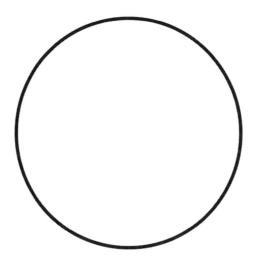

Figure 5-1. Representation of All Data, Information, and Knowledge in the Universe.

I would expect that each of the three circles that you drew were much smaller than the original, indicating that there is a lot of data, information, and knowledge that exists that neither Richard Dawkins, Richard Trayler, nor you possess. I would also expect that the sizes of the circles that you drew were different, indicating that there is probably a difference in the amount of data, information, and knowledge that each of us possess. Realistically, however, each of the three circles that you drew should have some overlap indicating common knowledge held by each of us. For example, each of us knows that George Washington was the first president of the U.S. and there are 50 states in the United States. However, there is still a lot of data, information, and knowledge that each of us possesses that is not possessed by the other two people. In other words, there is probably a lot that you and I know that Richard Dawkins does not, even though he is extremely well-educated.

The point of this test or exercise was to demonstrate that no matter how smart or well-educated someone is, you know some things that the other person does not. Furthermore, there is a lot of data, information, and knowledge that even the smartest human does not know. So, don't let anyone intimidate you intellectually, because you know a lot of things that the other person does not know and you are capable of evaluating facts and opinions and making decisions for yourself. Don't let anyone force you to believe something because "all educated people" believe in something.

On the topic of evolution Dawkins says that all scientists and educated people know evolution is true. Fortunately, "truth" is not determined by a majority vote by scientists and educated people. There was a time when all scientists and educated people believed the earth was the center of the universe and the sun orbited around the earth. There was a time when all scientists and educated people believed the earth was flat. You know that neither of these "facts" are true.

In reality, however, this is not really about what Richard Dawkins or Richard Trayler says or thinks, it is about you and your life now and for eternity. So, let's examine the following five areas and see if the evidence better supports Darwinian evolution, a key foundation of atheism, or Creationism, or as it is sometimes called, Intelligent Design:

1. In the Beginning
2. Order and Complexity
3. Irreducible Complexity
4. Fossil Record
5. Come Let Us Reason Together

1. In the Beginning.

The theory of evolution does not have a specific explanation for how life initially began. The idea of spontaneous generation of life is certainly appealing to evolutionists—although Louis Pasteur is credited with disproving that life spontaneously generates from non-living matter (in 1859, the same year that Darwin published his landmark book, *On the Origin of Species*). Nevertheless, in 1871, Darwin mused that maybe, somehow the first life forms spontaneously generated in "some warm little pond."

"It is often said that all the conditions for the first production of a living organism are now present, which could ever have been present. But if (and oh! what a big if!) we could conceive in some warm little pond, with all sorts of ammonia and phosphoric salts, light, heat, electricity, etc., present, that a protein compound was chemically formed ready to undergo still more complex changes, at the present day such matter would be instantly devoured or absorbed, which would not have been the case before living creatures were formed." [9]

Similarly, in 1924 Alexander Oparin and J.B.S. Haldane independently suggested that although Pasteur and others demonstrated that life does not spontaneously generate from non-living material, that perhaps in the beginning, life spontaneously generated in a "primordial soup" that existed in an atmosphere/environment that is different than is on the earth today. In conclusion, "there is no truly 'standard model' of the origin of life. Most currently accepted models draw at least some elements from the framework laid out by the Oparin-Haldane hypothesis." [10] (The probability of life occurring naturally will be addressed in the next section, "Order and Complexity.")

Although evolution does not have a good explanation for how life began, it does assert that as soon as life began the natural selection processes (evolution) began and ultimately resulted in life as we see it today. However, as you will soon see, there are some other areas in which evolution does not provide satisfactory answers.

Notes:
(a) For an interesting summary of various "scientific" explanations for the origin of life, ranging from spontaneous generation to Darwin's "warm little pond," to more modern hypotheses, see the article on abiogenesis in Wikipedia (http://en.wikipedia.org/wiki/Abiogenesis.

(b) The complete works of Charles Darwin can be viewed online at: http://darwin-online.org.uk/

(c) The Darwinism Refuted.com website provides information regarding "How the Theory of Evolution Breaks Down in the Light of Modern Science. (http://www.darwinismrefuted.com/molecular_biology_03.html)

(d) For detailed analyses of evolution and intelligent design read Philip E. Johnson's *Darwin on Trial* [11] and W.R. Bird's *The Origin of the Species Revisited.* [12] Both Johnson and Bird are attorneys and they analyze and present scientific information from a legal perspective. Johnson popularized the term "intelligent design" in his book *Darwin on Trial* and Bird was one of the attorneys that participated in the Edwards v. Aguillard case before the U.S. Supreme Court, which struck down the Louisiana law requiring equal time for presentation of evolution and creationism in public schools.

Regarding the origin of life, the Bible states that God created the universe and everything in it. A summary of the creation account from the Bible is shown in Table 5-1, below:

Table 5-1. Summary of the Genesis Creation Account.

Day	Event	Scripture
1	Creation of light and darkness	"Then God said, "Let there be light"; and there was light. God saw that the light was good; and God separated the light from the darkness. God called the light day, and the darkness He called night. And there was evening and there was morning, one day." Genesis 1:3-5
2	Creation of the heavens	"Then God said, "Let there be an expanse in the midst of the waters, and let it separate the waters from the waters." God made the expanse, and separated the waters which were below the expanse from the waters which were above the expanse; and it was so. God called the expanse heaven. And there was evening and there was morning, a second day." Genesis 1:6-8
3	Creation of land and sea	"Then God said, "Let the waters below the heavens be gathered into one place, and let the dry land appear"; and it was so. God called the dry land earth, and the gathering of the waters He called seas; and God saw that it was good. Then God said, "Let the earth sprout vegetation, plants yielding seed, and fruit trees on the earth bearing fruit after their kind with seed in them; and it was so. The earth brought forth vegetation, plants yielding seed after their kind, and trees bearing fruit with seed in them, after their kind; and God saw that it was good. There was evening and there was morning, a third day." Genesis 1:9-13

4	Creation of the sun, moon, and stars	"Then God said, "Let there be lights in the expanse of the heavens to separate the day from the night, and let them be for signs and for seasons and for days and years; and let them be for lights in the expanse of the heavens to give light on the earth"; and it was so. God made the two great lights, the greater light to govern the day, and the lesser light to govern the night; He made the stars also. God placed them in the expanse of the heavens to give light on the earth, and to govern the day and the night, and to separate the light from the darkness; and God saw that it was good. There was evening and there was morning, a fourth day." Genesis 1:14-19
5	Creation of birds and sea creatures	"Then God said, "Let the waters teem with swarms of living creatures, and let birds fly above the earth in the open expanse of the heavens." God created the great sea monsters and every living creature that moves with which the waters swarmed after their kind, and every winged bird after its kind; and God saw that it was good. God blessed them, saying, "Be fruitful and multiply, and fill the waters in the seas, and let birds multiply on the earth." There was evening and there was morning, a fifth day." Genesis 1:20-23

| 6 | Creation of land animals and man | "Then God said, "Let the earth bring forth living creatures after their kind: cattle and creeping things and beasts of the earth after their kind"; and it was so. God made the beasts of the earth after their kind, and the cattle after their kind, and everything that creeps on the ground after its kind; and God saw that it was good. Then God said, "Let Us make man in Our image, according to Our likeness; and let them rule over the fish of the sea and over the birds of the sky and over the cattle and over all the earth, and over every creeping thing that creeps on the earth." God created man in His own image, in the image of God He created him; male and female He created them. God blessed them; and God said to them, "Be fruitful and multiply, and fill the earth, and subject it; and rule over the fish of the sea and over the birds of the sky and over every living thing that moves on the earth." Then God said, "Behold, I have given you every plant yielding seed that is on the surface of all the earth, and every tree which has fruit yielding seed; it shall be food for you; and to every beast of the earth and to every bird of the sky and to everything that moves on the earth which has life, I have given every green plant for food; and it was so." God saw all that He had made, and behold, it was very good. And there was evening and there was morning, the sixth day." Genesis 1:26-31 |

| 7 | God rested | "Thus the heavens and the earth were completed, and all their hosts. By the seventh day God completed His work which He had done, and He rested on the seventh day from all His work which He had done. Then God blessed the seventh day and sanctified it, because in it He rested from all His work which God had created and made. This is the account of the heavens and the earth when they were created, in the day that the LORD God made earth and heaven." Genesis 2:1-4 |

As pointed out in Chapter 2, there are many areas of agreement between modern scientific understanding of the beginning of the universe and the biblical creation account. Although I addressed the apparent discrepancy between the scientific belief that the universe is billions of years old and that the biblical creation account indicates that God created the universe in six days by pointing out that the Hebrew word *yom* translated as "day" could mean a 24-hour period or an extended period of time. Nevertheless, since this is an important point, it may be helpful to consider Geisler and Howe's comments on the apparent conflict between science and the Genesis creation account:

"PROBLEM: The Bible says that God created the world in six days (Exodus 20:11). But modern science declares that it took billions of years. Both cannot be true.

SOLUTION: There are basically two ways to reconcile this difficulty.
First, some scholars argue that modern science is wrong. They insist that the universe is only thousands of years old and that God created everything in six literal 24-hour days (144 hours). In favor of this view they offer the following:

1. The days of Genesis each have "evening and morning," (cf. Gen. 1:5, 8, 13, 19, 23, 31), something unique to 24-hour days in the Bible.
2. The days were numbered (first, second, third, etc.), a feature found only with 24-hour days in the Bible.
3. Exodus 20:11 compares the six days of creation with the six days of a literal workweek of 144 hours.

4. There is scientific evidence to support a young age (of thousands of years) for the earth.

5. There is no way life could survive millions of years from day three (1:11) to day four (1:14) without light.

Other Bible scholars claim that the universe could be billions of years old without sacrificing a literal understanding of Genesis 1 and 2. They argue that:

1. The days of Genesis 1 could have a time lapse before the days began (before Gen. 1:3) or a time gap between the days. There are gaps elsewhere in the Bible (cf. Matt. 1:8, where three generations are omitted, with 1 Chron. 3:11-14).

2. The same Hebrew word "day" (*yom*) is used in Genesis 1-2 as a period of time longer than 24 hours. For example, Genesis 2:4 uses it of the whole six-day period of creation.

3. Sometimes the Bible uses the word "day" for long periods of time: "One day is as a thousand years" (2 Peter 3:8; cf. Ps. 90:4).

4. There are some indications in Genesis 1-2 that days could be longer than 24 hours:
   a) On the third "day" trees grew from seeds to maturity and they bore like seeds (1:11-12). This process normally takes months or years.
   b) On the sixth "day" Adam was created, went to sleep, named all the (thousands of) animals, looked for a help-meet, went to sleep, and Eve was created from his rib. This looks like more than 24 hours worth of activity.
   c) The Bible says God "rested" on the seventh day (2:2), and that He is still in His rest from creation (Heb. 4:4). Thus, the seventh day is thousands of years long already. If so, then other days could be thousands of years too.

5. Exodus 20:11 could be making a unit-for-unit comparison between the days of Genesis and a workweek (of 144 hours), not a minute-by-minute comparison.

CONCLUSION: There is no demonstrated contradiction of fact between Genesis 1 and science. There is only a conflict of interpretation. Either, *most* modern scientists are wrong in insisting the world is billions of years old, or else *some* Bible interpreters are wrong in insisting on only 144 hours of creation some several thousand years before Christ with no gaps allowing millions of years. But, in either case it is not a question of *inspiration* of Scripture, but of the *interpretation* of Scripture (and of the scientific data). [13]

To summarize, the Bible indicates that God created the universe and everything in it, including life forms in six creative episodes. These creative episodes appear to have had a beginning and end (evening and morning of each day). Because the Hebrew word for "day" can mean both a 24-hour time period as well as a longer than 24-hour period of time, we cannot conclude that these creative episodes represented a 24-hour time period, that necessarily followed one another in succession, without intervening time periods.

As you look at the variety of life forms on the earth, do you think that these just happened as a result of spontaneous generation of life followed by countless genetic mutations? In other words, is all life, including you, a descendant of slime from primordial soup? Or do you conclude, as I have, that the complexity of life strongly suggests an intelligent design? If there is intelligent design, then this requires an intelligent designer. I believe that the biblical creation account, although not as scientifically detailed as I would like, provides the best explanation for the origin of life. What do you believe?

2. Order and Complexity

As we observe the physical universe—the earth, moon, sun, planets, solar systems, stars, and galaxies—we see order and complexity. The earth orbits around the sun, the moon orbits around the earth, and seven other planets orbit around the sun to form our solar system. Likewise, as we observe life on earth, we see order and complexity. Humans and animals need oxygen to survive. When they inhale air, oxygen is bound to hemoglobin in their blood streams and is delivered to each cell in the body. The cells unload carbon dioxide into the blood, a byproduct of cellular function, and it is carried to the lungs and exhaled. Plants, conversely, take in carbon dioxide and exhale oxygen. When we look at the human body, we see order and complexity. The body has different types of cells to perform different functions, e.g., skeletal cells provide structure and support and muscle and nerve cells facilitate movement. When we look inside living cells, we see even more order and complexity.

The Darwinist or evolutionist tells us that all of the order and complexity that we observe in living beings (human, animal, and plant life) is the result of randomness and chance. The creationist (and the Bible) tells us that God created the universe and everything in it and point to order and complexity as the result of God's intellect and design. Which provides the best explanation?

Consider the following analogies:

1. What is the likelihood that a tornado (randomness and chance) could go through a junk yard and form a 747 airplane (order and complexity)? 14
2. What is the likelihood that if one million monkeys were given one million typewriters that without any outside coaching or prompting (to ensure randomness and chance), that one of the monkeys would produce a copy of one of Shakespeare's plays (order and complexity)? What if the monkeys were given a year? A hundred years? A thousand years? A million years?

I think you will agree that it is highly unlikely that a tornado could form a 747 and that monkeys could reproduce one of Shakespeare's plays. Evolutionists ask us to believe things that are even more unlikely to have happened than these two examples. Evolutionists say that randomness and chance produced everything in the universe. Creationists say that God created everything in the universe, which is consistent with biblical claims. Which seems more reasonable to you?

I think all of us would agree that the existing scientific knowledge is greater now than it has ever been in the history of mankind. Furthermore, we have the most sophisticated technology that the world has ever known. Isn't it interesting that with all of the knowledge and technology at the disposal of the foremost scientists in the world, that they have not been able to create life from the inanimate building blocks of life (carbon, oxygen, hydrogen, and nitrogen)? In spite of this, some of these same scientists ask us to believe that something they cannot do with all of their intelligence and resources—create life—just happened due to randomness and chance? Furthermore, they ask us to believe that the order and complexity of the human body is the result of countless genetic mutations (which are usually destructive to the resultant offspring), which are unguided, random, and occur by chance?

How can these same scientists look at their wristwatches and conclude that their watches are the product of intelligent design but look at their hands, which are infinitely more complex, and conclude they are the product of evolution, i.e., unguided natural selection (randomness and chance)? Take a few minutes to seriously consider the wonder of your hands—their skeletal components provide structure and support, the muscular system enables the fingers to flex and extend, the nervous system receives and transmits stimuli from the environment (e.g., hot, cold, sharp, dull, soft, hard) to your brain, the integration of the neuro-muscular system provides the ability to perform complicated tasks such as typing on a computer keyboard, the vascular system brings oxygen and nutrients to each cell and removes the waste products, and the skin encloses all of these to form your hands. Do you see evidence of intelligent design or randomness and chance?

Let's take some time to consider in more detail the complexity of living things, starting with a single cell. Since about 1,000 typical cells would fit inside the period at the end of this sentence, a typical cell must be very simple, right? [15] Wrong! Although some of my academic experience has enabled me to study in detail the anatomy (structure) and physiology (function) of the human body, which I find to be incredibly fascinating, you will probably be happy to know that the information presented below on the anatomy and physiology of a typical cell will be very superficial.

Figure 5-2 below shows the primary components of a typical cell. The structures and functions of some of these are summarized in Table 5-2.

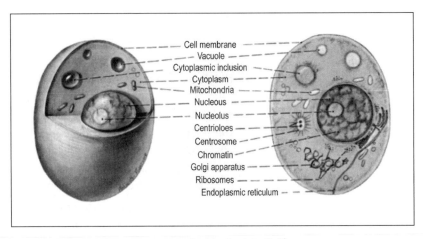

Figure 2. Primary Components of a Typical Cell. [16]

Table 5-2. Selected Structures and Function of a Typical Cell [17, 18]

Structure	Function
1. Cell Membrane	A semi-permeable covering that encloses the components of a cell and allows some molecules (e.g., nutrients) to enter and waste products to leave the cell.
2. Nucleus	The component of the cell that contains the majority of DNA in a cell and where proteins are synthesized.
a. Nuclear Membrane	A selective covering that allows entry and exit of only certain types of molecules into the nucleus.
b. Nucleoli	Small bodies within the nucleus that contain RNA, which is used in synthesizing proteins.
c. Chromosomes	Long strands of coiled DNA, protein, and RNA that contain genetic instructions for the cell. All human cells contain 23 pairs of chromosomes, with the exception of sex cells which contain 22 pairs plus an additional chromosome that determines gender (two "x" chromosomes—one from the male and one from the female—makes the offspring a female, whereas when an "x" chromosome from a female matches up with a "y" chromosome from a male, the offspring is a male.
3. Cytoplasm	Protoplasm that is outside of the nucleus and provides a "working area" for the other components of a cell.
a. Endoplasmic reticulum	Synthesizes protein for use inside the cell as well as exports it for use outside the cell.
b. Ribosomes	Dense aggregations of RNA, which is used in protein synthesis.

c. Golgi apparatus	Functions to concentrate, modify, and secrete proteins and carbohydrates.
d. Mitochondria	The "engine" of the cell, which breaks down glycogen and glucose into water and carbon dioxide to produce energy.

From a quick reading of the information in the table above, it can be concluded that the structure and function of each typical human body is incredibly complicated. But there is more for your consideration. If all of the DNA in a human body were straightened out and laid end to end, it would extend for 20 *billion* kilometers (12,427,413,268 miles)! [19]

There are approximately 3.2 billion base pairs of DNA that make up the 23 chromosomes in each cell. It is the information encoded in these 23 chromosomes and how they process and generate protein products that differentiate humans from all other life forms. A strand of DNA is in the form of a twisted ladder with the sides consisting of sugar-phosphates and the "rungs" consisting of thymine (T) and adenine (A) or guanine (G) and cytosine (C). The paired combinations are always TA, AT or GC, CG; no other combinations exist. Furthermore, "all of the nucleotides in a DNA chain must be of a certain molecular orientation ("right-handed," technically, dextroform) for the chain to work. [20]

Similarly, in order for DNA to produce specific proteins required to sustain life, it utilizes only 20 of the more than 80 amino acids and each of these must be oriented "left-handed" (levoform). The molecular orientation of right-handed or left-handed is termed "chirality" (additional information on this topic can be read at http://www.icr.org/article/evolution-hopes-you-dont-know-chemistry-problem-wi/). The existence of chirality adds significantly to the complexity of life. [21]

As you can see just from this very preliminary look at what goes on inside a typical cell, the cellular functions required to sustain life are amazingly complex. What do you think the likelihood that life happened by chance? Muncaster has listed some critical factors related to life originating from natural processes and the probability of them occurring.

Table 5-3. Factors Required for Origin of the First Cell and Their Probabilities of Occurring Naturally. [22]

Factor	Probability
Chirality	$1/10^{33,113}$
Life-specific amino acids in the right place	$1/10^{6,021}$
Correct specific amino acids in the right place	$1/10^{13,010}$
Correct material in the right place for each gene	$1/10^{60,155}$
Correct sequencing of genes	$1/10^{528}$
Total odds for naturalistic origin of the most simple conceivable bacterium (conservatively figured)	$1/10^{112,827}$

Muncaster puts these probabilities in perspective by stating that this would be equivalent to winning 16,119 state lotteries consecutively with one ticket in each or "picking a single pre-designated electron out of more than 1,300 universes as large as ours, assuming all matter was broken into subatomic particles." [22]

Doesn't the order and complexity of life support the belief in intelligent design more so than belief in evolution? Don't you agree that it looks like God has left His fingerprints on His creation?

> "For since the creation of the world His invisible attributes, His eternal power and divine nature, have been clearly seen, being understood through what has been made, so they are without excuse." Romans 1:20

3. Irreducible Complexity

The concept of irreducible complexity was introduced in 1996 by Dr. Michael Behe, a professor of biochemistry, in his book, *Darwin's Black Box: The Biochemical Challenge to Evolution*. Behe defines irreducible complexity as:

"By *irreducibly complex* I mean a single system composed of several well-matched, interacting parts that contribute to the basic function, wherein the removal of any one of the parts causes the system to effectively cease functioning. An irreducibly complex system cannot be produced directly (that is, by continuously improving the initial function, which continues to work by the same mechanism) by slight, successive modifications of a precursor system, because any precursor to an irreducibly complex system that is missing a part is by definition nonfunctional. An irreducibly complex biological system, if there is such a thing, would be a powerful challenge to Darwinian evolution." [23]

Dembski simplifies this definition by stating, "an integrated multipart functional system is irreducibly complex if removing any of its parts destroys the system's function." [24] In other words, there are some molecular systems that are so interdependent that all components must be fully formed, present, and functioning properly to accomplish its task. To illustrate this, consider the mousetrap shown in Figure 5-3.

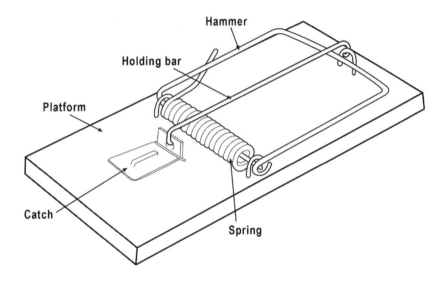

Figure 5-3. The Mousetrap Example of Irreducible Complexity.

As shown above, the typical mousetrap consists of five components: hammer, spring, catch, platform, and holding bar. In order for the trap to perform its specified function, all parts must be present and properly functioning. If any one of the components is not present or not working correctly, the mousetrap will not function properly.

Behe states that there are many such examples of molecular irreducible complexity in biological cells. His first example was a flagellar motor in a bacterium, as shown below in Figure 5-4.

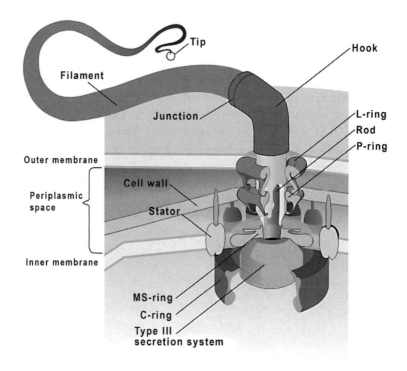

Figure 5-4. Biochemical Complexity and Irreducible Complexity of a Bacterial Flagellum.

Certainly, this flagellum is far more complicated than the mousetrap shown in the previous figure. However, the same concept applies—all components must be present and fully functioning in order to accomplish the task of propelling the bacterium around its environment.

Behe pointed out that if only some of the components of the flagellum evolve and others have not yet evolved that they would not represent an advantage to the bacterium. Consequently, according to the Darwinian theory of evolution, they would not be retained in the offspring as a beneficial adaptation.

Luskin lists six "molecular machines" that the majority of scientists agree represent irreducible complexity and another 34 which are still undergoing biochemical analysis that will most likely result in concluding that these also represent examples of irreducible complexity. Because of the highly technical nature, these will be listed below with comments on only a few. For more details, please see Luskin's article, "Molecular

Machines in the Cell" on the Discovery Institute's Center for Science and Culture (http://www.discovery.org/a/14791). [25]

Irreducibly Complex Molecular Machines: [25]

1. **Bacterial Flagellum**: The flagellum, as shown above in Figure 4, is a rotary motor in bacteria that drives a filament (propeller) to spin, much like an outboard motor. Amazingly, the flagellum is capable of spinning at speeds up to 100,000 rpm!
2. **Eukaryotic Cilium**: Eukaryotes are cells, such as plant and animal cells, that have a nucleus and other complex internal structures surrounded by a cellular membrane. The cilium is a hair-like structure that facilitates movement or sensory perception.
3. **Aminoacyl-tRNA Synthetases (aaRS)**
4. **Blood Clotting Cascade**: Normally, blood flows freely throughout the vascular system. However, when an injury to the vascular system occurs, a complex assembly of substrates, enzymes, protein cofactors, and calcium ions begins to form a blood clot to protect the organism from bleeding to death.
5. **Ribosome**: The ribosomes are the molecular machines within cells that utilize instructions from DNA to synthesize proteins for use within a cell.
6. **Antibodies and the Adaptive Immune System**: The immune system has the ability to identify foreign bodies and to produce antibodies to kill them to protect a cell and the entire organism.

Additional molecular machines that probably represent irreducibly complex molecular machines:

7. **Spliceosome**
8. **F_0F_1 ATP Synthase**
9. **Bacteriorhdopsin**
10. **Myosin**: Myosin is a molecular motor that converts chemical energy into mechanical energy and enables muscular contraction.
11. **Kinesin Motor**
12. **Tim/Tom Systems**
13. **Calcium Pump**
14. **Cytochrome C Oxidase**
15. **Proteosome**
16. **Cohesin**
17. **Condensin**
18. **ClpX**
19. **Immunological Synapse**

20. **Glideosome**
21. **Kex2**
22. **Hsp70**
23. **Hsp60**
24. **Protein Kinase C**
25. **SecYEG PreProtein Translocation Channel**
26. **Hemoglobin**: Red blood cells bind with oxygen molecules in the lungs, transport the oxygen to cells, release the oxygen, bind with carbon dioxide, and transport the carbon dioxide to the lungs, where it is released and the process begins again.
27. **T4 DNA Packaging Motor**
28. **Smc5/Smc6**
29. **Cytplasmic Dynein**
30. **Mitotic Spindle Machine**
31. **DNA Polymerase**
32. **RNA Polymerase**
33. **Kinetochore**
34. **MRX Complex**
35. **Apoptosome/Caspase**: These are molecular machines that cause cellular death. These function to destroy cells when they need to be replaced and to do so in an orderly manner.
36. **Type III Secretory System**
37. **Type II Secretion Apparatus**
38. **Helicase/Topoisomerase Machine**
39. **RNA degradasome**
40. **Photosynthetic system**

I think most objective readers will admit that this is a very impressive list of irreducibly complex molecular machines. Furthermore, most objective readers will admit that this concept presents a major obstacle to the theory of evolution. In fact, most objective readers will agree with Behe's conclusion:

"To a person who does not feel obliged to restrict his search to unintelligent causes, the straightforward conclusion is that many biochemical systems were designed. They were designed not by the laws of nature; not by chance and necessity; rather, they were planned. The designer knew what the systems would look like when they were completed, then took steps to bring the systems about. Life on earth at its most fundamental level, in its most critical components, is the product of intelligent activity. [26]

But how do evolutionists react to the concept of irreducible complexity? In a PBS interview of Richard Dawkins in 1996, he stated the following regarding Behe and the concept of irreducible complexity:

"He's a straightforward creationist. What he has done is to take a standard argument which dates back to the 19th century, the argument of irreducible complexity, the argument that there are certain organs, certain systems in which all the bits have to be there together or the whole system won't work...like the eye. Darwin answered (this)...point by point, piece by piece. But maybe he shouldn't have bothered. Maybe what he should have said is... maybe you're too thick to think of a reason why the eye could have come about by gradual steps, but perhaps you should go away and think a bit harder." [27]

Please allow me to set the record straight. In 1859, Charles Darwin did not have the slightest idea that irreducibly complex molecular machines existed within a cell; so, he could not have possibly "answered (this)... point by point, piece by piece." With all due respect to Richard Dawkins, this is another example of the intellectual bullying often employed by not only Dawkins but many in the scientific community when it comes to protecting the sanctity of the theory of evolution.

Dembski, a strong proponent of intelligent design and holder of four Master's degrees (statistics, mathematics, philosophy, and divinity) and two Ph.D. degrees (mathematics and philosophy), provides additional support for this statement and for the bias that exists within the scientific community.

"For research within an accepted framework, peer review is useful for quality control. But for radical new ideas and thinking outside the box, peer review is more often a hindrance than a help. That should come as no surprise given the nature of peer review. Peer review is primarily in the business of seeing that the standards, norms and practices of an established guild are respected. Only after they have been respected does the question of originality and innovation receive consideration. Peer review is essentially conservative. Peer review is therefore the last place we should expect to see a scientific revolution vindicated....

In the current intellectual climate it is impossible to get a paper published in the peer-reviewed biological literature if that paper explicitly affirms intelligent design or explicitly denies Darwinian and other forms of naturalistic evolution....

Overzealous critics of intelligent design regard it as their moral duty to keep biology free from intelligent design, even if that means taking extreme measures. I've known such critics to contact design theorists' employers and notify them of the "heretics" in their midst. Once "outed," the design theorists themselves get harassed and harangued with e-mails. Next, the press does a story mentioning their unsavory intelligent design associations. (The day one such story appeared, a close friend and colleague of mine mentioned in the story was dismissed from his research position at a prestigious molecular biology laboratory. He had worked in that lab for ten years.) Hereafter, the first thing that an Internet search of their names reveals is their connection with intelligent design.

...Lack of peer review has never barred the emergence of good science. Nor, for that matter, have peer-reviewed journals been the sole place where groundbreaking scientific work was done. As I noted, the peer-review process is inherently conservative, working nicely for filtering good incremental science from less rigorous work within an established paradigm, but it is lousy at opening its arms to paradigm revolutions. Thomas Kuhn, along with other eminent historians of science, has settled this point definitively: the old guard never opens its arms to a scientific revolution; they have too much invested in the old paradigm. The most important revolutions in science bypassed the peer-review process entirely and appeared in books. Copernicus's *De Revolutionibus*, Galileo's *On Two World Systems* and Newton's *Principia* are cases in point. None of these works were peer-reviewed. Nor was that book by a retiring English biologist from the nineteenth century—an unconventional work titled *On the Origin of Species*." [28]

In further support of the contention that many in the scientific community are biased against those who question the "fact" of evolution, consider the following "official disclaimer" statement that appears on the Lehigh University faculty webpage for Dr. Behe:

"My ideas about irreducible complexity and intelligent design are entirely my own. They certainly are not in any sense endorsed by either Lehigh University in general or the Department of Biological Sciences in particular. In fact, most of my colleagues in the Department strongly disagree with them." [29]

So, what do you think about the challenges presented by the concept of irreducible complexity to the theory of evolution? What do you think about what could be termed strong bias against (at best) or censorship of (at worst) ideas and hypotheses that challenge the validity of the theory of evolution? Since creationism or intelligent design cannot be taught in public schools and since there is some degree of censorship of topics and discussions in this area, it seems appropriate to recommend the following DVDs, websites, and books for additional information on atheism and evolution. The following represent good starting points:

Recommended DVDs (which can be purchased through http://www. arn.org/authors/behe.html):
- Darwin's Black Box: The Biochemical Challenge to Evolution,
- Science and Evidence for Design in the Universe,
- Intelligent Design: From the Big Bang to Irreducible Complexity,
- Unlocking the Mystery of Life,
- Irreducible Complexity: The Biochemical Challenge to Darwinian Theory, and
- Where Does the Evidence Lead?

Recommended Websites:
- http://www.arn.org/authors/behe.html
- http://www.discovery.org/
- http://www.parentcompany.com/default.asp
- http://www.designinference.com/
- http://www.creationscience.com/onlinebook/
- http://fixed-point.org/
- http://www.intelligentdesignanswers.com/
- http://www.talkorigins.org/origins/other-links-cre.html   (Lists several hundred creationist websites).

Recommended Books:
- Lennox, John C. *God's Undertaker: Has Science Buried God?* Oxford, England: Lion Hudson. 2009.
- Johnson, Philip E. *Darwin on Trial.* Downers Grove, IL: InterVarsity Press, 1991.
- Bird, W.R. *The Origin of the Species Revisited: The Theories of Evolution and of Abrupt Appearance.* Nashville, TN: Regency, 1991.
- Dembski, W. A. *The Design Revolution: Answering the Toughest Questions About Intelligent Design* (291). Downers Grove, IL: InterVarsity Press, 2004.

- Denton, Michael. *Evolution: A Theory in Crisis*. Chevy Chase, MD: Adler & Adler, Publishers, 1985.

4. Fossil Record

As stated earlier, the theory of evolution teaches that life began as a single cell. Over millions or billions of years and countless genetic mutations, more complex life forms evolved, eventually accounting for the diversity of life forms present today. A more complete explanation of biological evolution was provided by Thompson in the textbook, *Biology, Zoology, and Genetics*:

> "'Biological evolution,' in contrast to biological abrupt appearance, is the view held by the majority of scientists. It proposes that 'the first living cell 'evolved' into complex multicellular forms of life; these 'evolved' into animals without backbones. Fish evolved into amphibian, amphibian into reptiles, reptile into birds and mammals, early mammals into primates, and primates into man." [30]

Charles Darwin illustrated this concept in his book, *On the Origin of Species*, in what might be called the "evolutionary tree of life." A copy of his drawing that appeared in his book is shown below in Figure 5, along with a more modern-day depiction of the evolutionary tree of life.

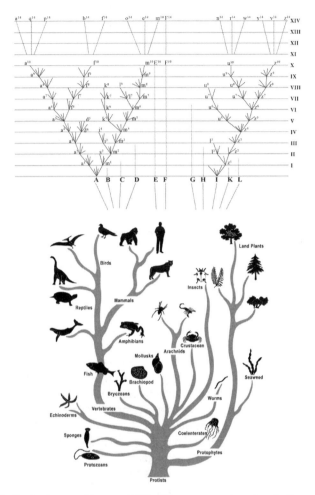

Figure 5-5. Evolutionary Trees of Life. The upper drawing is from Darwin's book *On the Origin of Species* published in 1859. [31] The lower drawing is a more modern depiction of the evolutionary tree of life.

Darwin explained the tree of evolutionary life as follows:

"The accompanying diagram will aid us in understanding this rather perplexing subject. Let A to L represent the species of a genus large in its own country; these species are supposed to resemble each other in unequal degrees, as is so generally the case in nature, and as is represented in the diagram by the letters standing at unequal distances.…

225

Let (A) be a common, widely-diffused, and varying species, belonging to a genus large in its own country. The little fan of diverging dotted lines of unequal lengths proceeding from (A) may represent its varying offspring. The variations are supposed to be extremely slight, but of the most diversified nature; they are not all supposed to appear simultaneously, but often after long intervals of time; nor are they all supposed to endure for equal periods. Only those variations which are in some way profitable will be preserved or naturally selected. And here the importance of the principle of benefit being derived from divergence of character comes in; for this will generally lead to the most different or divergent variations (represented by the outer dotted lines) being preserved and accumulated by natural selection. When a dotted line reaches one of the horizontal lines, and is there marked by a small numbered letter, a sufficient amount of variation is supposed to have been accumulated to have formed a fairly well-marked variety, such as would be thought worthy of record in a systematic work.

The intervals between the horizontal lines in the diagram may represent each a thousand generations; but it would have been better if each had represented ten thousand generations. After a thousand generations, species (A) is supposed to have produced two fairly well-marked varieties, namely a^1 and m^1. These two varieties will generally continue to be exposed to the same conditions which made their parents variable, and the tendency to variability is in itself hereditary, consequently they will tend to vary, and generally to vary in nearly the same manner as their parents varied. Moreover, these two varieties, being only slightly modified forms, will tend to inherit those advantages which made their common parent (A) more numerous than most of the other inhabitants of the same country; they will likewise partake of those more general advantages which made the genus to which the parent-species belonged a large genus in its own country. And these circumstances we know to be favourable to the production of new varieties.

If, then, these two varieties be variable, the most divergent of their variations will generally be preserved during the next thousand generations. And after this interval, variety a^1 is supposed in the diagram to have produced variety a^2, which will, owing to the principle of divergence, differ more from (A) than did variety a^1. Variety m^1 is supposed to have produced two varieties, namely m^2 and s^2, differing from each other, and more considerably from their common parent (A). We may continue the process by similar steps for any length of time; some of the varieties, after each thousand generations, producing only a single variety, but in a more and more modified condition, some producing two or three varieties, and some failing to produce any. Thus the varieties or modified descendants, proceeding from the common parent (A), will generally go on increasing in number and diverging in character. In the diagram the process is represented up to the ten-thousandth generation, and under a condensed and simplified form up to the fourteen-thousandth generation." [32]

More modern versions of the evolutionary tree of life show all living things evolving from a common ancestor. Note that man and all mammals are shown as having evolved from fishes. Likewise, birds are shown to have evolved from reptiles, which evolved from fishes.

If the theory of evolution is true, then there must be many transitional forms of living beings that are in the process of changing from one species to another. For example, there should be animals that have some features of a life form lower on the evolutionary tree and some features of a life form higher on the evolutionary tree. In other words, there should be some life forms that are part reptile and part bird, part mammal and part primate. As a matter of fact, if the theory of evolution is true, there should be many transitional or intermediate species and some of these should be numerous and survived for many years. [33] Examples of these transitional critters are shown below in Figure 5-6.

Figure 5-6. Transitional Critters.

Do you have one of these transitional critters for a pet? No? Do you know anyone who does? No? As you know, these transitional critters exist only because some creative people with a computer and some special software were able to merge photos of different animals to "create" images of these critters. Just as the transitional critters shown above do not exist today they did not exist in Darwin's time. And he knew it.

> "Sensing the lack of intermediate forms in the fossil record, Darwin confessed: "Geology assuredly does not reveal any such finely graduated organic change, *and this is perhaps the most obvious and serious objection which can be urged against the theory [of evolution]*" (Darwin, *Origin of Species*, 152, emphasis added). Darwin confessed that we do not find "an infinite number of those fine transitional forms which, on our theory, have connected all the past and present species of the same group into one long and branching chain of life" (ibid., 161). He attributed this to the scarcity of the "geological record as a history of the world imperfectly kept" (ibid.). [34]

Certainly, Darwin and his evolutionary colleagues had a valid point that the geological records of fossils were imperfectly kept. Additionally, there was the real possibility that further searching of the fossil record would turn up the missing links or fill in the gaps of the evolutionary tree with the predicted transitional life forms. [35]

During the 150 years since Darwin's time, there have been tremendous advancements in the field of paleontology and the study of fossils. In fact, there are now more than 200,000,000 fossils catalogued, representing more than 250,000 species. [36] According to scientists who are *not* supporters of creationism, there is general agreement that the fossil record is more than sufficient to draw objective conclusions regarding evolution.

> "Thus, according to Denton*, a molecular biologist, "[W]hen estimates are made of the percentage of living forms found as fossils, the percentage turns out to be surprisingly high, suggesting that the fossil record may not be as bad as it is often maintained. Of the 329 living families of terrestrial vertebrates 261 or 79.1% have been found as fossils, and, when birds (which are poorly fossilized) are excluded, the percentage rises to 87.8%.)" [37]

So, with an extensive, reasonably complete fossil record to study, what have the results been? Trouble, with a capital T, for the theory of evolution. The fossil record has raised three major problems related to the theory of evolution: (a) lack of expected transition forms; (b) sudden appearance of life forms; and (c) stasis.

(a) Regarding the lack of transitional life forms, consider the following quotes of evolutionary supporters catalogued by W.R. Bird in his book, *The Origin of Species Revisited: The Theories of Evolution and of Abrupt Appearance*:

"Simpson*, the noted Harvard paleontologist, acknowledges: "This *regular absence of transitional forms* is an *almost universal* phenomenon, as had long been noted by paleontologists. It is true of *almost all orders of classes of animals*, both vertebrate and invertebrate. A fortiori, *it is true also of the classes, themselves*, and of the *major animal phyla*, and it is apparently also true of *analogous categories of plants*." [38]

"Gould* states: 'The *extreme rarity of transitional forms* in the fossil record persists as the trade secret of paleontology. The evolutionary trees that adorn our textbooks have *data only at the tips* and nodes of their branches; the rest is inference, however reasonable, not the evidence of fossils.'" [39]

"Patterson* says: 'I fully agree with your comments on the *lack of direct illustration of evolutionary transitions in my book*. If I knew of any, fossil or living, I would certainly have included them....I will lay it on the line—*there is not one such fossil for which one could make a watertight argument*. The reason is that the statements about ancestry and descent are not applicable in the fossil record.'" [40]

"Kitts*concedes: 'Despite the bright promise that *paleontology* provides a means of 'seeing' evolution, it has presented some *nasty difficulties* for evolutionists, the most notorious of which is the presence of *"gaps"* in the fossil record. *Evolution requires intermediate forms between species and paleontology does not provide them*.'" [40]

So, what should we conclude from these statements? Consider the following quote:

"In fact, T.H. Huxley*, who was 'Darwin's bulldog' and chief exponent, wrote that 'if it could be shown that this fact [gaps between widely distinct groups] had always existed, the fact would be *fatal* to the doctrine of evolution.'" [40]

Note: "*" following the names of the scientists quoted above [and following] indicates "Scientists cited in this chapter, unless otherwise indicated, are not proponents of, and their quoted statements are not intended as endorsements of, either the theory of abrupt appearance or the theory of creation. However, their quoted statements are acknowledging data that some non-evolutionist scientists interpret as supporting the theory of abrupt appearance better than the theory of evolution." [41]

Geisler summarized the lack of transitional forms by stating, "The reality is that there are no missing links [transitional life forms], but a missing chain, with only a few links here and a few there." [42]

(b) What about the sudden appearance of life forms? One of the geological ages is known as the Cambrian Age. This age is thought to have been from 525 to 550 million years ago. During this age, there was an incredible explosion of life in which many new life forms appeared, including more than 100 fully-formed species of animals. [43] As you might suspect, this sudden explosion of fully formed species presents major problems to the theory of evolution, which calls for natural selection to gradually produce changes in one species that evolves into another different species. Johnson, a pro-creationist, comments,

"The single greatest problem which the fossil record poses for Darwinism is the "Cambrian explosion" of around 600 million years ago. Nearly all the animal phyla appear in the rocks of this period, without a trace of the evolutionary ancestors that Darwinists require. As Richard Dawkins puts it, "It is as though they were just planted there, without any evolutionary history." In Darwin's time there was no evidence for the existence of pre-Cambrian life, and he conceded in the *Origin of Species* that, "The case at present must remain inexplicable, and may truly be urged as a valid argument against the views here entertained." [44]

Since Johnson is a creationist, it is not surprising that he would be quick to point out the problems caused by the Cambrian explosion. However, many evolutionist supporters also admit the serious problems that the Cambrian explosion causes for evolutionist theory. Again, let's consider some of the evolutionist supporters' comments, as catalogued by Bird:

"Kemp*, curator of the University Museum at Oxford: '[P]alentology is now looking at exactly what it finds, not what it is told that it is supposed to find. As is now well known, most fossil species appear instantaneously in the record....'" [45]

"A similar point is made by Raup*, 'Instead of finding the gradual unfolding of life, what geologists of Darwin's time, and geologists of the present day, actually find is a highly uneven or jerky record; that is, species appear in the sequence very suddenly....'" [45]

Bird also documents statements from evolutionary scientists indicating the abrupt appearance of every major stage of Darwinianian evolution. This includes invertebrates, fish, reptiles, turtles, birds, mammals, primates, and man, which all appeared abruptly in the fossil records and they first appeared in complex form, as they appear today. [46]

So what did Charles Darwin say about the sudden appearance of fully formed living things?

"On the sudden appearance of whole groups of allied species—The abrupt manner in which whole groups of species suddenly appear in certain formations, has been urged by several palæontologists, for instance, by Agassiz, Pictet, and by none more forcibly than by Professor Sedgwick, as a fatal objection to the belief in the transmutation of species. If numerous species, belonging to the same genera or families, have really started into life all at once, the fact would be <u>fatal to the theory of descent with slow modification through natural selection</u>. For the development of a group of forms, all of which have descended from some one progenitor, must have been an extremely slow process; and the progenitors must have lived long ages before their modified descendants. But we continually over-rate the perfection of the geological record, and falsely infer, because certain genera or families have not been found beneath a certain stage, that they did not exist before that stage. We continually forget how large the world is, compared with the area over which our geological formations have been carefully examined; we forget that groups of species may elsewhere have long existed and have slowly multiplied before they invaded the ancient archipelagoes of Europe and of the United States. We do not make due allowance for the enormous intervals of time, which have probably elapsed between our consecutive formations—longer perhaps in some cases than the time required for the accumulation of each formation. These intervals will have given time for the multiplication of species from some one or some few parent-forms; and in the succeeding formation such species will appear as if suddenly created." [47] (underlining added for emphasis)

Darwin admitted that if it could be proven that many life forms suddenly appeared, without evidence of evolutionary change, this would be a fatal objection to his theory of evolution through natural selection. Although, there was merit in his proposing that there was the possibility that evolutionary ancestors of the life forms, which seemed to appear suddenly, would be found in the future. However, with 150 more years of paleontological research, the conclusion is even more compelling: life forms that exist today appeared fully formed and were not the process of evolutionary natural selection.

(c) Stasis presents another formidable challenge to the theory of evolution. Stasis means that there does not appear to be any changes in a species in the fossil record. The earliest fossils look much like the latest fossils of a species and currently living descendents. In other words, there is no evidence of gradual evolving from one species to another.

The fact of stasis has resulted in a new term being coined by evolutionary scientists: "living fossils," which means that over the course of their existence their appearance has not changed from their ancient ancestors. Consider the following statements, again listed by Bird:

"For reptiles, many crocodiles and alligators are 'living fossils' in Meyer's* words: 'Nile crocodiles and American alligators belong to a group of reptiles called broad-nosed crocodilians....They are living fossils in the sense that they resemble ancient forms in the shapes and ruggedness of their heads and bodies." [48]

"Among fish, bowfin fishes have changed 'next to nothing' in a history dated at 100 million years, according to Stanley*: 'As a first example, we can consider the bowfin fishes....No more than two bowfin species are known to have existed at any one time....What has happened to the bowfin fishes during their long history of more than one hundred million years? Next to nothing!...The bowfins of seventy or eighty million years ago must have lived very much as their lake dwelling descendants do today." [49]

"Among mammals, living fossils are also numerous. 'An Eocene bat looks just like a modern bat,' Mayr* concedes, and 'the bat's wings have not essentially progressed' in a period dated at 50 million years, Russell* points out.... Ancient squirrels 'differ in no important ways' from modern ones...." [48]

The fact of stasis is summarized by the following (evolutionary-supporting) scientists:

"Kemp*, curator of the University Museum at Oxford: 'As is now well known, most *fossil species appear instantaneously* in the record, persist for some millions of years *virtually unchanged*, only to disappear abruptly—the 'punctuated equilibrium' [pattern of Eldredge and Gould]....'" [45]

"A similar point is made by Raup*: '...*species* appear in the sequence *very suddenly*, show little or no change during their existence in the record, then abruptly go out of the record. And it is not always clear, in fact it's rarely clear, that the descendants were actually better adapted than their predecessors. In other words, biological improvement is hard to find....'" [45]

"Ager* writes that, 'whether at the level of orders or species, we find—over and over again—not gradual evolution, but the sudden explosion of one group at the expense of another.'" [45]

"It is characterized by Eldredge* and Tattersall* as 'the most obvious single fact about biological evolution—nonchange': Expectation colored perception to such an extent that *the most obvious single fact about biological evolution—nonchange*—has seldom, if ever, been incorporated into anyone's scientific notions of how life actually evolves. If ever there was a myth, it is that evolution is a process of constant change. The data, or basic observations, of evolutionary biology are *full of the message of stability*. Change is difficult and rare, rather than inevitable and continual. Once evolved, species with their own peculiar adaptations, behaviors, and genetic systems are remarkably conservative, *often remaining unchanged for several millions of years.*" [50]

Evolutionists from Darwin in 1859 to Dawkins in 2010 thought that the fossil record would provide undeniable scientific support of the theory of evolution. It does not. [52] The problems presented by lack of transitional life forms, sudden appearance of complex life forms, and the fact of species stasis, represent fatal flaws in the theory of evolution. It is up to the evolutionists to satisfactorily answer these scientifically documented facts before they can legitimately claim to be promoting the theory of evolution as scientific fact.

5. Come Let Us Reason Together

As you have read, the theory of evolution does not have an adequate explanation for the beginning of life. Although it has been proven scientifically that life does not spontaneously generate from non-living matter, many evolutionists still defend this as a possibility. The order and complexity of living things has been shown to be statistically impossible to occur due to randomness and chance. Furthermore, some biological systems have been shown to be so irreducibly complex that they could not have evolved over millions or even billions of years due to unguided natural selection. Finally, the problems of lack of transitional life forms, sudden appearance of fully formed living beings, and the fact that stasis or unchanging of life forms are well documented in the fossil record have not been satisfactorily addressed scientifically.

For the moment, let's set aside each of these fatal flaws associated with the theory of evolution and just think about what evolutionists want us to believe about natural selection and the diversity of life. What is the likelihood that randomness and chance could form life, even a simple single-cell organism, when modern day scientists have not been able to produce life in sophisticated scientific laboratories under carefully controlled conditions? Do you believe that a single-celled organism could evolve into the specialized organs, such as the heart, lungs, gastrointestinal tract, skeletal system, muscular system, brain, and nervous system, which are present in all animals?

For a moment, let's consider that if natural selection were able to produce the complex cells, organs, and systems in many life forms alive today, what is the likelihood, that a male *and* female of a specific species (e.g., a canine) would *evolve* at the *same time*, in the *same place*, so that they could procreate and continue their species (more canines)? Does this seem reasonable to you? If this does seem reasonable to you, then I should warn you to avoid people who want to sell you beachfront property in Arizona (just in case you are not aware of the location of the state of Arizona, it does not border an ocean and consequently, there is no beachfront property in this state)!

Kreeft and Tacelli summarize the scientific status of the theory of evolution by stating,

"The survival of the fittest presupposes the arrival of the fit. If Darwinians wish to extrapolate from their purely biological theory and maintain that all the vast order around us is the result of random changes, then they are saying something which no empirical evidence could ever confirm; which no empirical science could ever demonstrate; and which, on the face of it, is simply beyond belief." [52]

With these fatal flaws of the theory of evolution, why would eminent scientists still support the theory of evolution? Lennox provides an interesting insight by quoting Niles Eldredge, a paleontologist on the curatorial staff of the American Museum of Natural History, and then proposing a logical conclusion:

"In fact, Eldridge makes an astonishing admission, 'We paleontologists have said that the history of life supports [the story of gradual adaptive change] knowing all the while it does not.' But why? What conceivable reason could there be for members of an academic community to suppress what they know to be the truth—unless it were something which supported a worldview, which they had already decided was unacceptable?" [53]

Objectively, the scientific evidence and fossil record provide strong support to the theory of intelligent design. [54] I believe that Geisler and Howe concluded accurately when they wrote:

"There is no demonstrated contradiction of fact between Genesis 1 and science. There is only a conflict of interpretation. Either, *most* modern scientists are wrong in insisting the world is billions of years old, or else *some* Bible interpreters are wrong in insisting on only 144 hours of creation some several thousand years before Christ with no gaps allowing millions of years. But, in either case it is not a question of *inspiration* of Scripture, but of the *interpretation* of Scripture (and of the scientific data)." [13]

Moral Relativism

Now that we have dealt with the theory of evolution, let's turn our focus back to atheism. If, as atheism teaches, we all evolved from a common single-celled organism, then survival of the fittest or natural selection has blindly determined which life forms live and which become extinct. If this is true, then there is no basis for morality, or the concepts of good and evil. [55] Some atheists may object to this statement and claim that as mankind has evolved it has learned that some actions are beneficial to the species and others are not. Therefore, morality, good, and evil do exist. However, these same atheists quickly point out that there is no such thing as moral *absolutes.*

From a logical perspective, atheists must insist that there are no moral absolutes, because if they did not then this would lead to the following logical predicament:

"1. There are objective moral laws.
2. Moral laws come from a moral lawgiver.
3. Therefore, a moral lawgiver (God) exists." [56]

To admit that a moral lawgiver, God, exists would completely contradict their assertion that there is no God. So, they are left with the problem of moral relativism or situational ethics. This means that it is up to the individual to determine the appropriate moral or ethical action to take in a certain situation. With this perspective, how can one criticize the acts of cheating on class exams by school children? Of racism or violence in our society? Of corporate or political corruption? If there is general agreement that each of the factors listed should be controlled, then who decides what is right and wrong: parents, communities, churches, government officials? Who do you trust to make the best decisions regarding morality and ethics? Doesn't it look like the slippery slope of moral relativism or situational ethics should be avoided?

What about the concept of good and evil? Most everyone would agree that some acts are good and beneficial and that others are evil and destructive. In fact, some atheists use the presence of evil to "prove" that the God of the Bible does not exist. Their logic is summarized as:

"1. If God were all-good, he would destroy evil.
2. If God were all-powerful, he could destroy evil.
3. But evil has not been destroyed.
4. Therefore, God does not exist." [57]

This argument becomes invalidated by pointing out that at some point in the future God may destroy evil. [57] In fact, Chapter 7 provides details about when the Bible says God will destroy evil.

Man's Destiny Is Death

So, if you place your faith in atheism, what does atheism have in store for you? Death. Remember that according to atheism, you are a genetically mutated descendant of a single-celled organism that happened due to randomness and chance. There is nothing special about you. The only reason you are different from a mouse, a mutt, or a monkey is simply blind chance. There is no such thing as objective or absolute moral values, so go for all the gusto you can in this life because you will die, and that is all there is to say about you and the value of your life, according to atheism. [58] How do you feel about that? Do you want something better?

The Bible presents an entirely different perspective of you and the value of your life. You were created by God, in His image (see Genesis 1:26-27). Before you were even born, God knew you and had a plan for your life (see Psalm 139:14). God loves you so much He willingly sacrificed His Son to pay the debt of your sins (see John 3:16). Jesus promises eternal life to those who believe in Him:

> "...I am the resurrection and the life; he who believes in Me will live even if he dies." John 11:25

Jesus promised that we can have an eternal relationship with Him:

> "Do not let your heart be troubled; believe in God believe also in Me. In My Father's house are many dwelling places....I go to prepare a place for you. If I go and prepare a place for you, I will come again and receive you to Myself, that where I am, there you may be also." John 14:1-3

Which destiny do you choose: death or life? Death is eternal separation from God. Life is eternal relationship with God. The choice is yours. I pray that you will choose wisely because God will honor your decision.

References:

1. Lennox, John C. *God's Undertaker: Has Science Buried God*? Oxford: England, Lyon, 2009, p. 87.
2. Dawkins, Richard. The Richard Dawkins Foundation for Reason and Science website. http://richarddawkins.net/
3. _____. http://richarddawkins.net//pages/books.
4. _____. http://richarddawkins.net//pages/projects.
5. Lennox, John C. p. 210.
6. _____. p. 101.
7. _____. pp. 102-111.
8. _____. p. 99.

9. Darwin, Charles. written in 1871, published in Darwin, Francis, ed. 1887. *The Life and Letters of Charles Darwin, including an autobiographical chapter.* London: John Murray. Volume 3. p. 18)

10. Wikipedia. "Abiogenesis". (http://en.wikipedia.org/wiki/Abiogenesis).

11. Johnson, Phillip E. *Darwin on Trial.* Downers Grove, IL: InterVarsity Press, 1991.

12. Bird, W.R. *The Origin of the Species Revisited: The Theories of Evolution and of Abrupt Appearance.* Nashville, TN: Regency, 1991.

13. Geisler, N.L. & T. A. Howe. *When Critics Ask: A Popular Handbook on Bible Difficulties.* Wheaton, IL: Victor Books, 1992, pp. 32-33. Used by permission.

14. Hoyle, F. *The Intelligent Universe*, p. 129. As quoted by W.R. Bird's *The Origin of the Species Revisited: The Theories of Evolution and of Abrupt Appearance.* Nashville, TN: Regency, 1991, p. 77.

15. Muncaster, Ralph O. *Examine the Evidence: Exploring the Case for Christianity.* Eugene, OR: Harvest House Publishers, 2004. p. 89.

16. Jacob, Stanley W. and Clarice Ashworth Francone. *Structure and Function in Man.* Philadelphia, PA: W.B. Saunders Company, 1970, p. 19.

17. _____. pp. 20-23.

18. Vander, Arthur J., James H. Sherman, and Dorothy S. Luciano. *Human Physiology: The Mechanisms of Body Function.* New York, NY: McGraw-Hill, 1970, pp. 97-100, 113-114; 121-122.

19. Length of a Human DNA Molecule website. (http://hypertextbook.com/facts/1998/StevenChen.shtml)

20. Muncaster, Ralph O. p. 110.

21. Lennox, John C. p. 127.

22. Muncaster, Ralph O. p. 119.

23. Behe, Michael. *Darwin's Black Box.* New York, NY: Simon and Schuster, 1996, p. 39.

24. Dembski, W. A. *The Design Revolution: Answering the Toughest Questions About Intelligent Design.* Downers Grove, IL: InterVarsity Press, 2004, p. 291.

25. Luskin, Casey. "Molecular Machines in the Cell." Discovery Institute. June 11, 2010. http://www.discovery.org/a/14791

26. Behe, Michael. p. 193.

27. Dawkins, Richard. "On Evolution and Religion". Think Tank on PBS. November 8, 1996. http://www.simonyi.ox.ac.uk/dawkins/WorldOfDawkins-archive/Dawkins/Work/Interviews/thinktnk.shtml. Retrieved 2009-04-02.

28. Dembski, W. A. p. 300.

29. Lehigh University's Department of Biological Sciences Faculty website. (http://www.lehigh.edu/~inbios/faculty/behe.html)

30. Thompson, A. *Biology, Zoology, and Genetics.* 1983, as quoted by W.R. Bird. *The Origin of Species Revisited: Theories of Evolution and of Abrupt Appearance.* Nashville, TN: Regency, 1991, p. 42.

31. Darwin, Charles. *On the Origin of Species.* London, England: John Murray, 1859, p. 116.

32. Darwin, Charles. pp. 117-118.
33. Johnson, Phillip E. pp. 53-54.
34. Geisler, N.L. *Baker Encyclopedia of Christian Apologetics*. Grand Rapids, MI: Baker Books, 1999, p. 184.
35. Johnson, Phillip E. pp. 33-34.
36. Bird, W.R. p. 48.
37. Denton, Michael. *Evolution: A Theory in Crisis*. Chevy Chase, MD: Adler & Adler, Publishers, 1985, p. 189, as quoted by W.R. Bird, p. 49.
38. Bird, W.R. p. 57.
39. _____. p. 58.
40. _____. p. 59.
41. ____. p. 41.
42. Geisler, N.L. p. 184.
43. Muncaster, Ralph O. p. 50.
44. Johnson, Phillip E. p. 44.
45. Bird, W.R. p. 51.
46. Bird, W.R. pp. 54-55.
47. Darwin, Charles. pp. 303-304.
48. Bird, W.R. p. 67.
49. _____. p. 66.
50. _____. p. 69.
51. McDowell, Josh. *Josh McDowell's Handbook on Apologetics*. Nashville, TN: Thomas Nelson. 1997, Chapter 6. (Libronix Digital Library System version.)
52. Kreeft, Peter and Ronald K. Tacelli. *Handbook of Christian Apologetics: Hundreds of Answers to Crucial Questions*. Downers Grove, IL: InterVarsity Press, 1994, p. 57.
53. Lennox, John C. p. 114.
54. Geisler, N.L. p. 185.
55. Zacharias Ravi. *Can Man Live Without God?* Nashville, TN: W. Publishing Group, a Division of Thomas Nelson, Inc., 1994. pp. 32-44.
56. Geisler, N.L.,N.L. Geisler, & W.D. Watkins, W. D. (1989). *Worlds Apart: A Handbook on World Views*. Grand Rapids, Mich.: Baker Book House, 1989, p. 55.
57. _____. p. 58.
58. Zacharias Ravi. pp. 45-61.

Chapter 6

Secular Socialism: Why Is This So Dangerous?

In addition to my very strong belief in the Bible, I have strong views about America and politics. I am proud of America and proud to be an American. I strongly believe that God has blessed America in many ways and that the fundamental principles contained in the Declaration of Independence, the U.S. Constitution, and the Bill of Rights were based upon biblical principles and that these honor God. For example, the Declaration of Independence clearly recognizes and honors God when it states,

> "We hold these truths to be self-evident, that all men are created equal, that they are endowed by their Creator with certain unalienable Rights, that among these are Life, Liberty and the pursuit of Happiness. That to secure these rights, Governments are instituted among Men, deriving their just powers from the consent of the governed...." [1]

I believe that God actively guided our nation's founders in writing these documents, which provide the foundations of the American government. In my professional career, I have traveled to and done business in more than 40 countries. As a result of this international business experience, I have developed good friendships with many of my business partners and this has provided wonderful opportunities for me to get to know the people, cultures, business practices, and governmental philosophies/practices and their results in many countries. Consequently, I have been able to objectively compare these countries with the United States in many areas and always come to the same conclusion: the United States of America is unique among the nations of the world. After every international trip, I have always been grateful to return home to this great nation!

This chapter, however, was the most difficult for me to write. It breaks my heart to think and to say this, but I believe that America's best days are behind it. The reason for this is not because of enemies outside our border, of which there are many, but because of enemies within our borders, particularly "secular socialists." Due in large part to the complacency of the American people, secular socialists have gained tremendous power in this country and have pushed America so far down the slippery slope of secular socialism that it is unlikely that we can return to the guiding principles that began to form on July 4, 1776. Although I am an optimist by nature, I admit that this is a very pessimistic perspective, but I believe the facts that are presented in this chapter support this probable outcome, unless there is divine intervention.

So what does this have to do with biblical Christianity? The unifying principle of secular socialism is that government, not God, is the solution to man's needs. Furthermore, it demands that if you must believe in God, then keep Him personal, private, and out of public life. Because this is completely contradictory to what the Bible teaches, the secular socialists know that to gain complete power and control, biblical Christianity must be at least minimized and preferably eliminated from America (and eventually, the world). They will continue relentlessly in their quest for power and control and, unfortunately, they are much closer to achieving their goals than most Americans realize.

To provide perspective on the threat posed by secular socialism to both America and biblical Christianity, the following four topics will be discussed:

(1) Early American History: Embracing God;
(2) Recent American History: Turning Away From God;
(3) Secular Socialism: Incompatibility With Biblical Christianity; and
(4) Biblical Perspective and Response.

I trust that you, like I did, will find the facts presented in this chapter to be very thought-provoking and that they will enable you to see how far America has drifted away, or in some cases, pushed away, from the original intent of our Founding Fathers. Unfortunately, this has tremendously adverse implications regarding our freedom to believe and express our faith in Jesus Christ.

Early American History: Embracing God

In the beginning of this chapter, I stated that God has blessed America in many ways. If this is true, why? Do you remember that in Chapter 2, I pointed out that obedience to God's will brings blessings? I believe that America's blessings can be directly attributed to the obedience to God's will by America's discoverer, early settlers, and the Founding Fathers. I think you will be impressed with their commitment to biblical Christianity and their desire to be obedient to God's will. Consider some of the writings of these early "Americans":

> Note: The examples below are from David Barton's book, *Original Intent: The Courts, the Constitution, & Religion.* [2] and William J. Federer's book, *America's God and Country: Encyclopedia of Quotations.* [3] In my opinion, these books should be required reading for all Americans. More information about David Barton can be read on the website: http://www.wallbuilders.com/

Christopher Columbus (1451-1506), [4] discoverer of America:

> "[O]ur Lord opened to my understanding (I could sense his hand upon me) so it became clear to me that it [the voyage] was feasible....All those who heard about my enterprise rejected it with laughter, scoffing at me....Who doubts that this illumination was from the Holy Spirit? I attest that He [the spirit], with marvelous rays of light, consoled me through the holy and sacred Scriptures...they inflame me with a sense of great urgency....No one should be afraid to take on any enterprise in the name of our Savior if it is right and if the purpose is purely for His holy service....And I say that the sign which convinces me that our Lord is hastening the end of the world is the preaching of the Gospel recently in so many lands." [5]

Statements of early American settlers:

William Bradford (1590-1657): [6] "... a great hoe and inward zeal they had of laying some good foundation, or at least to make some way thereunto, for the propagating and advancing the Gospel of the kingdom of Christ in those remote parts of the world." [7]

John Winthrop (1588-1649) [8] "[W]e are a company professing ourselves fellow-members of Christ...knit together by this bond of love...[W]e are entered into covenant with Him for this work." [7]

Charters of early American settlements:

Virginia (1606): "[T]o make habitation...and to deduce a colony of sundry of our people into that part of America commonly called Virginia...in propagating of Christian religion to such people as yet live in darkness." [5]

Virginia (1609): (another charter): "[T]he principal effect which we can desire or expect of this action is the conversion...of the people in those parts unto the true worship of God and Christian religion." [5]

The Mayflower Compact (1620) stated: "Having undertaken for the glory of God and advancement of the Christian faith...[we] combine ourselves together into a civil body politic for...furtherance of the ends aforesaid." [7]

Massachusetts (1629): "[O]ur said people...be so religiously, peaceably, and civilly governed [that] their good life and orderly conversation may win and incite the natives of...[that] country to the knowledge and obedience of the only true God and Savior of mankind, and the Christian faith, which...is the principal end of this plantation [colony]." [7]

North Carolina (1662): "[E]xcited with a laudable and pious zeal for the propagation of the Christian faith...in the parts of America not yet cultivated or planted, and only inhabited by...people who have no knowledge of Almighty God." [9]

Colonial government constitutions:

Connecticut (1639): "[E]nter into combination and confederation together to maintain and preserve the liberty and purity for the Gospel of our Lord Jesus which we now profess...which, according to the truth of the said Gospel, is now practiced amongst us." [10]

New Hampshire (1639) "...do in the name of Christ and in the sight of God combine ourselves together to erect and set up among us such government as shall be to our best discerning agreeable to the will of God." [10]

New England Confederation (1643), which consisted of the colonies of Massachusetts, Connecticut, New Plymouth, and New Haven: "[W]e all came into these parts of America with one and the same end and aim, namely to advance the kingdom of our Lord Jesus Christ." [10]

Early American Educational Institutions:

Harvard (1636): "Let every student be plainly instructed and earnestly pressed to consider well the main end of his life and studies is to know God and Jesus Christ which is eternal life (JOHN 17:3) and therefore to lay Christ in the bottom as the only foundation of all sound knowledge and learning. And seeing the Lord only giveth wisdom, let everyone seriously set himself by prayer in secret to seek it of Him (PROVERBS: 2:3). Every one shall so exercise himself in reading the Scriptures twice a day that he shall be ready to give such an account of his proficiency there in." [11]

> "This is eternal life, that they may know You, the only true God, and Jesus Christ whom You have sent." John 17:3

> "For if you cry for discernment, Lift your voice for understanding." Proverbs 2:3

William and Mary College (1692): "[T]he youth may be piously educated in good letters and manners and that the Christian faith may be propagated... to the glory of Almighty God." [12]

Yale (1699): "[T]o plant, and under Divine blessing, to propagate in this wilderness the blessed reformed Protestant religion." [12]

Founding Fathers:

George Washington (1732-1799): the Father of the Country, General of the Revolutionary Army, and First President of the United States [13] speaking to members of the Delaware Indian tribe who brought three of their youths to be educated in American schools: "You do well to wish to learn our arts and ways of life, and above all, the religion of Jesus Christ. These will make you a greater and happier people than you are. Congress will do everything they can to assist you in this wise intention." [14]

Samuel Adams (1722-1803): [15] Father of the American Revolution, instigator of the "Boston Tea Party," and signer of the Declaration of Independence, member of the first Continental Congress, and Governor of Massachusetts, wrote in 1772: "The rights of the colonists as Christians...may be best understood by reading and carefully studying the institution of The Great Law Giver and Head of the Christian Church, which are to be found clearly written and promulgated in the New Testament." [15, 16]

John Quincy Adams (1767-1848): the sixth President of the United States, Senator, Congressman, U.S. Minister to France, and U.S. Minister to Britain, in 1811 wrote to his son: [17] "...for so great is my veneration for the Bible, and so strong my belief, that when duly read and meditated on, it is of all books in the world, that which contributes most to make men good, wise, and happy...I have myself, for many years, made it a practice to read through the Bible once every year...My custom is, to read four to five chapters every morning immediately after rising from my bed. It employs about an hour of my time....It is in the Bible, you must learn them [principles for good conduct and citizenship] and from the Bible how to practice them. Those duties are to God, to your fellow-creatures, and to yourself. 'Thou shalt love the Lord thy God, with all thy heart, and with all thy soul, and with all thy mind, and with all thy strength, and thy neighbor as thy self.' On these two commandments, Jesus Christ expressly says, 'hang all the law and the prophets'; that is to say, the whole purpose of Divine Revelation is to inculcate them efficaciously upon the minds of men...." [18] When asked which was his favorite Bible, he replied, "...any Bible that I can...understand. The New Testament I have repeatedly read in the original Greek, in the Latin, in the Geneva Protestant, in Sacy's Catholic French translations, in Luther's German translation, in the common English Protestant, and in the Douay Catholic translations. I take any one of them for my standard of faith...." [19]

Benjamin Franklin (1706-1790) [20] Diplomat to France and England, Governor of Pennsylvania, Founder of the University of Pennsylvania, inventor, publisher, and scientist, signer of the Declaration of Independence, the Articles of Confederation, and the Constitution, at the Constitutional Convention on June 28, 1787 spoke the following words, which were recorded by James Madison: "...In the beginning of the Contest with G. Britain, when we were sensible of danger, we had daily prayer in this room for Divine protection. Our prayers, Sir, were heard, and they were graciously answered. All of us who were engaged in the struggle must have observed frequent instances of a superintending Providence in our favor. To that kind Providence we owe this happy opportunity of consulting in peace on the means of establishing our future national felicity. And have we now forgotten that powerful Friend? Or do we imagine we no longer need His assistance? I have lived, Sir, a long time, and the longer I live, the more convincing proofs I see of this truth—that God Governs in the affairs of men. And if a sparrow cannot fall to the ground without His notice, is it probable than an empire can rise without His aid? We have been assured, Sir, in the Sacred Writings, that 'except the Lord build the House, they labor in vain that build it.' I firmly believe this; and I also believe that without his concurring aid we shall succeed in this political building no better than the Builders of Babel: We shall be divided by our partial local interests; our projects will be confounded, and we ourselves shall become a reproach and bye word down to future ages....I therefore beg leave to move—that henceforth prayers imploring the assistance of Heaven, and its blessing on our deliberations, be held in this Assembly every morning before we proceed to business, and that one or more of the clergy of this city be requested to officiate in that service." Franklin's motion to open the meetings of the Constitutional Congress was passed. In fact, prayers have opened both houses of the U.S. Congress, ever since." [21]

Thomas Jefferson, an architect, educator, scientist, third President of the U.S. and author of the Declaration of Independence (July 4, 1776) [22] wrote: "...We hold these truths to be self-evident, that all men are created equal. That they are endowed by their Creator with certain inalienable rights, that among these are life, liberty, and the pursuit of happiness." In 1798, he wrote, "No power over the freedom of religion...[is] delegated to the United States by the Constitution." [23]

Regarding his personal religious beliefs, Jefferson wrote on April 21, 1802:

"My views...are the result of a life of inquiry and reflection, and very different from the anti-Christian system imputed to me by those who know nothing of my opinions. To the corruptions of Christianity I am, indeed, opposed; but not to the genuine precepts of Jesus himself. I am a Christian in the only sense in which he wished any one to be; sincerely attached to his doctrines in preference to all others...." (November 4, 1820) "I hold the precepts of Jesus as delivered by Himself, to be the most pure, benevolent and sublime which have ever been preached to man...." (on the title page of his own Bible) "A more beautiful or precious morsel of ethics I have never seen; it is a document in proof that I am a real Christian; that is to say, a disciple of the doctrines of Jesus." [24]

Have you read enough to come to the conclusion that faith in the God and Jesus of the Bible were instrumental in the founding of America? If not, then may I suggest that you read Barton's *Original Intent* and Federer's *America's God and Country* [2] ? Do you think that the faith of the early settlers and Founding Fathers and their desire to be obedient to God were pleasing to God? Does it seem reasonable to propose that these were the reasons that God blessed America?

As you were reading these quotes, did they provide a new perspective about the founders of our nation and the role that God played in it? Did you think, as I did, that it would be wonderful if our governmental leaders of today had the strength of faith and willingness to openly share their faith as the early Founding Fathers did? Why is it that the vast majority of our leaders and citizens of our country do not or are not willing to speak so openly and favorably of their Christian beliefs? What has changed about our country that has lead to this? The next section addresses these questions and provides some answers.

Recent American History: Turning Away From God

Prior to doing research for this book, I did not fully appreciate the power of the U.S. Supreme Court. I just assumed that the members of the Supreme Court were very learned men and women who were committed to ensure that the laws of the land were consistent with the U.S. Constitution and that they looked to the writings of the Founding Fathers to ensure that their interpretation of the Constitution were consistent with the original intent. As you will soon see, my assumption regarding the commitment to ensure continued consistency with the original intent of the writers of the Constitution and Bill of Rights was very naïve and wrong.

It has often been said that the most important legacy of any U.S. president is the justices that he appoints to the U.S. Supreme Court. While the president has four or eight years to directly affect policy, the justices have a lifetime appointment and may serve many decades.

While the oaths of office for the president, vice president, and Congress all require that the person defend the U.S. Constitution, that requirement is not placed on Supreme Court justices. The oaths of offices are quoted below:

> **President:** "I do solemnly swear (or affirm) that I will faithfully execute the office of President of the United States, and will to the best of my ability, <u>preserve, protect, and defend the Constitution of the United States</u>." This is specified in the U.S. Constitution, Article II, Section I. [25] (underlining added by me)

Vice-President and Members of Congress: "I do solemnly swear (or affirm) that I will support and <u>defend the Constitution of the United States against all enemies, foreign and domestic</u>; that I will bear true faith and allegiance to the same; that I take this obligation freely, without any mental reservation or purpose of evasion; and that I will well and faithfully discharge the duties of the office on which I am about to enter: So help me God." This same oath has been administered since 1884. [25] (underlining added by me)

Supreme Court: "I, [NAME], do solemnly swear (or affirm) that I will administer justice without respect to persons, and do equal right to the poor and to the rich, and that I will faithfully and impartially <u>discharge and perform all the duties incumbent upon me</u> as [TITLE] under the Constitution and laws of the United States. So help me God." This oath is specified in Title 28, Chapter I, Part 453 of the United States Code. [25] (underlining added by me)

Did you notice that the oath of the Supreme Court justices only charges them to perform the duties prescribed by the Constitution and the laws of the United States, but does not require them to preserve or protect the Constitution? Furthermore, there is no guidance given to ensure a proper and consistent interpretation of the Constitution or the original intent of the Founding Fathers. This lack of guidance has lead to two basic interpretive schools of thought: "Strict Constructionism (i.e., remaining true to the original intent of the Founding Fathers and the documents they wrote, i.e., Declaration of Independence, U.S. Constitution, and Bill of Rights) and "Legal Positivism" (i.e., relativism).

John Eidsmoe, a constitutional scholar and law professor, provides the five major theses of "Legal Positivism":

"1. There are no objective, God-given standards of law, or if there are, they are irrelevant to the modern legal system.
2. Since God is not the author of law, the author of law must be man; in other words, the law is law simply because the highest human authority, the state, has said it is law and is able to back it up.
3. Since man and society evolve, therefore law must evolve as well.
4. Judges, through their decisions, guide the evolution of law.
5. To study law, get at the original sources of law: the decisions of judges." [26]

Notice some words that look like they belong in the previous chapter, under the topic of evolution: "There are no objective, God-given standards of law"; "Since God is not the author of law"; "Since man and society evolve"; "Judges...guide the evolution of law"; "The original sources of law...judges." Do you remember me saying that there is an unholy alliance between atheism and secular socialism? You will see more evidence of that as we consider the information in this and the following section.

Barton provides some additional insight into the concept of legal positivism:

"This philosophy ("positivism") was introduced in the 1870s when Harvard Law School Dean Christopher Columbus Langdell (1826-1906) applied Darwin's premise of evolution to jurisprudence. Langdell reasoned that since man evolved, then his laws must also evolve; and judges should guide both the evolution of law and the Constitution. Consequently, Langdell introduced the case-law study method under which students would study judges' decisions rather than the Constitution.

Under the case-law approach history, precedent, and the views and beliefs of the Founders not only became irrelevant, they were even considered hindrances to the successful evolution of society...." [27]

Isn't it an interesting irony that the first Christopher Columbus depended on God to discover America and Christopher Columbus Langdell applied a theory that demands unbelief in God to U.S. law? From my perspective, applying the theory of evolution to law is bound to produce problems, just as it has for biology. For starters, failing to recognize that there is a God and that He has given absolute laws is headed in the wrong direction. Have you ever heard of the Ten Commandments? Guess who originated these? It was God. Do you know why these are called "Commandments" and not "Suggestions"? These are God's laws. They are shown below for your consideration:

[1]   You shall have no other gods before Me.
[2]   You shall not make for yourself an idol.
[3]   You shall not take the name of the LORD your God in vain.
[4]   Remember the Sabbath day, to keep it holy.
[5]   Honor your father and your mother.
[6]   You shall not murder.

[7]   You shall not commit adultery.

[8]   You shall not steal.

[9]   You shall not bear false witness against your neighbor.

[10] You shall not covet your neighbor's house; you shall not covet your neighbor's wife or his male servant or his female servant or his ox or his donkey or anything that belongs to your neighbor. Exodus 20:3-17

Isn't it also interesting to note that these Ten Commandments form the basis for U.S. law and in fact are posted on the wall of the U.S. Supreme Court?

Do you remember that one of the problems associated with atheism is "moral relativism" (i.e., there are no moral absolutes, each individual determines what is right or wrong, depending upon the situation)? Now imagine what kinds of problems that can cause when a judge is given a lifetime appointment and has the power to interpret and *guide* the law based upon the situation! This provides an explanation for the following contradictory rulings:

"It is constitutional for congressional chaplains to pray ..., but unconstitutional for students to read those prayers."

"It is constitutional to display the Ten Commandments on public property ..., but unconstitutional either to allow students to see them ... or to display them at a courthouse."

"It is constitutional to begin public meetings with invocations ..., but unconstitutional to allow students to hear invocations in a public meeting."

"It was constitutional to display a crèche [nativity scene] and depict the origins of Christmas in 1984 .., but only five years later it was unconstitutional to do so." [28]

Have you heard the term, "judicial activism"? This term means that judges essentially make the laws to suit their particular political views. It is fair to say that this began when judges started utilizing the principle of legal positivism.

The foresight of our Founding Fathers is amazing. In fact, they warned against the concepts of judicial activism and legal positivism. Noah Webster (1758-1843), a master of word usage who learned more than 20 languages and compiled America's first dictionary, which defined more than 70,000 words, [29] warned that serious errors and misunderstandings can occur when original word meanings are ignored:

> "[I]n the lapse of two or three centuries, changes have taken place which in particular passages...obscure the sense of the original languages....The effect of these changes is that some words are...being now used in a sense different from that which they had...[and thus] present wrong signification or false ideas. Whenever words are understood in a sense different from that which they had when introduced....mistakes may be very injurious."

Similarly, when Thomas Jefferson was president, he warned Supreme Court Justice William Johnson:

> "On every question of construction, carry ourselves back to the time when the Constitution was adopted, recollect the spirit manifested in the debates, and instead of trying what meaning may be squeezed out of the text, or invented against it, conform to the probable one in which it was passed." [30]

Jefferson also wrote about the inherit dangers associated with giving judges too much power:

> "You seem...to consider the judges as the ultimate arbiters of all constitutional questions; a very dangerous doctrine indeed, and one which would place us under the despotism of an oligarchy. Our judges are as honest as other men, and not more so....and their power [is] the more dangerous, as they are in office for life and not responsible, as the other functionaries are, to the elective control. The Constitution has erected no such single tribunal, knowing that to whatever hands confided, with corruptions of time and party, its members would become despots." [31]

Additional support of original intent was recorded by James Madison (1751-1836) and Justices James Wilson (1742-1798) and Joseph Storey (1730-1781). [32] So, have the vagaries of legal positivism affected America and biblical Christianity? Yes, they have and from my perspective, very adversely. Consider the following U.S. Supreme Court cases related to Christianity, evolution, and abortion. Each case and ruling will be summarized and quotes of some of the Founding Fathers will be provided along with my commentary on the consequence of the ruling.

1. ***Everson v. Board of Education, 1947***. A New Jersey law allowed reimbursement to parents of children who took public buses to and from school. [33] Since some of the children attended parochial (church) schools, Mr. Everson objected and sued the school board claiming that the reimbursement represented state support of religion. [34]

Ruling: The reimbursements were not illegal since they were offered to all students and were made directly to the parents and not to any religious institution.

Consequence: The most significant aspect of this case is that for the first time, the justices used the term, "wall of separation between Church and State." "...In the words of Jefferson, the clause against establishment of religion by law was intended to erect "a wall of separation between Church and State." [34]

Subsequently this phrase has been used extensively to strike down religious activities and expressions previously considered constitutional. [35] Furthermore, this ruling laid the foundation for the U.S. Supreme Court to extend its control over all religious controversies, which seems to be contrary to the U.S. Constitution. [36]

Since this ruling has had far-reaching consequences in terms of the legal precedent it set, it is important to consider the related factors in more detail.

Founding Fathers' Writings: First Amendment to the Constitution (adopted June 15, 1790):

> "Congress shall make no law respecting an establishment of religion or prohibiting the free exercise thereof; or abridging the freedom of speech, or of the press; or the right of the people to peaceably to assemble and to petition the government for redress of grievances." [37]

Did you notice that this amendment refers only to Congress, i.e., the U.S. Congress? Consequently, it seems reasonable to conclude that the Founding Fathers intended religious matters to be under the control of the states and not the federal government. In fact, Barton states:

> "At the top of the ratified list was the amendment [the First Amendment] completely removing the subject of religion and religious expression from the jurisdiction of the federal government, thereby leaving it as it had been: in the hands of the states and the people. Therefore the Court's 1947 decision to federalize the First Amendment and apply it against the people and the states was a complete abrogation of that Amendment." [38]

Did you see the phrase "wall of separation between Church and State" in the First Amendment? This phrase is not part of the first amendment. This phrase was used by Thomas Jefferson in a letter to the Danbury Baptist Church in response to their congratulating him on being elected the third president of the U.S.

Thomas Jefferson's letter to the Danbury Baptist Church:

"Gentlemen, The affectionate sentiments of esteem and approbation which you are so good as to express towards me on behalf of the Danbury Baptist Association give me the highest satisfaction....Believing with you that religion is a matter which lies solely between man and his God; that he owes account to none other for this faith or his worship; that the legislative powers of government reach actions only and not opinions, I contemplate with sovereign reverence that act of the whole American people which declared that their legislature should "make no law respecting an establishment of religion or prohibiting the free exercise thereof," thus building a <u>wall of separation between Church and State</u>. Adhering to this expression of the supreme will of the nation in behalf of the rights of conscience, I shall see with sincere satisfaction the progress of those sentiments which tend to restore to man all his natural rights, convinced he has no natural right in opposition to his social duties. I reciprocate your kind prayers for the protection and blessing of the common Father and Creator of man, and tender you for yourselves and your religious association assurances of my high respect and esteem." [38] (underlining was added by me for emphasis)

Neither Thomas Jefferson nor any of the other Founding Fathers intended for the federal government to establish a national religion. Likewise, they did not intend for the federal government to regulate, restrict, limit, or interfere with the free exercise of religion. [39] On the contrary, the Founding Fathers agreed that the following aspects of religion, developed by Benjamin Franklin, should be taught in all public schools:

"1. There exists a Creator who made all things and mankind should recognize and worship him.
2. The Creator has revealed a moral code of behavior for happy living which distinguishes right from wrong.
3. The Creator holds mankind responsible for the way they treat each other.
4. All mankind live beyond this life.
5. In the next life mankind are judged for their conduct in this one." [40]

2. ***McCollum v. Board of Education, 1948.*** Illinois public schools offered elective classes for children in grades 4-9 if the children had written permission from the children's parents. These classes were taught by non-school employees, who were subject to the approval and supervision of the superintendent of schools.

Ruling: These voluntary, elective classes were ruled unconstitutional, citing the "wall of separation between Church and State."

Consequence: This removed all religious education from public schools. Barton commented,

> "The Court ruled in favor of a single atheist **not** involved in the classes but who was **personally** offended by religion and therefore did not want **any** students taught religious principles. This decision foreshadowed what was soon to become routine: a single individual, unable to advance his or her goals through legitimate political and legislative means, convincing a willing Court to violate the rights of the overwhelming majority of its citizens in order to accommodate the wishes of that individual." [41]

Founding Fathers' Writings: The Northwest Ordinance, which set forth requirements for statehood, was passed by the House on July 21, 1789, the Senate on August 4, 1789, and signed by President Washington on August 7, 1789, in Article III stated,

> "Religion, morality, and knowledge, being necessary to good government and the happiness of mankind, schools and the means of education shall forever be encouraged." [42]

Thomas Jefferson wrote in his plan for public education in Virginia,

> "[I]n my catalogue, considering ethics, as well as religion, as supplements to law in the government of man, I had placed them in that sequence." [43]

Gouverneur Morris (1752-1816), writer of the final draft of the Constitution, member of the Continental Congress, U.S. Minister to France, and U.S. Senator, [44] wrote

> "Religion is the only solid basis of good morals; therefore education should teach the precepts of religion and the duties of man towards God." [45]

3. ***Engel v. Vitale, 1962***. New York state schools allowed students to voluntarily pray the following prayer, at the beginning of each school day:

"Almighty God, we acknowledge our dependence upon Thee, and we beg Thy blessings upon us, our parents, our teachers and our Country." [46]

Ruling: This prayer, and all prayers in public schools, are unconstitutional. [47] Furthermore, the Court said that,

"[A] union of government and religion tends to destroy government and to degrade religion." [48]

Consequence: This ruling removed all prayers from public schools. [48] It is interesting to note that this was the first case in which the U.S. Supreme Court did not cite any previous case laws to support its ruling. [49] Barton provides the following comments:

"The Court had failed to cite even a single precedent to justify its prohibition of New York's voluntary prayers—a significant departure from a bedrock rule of jurisprudence. Why did it fail to cite precedent cases? There were none which would support its decision. For 170 years following the ratification of the Constitution and Bill of Rights, no Court had ever struck down any prayer, in any form, in any location. While the Court invoked no judicial precedent to sustain its decision, it did employ some strategic psychological rhetoric. Recall the Court's comment that '...these principles were so **universally recognized**... (emphasis added [by Barton]).

Lacking precedent, the Court simply alleged a widespread public support; that is, since "everybody" knew school prayer was wrong, the Court needed cite no precedent." [50]

Founding Fathers' Writings: Regarding the statement that "a union of government and religion tends to destroy government and degrade religion," consider the following statements by the Founding Fathers:

George Washington: "[T]rue religion affords to government its surest support." [48]

John Adams (1735-1826), who served for eight years as vice president under George Washington and was the second U.S. president: [51] "[R]eligion and virtue are the only foundations...of republicanism and of all free governments." [48]

Thomas Jefferson: "[The] liberty to worship our Creator in the way we think most agreeable to His will [is] a liberty deemed in other countries incompatible with good government and yet proved by our experience to be its best support." [52]

4. ***School District of Abington Township v. Schempp, 1963.*** (a similar case brought by Madalyn Murray O'Hair was combined with this case before the Supreme Court). [53] A Pennsylvania law required students in public school to read at least 10 verses from the Bible and recite the Lord's Prayer. However, students could be excluded from this requirement by a written note from their parents.

Ruling: This law was struck down as being unconstitutional.

Consequence: This effectively removed prayer and Bible reading from public schools.

Founding Fathers' Writings:

Benjamin Rush (1745-1813), signer of the Declaration of Independence, Surgeon General of the Continental Army, and Treasurer of the U.S. Mint, [54] wrote, "The great enemy of the salvation of man, in my opinion, never invented a more effectual means of extirpating [extinguishing] Christianity from the world than by persuading mankind that it was improper to read the Bible at schools. [T]he Bible, when not read in schools, is seldom read in any subsequent period of life....[It] should be read in our schools in preference to all other books from its containing the greatest portion of that kind of knowledge which is calculated to produce private and public temporal happiness. [55]

5. ***Stone v. Graham, 1980***. A Kentucky state law required posting the Ten Commandments on the wall in each classroom.

Ruling: This state law was declared unconstitutional.

Consequence: "The Court's decision in this case not only struck down a passive, non-coercive display; it also reflected the hostility which has become characteristic of the Court's decisions on these issues." [56]

Founding Father's Writings:

Noah Webster: "All the miseries and evils which men suffer from vice, crime, ambition, injustice, oppression, slavery and war proceed from their despising or neglecting the precepts contained in the Bible." [56]

John Quincy Adams wrote: "The law given from Sinai was a civil and municipal as well as a moral and religious code....laws essential to the existence of men in society and most of which have been enacted by every nation which ever professed any code of laws. Vain indeed would be the search among the writings of profane antiquity [secular history]...to find so broad, so complete and so solid a basis for morality as this Decalogue [Ten Commandments] lays down." [57]

6. *Edwards v. Aguillard, 1987*. A Louisiana law mandated teaching of "creation science" along with the theory of evolution in public schools. Although schools were not forced to teach either creation or evolution, if one was taught, then the other must be taught also.

Ruling: The law was ruled unconstitutional. The rationale given was:

First, it was not enacted to further a clear secular purpose. Second, the primary effect of the law was to advance the viewpoint that a "supernatural being created humankind," a doctrine central to the dogmas of certain religious denominations. Third, the law significantly entangled the interests of church and state by seeking "the symbolic and financial support of government to achieve a religious purpose." [58]

Consequence: This stifles academic analysis of the claims of both evolution and creationism. Furthermore, it implicitly promotes the "religion" of atheism.

Founding Fathers' Writings: The Declaration of Independence, itself, clearly documents that the founders believed in creation:

"We hold these truths to be self-evident, that all men are created equal, that they are endowed by their Creator with certain unalienable rights, that among these are life, liberty and the pursuit of happiness." [1]

The Bible leaves no doubt that the universe and everything in it was created by God:

> "In the beginning God created the heavens and the earth."
> Genesis 1:1

7. **Roe v. Wade, 1973.** This was a landmark case regarding a woman's right to terminate pregnancy by abortion.

Ruling: The court held that a woman's right to an abortion fell within the right to privacy. The ruling indicated that a woman had total autonomy over pregnancy during the first trimester and defined increasing levels of state control during the second and third trimesters. [59]

Consequence: The life of a child is not protected. Realistically, since the Constitution does not comment on abortion, in keeping with the spirit of the Constitution, it would have been appropriate for the Supreme Court to leave the decision to the legislative and democratic processes of each state, rather than issuing an all-encompassing judicial edict. In 1976, Congress passed the Hyde Amendment, which prevents federal funds from being used for abortions, except in the case of rape, incest, or danger to the life of the mother. [60]

Founding Fathers' Writings: The founding fathers did not address the topic of abortion. However, based upon their reverence for and belief in Christian principles of God creating man in His image, God knowing and loving each person even before they were born, and the commandment against murder, it is clear that they would not have supported legalizing abortion.

"In the American governing philosophy set forth in the Declaration (and then subsequently secured in the Constitution), protecting the right to life is so important that it is the first of the three specifically-enumerated inalienable rights (others were subsequently specified in the Bill of Rights). Our governing documents also make clear that the most important function of government is to protect inalienable rights." [61]

"American government was established on the thesis that certain rights come from God rather than men and that government is to protect those rights inviolable. So long as the recognition remains that God-given rights cannot be infringed, then those rights will remain safe; if that conviction is lost, government will then begin to regulate, alter, and even repeal those rights." [62]

"Thomas Jefferson's clarion warning from two centuries ago still rings true today: '[C]an the liberties of a nation be thought secure when we have removed their only firm basis: a conviction in the minds of the people that these liberties are of the gift of God? That they are not to be violated but with His wrath? Indeed I tremble for my country when I reflect that God is just and that His justice cannot sleep forever." [62]

"For You formed my inward parts; You wove me in my mother's womb. I will give thanks to You, for I am fearfully and wonderfully made; Wonderful are Your works, and my soul knows it very well.... Your eyes have seen my unformed substance; and in Your book were all written the days that were ordained for me, When as yet there was not one of them." Psalm 139:13, 16

"Thus says the LORD who made you and formed you from the womb." Isaiah 44:2

"They profess to know God, but by their deeds they deny Him, being detestable and disobedient and worthless for any good deed." Titus 1:16

Barton provides the following, which is certainly worthy of your careful consideration:

"In fact, experience regularly attests that if a government leader is willing to violate the foremost of all inalienable rights (the right to life), then he will also disregard other inalienable rights. That is, if a leader does not support the inalienable right to life, then he will almost certainly be wrong on the protection of private property (as guaranteed in the Fifth Amendment to the Constitution), the biblical right of self defense (the right to keep and bear arms guaranteed in the Second Amendment), the right of religious expression (guaranteed in the First Amendment), the sanctity of the home (guaranteed in the Third Amendment), etc. In short, if a leader refuses to recognize the role of God in the creation of life and does not pledge himself to protect that first of all inalienable rights, then all other individual rights are also in danger. (Barack Obama has never voted to protect unborn life either as a state senator in Illinois or as a U.S. Senator. Furthermore, he is a sponsor of the deplorable Freedom of Choice Act (FOCA), a federal law that would prohibit all restrictions on abortion, including even the current state bans on partial-birth abortions as well as parental consent and parental notification laws.)" [62]

So other than severely limiting religious expression (particularly Christianity), banning teaching the theory of intelligent design, and legalizing abortion, have there been any other negative consequences to these relativistic rulings that contradict the intent of the Founding Fathers? Yes, as shown in Figure 1 below, there have been significant increases in measures of immorality, family instability, and violent behavior accompanied by a decline in student educational performance. [63]

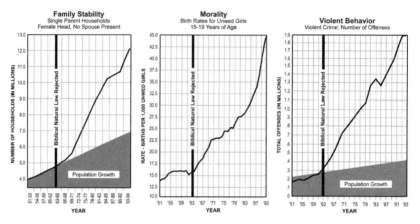

Figure 6-1. Relationship Between Societal Factors and the Supreme Court's Ruling Against Teaching Biblical Principles in Public Schools. [63]

W. Cleon Skousen's closing words of his book, *The Five Thousand Year Leap: 28 Great Ideas That Changed the World,* [64] are very appropriate for closing this section,

> "In our day of accelerating crimes of violence, narcotics addiction, billion-dollar pornography sales, hedonistic sexual aberrations, high divorce rates, and deteriorating family life, the American people might well recall the stirring words of Daniel Webster when he spoke to the New York Historical Society, February 22, 1852:
>
> > "Unborn ages and visions of glory crowd upon my soul, the realization of all which, however, is in the hands and good pleasure of Almighty God; but, under his divine blessing, it will be dependent on the character and virtues of ourselves and of our posterity...if we and they shall live always in the fear of God, and shall respect his commandments...we may have the highest hopes of the future fortunes of our country....It will have no decline and fall. It will go on prospering....**But if we and our posterity reject religious instruction and authority, violate the rules of eternal justice, trifle with the injunctions of morality, and recklessly destroy the political constitution which holds us together, no man can**

tell how sudden a catastrophe may overwhelm us, that shall bury all our glory in profound obscurity. Should that catastrophe happen, let it have not history! Let the horrible narrative never be written!"

Unfortunately, unless the present generation of American leadership returns to fundamental values, that history is being written right now." [64] (emphasis added by me)

These are sobering words, indeed. Based upon the Supreme Court decisions cited above, it certainly appears that the Supreme Court has ignored Daniel Webster's warning and that, consequently, America is well on its way to what Webster described as the "profound obscurity." Unfortunately, this journey to America's demise is being accelerated by the present American leadership, which has no intention of returning to the fundamental principles and values that were given to us by the Founding Fathers.

Secular Socialism: Incompatible With Biblical Christianity

I realize that these are harsh words regarding the present American leadership and the impending demise of America. I am well aware that as a Bible-believing Christian, I am commanded to be obedient to the government and even to pray for its leaders:

> "Every person is to be in subjection to the governing authorities. For there is no authority except from God, and those which exist are established by God." Romans 13:1

> "But I say to you, love your enemies and pray for those who persecute you." Matthew 5:44

However, I am also aware of the righteous anger that Jesus directed toward the religious leaders who were leading the people astray.

> "But woe to you, scribes and Pharisees, hypocrites, because you shut off the kingdom of heaven from people; for you do not enter in yourselves, nor do you allow those who are entering to go in." Matthew 23:13

Additionally, I know that the Old Testament prophets often criticized their leaders for not being obedient to God and that their prophetic messages had four principle themes: (a) expose the sinful practices of men, (b) call the people back to God, (c) warn the people of coming judgment, and (d) inform the people of the coming Messiah. [65]

> "Then the LORD sent Nathan to David....Why have you despised the word of the LORD by doing evil in His sight?...Then David said to Nathan, "I have sinned against the LORD" And Nathan said to David, "the LORD also has taken away your sin...." 2 Samuel 12:7

> Yet you, his son, Belshazzar, have not humbled your heart, even though you knew all this, but you have exalted yourself against the Lord of heaven...." Daniel 5:22-23

Certainly, I am not claiming to have the authority to condemn the leaders of our country that Jesus had to condemn the leaders of the Jewish nation, nor am I claiming to be a modern-day prophet. However, I believe it is appropriate for me to point out the attitudes and actions of our leaders and American citizens that are not consistent with biblical principles (and as a matter of fact, not consistent with the intent of America's Founding Fathers) and encourage our leaders and citizens to turn to God. That is the purpose of the remainder of this chapter.

The good news is that if our leaders and citizens turn to God, He will forgive them. Conversely, if they do not, then there will be divine consequences—as demonstrated in Daniel's account of Belshazzar. The rest of the story of Belshazzar will be told at the end of this chapter.

Before discussing secular socialism and the stranglehold that it now has on America, let's consider Daniel Webster's warning, quoted above, in a little more detail and see if there is evidence that America is clearly on the road to what he termed "profound obscurity":

Rejection of religious instruction and authority...yes, all religious instruction in schools is forbidden;

Violate rules of eternal justice...yes, more than 45 million babies have been aborted since *Roe v. Wade*;

Trifle with injunctions of morality...yes, some schools are now giving condoms to elementary children; and

Recklessly destroy the political constitution...yes, legal positivism or relativity.

Add to these factors the financial debt of the U.S., which is currently (as of July 2010) more than $13 trillion dollars, which is a debt of more than $42,000 per citizen and more than $119,000 per taxpayer. Unfortunately, that is not the end of the story—it gets worse! The total U.S. unfunded liabilities, which include Social Security, Medicare, and prescription drugs (Medicare Part D) is more than $109 trillion dollars, which is more than $354,000 per citizen and more than $1,000,000 per taxpayer. [66] For the current numbers, log on to the U.S. National Debt Clock website: http://www.usdebtclock.org/.

The famous quote of the Apollo 13 astronauts' famous statement seems appropriate, "Houston, we have a problem." [67] To paraphrase: "America, we have a problem!" This section presents information on this problem in the following three areas:

1. What is secular socialism?
2. Who are its leaders?
3. Why is it so deadly?

What Is Secular Socialism?

Sometimes breaking down a word or phrase into its components and defining them can provide a better understanding of the meaning of a given word or phrase. For example, the word "politics" can be broken into its component parts: "poli," which means "many," and "tics," which means "blood sucking insect"! Therefore, it could be concluded that the word "politicians" refers to many blood sucking policy makers! Since this chapter has been somewhat depressing, I thought a little humor might be appreciated. If any politicians were offended by this joke, I apologize for this humor at their expense (even though it is not difficult to find politicians to whom this definition applies).

Seriously, you are probably familiar with the terms "liberalism" and "conservatism" when used in a political context. To make sure we are all thinking about the correct definition of these words, the Merriam-Webster's definitions are:

Liberalism: "a political philosophy based on belief in progress, the essential goodness of the human race, and the autonomy of the individual and standing for the protection of political and civil liberties." [68]

Conservativism: "tending or disposed to maintain existing views, conditions, or institutions: Traditional." [68]

It seems that people who previously identified themselves as "liberals" now prefer the term "progressives." After all, "progressive" sounds much more impressive and gives the impression that these people and their philosophies will lead to progress. From my biased perspective, I think a more accurate term would be "regressive" because these people and philosophies are regressing to a form of government that has never had long-term success. But more about that later.

Bill O'Reilly, in his book *Culture Warrior*, has more accurately described the philosophy of the liberals/progressives as "secular progressive." [69] He makes a very compelling case that because the current day liberal/progressive philosophies must eliminate God from public life that they are secular in nature.

"Almost every social change the secular-progressive [S-P] movement wants to achieve is opposed by religious Americans. Therefore, the more the S-Ps can diminish religious influence in America, the faster their agenda can become a reality.... So for the S-P agenda to succeed, religion in America must be deemphasized, just as it already has been in Western Europe and Canada, where secular-progressives have made huge gains. Looking at the entire battle zone, we can see that the American S-P generals have learned that goal number one is to secularize the American public school system in order to drive children away from religion and into the S-P camp." [70]

O'Reilly provides additional insight into the philosophy by providing his version of the secular progressive commandments:

"Thou Shalt Not Make Any Judgment Regarding Most Private Personal Behavior. Man/Woman Is the Master/Mistress of the Universe and His/Her Gratification Is Paramount.

Thou Shalt Not Worship or Acknowledge God in the Public Square, for Such an Exposition Could Be Offensive to Humankind.

Thou Shalt Take From the Rich and Give to the Poor. No Private Property is Sacrosanct.

Thou Shalt Circumvent Mother and Father in Personal Issues Such as Abortion and Sex Education in Public Schools.

Thou Shalt Kill if Necessary to Promote Individual Rights in Cases of Abortion and Euthanasia.

Thou Shalt Be Allowed to Bear False Witness Against Thy Neighbor if That Person Stands Against Secular Humanism.

Thou Shalt Not Wage Preemptive War in Any Circumstance.

Thou Shalt Not Impede the Free Movement of Any Human Being on Earth. All Countries Should be Welcoming Places Without Borders.

Thou Shalt Not Prohibit Narcotics or Impede Personal Gratification in This Area.

Thou Shalt Not Limit the Power of Government in Order to Provide "Prosperity to All." [71]

Although these are written in a somewhat humorous style, examples to support each of these commandments are plentiful. It is obvious, even with just a cursory reading, that these commandments are clearly incompatible with the Ten Commandments and biblical principles.

O'Reilly bluntly states, "Socialism has never worked anywhere in the world." [72] From my experience, I have seen that socialism breaks down the work ethic of a people and replaces it with an entitlement attitude. The people believe that the government owes them health care, a shorter workweek, extensive vacations, large retirement pensions.... For example, I have observed that many of my European friends have the attitude that their vacation always takes precedence over their work responsibilities. When they go on vacation they don't really care about what is left undone at work. They don't check voice mail, email messages, or follow up on work-related items. They think that the government and employer *owe* them their uninterrupted vacations.

Newt Gingrich, former Speaker of the U.S. House of Representatives and best-selling author, has written a book, *To Save America: Stopping Obama's Secular Socialist Machine*, in which he says that the current day "liberals/progressives/secular progressives" are better described as "secular socialists." Let's again turn to the dictionary for the meanings of these words:

Secular means "of or relating to the worldly or temporal" [68]

Socialism means "any of various economic and political theories advocating collective or governmental ownership and administration of the means of production and distribution of goods....a stage of society in Marxist theory transitional between capitalism and communism and distinguished by unequal distribution of goods and pay according to work done." [68]

I would summarize the fundamental principle of secular socialism as, "Government, not God, provides the answer to all of man's problems. If you must believe in God, then keep him locked up in a box and do not let Him out in public." This is clearly not what the Founding Fathers believed and it certainly is not compatible with biblical Christianity.

Gingrich lists 10 fundamental differences between the principles of our Founding Fathers and the social secularists:

"1. Work versus theft
2. Productivity versus union work rules and bureaucracy
3. Elected representation versus bureaucrats and judges
4. Honesty versus corruption
5. Low taxes with limited government versus high taxes with big government
6. Private property versus government controls
7. Localism versus Washington control
8. American energy versus environmental extremism
9. Conflict resolution versus litigation
10. Religious belief versus oppression" [73]

Since my desire is not to write a book on politics, I'll not discuss these differences. If you are interested in more detail and justification of these differences, then I direct you to Speaker Gingrich's book. He is far more capable at discussing these differences than I am.

Who are its leaders?

Yes, President Barack Obama is the current, visible leader of the secular socialist movement. Yes, Nancy Pelosi, Speaker of the U.S. House of Representatives, and Harry Reid, the U.S. Majority Leader of the Senate, and the majority of the members of the Democratic National Party are either secular socialists or are actively supporting its policies for political gain. Yes, many members of academia, the elite news media, union leaders, trial lawyers, the bureaucracy, the courts, and lobbyists at the state and federal levels are secular socialists. [69, 74] If you have any disagreements with these statements, then consider their attitudes and actions documented in the next section.

Having said this, I am certainly aware that the secular socialists will immediately react by saying that since I have said something critical about President Obama that I am racist! Just to set the record straight (not that it will matter to the secular socialists), I am not racist. I believe, as our Founding Fathers did and as the Bible teaches, that *all* men are created equal before God. Furthermore, I know that Jesus Christ, the Savior and Lord of my life, loved Barack Obama enough to die for him.

> "For God so loved the world, that He gave His only begotten Son, that *whoever* believes in Him shall not perish, but have eternal life." John 3:16

So, I'll say it once again—I am not racist.

Now back to the leadership of the secular socialist movement. Unfortunately, there are several immensely wealthy people pouring millions of dollars into the support of the secular socialist agenda. These include billionaires George Soros and Peter Lewis. O'Reilly warns of their power:

> "To sum up, Soros is a smart, ruthless ideologue who will stop at nothing to advance the secular-progressive [secular socialist] offensive. He has no scruples, ethics, or sense of fair play....For traditional-minded Americans, George Soros is public enemy number one. Without his unlimited cash (along with that of Peter Lewis), the S-P movement could not attack so readily and so effectively—and with such venom. Soros envisions a libertine society that soaks the rich (except for him) and forms no judgments on personal behavior. His one-world philosophy would obliterate the uniqueness of America and downsize its superpower status. His secular approach would drastically diminish Judeo-Christian philosophy in America and encourage his own spiritual philosophy: atheism. George Soros is truly an imposing force, and his elite media allies are making him even more so. We ignore him at our peril." [75]

Why is secular socialism so deadly?

Gingrich provides considerable insight into the answer to this question by stating:

"America as we know it is now facing a mortal threat.

The Left have expanded their power through their control of academia, the elite news media, union leaders, trial lawyers, the bureaucracy, the courts, and lobbyists at the state and federal levels. They share a vision of a secular, socialist America run for the interests of the members of the political machine that keeps them in power. It will be an America where government dominates the people rather than represents them. In short, they want to use government power to change who we are and how we think.

This danger to America is greater than anything I dreamed possible after we won the Cold War and the Soviet Union disappeared in December 1991. We stand at a crossroads: either we will save our country or we will lose it." [74]

Consider the following five factors that combine to make secular socialism deadly to the American way of life and the American dream:

1. Political Power
2. Money
3. Rules for Radicals
4. Word Games
5. Policies and Philosophies

Although any one of these, in the wrong hands, could present major problems, the combination of all of these in the hands of secular socialists is indeed deadly.

1. Political Power. The Founding Fathers set up a system of government that operated under a system of checks and balances. The system was designed to ensure that neither the executive, legislative, nor judicial branch of the federal government would gain too much power since the other two branches would be able to offset and balance any undue or unconstitutional quest for power. The elections of 2008 did not provide the desired balance of power envisioned by our Founding Fathers. The secular socialists have taken control of the executive and legislative branches of our government. The visible leader of the secular socialist movement is the President of the United States of America, Barack Obama, who is supported by a majority of U.S. Congressmen and U.S. Senators. As the Founding Fathers understood, concentration of power leads to corruption and abuse of power.

"But secular socialists know the bigger and more powerful government gets, the more politicians can use its power to benefit their supporters. In other words, secular socialism doesn't win power because it's a compelling vision for the future; it's just a convenient way to pay off members of their coalition and bribe new ones into joining. And the more power secular socialist politicians have, both in elected positions and in the bureaucracies, the better these coalition members can be fed from the public trough." [76]

There is considerable truth in the saying that "Power corrupts and absolute power corrupts absolutely."

> "The fool has said in his heart, 'There is no God;' They are corrupt, and have committed abominable injustice.... Psalm 53:1

2. Money. The power of money in politics cannot be overstated. Funding by Soros and others enabled the secular socialist political machine to succeed in getting a candidate with virtually no executive experience, no business experience, very questionable personal and political relationships, and the most liberal voting record of any U.S. Senator elected as President of the United States. In fairness, however, Barack Obama is very good at reading teleprompters and delivering compelling speeches.

> "For the time will come when they will not endure sound doctrine; but wanting to have their ears tickled, they will accumulate for themselves teachers in accordance to their own desires, and will turn away their ears from the truth and will turn aside to myths." 2 Timothy 4:3-4

Remember that during the 2008 presidential campaign, candidate Obama's message was "Hope and Change." He promised to transform the U.S. Now that he has the political power and the financial resources of the secular socialist billionaires, he is making good on that promise through his secular socialist agenda. Many of the American people who voted for him, however, are realizing that the "Hope and Change" and transformation of America promised by candidate Obama are not what they envisioned.

You might be interested to know that since President Obama took office on January 20, 2009 to March 31, 2010, numerous secular socialists have visited the White House, including George Soros—at least five visits; Peter Lewis—at least six visits, Andy Stern, president of the Service Employees International Union (SEIU)—at least 47 visits; Anna Burger, secretary-treasurer of SEIU—at least 53 visits; Richard Trumka, president of AFL-CIO—at least 29 visits; Leo Gerard, president of International United Steel Workers Union—at least 13 visits; John Podesta, president of liberal think tank, Center for American Progress—at least 39 visits; Cass Sunstein, law professor at University of Chicago—at least 11 visits; and Cecile Richards, president of Planned Parenthood and former deputy chief of staff for Nancy Pelosi—at least five visits. [77] It is fair to conclude that the secular socialist agenda is well-represented by these frequent White House visitors.

I hope and pray that the secular socialists in the government will prove to be as inefficient and wasteful in spending the secular socialist's donations as the federal government is in spending our tax dollars. On July 22, 2010, President Obama signed legislation intended to reduce the erroneous payments made by the federal government:

> "Almost $110 billion was paid by the government in 2009 to the wrong person, in the wrong amount or for the wrong reasons, according to a White House release....In the past three years the government paid benefits totaling more than $180 million to approximately 20,000 Americans who had died, according to the statement. More than $230 million in benefits were paid to about 14,000 fugitives or people in jail who were ineligible for them, the release said." [78]

Another example of the government's waste is the monthly rent paid for Speaker Nancy Pelosi's office in San Francisco. The rent for her office is $18,736.00 per month! [79] Does this look like good stewardship of your and my tax dollars?

3. Rules for Radicals. The "bible" of secular socialists is *Rules for Radicals* by Saul Alinsky. [80, 81] According to Gingrich,

> "Barack Obama taught courses on Alinsky's techniques for community organizing groups. So his endorsement of these tactics of fundamental dishonesty is a matter of a public record." [82]

The "Rules for Radicals" website states:

"Obama learned his lesson well. I am proud to see that my father's model for organizing is being applied successfully beyond local community organizing to affect the Democratic campaign in 2008. It is a fine tribute to Saul Alinsky as we approach his 100th birthday." DAVID ALINSKY, son of Saul Alinsky.

Obama helped fund 'Alinsky Academy': "The Woods Fund, a nonprofit on which Obama served as paid director from 1999 to December 2002, provided startup funding and later capital to the Midwest Academy.... Obama sat on the Woods Fund board alongside William Ayers, founder of the Weather Underground domestic terrorist organization....'Midwest describes itself as 'one of the nation's oldest and best-known schools for community organizations, citizen organizations and individuals **committed to progressive social change**.' ... Midwest teaches Alinsky tactics of community organizing." [81]

Additional information about Alinsky's rules, from the Rules for Radical's website, are provided below:

"Alinsky's tactics were based, not on Stalin's revolutionary violence, but on the Neo-Marxist strategies of Antonio Gramsci, an Italian Communist. Relying on gradualism, infiltration and the dialectic process rather than a bloody revolution, Gramsci's transformational Marxism was so subtle that few even noticed the deliberate changes.

Like Alinsky, Mikhail Gorbachev followed Gramsci, not Lenin. In fact, Gramsci aroused Stalin's wrath by suggesting that Lenin's revolutionary plan wouldn't work in the West. Instead the primary **assault** would be on **biblical absolutes** and Christian values, which must be crushed as a social force before the new face of Communism could rise and flourish.

Malachi Martin gave us a progress report:

"By 1985, the influence of traditional Christian philosophy in the West was weak and negligible....Gramsci's master strategy was now feasible. Humanly speaking, it was no longer too tall an order to **strip large majorities** of men and women in the West of those last vestiges that remained to them of Christianity's transcendent God." [81]

As indicated above, biblical Christianity in America was clearly the target for Lenin's communist plans and it remains so for secular socialists. One of the key principles taught by Alinsky is that the "ends justify the means." This means that they will use whatever means necessary to accomplish their goals. Yes, this even means that they will lie when it serves their purpose.

For example, consider that candidate Obama stated at least eight times that if he were elected president that he would pursue a national healthcare plan and that the discussions and negotiations associated with this would be televised and that the nation would have 72 hours to read any bill before it was passed. Not only were the healthcare negotiations not televised on C-SPAN, the nation was not given 72 hours to read the 2,000+ page bill before it was passed.

Sadly, most of the congressmen who voted in support of the bill had not read the bill, either. Speaker Pelosi even told the American people to "trust us, you will like it when you see the details." [83, 84]

4. Word Games. Another tactic used by the secular socialists is to change the use of commonly accepted words and phrases and attach new meanings to them. So, what they say is really not what is typically meant or understood. Examples of this include:

(a) *Christian*: the common meaning of this word is one who has placed his/her faith in the gospel of Jesus Christ. However, when Barack Obama claims that he is a Christian, it is important to see if his beliefs are consistent with biblical teaching. For 20 years Barack Obama attended Trinity United Church of Christ in Chicago, whose pastor is Reverend Jeremiah Wright. [85] This church is a part of the United Church of Christ denomination.

"The United Church of Christ (UCC)—the Christian denomination of 1.2 million members recently made famous by Barack Obama and the Rev. Jeremiah Wright—provides a clear illustration of a non-biblical "Christian" group. The UCC was the first denomination to ordain an openly gay minister and to call for recognition of homosexual marriages (in 1976),[1] and currently some 200 openly homosexual UCC clergy serve in its various ministries or pastorates.[2] The UCC is also a strong advocate of abortion, openly endorsing abortion-on-demand a full two years before the *Roe v. Wade* decision of 1973;[3] they even oppose the ban on partial-birth abortions.[4] The UCC also holds positions that favor Palestinians above Jews (the Jewish Anti-Defamation League is uncomfortable with their position toward Israel),[5] and the UCC doesn't celebrate the "sexist" God of the Bible but instead uses gender-neutral images of God that can be either "he," "she," or whatever the individual wants Him to be.[6] Believing that "God speaks in new ways every day" and that "doctrine and the intent of the Bible are affected by culture and context,"[7] the UCC does not embrace fixed absolutes from the Scriptures (especially on moral issues) but rewrites the Bible to match whatever position they embrace at that time. Clearly, this denomination, while officially considered Christian, is certainly not biblical; there unfortunately are other Christian and Jewish groups and individuals that have also rejected traditional biblical truths and standards." [86] (The reference numbers shown above are in Barton's book and are not reproduced in this book.

The ordination of openly gay people to positions of leadership in the church, support of homosexual marriage, support of abortion, support of Palestinians over Jews, modification of biblical text to be "non-sexist," and teaching against absolute truth from the Scriptures are all contradictory to direct biblical principles. Therefore, the UCC cannot be considered a denomination of biblical Christianity.

It is important to remember that just as going into a garage does not make you a car, neither does going into a church make you a Christian. Be very skeptical of politicians (or anyone else) who claim to be Christians but who do not act according to biblical teachings. Considering that the Obama family has now lived in Washington, D.C. for more than 18 months but have yet to select a church to attend to worship God can lead to legitimate questions about his commitment to Christianity.

> "Let us hold fast the confession of our hope without wavering, for He who promised is faithful; and let us consider how to stimulate one another to love and good deeds, not forsaking our own assembling together, as is the habit of some, but encouraging one another; and all the more as you see the day drawing near." Hebrews 10:23-25

(b) *Gospel*: The gospel of Jesus Christ is:

> "For I delivered to you as of first importance what I also received, that Christ died for our sins according to the Scriptures, and that He was buried, and that He was raised on the third day according to the Scriptures." 1 Corinthians 15:3-4

That is the gospel—no more, no less.

In interviews on April 26, 2005, January 13, 2006, and January 21, 2010, Reverend Jim Wallis, a spiritual and political advisor to President Obama, stated that the gospel is about redistribution of wealth. He believes it is the government's responsibility to take care of the poor. [87]

> "But even if we, or an angel from heaven, should preach to you a gospel contrary to what we have preached to you, he is to be accursed! Galatians 1:8

Regarding the responsibility to take care of the poor, the Bible is very clear that this is a personal responsibility of believers, not the government's responsibility.

> "Then the King [Jesus] will say to those on His right, 'Come, you who are blessed of My Father, inherit the kingdom prepared for you from the foundation of the world. 'For I was hungry, and you gave Me something to eat; I was thirsty, and you gave Me something to drink; I was a stranger, and you invited Me in; naked, and you clothed Me; I was sick, and you visited Me,; I was in prison, and you came to me.' Then the righteous will answer Him, 'Lord, when did we see You hungry, and feed You, or thirsty, and give You something to drink? And when did we see You a stranger, and invite you in, or naked, and clothe you? When did we see You sick, or in prison, and come to You? The King will answer and say to them, 'Truly I say to you, to the extent that you did it to one of these brothers of Mine, even the least of them, you did it to Me.'" Matthew 34-40

(c) *Social Justice*: This is the concept that it is the government's responsibility to ensure equality between all members of society and encompasses the concepts of caring for the poor and less fortunate, as well as redistribution of wealth. The Founding Father's convictions regarding helping the needy are summarized below:

"1. Do not help the needy completely. Merely help them to help themselves.
2. Give the poor the satisfaction of "earned achievement" instead of rewarding them without achievement.
3. Allow the poor to climb the "appreciation ladder," from tents to cabins, cabins to cottages, cottages to comfortable houses.
4. Where emergency help is provided, do not prolong it to the point where it becomes habitual.
5. Strictly enforce the scale of "fixed responsibility." The first and foremost level of responsibility is with the individual himself; the second level is the family; then the church; next the community; and finally the country, and in a disaster or emergency, the state. Under no circumstances is the federal government to become involved in public welfare. The Founders felt it would corrupt the government and also the poor. No Constitutional authority exists for the federal government to participate in charity or welfare." [88]

The Bible teaches that caring for those in need (financial and physical) is an individual believer's responsibility, not the government's responsibility.

"Jesus replied and said, 'A man was going down from Jerusalem to Jericho, and fell among robbers, and they stripped him and beat him, and went away leaving him half dead. And by chance a priest was going down on that road, and when he saw him, he passed by on the other side. Likewise a Levite also, when he came to the place and saw him, passed by on the other side. But a Samaritan, who was on a journey, came upon him; and when he saw him, he felt compassion, and came to him and bandaged up his wounds, pouring oil and wine on them; and he put him on his own beast, and brought him to an inn and took care of him. On the next day he took out two denarii and gave them to the innkeeper and said, 'Take care of him; and whatever more you spend, when I return I will repay you.' Which of these three do you think proved to be a neighbor to the man who fell into the robbers' hands? And he said, 'The one who showed mercy toward him.' Then Jesus said to him, 'Go and do the same.'" Luke 10:30-37

The government's idea of providing social justice includes redistribution of wealth—taking from those who have and giving it to those who do not. This fosters entitlement attitudes and class warfare. [89] Neither of these are biblical principles. Furthermore, a strong case can be made that this violates two of the Ten Commandments: "You shall not steal" and "You shall not covet."

(d) *Fairness*. The concept of "fairness" or freedom from impartiality, prejudice, or favoritism is part of the American heritage. [68, 90] This concept was incorporated into the Declaration of Independence's words, "all men are created equal" and "that they are endowed with certain unalienable rights." This means that all men are created with equal *opportunity* to utilize their rights to life, liberty, and pursuit of happiness. Secular socialists, however, modify this to mean all men should have equal *outcomes*, regardless of effort. This difference is as significant as the difference between day and night.

The concept of equal opportunity encourages personal responsibility, self-discipline, and accountability. It permits failure, but it also encourages striving for excellence, rewards success, and enhances self-esteem. It is the foundation of free enterprise and capitalism. [90]

On the other hand, the concept of equal outcomes destroys initiative, fosters laziness, dependence, and mediocrity. People learn to depend upon governmental control, regulation, and redistribution of wealth to support "equal rewards for unequal results." It also creates class warfare and is the foundation for socialism and communism.

As you probably suspect, neither the Founding Fathers nor the Bible support the secular socialists' modification of the word "fairness" to mean "equal outcome." For example, in the "gospel" section above, I quoted a portion of one of Jesus' parables to demonstrate that it is our individual responsibility to care for those less fortunate among us. There is, however, more to this parable:

> "Then the King [Jesus] will say to those on His right, 'Come, you who are blessed of My Father, inherit the kingdom prepared for you from the foundation of the world....Then He will say also to those on His left, 'Depart from Me, accursed ones, into the eternal fire which has been prepared for the devil and his angels." Matthew 25:34, 41

This parable supports the validity of equal opportunity to serve, but not equal outcomes for the servants. Rewards for service are clearly dependent upon results. (This concept and how it applies to eternal life will be presented in detail in the next chapter.)

As usual, secular socialists are completely ignoring the intent of the Founding Fathers and sound biblical principle. They are using their version of fairness to help those who are less fortunate among us to achieve social justice. They are also trying, unsuccessfully so far, to use it to control the media through the "Fairness Doctrine." The original Fairness Doctrine was issued by the U.S. Federal Communications Commission (FCC) in 1949 and it required radio broadcasters to provide a reasonable (i.e., fair) opportunity for conflicting views to be broadcasted. [91]

Since the FCC is an independent regulatory agency, it has the authority to regulate the electronics communication media (radio, television, wire, satellite, and cable) [92] without executive or legislative action. [91] In 1987, the FCC rescinded this law due to concerns about its constitutionality. [92] Shortly thereafter, the Democrat controlled congress passed a bill to reinstate the Fairness Doctrine; however, this was vetoed by President Reagan. [91]

Passing a law to reinstate the Fairness Doctrine, with strategic modifications, is high on the list of priorities for secular socialists. [92] If passed, this would provide governmental control over the programming content of the electronic communications media. In other words, this would allow secular socialists to effectively minimize or eliminate pesky programs that promoted conservative and Christian perspectives.

(e) *Comprehensive Immigration Reform*: This sounds like a fair and far-reaching way to solve the illegal immigration problem in the U.S. However, the secular socialists use this term to support their relentless quest for political power. Consider the current debates that focus on two ends of the illegal immigration controversy: Arizona's SB 1070 law and "sanctuary cities."

On April 23, 2010, Arizona's Governor Janet Brewer signed into law the senate bill known as SB 1070, which gives the Arizona law enforcement officers the right to determine the legal status of any person stopped during a lawful contact. This law was designed to fully support and cooperate with the federal immigration laws. [94] Nevertheless, the U.S. Department of Justice filed a lawsuit against the state of Arizona on

July 6, 2010, claiming that the Arizona law preempted exclusive federal right to enforce immigration policy. [95]

At the other end of the spectrum are cities in the U.S. that have decided not to allow their municipal funds to be used to support or enforce federal immigration laws. The term "sanctuary cites" is applied to these, since, in effect, they are safe sanctuaries for illegal immigrants. [96] As of May 2007, sanctuary cities included: Los Angeles, CA; San Francisco, CA; Miami, FL; Chicago, IL; Minneapolis, MN; Albuquerque, NM; Austin, TX; Houston, TX; Seattle, WA, and Washington, D.C. [97] Although these and other sanctuary cities have openly refused to support and enforce federal law, the U.S. Department of Justice has not filed lawsuits against any of these cities because of their sanctuary city policies.

What is the explanation of these bizarre actions by the U.S. Department of Justice? Politics. Realistically, the Republicans are afraid to address this problem for fear of alienating the large and growing Latino population in the U.S. On the other hand, President Obama and the Democrats (many of whom are secular socialists) are lustily looking at the 12 million-plus illegal aliens currently in the U.S. as future voters that will support their secular socialist agenda. The secular socialists know that if they can find a way to grant amnesty to these 12 million illegal aliens, that there is a high probability that the majority of these would return the favor by being lifetime Democratic voters. If (or when) this happens, it will permanently change the political landscape in the U.S. So, beware when you hear President Obama promoting the "compassionate" need to pass comprehensive immigration reform.

So, what is the biblical answer to the illegal immigration problem facing America?

> "Every person is to be in subjection to the governing authorities...." Romans 13:1

> "Submit yourselves for the Lord's sake to every human institution...." 1 Peter 2:13

> "Remind them to be subject to rulers, to authorities, to be obedient, to be ready for every good deed." Titus 3:1

Since nothing in the current U.S. immigration laws contradicts biblical teaching, Christians are to submissively obey current U.S. immigration law. Furthermore, we are to support and obey federal laws. Harboring or assisting the person to break U.S. laws is not consistent with biblical principles. If we know of someone residing illegally in the U.S., it is our responsibility to assist in the resolution of this breach of law. This might include counseling the person, informing the legal authorities, referring the person to an immigration attorney, or even assisting the person to leave the U.S. [98]

5. Policies and Philosophies. Some of the most noteworthy policies and philosophies expressed by our federal government under the Obama administration are summarized below. When appropriate, quotes from the Founding Fathers and the Bible are included.

(a) There have been several significant new *policies* passed during the first couple years of the Obama Administration. These include the American Recovery and Reinvestment act of 2009; The Affordable Care Act of 2010 (Obama Healthcare); and the Dodd-Frank Wall Street Reform and Consumer Protection Act of 2010 (financial reform). Although there have been and will continue to be many arguments regarding the necessity and the details of these bills, there is no doubt that they have substantially increased the power and reach of the federal government— and the secular socialists. This is certainly not what the Founding Fathers had in mind.

Jefferson warned of loss of local (state) control and concentration of power in Washington (federal government):

"[T]aking from the States the moral rule of their citizens, and subordinating it to the general authority [federal government]...would...break up the foundations of the Union....I believe the States can best govern our home concerns and the general [federal] government our foreign ones. I wish, therefore... never to see all offices transferred to Washington, where, further withdrawn from the eyes of the people, they may more secretly be bought and sold as at market." [99]

(b) *Illegal immigration* continues to be a major problem for the U.S., especially in the border states. With more than 12 million illegal immigrants in the U.S., it is clear that the U.S. government has failed to fulfill its responsibility to protect its citizens. Do you find it ironic that the Department of Justice has filed lawsuits against the state of Arizona for trying to assist the federal government in controlling illegal immigration but the Department of Justice does not prosecute sanctuary cities who are clearly defying federal immigration law? The political reality is that the Republicans are afraid of doing something that might alienate Latino voters and President Obama and the Democrats are ogling the 12 million illegals as potential future Democratic voters. Undoubtedly, President Obama's "comprehensive immigration reform" will be designed to offer significant benefits to the Democratic party, in general, and secular socialists, in particular.

(c) *Taxation and redistribution of wealth* is a major political tool for the secular socialists—take from the rich and give to the poor. From my perspective, redistribution of wealth is the politically correct way to refer to "legalized theft." It promotes class warfare—rich vs. poor—and it fosters an entitlement attitude amongst the recipients. Politically, since there are more poor folks than rich folks, it helps ensure that the secular socialists will stay in power. Certainly, the Founding Fathers were adamantly opposed to this philosophy and it is unbiblical. For example, Samuel Adams wrote:

"The Utopian schemes of leveling [redistribution of the wealth] and a community of goods [central ownership of the means of production and distribution], are as visionary and impractical as those which vest all property in the Crown. [These ideas] are arbitrary, despotic, and in our government, unconstitutional." [100]

Summarizing the Founding Father's writings regarding redistribution of wealth, Skousen states,

"The American Founders recognized that the moment the government is authorized to start leveling the material possessions of the rich in order to have an "equal distribution of goods," the government thereafter has the power to deprive any of the people of their "equal" rights to enjoy their lives, liberties, and property." [101]

Jesus' parable of the talents emphasizes the importance of properly utilizing one's talents and being rewarded for wise use of them:

"For it is just like a man about to go on a journey, who called his own slaves and entrusted his possessions to them. To one he gave five talents, to another, two, and to another one, each according to his own ability; and he went on his journey. Immediately the one who had received five talents went and traded with them, and gained five more talents. In the same manner the one who had received the two talents gained two more. But he who received the one talent went away, and dug a hole in the ground and hid his master's money. Now after a long time the master of those slaves came and settled accounts with them. The one who had received the five talents came up and brought five more talents, saying, 'Master, you entrusted five talents to me. See, I have gained five more talents.' His master said to him, 'Well done, good and faithful slave. You were faithful with a few things, I will put you in charge of many things; enter into the joy of your master.' Also the one who had received the two talents came up and said, 'Master, you entrusted two talents to me. See, I have gained two more talents.' His master said to him, 'Well done, good and faithful slave. You were faithful with a few things, I will put you in charge of many things; enter into the joy of your master.' Also the one who had received one talent came up and said, 'Master, I knew you to be a hard man, reaping where you did not sow and gathering where you scattered no seed. And I was afraid, and went away and hid your talent in the ground. See, you have what is yours.' But his master answered and said to him, 'You wicked, lazy slave, you knew that I reap where I did not sow and gather where I scattered no seed. Then you ought to have put my money in the bank, and on my arrival I would have received my money back with interest. Therefore take away the talent from him, and give it to the one who has the ten talents. For to everyone who has, more shall be given, and he will have an abundance; but from the one who does not have, even what he does have shall be taken away. Throw out the worthless slave into the outer darkness; in that place there will be weeping and gnashing of teeth." Matthew 25:14-30

(d) *Abortion* rights have a strong supporter in President Obama. On January 23, 2009, President Obama signed the Mexico City Policy, which provides U.S. funding for international agencies providing abortion services. It is estimated that there are more than 45 million abortions performed annually outside the U.S. [102]

From 1973 through 2005, there have been more than 45 million abortions performed in the United States. In 2005, there were 1.21 million abortions performed in the U.S. Twenty-two percent of all pregnancies in the U.S. end in abortion. [102]

The Founding Fathers did not specifically address the topic of abortion. However, given their reverence for and dependence upon the Bible and Christianity, it is reasonable to conclude that they would not have supported the constitutionality of abortion. The Declaration of Independence states,

"We hold these truths to be self-evident, that all men are created equal, and that they are endowed by their creator with certain unalienable rights, that among these are life, liberty, and the pursuit of happiness. ..." [1]

The fact that they recognized that all men are created by God and that the first inalienable right listed is life indicates that they recognize the sanctity of life. Additionally, they were well aware of the Ten Commandments, one of which specifically states, "You shall not murder."

Although it is not politically correct to say this, abortion is the killing (murder) of an innocent human life. An aborted child is a person that was created by God, in His image, whom He knew and loved:

> "For You formed my inward parts; You wove me in my mother's womb. I will give thanks to You, for I am fearfully and wonderfully made; Wonderful are Your works, And my soul knows it very well. My frame was not hidden from You, When I was made in secret, And skillfully wrought in the depths of the earth; Your eyes have seen my unformed substance; and in Your book were all written the days that were ordained for me, When as yet there was not one of them."
> Psalm 139:13-16

(e) The U.S. *relationship with Israel* is not clear. It is difficult to know what President Obama's commitment is to the nation of Israel. Although he says that the relationship is strong, actions will speak louder than words and so far his actions have not been convincing. He would be wise to recall God's promise to Abraham relating to those who support Israel:

"And I will bless those who bless you [the nation of Israel], and the one who curses you I will curse." Genesis 12:3

It is interesting to note that the modern day nation of Israel was formed on May 14, 1948, at the stroke of midnight in Jerusalem. Eleven minutes later, President Truman announced the United States' recognition and support of the nation of Israel. Perhaps this is another reason why God has chosen to bless the U.S. [103]

Most Americans would agree with me that God has graciously blessed America in many ways. The evidence strongly suggests that the reasons for God's blessings originated with the intention of Christopher Columbus and the early American settlers who wanted to glorify God and to spread the gospel of Jesus in the new land. This God-honoring spirit continued with the amazing visionary leadership provided by the United States' Founding Fathers, who were clearly dependent upon and obedient to the Holy Spirit's guidance in establishing a country and governmental system that was based upon biblical principles. God blesses obedience to Him.

In spite of God's obvious blessings on our country, many Americans don't realize how truly unique and blessed America is among the nations of the world. We have become distracted by living the American dream and have not protected the foundations of our nation with vigilance. Our complacency has allowed the unholy alliance of atheism and secular socialism to not only infuse their deadly philosophies into America's educational and governmental systems, but in fact they now control these systems. In addition, the majority of America's mainstream media is supportive of the secular socialist agenda, as demonstrated by the slanted coverage of the Obama presidential candidacy and subsequent coverage.

Perhaps after reading about the "progress" made by atheism and secular socialism in Chapters 5 and 6, many Americans will agree with my assessment that the best days of America appear to be behind it. [104-106] The atheist and secular socialist agenda is accelerating toward its goals of a godless society, ruled by a socialistic government, which will lead to communism. However, as I indicated at the beginning of this chapter, the atheist and secular socialist agenda can be defeated, but it will require divine intervention. Ironically, this divine intervention will utilize "hope and change" to put America back on the right (i.e., God honoring) path.

Before explaining how God may choose to perform a modern day miracle in America with hope and change, I would like to use an analogy that I think is relevant. The analogy is the instructions for "how to boil a frog." If, for some reason, you wanted to boil a live frog, you cannot succeed by putting the frog into a pot of boiling water because he will instantly know the water is too hot and jump out of it. However, if you put the frog into the pot of water at room temperature, he will feel comfortable and not jump out. Then if the water is gradually heated up, the frog will adapt to the increasing temperature and not jump out of the pot. Eventually, the water temperature will heat up so much it will start to boil and it will be too late for the frog to jump out of the pot and save himself.

This has been the strategy of atheists and secular socialists. Slowly, gradually, incrementally, they infused their godless philosophies into the American culture and educational system. Additionally, the Supreme Court cases presented in this chapter have shown how the court overstepped its constitutional boundaries with the Everson case by incorrectly interpreting Jefferson's letter regarding the separation of church and state. Although some Americans objected to this ruling, the majority did not (thereby choosing to remain in the pot, even though the water temperature was increasing). Subsequent court rulings barring religious teaching, praying, Bible reading, posting the Ten Commandments, and teaching intelligent design in the public schools, further increased the water temperature in the American pot.

The *Roe v. Wade* case legalizing abortion further increased the temperature of the water in the American pot, but still the majority of Americans ignored the ramifications of these rulings. Ignoring the intent of the Founding Fathers to maintain a system of checks and balances among the branches of the federal government, the American people elected the most ardent supporters of secular socialism to the executive branch and legislative branch of government that this nation has ever seen. This has enabled the secular socialists to control and significantly increase the water temperature in the American pot. The temperature of the water in the American pot is now close to the boiling point and the future of America is in serious jeopardy!

The divine intervention may be manifested in surprising ways. For example, God may be using the secular socialists to bring an end to their unquenchable quest for power through their own actions. Their lust for power and enthusiastic exuberance expressed with the passage of the "Obama-Pelosi-Reid healthcare bill" and the "Dodd-Frank financial reform bill" effectively turned up the dials on the stove controlling the temperature of the water in America too high and too fast. The majority of Americans are now realizing this water is getting too hot and we need to jump out of this pot! Many Americans are realizing that the "hope and change" and the transforming of America that candidate Obama promoted on the campaign trail are not what they envisioned and are clearly not what the Founding Fathers' established. Consequently, many Americans are getting ready to jump out of the almost boiling water of the American pot.

If Americans do jump out of the almost boiling pot of water, where can they land to ensure their long-term safety? There is only one place to land that offers the security and hope for a better future that Americans desire and that is on the Bible! Do you remember Jesus' promise in John 8:32: "And you will know the truth and the truth will make you free"? This verse has both temporal and eternal ramifications. From the temporal perspective, Americans need to determine whether they want to continue on the road to socialism and communism or change directions and return to the form of government designed by America's Founding Fathers, which was based upon biblical principles. In order to do so, it will be necessary to get the true facts about our Founding Fathers and their beliefs and philosophies, as well as facts about other forms of government.

I must admit that I am not particularly interested in government and politics. In spite of this, over the past several years I have become aware of the fact that atheism and secular socialism have insidiously infiltrated our government, educational system, and media. Consequently, it is difficult to obtain valid sources of "truth." Certainly the only source of TRUTH is the Bible. Additionally, I have found several sources of valid information about the Founding Fathers and their views on governmental systems. In fact, I have quoted extensively from some of these in this chapter, notably books by David Barton, (*Original Intent*)[2], William J. Federer (*America's God and Country*) [3], and W. Cleon Skousen (*The Five Thousand Year Leap*)[107].

I have also found that the most reliable source of current news is the Fox News channel. I believe that they live up to their clam: presenting news in a manner that is fair, balanced, and unafraid. Furthermore, I have found that the facts presented by Glenn Beck in his television program on Fox News are accurate, informative, compelling, and motivating. I challenge you to do as I have done: read these books (starting with the

Bible), watch the Fox News channel (especially Glenn Beck to gain additional and current insight into the secular socialist activities) and objectively evaluate their coverage and commentaries and compare them to the other news sources. Then based upon objective data, you, I, and our fellow Americans can make informed decisions regarding the future of this country and determine appropriate courses of action to ensure that the will of the people, not the will of the politicians, be done.

Biblical Perspective and Response

With all of these facts about secular socialism in mind, here is a scary thought: President Barack Obama and the Democratic congressional majority are in place because God ordained them to be elected! The Bible is very clear that human governments are in place because God wanted them to be there:

> "Every person is to be in subjection to the governing authorities. For there is no authority except from God, and those which exist are established by God." Romans 13:1

Why would God want a government that does not honor Him to be in charge of the U.S.? Perhaps Thomas Jefferson's warning is coming true:

> '[C]an the liberties of a nation be thought secure when we have removed their only firm basis: a conviction in the minds of the people that these liberties are of the gift of God? That they are not to be violated but with His wrath? Indeed I tremble for my country when I reflect that God is just and that His justice cannot sleep forever." [62]

Do you remember earlier in this chapter that I quoted from Daniel, the Old Testament prophet, and his words to Belshazzar? Well, as promised, here is the rest of the story:

> "O king, the Most High God granted sovereignty, grandeur, glory and majesty to Nebuchadnezzar your father. Because of the grandeur which He bestowed on him, all the peoples, nations and men of every language feared and trembled before him; whomever he wished he killed and whomever he wished he spared alive; and whomever he wished he elevated and whomever he wished he humbled. But when his

heart was lifted up and his spirit became so proud that he behaved arrogantly, he was deposed from his royal throne and his glory was taken away from him....Yet you, his son, Belshazzar, have not humbled your heart, even though you knew all this, but you have exalted yourself against the Lord of heaven....But the God in whose hand are your life-breath and all your ways, you have not glorified....Now this is the inscription that was written out: 'MENE, MENE, TEKEL, UPHARSIN.' This is the interpretation of the message: 'MENE' —God has numbered your kingdom and put an end to it. 'TEKEL' —you have been weighed on the scales and found deficient. 'PERES' —your kingdom has been divided and given over to the Medes and Persians....That same night Belshazzar the Chaldean king was slain. So Darius the Mede received the kingdom at about the age of sixty-two." Daniel 5:17-31

It could be that as the Babylonian empire experienced and Jefferson warned, there is a limit to God's patience. Perhaps His patience with America's sinful ways has reached its limit and America's end is near.

The area of biblical prophecy is one that I find extremely fascinating and thought-provoking and it will be the subject of the following chapter. When I began studying biblical prophecies related to the end times I realized that the United States of America is not mentioned, either explicitly or implicitly, in the Bible. My first thought was how could it be that God would not mention the U.S., the most powerful nation on the earth, as playing a major role in the events leading to the end of the world as we know it? Was it an oversight on God's part or did He not know about the U.S. and its superpower status? "No" and "No" are the answers to both of those questions.

My next thought was that the rapture will occur and this will have devastating consequences on the U.S. and will cause it instantly to lose its superpower status. Certainly, this is a reasonable and possible biblical scenario. However, the more I have studied and considered the effects of atheism and secular socialism on the U.S., the more I think it is possible that God will simply allow America to rot from within as a result of its godless beliefs and unsustainable financial debt. In other words, the U.S. will be robbed of its position as the preeminent nation on earth because we have turned our back on God. This, too, is consistent with biblical principles and appears to be the course that America is currently taking. If the U.S. continues on this course, it will have tremendously adverse consequences for our country, as well as for biblical Christianity. However, if the American people repent and turn back to God, which would be a modern day miracle, He will forgive us.

> "and My people who are called by My name humble themselves and pray and seek My face and turn from their wicked ways, then I will hear from heaven, will forgive their sin and will heal their land." 2 Chronicles 7:14 (For both of his presidential inaugurations, President Ronald Regan had the Bible opened to this verse.)

> "Blessed is the nation whose God is the Lord...." Psalm 33:12

Summary and Recommendations Regarding

Competing Worldviews

The preceding three chapters presented information about Islam, atheism, and secular socialism. The information was presented so that you could examine and compare the teachings of these three religions/worldviews with biblical Christianity. So with this information in mind, what is the source of these religions/worldviews? There are only two choices: God or Satan. As documented in the preceding chapters, none of these three religions/worldviews are compatible with the Bible. Consequently, one must conclude that they are not from God, but from Satan. Whose side do you want to be on? Chapter 7 will focus on biblical prophecy and who ultimately will prevail: God or Satan. Hopefully, you will make the right choice.

Warning to Muslims, Atheists, and Secular Socialists

I strongly advise Muslims, atheists, and secular socialists to turn from your man-made religion and worldviews and turn to the true God, as described in the Bible. There are several reasons for my recommendation:
Firstly,

"Do not be deceived, God is not mocked; for whatever a man sows, this he will also reap. For the one who sows to his own flesh will from the flesh reap corruption, but the one who sows to the Spirit will from the Spirit reap eternal life." Galatians 6:6

Secondly,

"Not everyone who says to me, 'Lord, Lord,' will enter the kingdom of heaven, but he who does the will of My Father who is in heaven will enter. Many will say to Me on that day, 'Lord, Lord, did we not prophesy in Your name, and in Your name cast out demons, and in Your name perform many miracles.' And then I will declare to them, 'I never knew you, DEPART FROM ME, YOU WHO PRACTICE LAWLESSNESS.'" Matthew 7:21-22.

Finally, there will come a time when you (and everyone else) will acknowledge Jesus as Lord.

"For this reason also, God highly exalted Him, and bestowed on Him the name which is above every name, so that at the name of Jesus EVERY KNEE WILL BOW, of those who are in heaven and on earth and under earth, and that every tongue will confess that Jesus Christ is Lord, to the glory of God the Father." Philippians 2:8-10

This particular acknowledgment, however, will come at the Great White Throne Judgment (see Chapter 7 for details). If you cannot also add that you have accepted Jesus as your personal Savior, according to the Bible, you will spend eternity in hell.

Biblical Christianity's Perspective

For the Christian, we may take comfort in knowing that God is in control and He is sovereign over the affairs of this world. [108]

"Your kingdom is an everlasting kingdom, and Your dominion endures throughout all generations." Psalm 145:13

God has warned us that men (and governments) will turn from Him until the return of Jesus. [108]

> "But the Spirit explicitly says that in later times some will fall away from the faith, paying attention to deceitful spirits and doctrines of demons." 1 Timothy 4:1

> "But realize this, that in the last days difficult times will come. For men will be lovers of self, lovers of money, boastful, arrogant, revilers, disobedient to parents, ungrateful, unholy, unloving, irreconcilable, malicious gossips, without self-control, brutal, haters of good, treacherous, reckless, conceited, lovers of pleasure rather than lovers of God, holding to a form of godliness, although they have denied its power; Avoid such men as these." 2 Timothy 3:1-5

It is important for us to remember that our citizenship is in heaven and we are just passing through this life on earth. [109]

> "For our citizenship is in heaven, from which also we eagerly wait for a Savior, the Lord Jesus Christ." Philippians 3:20

So with these perspectives in mind, what should biblical Christians do while we are on this earth? This is the topic that will be addressed in detail in Chapter 8, but for now consider the following:
Trust in the Lord:

> "Trust in the LORD with all your heart and do not lean on your own understanding. In all your ways acknowledge Him and He will make your paths straight." Proverbs 3:5-6

> "But seek first His kingdom and His righteousness, and all these things will be added to you." Matthew 6:33

Ensure that you are following biblical principles:

"See to it that no one takes you captive through philosophy and empty deception, according to the tradition of men, according to the elementary principles of the world, rather than according to Christ." Colossians 2:8

"Beloved, do not believe every spirit, but test the spirits to see whether they are from God, because many false prophets have gone out into the world. By this you know the Spirit of God: every spirit that confesses that Jesus Christ has come in the flesh is from God." 1 John 4:1

Walk worthy of your high calling:

"Therefore I, the prisoner of the Lord, implore you to walk in a manner worthy of the calling with which you have been called, with all humility and gentleness, with patience, showing tolerance for one another in love, being diligent to preserve the unity of the Spirit in the bond of peace." Ephesians 4:1-3

Pray for our leaders and all men for their salvation:

"First of all, then, I urge that entreaties and prayers, petitions and thanksgivings, be made on behalf of all men, for kings and all who are in authority, so that we may lead a tranquil and quiet life in all godliness and dignity. This is good and acceptable in the sight of God our Savior, who desires all men to be saved and to come to the knowledge of the truth. For there is one God, and one mediator also between God and men, the man Christ Jesus, who gave Himself as a ransom for all...." 1 Timothy 2:1-6

Pray for our country:

> "and My people who are called by My name humble themselves and pray and seek My face and turn from their wicked ways, then I will hear from heaven, will forgive their sin and will heal their land." 2 Chronicles 7:14

Share the reason for your hope and joy:

> "But even if you should suffer for the sake of righteousness, you are blessed. AND DO NOT FEAR THEIR INTIMIDATION, AND DO NOT BE TROUBLED, but sanctify Christ as Lord in your hearts, always being ready to make a defense to everyone who asks you to give an account for the hope that is in you, yet with gentleness and reverence." 1 Peter 3:14-15

My Conviction

After reading the chapters on Islam, atheism, and social secularism, you are probably questioning my sanity. Why would anyone say these things, which will certainly expose, offend, and probably anger people who are Muslims, atheists, and secular socialists? I realize that there is a strong probability that I will be persecuted and maybe even killed because of the words I have written about these three "religions" that stand against biblical Christianity. Why would I do this? There are three primary reasons:

1. You and your eternal destiny are worth any persecution that I may encounter and you deserve to know the truth.

    > "and you will know the truth, and the truth will make you free." John 8:32

2. My desire is to please God and not men.

    > "Whatever you do, do your work heartily, as for the Lord rather than for men, knowing that from the Lord you will

receive the reward of the inheritance. It is the Lord Christ whom you serve. Colossians 3:23-24

3. In the event that I am killed because of my belief in Jesus and willingness to speak out for Him, then I will be honored to join the more than 70,000,000 people who have died as martyrs to seal their faith in Jesus. [110] I believe there is considerable wisdom in the words of missionary Jim Elliott, who said prior to his martyrdom, "He is no fool who gives up what he cannot keep to gain what he cannot lose." [111]

"This is My commandment, that you love one another, just as I have loved you. Greater love has no one than this, that one lay down his life for his friends." John 15:12-13

References:

1. United States Government. "Declaration of Independence." http://www.archives.gov/exhibits/charters/declaration_transcript.html.
2. Barton, David. *Original Intent: The Courts, the Constitution, & Religion.* Aledo, TX: Wallbuilders, 3rd Printing, 2010.
3. Federer, William J. *America's God and Country: Encyclopedia of Quotations.* Coppell, TX: FAME Publishers, 1994/
4. _____. p. 113.
5. Barton, David. *Original Intent.* p. 82.
6. Federer, William J. *America's God and Country.* p. 62.
7. Barton, David. *Original Intent.* p. 83.
8. Federer, William J. *America's God and Country.* p. 699.
9. Barton, David. *Original Intent.* p. 84.
10. _____. p. 85.
11. _____. p. 87.
12. _____. p. 88.
13. Federer, William J. *America's God and Country.* p. 634.
14. _____. p. 91.
15. Federer, William J. *America's God and Country.* pp. 21- 22.
16. Barton, David. *Original Intent.* p. 96.
17. Federer, William J. *America's God and Country.* p. 15.
18. _____. p. 16.
19. _____. pp. 17-18.
20. _____. p. 239.
21. _____. pp. 248-249.

22. _____. p. 322.
23. _____. pp. 322-323.
24. _____. p. 326.
25. Gill, Kathy. "About.com: US Politics. Oaths of Office For Federal Officials." http://uspolitics.about.com/od/usgovernment/a/oaths_of_office.htm.
26. Barton, David. *Original Intent*. p. 233.
27. _____. pp. 233-234.
28. _____. p. 239.
29. _____. p. 27.
30. Federer, William J. *America's God and Country*. p. 331.
31. _____. p. 330.
32. Barton, David. *Original Intent*. pp. 28-29.
33. U.S. Supreme Court Media: OYEZ. *Everson v. Board of Education*. http://www.oyez.org/cases/1940-1949/1946/1946_52.
34. Wikipedia. *Everson v. Board of Education*. http://en.wikipedia.org/wiki/Everson_v._Board_of_Education.
35. Barton, David. *Original Intent*. p. 14.
36. _____. p. 22.
37. Barton, David. *Documents of Freedom: The Declaration of Independence, The Constitution of the United States, George Washington's 'Farewell Address'*. Aledo, TX: Wallbuilders, 3rd Edition, 1st Printing, 2007, p. 28.
38. Barton, David. *Original Intent*. p. 23.
39. _____. pp. 51-52.
40. Skousen, W. Cleon. *Five Thousand Year Leap: 28 Great ideas That Changed the World*. Franklin, TN: American Documents Publishing, Inc., 2009, p. 61.
41. Barton, David. *Original Intent*. p. 161.
42. _____. p. 47.
43. _____. p. 158.
44. Federer, William J. *America's God and Country*. p. 455.
45. Barton, David. *Original Intent*. p. 159.
46. _____. p. 161.
47. U.S. Supreme Court Media: OYEZ. *Engel v. Vitale*. http://www.oyez.org/cases/1960-1969/1961/1961_468.
48. Barton, David. *Original Intent*. p. 162.
49. _____. p. 164.
50. _____. p. 165.
51. Federer, William J. *America's God and Country*. p. 4.
52. _____. p. 163.
53. Wikipedia. "Madalyn Murray O'Hair." http://en.wikipedia.org/wiki/Madalyn_Murray_O'Hair.
54. Federer, William J. *America's God and Country*. p. 543.
55. Barton, David. *Original Intent*. p. 168.
56. _____. p. 181.
57. _____. p. 178.

58. U.S. Supreme Court Media: OYEZ. *Edwards v. Aguillard*. http://www.oyez. org/cases/1980-1989/1986/1986_85_1513.

59. U.S. Supreme Court Media: OYEZ. *Roe v. Wade*. http://www.oyez.org/ cases/1970-1979/1971/1971_70_18.

60. Wikipedia. *Roe v. Wade*. http://en.wikipedia.org/wiki/Roe_v._Wade.

61. Barton, David. *The Bible, Voters, and the 2008 Election*. Aledo, TX: Wallbuilders, 1st Edition, 1st Printing, 2008, p. 13.

62. _____. pp. 14-15.

63. Barton, David. *Original Intent*. pp. 248-252.

64. Skousen, W. Cleon. *Five Thousand Year Leap*. p. 252.

65. Wilkinson, Bruce and Kenneth Boa. *Talk Thru the Bible*. Nashville, TN: Thomas Nelson Publishers, 1983, p. 186.

66. U.S. National Debt Clock: Real Time. "US Debt Clock.org." http://www. usdebtclock.org/.

67. The Phrase Finder. "Houston, we have a problem." http://www.phrases.org. uk/meanings/houston-we-have-a-problem.html.

68. Merriam-Webster, I. *Merriam-Webster's Collegiate Dictionary*. Springfield, Mass., U.S.A.: Merriam-Webster, 1996.

69. O'Reilly, Bill. *Culture Warrior*. New York, NY: Broadway Books, 2006.

70. _____. pp. 80-81.

71. _____. pp. 69-70.

72. _____. p. 203.

73. Gingrich, Newt. *To Save America: Stopping Obama's Secular-Socialist Machine*. Washington, D.C.: Regnery Publishing, Inc. p. 7.

74. _____. p. 2.

75. O'Reilly, Bill. *Culture Warrior*. pp. 40-41.

76. Gingrich, Newt. *To Save America*. p. 52.

77. Eisen, Norm. White House Visitor Records Online. "More than 450,000 White House Visitor Records Online." June 25, 2010, http://www.whitehouse.gov/ blog/2010/06/25/more-450000-white-house-visitor-records-online.

78. Brower, Kate Anderson. "Obama Signs Law Aimed at Cutting Billions in Improper Government Payments." Bloomberg. July 22, 2010, http://www. bloomberg.com/news/print/2010-07-22/obama-signs-law-aimed-at-cut- ting-billions-in-improper-government-payments.html.

79. Fox News.com. "Pelosi's New District Office Costs $18,736 a Month." http:// www.foxnews.com/politics/2010/06/14/pelosis-new-district-office-report- edly-costs-month/, June 14, 2010.

80. Gingrich, Newt. *To Save America*. pp. 46-48.

81. Rules for Radicals website. http://www.crossroad.to/Quotes/communism/ alinsky.htm.

82. Gingrich, Newt. *To Save America*. p. 49.

83. Breitbart TV website. "The C-SPAN Lie? See Eight Clips of Obama Promising Televised Healthcare Negotiations." http://www.breitbart.tv/the-c-span-lie- did-obama-really-promise-televised-healthcare-negotiations/.

84. The Heritage Foundation: The Foundry website. "Video of the Week: "We have to pass the bill so you can find out what is in it." http://blog.heritage. org/2010/03/10/video-of-the-week-we-have-to-pass-the-bill-so-you-can-find-out-what-is-in-it/, March 10, 2010.

85. Ross, Brian and Rehab El-Buri. "Obama's Pastor, Rev. Jeremiah Wright, Has a History of What Even Obama's Campaign Aides Say is 'Inflammatory Rhetoric'. ABC News Website, http://abcnews.go.com/Blotter/DemocraticDebate/ story?id=4443788&page=1, March 13, 2008.

86. Barton, David. *The Bible, Voters, and the 2008 Election*. p. 3.

87. Blue Collar Philosophy Website. "Jim Wallis Says The Gospel is About The Redistribution of Wealth (Video)." http://www.bluecollarphilosophy. com/2010/07/jim-wallis-says-gospel-is-about.html, July 21, 2010.

88. Skousen, W. Cleon. *Five Thousand Year Leap*. p. 91.

89. O'Reilly, Bill. *Culture Warrior*. p. 204.

90. Olasky, Marvin. "More Than Money." *World Magazine*, Asheville, NC, Vol. 25, No. 13, July 3, 2010, pp. 37-42.

91. Thierer, Adam. "Why The Fairness Doctrine Is Anything But Fair. The Heritage Foundation website: http://www.heritage.org/Research/Reports/1993/10/ EM368-Why-The-Fairness-Doctrine-Is-Anything-But-Fair.

92. Federal Communications website: http://www.fcc.gov/aboutus.html

93. Gattuso, James. "Back to Muzak? Congress and the Un-Fairness Doctrine." The Heritage Foundation website: http://www.heritage.org/Research/ Reports/2007/05/Back-to-Muzak-Congress-and-the-Un-Fairness-Doctrine.

94. State of Arizona. "Senate Bill 1070". State of Arizona website: http://www. azleg.gov/legtext/49leg/2r/bills/sb1070s.pdf.

95. Wikipedia. "Arizona SB 1070." http://en.wikipedia.org/wiki/Support_ Our_Law_Enforcement_and_Safe_Neighborhoods_Act#Department_of_ Justice_lawsuit.

96. Wikipedia. "Sanctuary Cities." http://en.wikipedia.org/wiki/Sanctuary_city.

97. The Voice website. "List of US Sanctuary Cities" http://thevoice. name/?p=3926

98. John McArthur and the Leadership Team at Grace Community Church. *Right Thinking in a World Gone Wrong: A Biblical Response to Today's Most Controversial Issues*. Eugene, OR: Harvest House Publishers, 2009, p. 170.

99. Barton, David. *Original Intent*. p. 267.

100. Skousen, W. Cleon. *Five Thousand Year Leap*. p. 27.

101. _____. p. 88.

102. Guttmacher Institute. "Facts on Induced Abortion in the United States." May 2010, http://www.guttmacher.org/pubs/fb_induced_abortion.html.

103. Palestine Facts Website. "Israel's Independence – US Recognizes Israel" http://www.palestinefacts.org/pf_independence_recognition_us.php.

104. Yahoo News. "Majority of Americans lack faith in Obama: poll" http://news. yahoo.com/s/nm/us_obama_poll, July 13, 2010.

105. Zacharias, Ravi. *Can Man Live Without God?* Nashville, TN: W. Publishing Group, a Division of Thomas Nelson, Inc., 1994, p. 33.

106. Graham, Billy. *Storm Warning*. Nashville, TN: Thomas Nelson, 2010.

107. Skousen, W. Cleon. *Five Thousand Year Leap: 28 Great ideas that Changed the World*. Franklin, TN: American Documents Publishing, Inc., 2009.

108. John McArthur, et al., *Right Thinking in a World Gone Wrong*. P.124.

109. _____. p. 174.

110. Graham, Billy. *Storm Warning*. Nashville, TN: Thomas Nelson, 2010, p. 157.

111. Elliot, Jim, as quoted in Graham, Billy. *Storm Warning*. Nashville, TN: Thomas Nelson, 2010, p. 157.

PART 3

THE FUTURE

So, how does the story end? Actually, this story does not have an ending—it continues forever and it certainly gives new meaning to the phrase "and they lived happily ever after!"

Early in my sales career, one of my trainers and mentors asked me, "What is the favorite radio station of all prospects and buyers?"

Since I like country music, I immediately thought of the call letters of my favorite country radio station, but I knew that is not what he had in mind, so I replied, "I don't know. What is it?"

He replied, "It is WIIIFM. Which stands for '*What Is In It For Me*'."

I think he was right. It is human nature to want to know how things will benefit us. I think the same is true of you and your decision to place your faith in the gospel. *What is in it for me*?

I am glad you asked, because the decision to place your faith in the gospel of Jesus Christ pays dividends in this life, at the Bema Judgment of Jesus, in the Millennial Kingdom, and forever in the Eternal State. In fact, these benefits are guaranteed. Do you have any other investments that promise and deliver these kinds of return on your investment? When you understand and appreciate the return on your investment and realize that your friends and neighbors can also take advantage of this richly-rewarding opportunity, you will want to share the Good News with them.

These are the topics that will be discussed in the following three chapters. Chapter 7 provides information on God's plan for the future, as indicated in yet-to-be fulfilled biblical prophecies, and how these benefit you. Chapter 8 encourages you to make a personal decision to place your faith in the gospel and provides an overview of how God will bless you for that decision. Chapter 9 will help you understand how to effectively share your faith and the gospel with others.

Sooner or later, you will have questions about the eternal destiny of unborn children who are aborted or miscarried, children who die before they can understand the gospel, and people who have never heard of Jesus or the gospel. The Epilogue will provide answers to these questions.

Chapter 7

Biblical Prophecy: What Is Coming?

You may be wondering why I would include a chapter on biblical prophecy in this book. I'll answer this question by providing an answer from two different perspectives: first a worldly perspective and then a biblical perspective. From the worldly perspective, would you like to win the lottery? If you knew in advance the numbers that would be selected in the lottery, you could utilize this knowledge to select the winning numbers and instantly become a multi-millionaire! Most people would be excited about winning millions of dollars. Realistically, however, if you have placed your faith in Jesus as your Savior, you have already won something far more valuable than the lottery. If you knew what God has planned for the future, you could take advantage of this information and live your life accordingly to ensure that you fully benefit, now and in the future, from this special prophetic knowledge. So, let's see what the Bible says is coming in the future.

Purpose of Prophecy

More than 25% of the Bible was prophetic at the time it was written. [1] In fact, Walvoord has identified more than 1,000 prophecies in the Bible, of which approximately half have been fulfilled already and we have good reason to believe that the rest will be fulfilled in the future (many of which we will witness). [1,2] With God's emphasis on prophecy, it is reasonable to conclude that God had some good and specific reasons for including prophecy in the Bible.

As Walvoord and Ryrie, two very respected academic theologians who devoted the majority of their lives studying and teaching the Bible, point out, God's purposes of prophecy were to (1) demonstrate His knowledge of and control of the future, (2) keep us from false doctrines and false hope, (3) warn people of the consequences of their sin, (4) call us to repent and to return to Him, and (5) provide a source of joy in times of tribulation and affliction. [3, 4] It is in this spirit that I present the information in this chapter.

There are more than 500 prophecies yet to be fulfilled. The most significant of these are summarized below:

Table 7-1. "Major Events of Unfulfilled Prophecy"

#	Prophecy	Reference
1	Rapture of the church*	1 Cor. 15:51-58; 1 Thess. 4:13-18
2	Revival of the Roman Empire; 10-nation confederacy formed	Dan. 7:7, 24; Rev. 13:1; 17:3, 12-13
Tribulation Begins*		
3	Rise of the Antichrist: the Middle East dictator	Dan. 7:8; Rev. 13:1-8
4	The seven-year peace treaty with Israel: consummated seven years before the second coming of Christ	Dan. 9:27; Rev. 19:11-16
5	Establishment of a world church	Rev. 17:1-15
6	Russia springs a surprise attack on Israel four years before the second coming of Christ	Ezek. 38-39
7	Peace treaty with Israel broken after three-and-a-half years: beginning of world government, world economic system, world atheistic religion, final three-and-a-half years before second coming of Christ	Dan. 7:23; Rev. 13:5-8, 15-17; 17:16-17
8	Many Christians and Jews martyred who refuse to worship world dictator	Rev. 7:9-17; 13:15
9	Catastrophic divine judgments represented by seals, trumpets, and bowls poured out on the earth	Rev. 6-18

10	World war breaks out focusing on the Middle East: Battle of Armageddon	Dan. 11:40-45; Rev. 9:13-21; 16:12-16
11	Babylon destroyed	Rev. 18
Tribulation Ends		
12	Second coming of Christ*	Matt. 24:27-31; Rev. 19:11-21
13	Judgment of wicked Jews and Gentiles	Ezek. 20:33-38; Matt. 25:31-46; Jude 14-15; Rev. 19:15-21;20:1-4
14	Satan bound for 1,000 years	Rev. 20:1-3
15	Resurrection of Tribulation saints and Old Testament saints	Dan. 12:2; Rev. 20:4
16	Millennial kingdom begins*	Rev. 20:5-6
17	Final rebellion at the end of the millennium	Rev. 20:7-10
18	Resurrection and final judgment of the wicked: Great White Throne judgment	Rev. 20:11-15
19	Eternity begins: new heaven, new earth, New Jerusalem*	Rev. 21:1-2

* = Additional information on these prophecies will be provided later in this chapter.

Table 7-2. "Predicted Order of Prophetic Events Related to Israel" [6]

Order	Event
1.	The holocaust and suffering of Jews in Germany in World War II lead to worldwide sympathy for a homeland for the Jews.
2.	United Nations recognizes Israel as a nation and allows 5,000 square miles of territory, excluding ancient Jerusalem in 1948.
3.	Israel, though immediately attacked by those nations surrounding her, achieves increases in territory in subsequent wars.
4.	Though Russia at the beginning was sympathetic to Israel, the United States becomes her principal benefactor and supplier of military aid and money.

5.	Israel makes amazing strides forward in reestablishing her land, its agriculture, industries, and political power.
6.	In the series of military tests, Israel establishes that she has a superior army to that of surrounding nations.
7.	Arab power opposing Israel is sufficient to keep Israel from having peaceful coexistence with other nations in the Middle East.
8.	Israel continues in the state of confusion and conflict until the church is raptured.
9.	With the formation of the 10-nation confederacy by the Gentile ruler in the Middle East, Israel is forced to accept a seven-year peace settlement.
10.	The world and the Jewish people celebrate what appears to be a permanent peace settlement in the Middle East.
11.	Israel prospers and many return to Israel after the peace is settled.
12.	Toward the close of the three-and-a-half years of peace, Russia accompanied by several other nations attempts to invade Israel but is destroyed by a series of judgments from God.
13.	After three-and-a-half years of peace, the covenant is broken and the Middle East ruler becomes a world dictator and a principal persecutor of Israel.
14.	The world dictator desecrates the temple of Israel and sets up an idol of himself to be worshiped.
15.	Worldwide persecution of the Jews begins, and in the land two out of three perish.
16.	A Jewish remnant emerges who puts their trust in Christ.
17.	Though the world ruler massacres both Jews and Gentiles who fail to worship him as God, some survive from both Jews and Gentiles and are rescued by Christ.
18.	The second coming of Christ rescues persecuted Jews and Gentiles and brings judgment upon all wickedness in the world and unbelievers.

19.	The promised kingdom on earth with Jesus as Israel's Messiah and David as her regent prince begins with godly Israel being regathered from all over the world to inhabit her Promised Land.
20.	For 1,000 years Israel experiences unusual blessing as the object of Christ's favor.
21.	With the end of the millennial kingdom and the destruction of the present earth, godly Israel has its place in the eternal state and the new heaven and the new earth.
22.	Those among Israel who are saved are placed in the New Jerusalem in the new earth.

In this chapter the following major categories of biblical prophecy will be reviewed: Rapture, Tribulation, Christ's Second Coming, Millennial Kingdom, and the Eternal State. My intent is to provide a sufficient amount of information about these categories so that you will have a good understanding of these prophecies. With this information, then you can make informed decisions about how to live your life in light of these coming events. Hopefully, after reading this information, you will be motivated to gain additional knowledge about biblical prophecy and if so, then I recommend the following books:

1. Jeremiah, David. *What In The World Is Going On?* This is an excellent book to begin your quest for additional knowledge about biblical prophecy. I think you will find it to be very readable and very informative. [7]
2. Walvoord, John F. *Major Bible Prophecies: 37 Crucial Prophecies That Affect You Today.* As indicated in the title, Walvoord selects and explains 37 prophecies that have particular relevance to each of us. [8]
3. Walvoord, John F. *The Prophecy Knowledge Handbook.* Dr. Walvoord began this comprehensive book (809 pages) with principles to be used in biblical and prophetic interpretation, then methodically identified and discussed more than 1,000 prophecies in the Bible, from Genesis through Revelation. [9]
4. Pentecost, J. Dwight. *Things To Come: A Study in Biblical Eschatology.* Dr. Pentecost provides not only his own insight on biblical prophecy, but also quotes other scholars extensively in this text of 633 pages. [10]

The Revelation of Jesus to John

As we progress through this chapter and as you study more about Bible prophecy, you will quickly see that the last book in the Bible, *"The Revelation to John,"* or as it is commonly referred to, *"Revelation,"* is an extremely important source of information about future prophetic events. Revelation was written by the apostle John probably around AD 95 to 96 and records Jesus' revelation of future events to John. [11] Since this book provides the most detailed information about future events it may be helpful to provide some information about this book and its prophecies.

There is only one book in the Bible that directly promises a blessing to those who read, hear, and heed its words: the book of Revelation.

"Blessed is he who reads and those who hear the words of the prophecy, and heed the things which are written in it; for the time is near." Revelation 1:3

Interestingly, the book of Revelation is one of the least read and least understood books in the entire Bible, or certainly in the New Testament. There are several reasons for this: there is extensive use of symbolism in the book, making it difficult to understand; there have been many conflicting interpretations proposed to explain its contents; and the chronological flow of the prophecy is interrupted by several parenthetical sections. These tend to confuse and discourage many readers.

Regarding the extensive use of symbolism in Revelation, try to imagine how you would respond if Jesus appeared to you in His glorified form, told you about things which would happen 2,000 years in the future, and then told you to write about these things! How would you write about the things that you had never seen or even imagined and some of which you did not clearly understand?

That is exactly what happened to the apostle John. When one considers that the apostle John, the author of Revelation, was trying to describe things which Jesus told him would occur several thousand years in the future, things which he had never seen or even imagined before, it is not surprising to see the extensive use of symbolism that is found in this book. In most cases, however, the meaning of the symbolism is explained in the context of the verse or in other passages in the Bible. Fortunately, many good commentaries have been written on this book, which provide explanations of the symbolism and explain these prophecies of Jesus. One of the commentaries that I have found to be particularly helpful is by John F. Walvoord, *The Revelation of Jesus Christ*. [12] When you begin

306

reading and studying Revelation, I highly recommend that you have his commentary close by and consult it frequently!

If you decide to receive the blessings promised by reading and heeding the words of Revelation, perhaps a few additional comments will be helpful. Generally speaking, Revelation is written in a chronological order. In fact, the divine outline for this book is given in 1:19 and consists of the past (chapter 1), the present (chapters 2 and 3), and the future (chapters 4-22). Furthermore, the "Seal Judgments" (chapter 6), the "Trumpet Judgments" (chapters 8 and 9), and the "Bowl Judgments" (chapter 16) provide the chronological framework for the seven-year tribulation period. Chapter 20 describes the Millennial Kingdom and Chapters 21 and 22 describe the Eternal State.

The chronological flow is interrupted by several parenthetical sections that provide insight into various events occurring on earth and heaven during and after the tribulation period. I have found that studying the tribulation period without putting these parenthetical sections in proper chronological order is somewhat like looking at individual pieces of a puzzle and trying to get some idea of the picture. However, when all of the pieces of the puzzle are arranged in their proper place, it is much easier to see and appreciate the big picture. Placing these events in proper chronological sequence is challenging, but will be very rewarding.

With these things in mind, perhaps the general outline of Revelation below and the probable (in my opinion) chronological order of events of the seven-year tribulation shown in Table 7-3 will facilitate your future study of the future, as told in Revelation.

I. Introduction (1:1-3)
II. "The things which you have seen" (1:4-20)
III. "The things which are" (2:1-3:22)
IV. "The things which shall take place after these things" (4:1-22:21)
 A. Prologue (The Pre-Tribulation Period) (4:1-5:14)
 B. The Tribulation Period (6-18)
  1. The First 3 1/2 years
  2. The Last 3 1/2 years
 C. The Second Coming of Christ (19)
 D. The Millennium (20:1-15)
 E. The Eternal State (21:1-22:21)

Table 7-3. Probable Chronological Order of the Major Events of the Tribulation.

#	Event	Chapter:Verse
First 3 1/2 Years of the Tribulation		
1	1st Seal: The Antichrist	6:1-2
2	Emergence of the Beast out of the Sea	13:1-2
3	The Two Witnesses Begin Their Ministry	11:1-6
4	2nd Seal: War	6:3-4
5	Destruction of Ecclesiastical Babylon	17:1-18
6	3rd Seal: Famine	6:5-6
7	4th Seal: Death	6:7-8
8	5th Seal: Martyred Souls in Heaven	6:9-11
9	6th Seal: The Day of Divine Wrath	6:12-17
10	Sealing of 144,000	7:1-8
11	7th Seal: The Beginning of the Trumpets	8:1-6
12	1st Trumpet: Destruction of 1/3 of the Vegetation	8:7
13	2nd Trumpet: Destruction of 1/3 of the Sea Life	8:8-9
14	3rd Trumpet: Destruction of 1/3 of the Fresh Water	8:10-11
15	4th Trumpet: Destruction of 1/3 of the Light Sources	8:12-13
16	Satan Cast out of Heaven by Michael, the Archangel	12:7-9
17	Announcement of the Coming Day of Satan's Wrath	12:10-12
The Last 3 1/2 Years of the Tribulation		
18	Desecration of the Temple by the Antichrist	13:5-6
19	Worldwide Dominion of the Antichrist	13:3-7
20	The False Prophet and Worship of the Antichrist	13:11-18
21	Persecution of Israel	13:12-13
22	Divine Protection of Israel	13:14-16
23	Persecution of the Saints	13:7

24	5th Trumpet: Key to Abyss Given to Satan, Demonic Torment	9:1-11
25	Death and Resurrection of the Two Witnesses	11:7-12
26	The Angel Preaches the Gospel to all People Groups	14:6-7
27	6th Trumpet: Army of 200,000,000	9:13-21
28	The Mighty Angel With the Little Book	10:1-11
29	Prophecy of the Coming Fall of Political Babylon	14:8
30	7th Trumpet: Christ's Reign Foreseen	11:15-19
31	1st Bowl: Malignant Sores on Worshipers of Antichrist	16:2
32	2nd Bowl: Sea Became Like Blood and All Sea Life Died	16:3
33	3rd Bowl: Rivers and Springs Became Blood	16:4-4
34	4th Bowl: Sun Scorched Men With Fierce Heat	16:8-9
35	5th Bowl: Kingdom of the Antichrist Was Darkened	16:10-11
36	The Fall of Political Babylon	18:1-19
37	6th Bowl: Euphrates River Dried Up	16:12
38	Gathering of the Armies of the World at Armageddon	16:13-16
39	7th Bowl: Great Earthquake and Hail ("It Is Done")	16:17-21
40	Second Coming of Christ	19:11-16
41	Beast and False Prophet Are Thrown Into the Lake of Fire	19:20
42	Destruction of the Armies of the World at Armageddon	19:21
43	Satan Bound for 1,000 Years	20:1-3
44	The Millennial Kingdom Begins	20:4

In fairness to you, there is disagreement among Bible-believing Christians about how and when some of the events listed above and discussed below will take place. Nevertheless, most will agree with the majority of the chronology depicted above.

My perspective on biblical prophecy is that it can best be understood from a normal (i.e., literal) interpretation and that the prophecies will be literally fulfilled. This was true for the more than 500 prophecies which have already been fulfilled and should be true for the future prophecies. My "interpretative framework" regarding future prophecies can best be defined as "dispensational," "pretribulational," and "premillennial." [13] Definitions of these technical terms are:

Dispensational: "A dispensation is a distinguishable economy in the outworking of God's purpose." [14] In other words, a dispensational view is that God's plan for mankind has different administrations, programs, or economies for different people, at different times. (e.g., The program for Israel is different from the program for the church (believers in Jesus). Although dispensationalists believe that there are several different programs presented throughout the Bible, they emphasize that the underlying purpose of all of these is to bring glory to God. [15]

Pretribulational: the rapture of believers will occur before the Tribulation; [16] (The terms "rapture" and "Tribulation" will be defined in the respective sections below).

Premillennial: Jesus' literal second coming will occur before the Millennial Kingdom, which is the literal 1,000-year reign of Jesus on the earth. [17]

Ryrie summarizes this interpretative framework as:

"Dispensationalism is the belief "that the promises made to Abraham and David are unconditional and have had or will have a literal fulfillment. In no sense have these promises made to Israel been abrogated or fulfilled by the Church, which is a distinct body in this age having promises and a destiny different from Israel's. At the close of this age, premillennialists believe that Christ will return for His Church, meeting her in the air (this is not the Second Coming of Christ), which event, called the rapture or translation, will usher in a seven-year period of tribulation on the earth. After this, the Lord will return to the earth (this is the Second Coming of Christ) to establish His kingdom on the earth for a thousand years, during which time the promise to Israel will be fulfilled." [18]

Figure 7-1 below illustrates the major events to be fulfilled in the future and places them in order, according to the dispensational, pretribulational, premillennial perspective. [19]

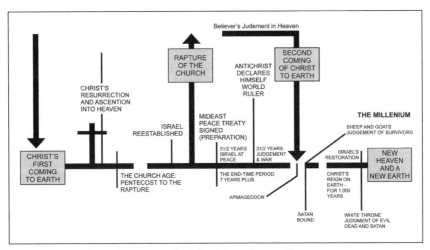

Figure 7-1. Order of Events of Biblical Prophecy. [19]

Figure 7-1 shows the major events of biblical prophecy, beginning almost 2,000 years ago with Jesus' first coming to earth and ends with the creation of the new heaven and earth at the beginning of the Eternal State. Moving from left to right along the time line, the crucifixion of Jesus is signified by the cross, which is followed by His resurrection and ascension to heaven. We are currently living in the Church Age, which began with the Holy Spirit indwelling those who placed their faith in Jesus following His ascension. The Church Age, which includes the nation of Israel being established in 1948, will end with the Rapture, at which time Jesus will remove all Christians from the earth and take them to heaven. Soon after the Rapture, a seven-year period of time will begin that is called the tribulation.

The tribulation period will be the most turbulent and violent time during the history of the world. During the tribulation, the world will be controlled by the Antichrist, a person totally dedicated to implementing Satan's plan for the world. In addition, during this time, God will be pouring His wrath upon the earth and its inhabitants as a consequence of their sins. Fortunately, God's mercy will stop the Antichrist's plans and the destruction of the earth at the battle of Armageddon with the second coming of Jesus. When Jesus returns to the earth, Satan will be captured and bound for 1,000 years. Shortly, after Jesus' second coming, He establishes the Millennial Kingdom on earth, which He rules. The Great White Throne Judgment is the judgment of Satan, demons, and the unbelieving people of all times. Then God creates the new heaven and new earth, which will be inhabited by all the people and angels who have placed their faith in God throughout all of the history of the world.

Regarding the order of events of biblical prophecy, I realize that some of my brothers and sisters in Christ may disagree with some of the timing of events as shown in Table 7-3 and Figure 7-1 above. Since our interpretation of the occurrence or the timing of these events does not affect the truth of the gospel, I recommend that we respect one another's views and agree that it is okay to disagree on the non-essentials of our faith.

Rapture
What is it?

The rapture refers to an event described by the apostle Paul in First Thessalonians 4:13-18 and First Corinthians 15:50-52.

> "But we do not want you to be uninformed, brethren, about those who are <u>asleep</u> [dead], so that you will not grieve as do the rest who have no hope. For if we believe that Jesus died and rose again, even so God will bring with Him those who have fallen <u>asleep</u> in Jesus. For this we say to you by the word of the Lord, that we who are alive and remain until the coming of the Lord, will not precede those who have fallen <u>asleep</u>. For the Lord Himself will descend from heaven with a shout, with the voice of the archangel and with the trumpet of God, and the dead in Christ will rise first. <u>Then we who are alive and remain will be **caught up** together with them in the clouds to meet the Lord in the air</u>, and so we shall always be with the Lord. Therefore comfort one another with these words." 1 Thessalonians 4:13-18. (emphasis added by me)

> "Now I say this, brethren, that flesh and blood cannot inherit the Kingdom of God; nor does the perishable inherit the imperishable. Behold, I tell you a mystery; we will not all <u>sleep</u> [die]; but <u>we will all **be changed**, in a moment, in the twinkling of an eye</u>, at the last trumpet; for the trumpet will

sound and the dead will be raised imperishable, and we will be changed." 1 Corinthians 15:50-52 (emphasis added by me)

If you read these two verses closely, you noticed that the word *rapture* does not appear in either of these verses. In fact, the word is not found anywhere in the Bible. Our word *rapture* comes from the Greek word translated in First Thessalonians 4:17 as "caught up." This word also communicates "to snatch out or away speedily." In other words, Jesus will come to the earth and call all who believe in Him, both those believers who have died and those who are alive, and they will join Him in heaven. This will happen instantaneously in a specific order:

(1) The bodies of those believers who have already died will be resurrected, transformed into a new resurrection body, and be reunited with their spirits (2 Cor. 5:8 and Phil. 1:20-24 teach that the believer's spirit goes to be with the Lord at the instant of physical death). (1 John 3:1-3; Rom. 8:29; Phil. 3:20-21)]
(2) The resurrected believers will be joined by those believers who are alive at the time of this event, and
(3) The resurrected believers and the raptured believers will join Jesus. [20, 21]

WOW! What a wonderful promise!

One other point deserves your consideration. Did you notice that the apostle Paul used the words "asleep" and "sleep" to describe those believers who had died? What a wonderful way to put our physical death in perspective—death is not the end, just a temporary resting state from which we will awake in the future! With these thoughts in mind, now you can understand why Paul finished his message to the Thessalonians quoted above with the words, "Therefore comfort one another with these words." These can provide a great source of comfort to each of us.

You may wonder if there are any other examples in the Bible of people being raptured. Yes, Enoch, Elijah, Paul, and Jesus had experiences similar to that described as being raptured: [22]

"By faith Enoch was taken up so that he would not see death; AND HE WAS NOT FOUND BECAUSE GOD TOOK HIM UP...." Hebrews 11:5

"As they were going along and talking, behold, there appeared a chariot of fire and horses of fire which separated the two of them. And Elijah went up by a whirlwind to heaven." 2 Kings 2:11

"I know a man in Christ [Paul] who fourteen years ago—whether in the body I do not know, or out of the body I do not know, God knows—such a man was *caught up* to the third heaven. And I know how such a man—whether in the body or apart from the body I do not know, God knows—was *caught up* into Paradise and heard inexpressible words, which a man is not permitted to speak." 2 Corinthians 12:2-4

"And as they were gazing intently into the sky while He was going, behold, two men in white clothing stood beside them. They also said, "Men of Galilee, why do you stand looking into the sky? This Jesus, who has been taken up from you into heaven, will come in just the same way as you have watched Him go into heaven." Acts 1:10-11

These are examples of how God has performed miracles similar to the rapture to accomplish His divine purpose and he will do so again in the future. The divine purpose of the rapture is for Jesus to take believers out of the world to His Father's house he has prepared for them. As you will see, this is a tremendous blessing for us, because it will not only unite believers of all times with Jesus and God, but will save believers (biblical Christians) from the terrible consequences of the tribulation. [23]

When does it occur?

This certainly sounds exciting; so when will it occur? The Bible is very direct in saying that no one knows when the rapture (or the following events called "The Day of the Lord") will occur. [24]

"But of that day or hour no one knows, not even the angels in heaven, nor the Son, but the Father alone. Take heed, keep on the alert; for you do not know when the appointed time will come." Mark 13:32-33

"You too, be ready; for the Son of Man is coming at an hour that you do not expect." Luke 12:40

"For you yourselves know full well that the day of the Lord will come just like a thief in the night. While they are saying, "Peace and safety!" then destruction will come upon them suddenly like labor pains upon a woman with child, and they will not escape....For God has not destined us for wrath, but for obtaining salvation through our Lord Jesus Christ, who died for us, so that whether we are awake or asleep, we will live together with him. 1 Thessalonians 5:2-3, 9-10

So, no one knows when the rapture will occur. However, there are no other prophetic events on God's schedule that must occur before the rapture can occur. So, be ready—the rapture could occur today! Are you ready?

Here are some recommendations from the New Testament that will help you prepare for and look forward to the rapture: [3]

1. Trust in God and Jesus

"Do not let your heart be troubled; believe in God, believe also in Me. In My Father's house are many dwelling places; if it were not so, I would have told you; for I go to prepare a place for you. If I go and prepare a place for you, I will come again and receive you to Myself, that where I am, there you may be also." John 14:1-3

2. Encourage each other

"Therefore comfort one another with these words." 1 Thessalonians 4:18

3. Serve Jesus faithfully now

"Beloved, now we are children of God, and it has not appeared as yet what we will be. We know that when He appears, we will be like Him, because we will see Him just as He is. And everyone who has this hope fixed on Him purifies himself, just as He is pure." 1 John 3:2-3

4. Stand Firm

"Therefore, my beloved brethren, be steadfast, immovable, always abounding in the work of the Lord, know that your toil is not in vain in the Lord." 1 Corinthians 15:58

5. Wait Patiently

"Therefore be patient, brethren, until the coming of the Lord. The farmer waits for the precious produce of the soil, being patient about it, until it gets the early and late rains. You too be patient; strengthen your hearts, for the coming of the Lord is near." James 5:7-8

Walvoord summarizes these by stating:

"We are to look forward eagerly to that day, as we are told in Romans 8:25; 1 Corinthians 1:7; Philippians 3:20; and Hebrews 9:28. These five exhortations show us that the truth of the soon-to-come rapture motivates us to set aside anxiety, to be comforted and encouraged, to be morally pure, to serve the Lord faithfully and diligently, and to be patient. [3]

Remember that our salvation is by grace, but our works will be judged by Jesus when we join Him in heaven. This leads us to the next topic.

What happens to those raptured?

One of the first things that will happen to those of us who join Jesus at the time of the rapture is that our bodies will be transformed from perishable to imperishable. The description of Jesus' resurrected body provides some insight into what our imperishable bodies may be like. Since Jesus was recognizable to those who saw him after his resurrection, it seems reasonable to assume that we may retain some features of our individual identity, including voices that sound like our current voices. Jesus could enter a room without going through the door, he ate, and since he was about 33 years old when he died, some have suggested that our new heavenly bodies may have these same attributes. [25]

There are two events that involve those raptured that have special significance in God's plan for the future. These are the judgment of believers and uniting with Jesus as His bride. [26] We, as believers in Jesus, form the church, which will be presented to Jesus as His bride. We will then be forever united with Jesus and will continue to serve and worship Him as a special entity in heaven during the tribulation period, rule with Him during the Millennial Kingdom, and be with Him in the Eternal State. [27]

As clearly stated in Hebrews, everyone will be judged after they die, and this includes those who were raptured and did not experience normal physical death.

> "And inasmuch as it is appointed for men to die once and after this comes judgment." Hebrews 9:27

The apostle Paul tells us about the judgment that believers will undergo.

> "For we must all appear before the judgment seat of Christ, so that each one may be recompensed for his deeds in the body, according to what he has done, whether good or bad." 2 Corinthians 5:10

It is important to emphasize that this judgment has nothing to do with our salvation and eternal destiny. Our salvation and eternal destiny were sealed when we placed our faith in Jesus as our Savior. However, at the Judgment Seat of Christ (sometimes referred to as the Bema Seat Judgment), our works will be evaluated. This point is emphasized by Walvoord and Pentecost, respectively: [28, 29]

> "The purpose of the judgment seat of Christ, then will be to determine not the extent of believers' sins but rather the quality of their service for God while on earth." [28]

> "It is not the Lord's purpose here to chasten His child for his sins, but to reward his service for those things done in the name of the Lord." [29]

The verdict declared by Jesus will be rewards received or rewards lost. [29] The apostle Paul provided several illustrations about how Jesus will determine the verdict. The first is an illustration of a building and the materials used to build upon the foundation.

> "According to the grace of God which was given to me, like a wise master builder I laid a foundation, and another is building on it. But each man must be careful how he builds on it. For no man can lay a foundation other than the one which is laid, which is Jesus Christ. Now if any man builds on the foundation with gold, silver, precious stones, wood, hay, straw, each man's work will become evident; for the day will show it because it is to be revealed with fire, and the fire itself will test the quality of each man's work. If any man's work which he has built on it remains, he will receive a reward. If any man's work is burned up, he will suffer loss; but he himself will be saved, yet so as through fire." 1 Corinthians 3:10-15

In this illustration, the foundation is the person's faith in the gospel. Gold represents whatever a Christian does to glorify or bring glory to God. Silver represents sharing the gospel with others, either directly or indirectly through supporting others involved in evangelism by prayers and gifts. Costly stones probably represent what a believer does to grow and mature in faith in Jesus. On the other hand, wood, hay, and straw represent things done according to the world's standards and not God's. These are of no eternal value and will be destroyed. [30]

A second illustration Paul used indicates that each one of us will testify on our own behalf.

> "So then each one of us will give an account of himself to God." Romans 14:12

Walvoord comments on this illustration by stating:

This illustration is built on the laws of a trustee. A trustee is responsible to administer something that belongs to another. He is legally bound to give an account in due time of how he managed his trusteeship. The Christian life, by its nature, is a trust from God. All we have has been made possible by God, whether it is physical life, natural gifts, spiritual talents, opportunities, environment, or education. These provisions and many others God gives us are our responsibilities, and the Lord's question to us at the judgment seat of Christ will be, "What have you done with what I have given you?"

This illustration points out several important truths. First, a Christian will not be judged competitively with other Christians. Second, believers will not be held responsible for things we did not possess, gifts we did not receive, or opportunities that were not before us. God gives every believer equal opportunity for spiritual victory. Third, we are responsible to use properly what God has entrusted to us. Thus a person with great talents or great resources is held accountable for far more than one who has few talents. [31]

Imagine what it will be like to stand before the Creator of the universe, the Lord of Lords, the King of Kings, the Son of God, Jesus, and tell Him what you did with the life that He "loaned" to you. No matter how good or bad we think we have been, I think each of us will be humbled and will have trouble finding appropriate words at that moment. Now is the time to commit to fully utilizing the talents and gifts that the Lord has entrusted to you, to bring glory, honor, praise, and worship to God.

What happens to those left behind?

Chaos and confusion will rule the earth following the rapture. As tragic as the terrorist attacks were and as much chaos and death as they caused, the attacks of 9-11 will be insignificant in comparison to the events following the rapture.

"The translation [rapture] of the church will be worldwide, for there are true believers in Jesus Christ in every country on earth, and they all shall be "taken." Every country will find itself in turmoil. Each government will have to act as quickly as possible to prevent a wild tide of anarchy and terrorism.... Millions of people will suddenly disappear from the face of the earth....From all walks of life, and from virtually every phase of life, there shall be people missing.

The freeways, subways, airports, and streets will be in shambles as many engineers, pilots, bus drivers and a multitude of private car owners shall suddenly be caught up out of this world. It will be many days before they can unscramble the mangled cars, trains, and fallen aircraft.

Remaining millions of people will be wailing, dazed and shaken by the event. They shall be frantically striving to locate loved ones in all of the rubble of broken cars and amid broken storefronts and smashed residences.

Communications will be greatly disrupted. Many key persons shall disappear and much of the lines of communications... will be broken....Distraught and searching multitudes will jam and overload the communication lines and systems that do remain.

... Policemen, firemen, and rescue crews will work around the clock. Hospitals will overflow. Emergency shelters and first-aid stations will be inadequate. The Red Cross and all other emergency units, plus the army facilities will still not be enough.

Opportunists will add to the confusion and the misery by looting and killing. They shall feel that under such a total emergency they can get away with anything. CHAOS WILL BE ON EVERY HAND." [32]

There will be a shift in balance of world power. Realistically, there will be more people raptured from the U.S. than there will be from Muslim countries, such as Iran, Iraq, Saudi Arabia, and other Middle Eastern countries. The world's 1.6 billion Muslims will not be touched, but all of the world's biblical Christians will disappear suddenly from the earth. The governments of China and Russia will be largely intact. The U.S. will no longer be a world power.

The events that will transpire during the tribulation are not ones that any of us would want our family and friends to experience. Consequently, let this motivate each of us to share the Good News of the gospel with them!

God has given mankind intellect and freedom of choice. He has chosen to use us to share the good news of His holiness, love, and mercy, as well as to warn of His righteousness, justice, and coming wrath. Let's ensure that we do our part to make sure our family and friends have the knowledge of God and His prophetic timetable, so that they can make informed decisions regarding their future.

Tribulation

The tribulation is the coming seven-year period during which the Jewish people, God's chosen people, fight for their survival, while their existence is threatened by Satan's forces, led by his supreme commander, the Antichrist. Further complicating the situation will be the fact that during this time they will also be tested, tried, and tempered by God. Satan's previous plans to thwart God's promises to Abraham and David and to distract Jesus from His obedience to God's redemptive plan have all failed. Since Satan knows biblical prophecy and knows that he is running out of time to steal and receive the worship that rightfully belongs to God, he is desperate.

So, Satan, his demonic forces, and the rebellious people on earth who are loyal to him use deceit, destruction, and death to try to derail God's plan. However, God uses Satan's activities as well as a series of 21 judgments and His direct intervention to restore and rebuke the Jewish people and then to refine and protect a select remnant of the Jewish people. Even through the chaos of this man-made hell of the tribulation period, God's sovereignty, righteous wrath, and mercy are clearly seen.

This section will highlight some of the information about the Antichrist, the judgments of God, and the battle of Armageddon.

Antichrist: *Who is he, where will he come from, is he alive today?*

The destruction and chaos caused by the rapture sets the stage for the coming Antichrist. In times of crisis and chaos, people want a strong leader. Additionally, they will unite to face a common threat and they will give up freedom for security. [33] The Antichrist will rise to power promising to provide the safety and security the world will desperately desire following the rapture.

The Antichrist will be Satan's supreme commander on the earth during the tribulation period. He will emerge onto the world scene from the revived Roman Empire, which dominated the world during and shortly after the time of Jesus.

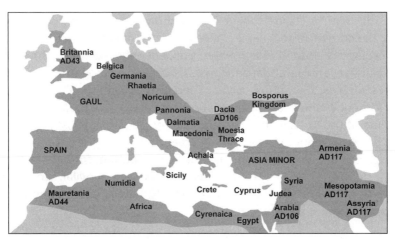

Figure 7-2. Map of the Roman Empire, Around the Time of Jesus. [34]

At its height, the Roman Empire was huge and as shown above included many of the modern-day European, Middle Eastern, and Northern African nations. It is from one of these nations that the Antichrist will emerge.

Satan has had thousands of years to observe the human race and he knows the ideal characteristics in a person to select as his supreme commander. The Antichrist will be a very handsome, attractive man, a charismatic leader, a gifted orator, and a master politician. Through political manipulations, he will gain power over three nations initially and eventually over a total of 10 nations in the revived Roman Empire. He will be totally devoted to Satan and rises to power with Satan's help. The Antichrist will initially gain power through peaceful means, but when necessary he will show his true nature as an evil, lawless man. He will rule with an iron fist, crush and devour nations, persecute God's people, exalt himself above all others, demand to be worshiped, and blaspheme God. [33, 35] (Daniel 9:27, 7:19, 21; 11:37; 2 Thessalonians 2:2-4; Revelation 13:5)

Dr. David Jeremiah comments on the evil nature of the Antichrist:

> "Although all the believers of the present age will be taken to heaven before the reign of this man, new converts will come to Christ during the years of tribulation. This will infuriate the Antichrist, and he will take out his wrath on those new Christians. Many followers of Christ will be martyred for their faith....It would be easier for the saints during the tribulation if they were simply killed outright, but instead they will be "worn out"—mercilessly tortured by this unthinkably cruel man." [36]

Is the Antichrist alive today? Probably, or at least several people who could become the Antichrist are alive today. Satan knows that the rapture will occur, but doesn't know when. Consequently, he has had and currently has several potential antichrists ready and waiting to step into history as soon as the rapture occurs. Therefore, it is reasonable to assume that someone who could become the Antichrist is alive today! [33]

One of the Antichrist's first actions after gaining political power is to offer a peace treaty to Israel. Today, Israel is in a very precarious position among the nations of the world. Following the rapture, their situation will be much worse because the U.S. will be unable or unwilling to protect them. Consequently, it is easy to see why Israel will desperately want a peace agreement after the rapture.

> "Israel is one of the smallest nations on earth. It is one-nineteenth the size of California and roughly the size of our [U.S.] third smallest state, New Jersey.

Israel is 260 miles at its longest, 60 miles at its widest, and between three and nine miles at its narrowest. The nation of Israel is a democratic republic surrounded by 22 hostile Arab/Islamic dictatorships that are 640 times her size and 60 times her population." [37]

The Antichrist will forge a peace treaty with Israel that will establish Israel's borders, normalize trade relations with her neighbors, and promise protection from outside attacks. The treaty also allows the Jews to rebuild their temple in Jerusalem and to reinstitute the sacrificial system given to them by God in the Old Testament times. This enables the Jews to live in peace, for a while... [38]

As predicted in the Old Testament book of Ezekiel (chapters 38 and 39), numerous nations decide to ignore the peace treaty and attack Israel. These nations will be Russia and several Islamic nations. Figure 7-3 below shows the nations that will join together to attack Israel.

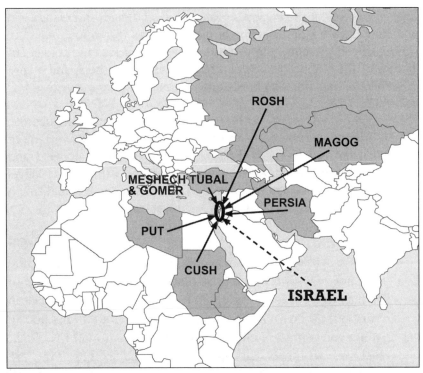

Figure 7-3. Russian/Islamic Invasion of Israel.

The map above shows the names of these countries at the time of Ezekiel. [39] The biblical names and the modern-day names of the invading countries are: "Rosh" (Russia); "Magog" (Kazakhstan, Kyrgyzstan, Uzbekistan, Turkmenistan, Tajikistan, Azerbaijan, Georgia, and possibly Afghanistan); "Mesheck and Tubal" (Turkey); "Cush" (Ethiopia and Sudan); "Put" (Libya); "Gomer" (Turkey and possibly Germany); and "Persia" (Iran). Also likely to join the invasion are Syria, Lebanon, and Jordan. [40, 41] Ezekiel also indicates that the following countries will not join in the planned invasion of Israel: Saudi Arabia, Yemen, Oman, Kuwait, and United Arab Emirates. [42]

The motivation for the invasion will be for the invaders to take control of the land and wealth of Israel and to slaughter all Jews. As you consider these reasons, it is easy to understand why, with the exception of Russia, all of these countries are Islamic countries. The Islamic hatred of the Jews will certainly manifest itself in this planned invasion. [43]

The Israelites are so outnumbered there is no human possibility that they can defeat the invaders. However, God directly intervenes and completely destroys the invading armies. He does this in four ways: an earthquake will kill many, the resulting confusion causes the soldiers to kill some of their comrades, debilitating disease kills others, and finally, torrential rain, hail, fire, and brimstone kills the rest of the invaders. [41, 44] (Ezekiel 38:19-22)

Soon after the defeat of the invading nations, the Antichrist goes into the Jewish temple in Jerusalem and as prophesied by the Old Testament prophet, Daniel (9:27; 11:31; 12:11), stops all sacrifices to God and demands to be worshiped. Additionally, he begins a campaign to kill all the Jews. [35] Both Daniel and Jesus warned that this action would result in serious consequences. Consider Jesus' words of warning:

> "Therefore when you see the ABOMINATION OF DESOLATION which was spoken of through Daniel the prophet, standing in the holy place....then those who are in Judea must flee to the mountains. Whoever is on the housetop must not go down to get the things out that are in his house. Whoever is in the field must not turn back to get his cloak. But woe to those who are pregnant and to those who are nursing babies in those days! But pray that your flight will not be in the winter, or on a Sabbath. For then there will be a great tribulation, such as has not occurred since the beginning of the world until now, nor ever will. Unless those days

had been cut short, no life would have been saved; but for the sake of the elect those days will be cut short." Matthew 24:15

Judgments of God

As mentioned earlier, during the tribulation God unleashes His judgment upon the earth and the people with a series of 21 judgments. These are in three groups of seven judgments, referred to as the Seal, Trumpet, and Bowl judgments. These judgments begin with the Seal judgments and proceed through the Bowl judgments. These are summarized below in Table 7-4.

Table 7-4. The Judgments of the Tribulation.

Judgment	Result	Chapter:Verse
Seal Judgments		
1st	Appearance of the Antichrist	6:1-2
2nd	War	6:3-4
3rd	Famine	6:5-6
4th	Death	6:7-8
5th	Martyred Souls in Heaven	6:9-11
6th	The Day of Divine Wrath	6:12-17
7th	Beginning of the Trumpets	8:1-6
Trumpet Judgments		
1st	Destruction of 1/3 of the Vegetation	8:7
2nd	Destruction of 1/3 of the Sea Life	8:8-9
3rd	Destruction of 1/3 of the Fresh Water	8:10-11
4th	Destruction of 1/3 of the Light Sources	8:12-13
5th	Key to Abyss Given to Satan, Demonic Torment	9:1-11
6th	Army of 200,000,000	9:13-21
7th	Christ's Reign Foreseen	11:15-19

Bowl Judgments		
1st	Malignant Sores on Worshipers of Antichrist	16:2
2nd	Sea Became Like Blood and All Sea Life Died	16:3
3rd	Rivers and Springs Became Blood	16:4-4
4th	Sun Scorched Men With Fierce Heat	16:8-9
5th	Kingdom of the Antichrist Was Darkened	16:10-11
6th	Euphrates River Dried Up	16:12
7th	Great Earthquake and Hail ("It Is Done")	16:17-21

These judgments will demonstrate God's omnipotence and righteousness. Their primary purpose is to discipline the nation of Israel, purge Israel of rebels and unbelievers, and bring Israel to faith in Jesus. [45] Secondarily, these serve to pour out judgment on unbelieving people and nations. [46]

As you read about these judgments (and certainly, if you were to experience them), there is no doubt that these are directly from God. The appropriate response would be to repent and ask God for forgiveness. Incredibly, however, most people living through these judgments will not repent, thereby exposing the wickedness and evil of mankind, when it seeks its will and not God's will.

> "The rest of mankind, who were not killed by these plagues, *did not repent* of the works of their hands, so as not to worship demons, and the idols of gold and of silver and of brass and of stone and of wood, which can neither see nor hear nor walk; and they *did not repent* of their murders nor of their sorceries nor of their immorality nor of their thefts." Revelation 9:20-21 (emphasis added by me)

> "Men were scorched with fierce heat; and *they blasphemed the name of God* who has the power over these plagues, and they **did not repent**, so as to give Him glory....and *they blasphemed the God of heaven* because of their pains and their sores; and *they*

did not repent of their deeds." Revelation 16:9, 11 (emphasis added by me)

Armageddon

During the tribulation period, the Antichrist expands his power from being the leader of the revived Roman Empire, to a world leader, to an oppressive global dictator, and to demanding to be worshiped as God. [47] His harsh and cruel actions produced turmoil and discontent among many people in the world. Consequently, many nations begin assembling their armies to rebel against the Antichrist and his forces, which was predicted by biblical prophecy.

The first force that attacks the Antichrist's forces are from the South, composed of troops from Egypt and other African nations. Then Russia, although defeated about four years previously when it and the Islamic forces tried to attack Israel, will send its army to fight the Antichrist. As the Antichrist is battling these forces, he receives word that an army of 200,000,000 soldiers is coming from China to attack him. [48]

Walvoord summarizes the biblical perspective of this massive war:

"According to Revelation 16:13-14, the armies of the world will gather by demonic influence. The world ruler, who was established and aided in his control of the entire world by the power of Satan, now will be attacked by armies that have been inspired to come to battle by demons sent forth from Satan....This demonic sorcery will deceive the kings of the earth into joining the world rebellion with the prospect of gaining world power.... Although from their point of view they are gathered to fight it out for world power, the armies of the world will actually be assembled by Satan in anticipation of the second coming of Christ. The entire armed might of the world will be assembled in the Middle East, ready to contend with the power of Christ as He returns from heaven....The armies of the world are by no means equipped to fight the armies of heaven. Still Satan will assemble the nations for this final hour, and in fact, the nations will choose to side with Satan and oppose the second coming of Christ....These events will give the nations their choice and allow Satan his desperate bid to oppose Christ's second coming." [49]

The focal point of this war is a valley near Mt. Megiddo in northern Israel. It is about 14 miles wide and 20 miles long. Although it is too small to contain the millions of men assembled in the region, it will be the geographical focal point for the "Battle of Armageddon."

Jesus' Second Coming

So what happens next? As David Jeremiah points out, the Bible is very clear that Jesus will return to the earth a second time.

> "Although Christians are most familiar with the first coming of Christ, it is the second coming that gets the most ink in the Bible. References to the second coming outnumber references to the first by a factor of eight to one. Scholars count 1,845 biblical references to the second coming, including 318 in the New Testament. His return is emphasized in no less than 17 Old Testament books and seven out of every 10 chapters in the New Testament. The Lord Himself referred to His return 21 times. The second coming is second only to faith as the most dominant subject in the New Testament." [50]

The book of Revelation informs us that Jesus returns to earth at the Battle of Armageddon. Walvoord's introduction to the biblical text in Revelation is very appropriate:

> "As contending armies pause in their conflict, the heavens will open and Christ will begin the majestic procession from heaven to earth. The words of this prophecy are the most dramatic to be found anywhere in world literature." [51]

> "And I saw heaven opened, and behold, a white horse, and he who sat on it is called Faithful and True, and in righteousness He judges and wages war. His eyes are a flame of fire, and on His head are many diadems; and He has a name written on Him which no one knows except Himself. He is clothed with a robe dipped in blood, and His name is called the Word of God. And the armies which are in heaven, clothed in fine linen, white and clean, were following Him on white horses. From His mouth comes a sharp sword, so that with it He may strike down the nations, and he will rule them with a rod of iron; and He treads the wine press of the fierce wrath of God, the Almighty. And on His robe and on His thigh He has a name written, "KING OF KINGS, AND LORD OF LORDS." Revelation 19:11-16

What an awesome sight—Jesus returning to the earth as the King of Kings and the Lord of Lords, followed by millions of angels, all riding white horses as a sign of victory. The purpose of Jesus' second coming is to judge the world and to remove all who oppose Him. With a word from Jesus, all of the armies gathered at Armageddon will be slain, as will all the unbelievers in the world. The Antichrist and the false prophet who had performed miraculous signs on his behalf will be thrown into the lake of fire for eternal punishment. [52] Additionally, Satan will be captured, bound, and removed from the earth. [53] In other words, Jesus will destroy or remove "every hostile force that would challenge His right to rule as Messiah over the earth." [54] These events usher in the literal reign of Jesus on earth, which is referred to as the Millennial Kingdom.

Millennial Kingdom

At the end of the tribulation period, the earth will be in shambles. The judgments of God as well as the destruction caused by the Antichrist will have almost demolished the earth. The only people who remain alive will be those believers, both Jews and Gentiles, who have been persecuted and tortured by the Antichrist and his followers. What a sorry state of affairs! Does it look like it is time to push the "RESET" button and start all over?

Jesus will use His creative powers to restore and renew the earth. The beauty and richness of the renewed earth will exceed that of today and will equal that of the original creation. [55]

Jesus will also establish a world government, which will be located in Jerusalem. The government will be a theocracy, headed by Jesus and will fulfill the Davidic Covenant: [56]

> "I will also appoint a place for My people Israel and will plant them, that they may live in their own place and not be disturbed again, nor will the wicked afflict them any more as formerly....I will raise up your descendant after you [Solomon], who will come forth from you, and I will establish his kingdom. He shall build a house for My name, and I will establish the throne of his kingdom forever.... Your house and your throne shall be established forever." 2 Samuel 7:10, 12b-13, 16

Jesus will sit on this throne and rule the entire earth. His reign will extend from the Millennial Kingdom and continue in the Eternal State, fulfilling the prophecy that David's throne shall be established forever. [57]

Jesus will be assisted in ruling the earth by believers who died or were raptured prior to the start of the Millennial Kingdom. [58, 59] The privilege of ruling with Jesus will be granted to some of the believers at the Bema Judgment in recognition of their faithful stewardship of their life on earth. (See Chapter 8 for more details on the rewards given to believers at the Bema Judgment)

The people who will inhabit the Millennial Kingdom are the adult believers, both Jew and Gentile, who survive the tribulation. [60] With their faith clearly focused on Jesus, living under His righteous government in the rejuvenated earth, they will prosper spiritually and materially. They will enjoy a standard of living that exceeds anything the world has ever seen. They will have children and through the generations, will repopulate the earth. The life on earth during this time is characterized by its righteousness, joy, and peace. [61]

The initial inhabitants of the Millennial Kingdom will be believers in Jesus (i.e., biblical Christians). However, their children will have the freedom to accept or reject Jesus as their personal Savior. Unbelievably, some will choose not to place their faith in Jesus, even in this near-perfect environment.

At the end of the thousand years of the Millennial Kingdom, Satan will be released and allowed to tempt those living in the Millennial Kingdom to rebel against God. The fact that some will choose to follow Satan clearly demonstrates the sinful nature of man, even under the most ideal environment: the Millennial Kingdom. [62] Satan will lead these in rebellion against Jesus and will be immediately defeated.

Following the defeat of Satan, the Great White Throne Judgment will occur. At this judgment, all unbelievers of all times will be raised from the dead and brought before Jesus, who will be sitting on the Great White Throne of Judgment. Although all unbelievers will be gathered before Jesus, each will be individually judged according to their words and works. [63-66]

"Then I saw a great white throne and Him who sat upon it, from whose presence earth and heaven fled away, and no place was found for them. And I saw the dead, the great and the small, standing before the throne, and books were opened; and another book was opened which is the book of life; and the dead were judged from the things which were written in the books, according to their deeds....And if anyone's name was not found written in the book of life, he was thrown into the lake of fire." Revelation 20:11-12, 15

According to other passages, there are varying degrees of eternal punishment in the lake of fire (e.g., Matthew 11:22; Luke 20:47). [67] In spite of the fact that there will be varying degrees of punishment for unbelievers, the thought of eternal punishment for all unbelievers is difficult to accept. Walvoord provides some guidance in placing this in proper perspective:

"It is only human to try to find some escape from the rigidity of eternal punishment, but if one dies without salvation, there is no escape. The Bible clearly pictures eternal punishment as continuing forever, just as heaven will continue forever for those who are saved. As heaven will constitute an eternal reminder of the grace of God, so the lake of fire will constitute an eternal reminder of the righteousness of God....Though the doctrine of eternal punishment is repugnant to the unsaved world and troubles even those who are saved, a thorough appreciation of the destiny of the wicked will do much to further zeal for preaching the gospel and for winning souls for Christ. At the same time it causes Christians to worship and praise God for His grace as manifested in the death and resurrection of Jesus Christ." [68]

"The Word of God makes plain that God so loved the world that He gave His Son, and that all who avail themselves of the grace of God are immeasurably blessed in time and eternity. On the other hand, the same Word of God states plainly that those who spurn God's mercy must experience His judgment without mercy. How foolish it is to rest in the portions of the Word of God that speak of the love of God and reject the portions that deal with His righteous judgment. The present age reveals the grace of God and suspended judgment. The age to come, while continuing to be a revelation of the grace of God, will give conclusive evidence that God brings every evil work into judgment and that those who spurn His grace must experience His wrath." [69]

I believe it is fair to say that those who choose to ignore the grace and mercy of God, demonstrated by the crucifixion and resurrection of Jesus, also choose to reject God's grace and mercy throughout eternity. God will honor both of these choices. Let this motivate us to share the gospel with others, so at least they can make an informed decision on how they will live their lives on earth and where they will spend eternity.

Eternal State

After the Great White Throne Judgment, God will destroy the universe and replace it with a new heaven and new earth: [70]

> "...the heavens will pass away with a roar and the elements will be destroyed with intense heat, and the earth and its works will be burned up....the heavens will be destroyed by burning, and the elements will melt with intense heat!" 2 Peter 3:10, 12

> "Then I saw a new heaven and a new earth; for the first heaven and the first earth passed away, and there is no longer any sea." Revelation 21:1

The apostle John wrote about the centerpiece of the new earth and new heaven:

> "And he carried me away in the Spirit to a great and high mountain, and showed me the holy city, Jerusalem, coming down out of heaven from God, having the glory of God. Her brilliance was like a very costly stone, as a stone of crystal-clear jasper. It had a great and high wall, with twelve gates, and at the gates twelve angels; and names were written on them which are the names of the twelve tribes of the sons of Israel....The city is laid out as a square, and its length is as great as the width....fifteen hundred miles; its length and width and height are equal....I saw no temple in it, for the Lord God the Almighty and the Lamb [Jesus] are its temple....And the city has no need of the sun or of the moon to shine on it, for the glory of God has illumined it, and its lamp is the Lamb [Jesus]. The nations will walk by its light, and the kings of the earth will bring their glory into it." Revelation 21:10-12, 16, 22-24

Every believer (biblical Christian) in history, from Adam to the last person saved in the Millennial Kingdom will reside in New Jerusalem, with God the Father, God the Son, and God the Holy Spirit. [71] In the New Jerusalem, there will be no sin, mourning, pain, or death.

"And I heard a loud voice from the throne, saying, "Behold, the tabernacle of God is among men, and He will dwell among them, and they shall be His people, and God Himself will be among them, and He will wipe away every tear from their eyes; and there will be no longer any death; there will no longer be any mourning, or crying, or pain; the first things have passed away." Revelation 21:3-4

The Bible does not provide a detailed description about life in the Eternal State. However, based upon glimpses provided in various verses, life in the Eternal State can be summarized as a life of fellowship with God (1 Corinthians 13:13; John 14:3; Revelation 22:4), rest (Revelation 14:13), full knowledge (1 Corinthians 13:12), holiness (Revelation 21:27), joy (Revelation 21:4), service to God (Revelation 22:3), abundance (Revelation 21:6), glory (2 Corinthians 4:17; Colossians 3:4), and worship (Revelation 19:1). [72] I am looking forward to this incredible eternal life with God. How about you?

Biblical prophecy provides assurance that God is in control of the universe and everything in it. Prophecy should also call our attention to the fact that *"Life is short, compared to eternity."* Each of us is accountable to God for the decisions we make and hopefully you will accept the marvelous grace of God and place your faith in Jesus.

In closing this chapter, let me remind you of the opening promise in the book of Revelation:

"Blessed is he who reads and those who hear the words of the prophecy, and heed the things which are written in it; for the time is near." Revelation 1:3

References:

1. Walvoord, John F. *The Prophecy Knowledge Handbook*. Wheaton, IL: Victor Books, 1990, p. 10.
2. _____. pp. 648-769.
3. Walvoord, John F. "Part X: End Times". *Understanding Christian Theology*. Swindoll, Charles R. and Roy B. Zuck (general editors). Nashville, TN: Thomas Nelson Publishers, 2003, p. 1,370.
4. Ryrie, Charles C. *The Basis of the Premillennial Faith*. Neptune, NJ: Loizeaux Brothers, 4th printing, 1989, p. 16.

5. Walvoord, John F. *The Prophecy Knowledge Handbook.* p. 551.
6. _____. pp. 382-383.
7. Jeremiah, David. *What in the World Is Going On? 10 Prophetic Clues You Cannot Afford to Ignore.* Nashville, TN: Thomas Nelson, 2008.
8. Walvoord, John F. *Major Bible Prophecies: 37 Crucial Prophecies That Affect You Today.* Grand Rapids, MI: Zondervan Publishing House, 1991.
9. Walvoord, John F. *The Prophecy Knowledge Handbook.* Wheaton, IL: Victor Books, 1990.
10. Pentecost, J. Dwight. *Things to Come: A Study in Biblical Eschatology.* Grand Rapids, MI: Academie Books, 1964.
11. Dennis, Lane T. (Executive Editor) and Wayne Grudem (General Editor). *ESV Study Bible, English Standard Version.* Wheaton, IL: Crossway Bibles, 2008, p. 2,453.
12. Walvoord, John F. *The Revelation of Jesus Christ.* Chicago, IL: Moody Press, 1966.
13. Walvoord, John F. *The Prophecy Knowledge Handbook.* pp. 11-17.
14. Ryrie, Charles C. *Dispensationalism.* Chicago, IL: Moody Publishers, 2007, p. 33.
15. _____. p. 46.
16. Pentecost. pp. 193-218.
17. Ryrie, Charles C. *The Basis of the Premillennial Faith.*
18. _____. p. 12.
19. Walvoord, John F. *The Prophecy Knowledge Handbook.* p. 385.
20. Jeremiah, David. pp. 108, 110.
21. Walvoord, John F. *The Prophecy Knowledge Handbook.* pp. 482-483.
22. Jeremiah, David. pp. 109.
23. Walvoord, John F. *Major Bible Prophecies.* p. 268.
24. Grudem, Wayne. *Systematic Theology: An Introduction to Bible Doctrine.* (Electronic version, Copyright 1997, 2004 Wayne Grudem and John Hughes; published by Bits & Bytes, Inc., Whitefish, MT. Print version: Leicester, Great Britain: Inter-Varsity Press and Grand Rapids, MI: Zondervan Publishing House, 1994, pp. 1,095-1,096.
25. Walvoord, John F. in *Understanding Christian Theology.* p. 1,273.
26. Pentecost. p. 219.
27. Walvoord, John F. in *Understanding Christian Theology.* p. 1,248.
28. _____. p. 1,277.
29. Pentecost. pp. 222-223.
30. Walvoord, John F. in *Understanding Christian Theology.* p. 1,278.
31. _____. p. 1279.
32. Taylor, Charles, as quoted by Tan, P.L., *Encyclopedia of 7700 Illustrations: A Treasury of Illustrations, Anecdotes, Facts and Quotations for Pastors, Teachers, and Christian Workers.* Garland, TX: Bible Communications, 1996, Item 4885. (Libronix electronic version)

33. Dyer, Charles H. *Prophecy in Light of Today*. Chicago, IL: Moody Press, 2002, pp, 14-31.
34. New Testament World and Times website. "The Roman Empire at its Greatest Extend, c. AD 117." http://www.ccel.org/bible/phillips/CN600NTWORLD.htm.
35. Jeremiah, David. pp. 141-160.
36. _____. p. 151.
37. _____. p. 174.
38. Walvoord, John F. *Major Bible Prophecies*. p. 319.
39. Jeremiah, David. p. 173.
40. _____. pp. 162-171.
41. Naam, Samuel. "The Future of Islamic Fundamentalism." in Dyer, Charles H. *Prophecy in Light of Today*. Chicago, IL: Moody Press, 2002, pp. 55-69.
42. _____. p. 172.
43. _____. pp. 175-176.
44. _____. pp. 178-179.
45. Rydelnik, Michael. "Ground Zero." in Dyer, Charles H. Prophecy in Light of Today. Chicago, IL: Moody Press, 2002, pp, 43-44.
46. Pentecost. pp. 237-238.
47. Jeremiah, David. p. 202.
48. Walvoord, John F. with Mark Hitchcock. *Armageddon, Oil, and Terror: What the Bible Says About the Future of America, the Middle East, and the End of Western Civilization*. Carol Stream, IL: Tyndale House Publishers, Inc., 2007, p. 174.
49. _____. pp. 174-176.
50. Jeremiah, David. p. 217.
51. Walvoord, John F. with Mark Hitchcock. *Armageddon, Oil, and Terror*. pp. 179-180.
52. Walvoord, John F. *Major Bible Prophecies*. p. 382.
53. _____. p. 383.
54. Pentecost. p. 358.
55. Walvoord, John F. *Jesus Christ Our Lord*. Chicago, IL: Moody Press, 1969, p. 280.
56. Pentecost. p. 476.
57. Walvoord, John F. *Major Bible Prophecies*. p. 390.
58. Pentecost. pp. 495-502.
59. Walvoord, John F. *Major Bible Prophecies*. pp. 384-385.
60. _____. p. 387.
61. Walvoord, John F. *Jesus Christ Our Lord*. p. 285.
62. Lutzer, Erwin W. "When All Hell Breaks Loose." in Dyer, Charles H. Prophecy in Light of Today. Chicago, IL: Moody Press, 2002, p. 81.
63. Pentecost. p. 424.
64. Walvoord, John F. in *Understanding Christian Theology*. p. 1,340.
65. Walvoord, John F. *Major Bible Prophecies*. p. 408.

66. Ryrie, Charles C. *Basic Theology*. Wheaton, IL: Victor Books, 5th Printing, 1988, p. 518.
67. Grudem, Wayne. *Systematic Theology*. p. 1,142.
68. Walvoord, John F. *Major Bible Prophecies*. pp. 411-412.
69. Walvoord, John F. *The Revelation of Jesus Christ*. p. 281.
70. Walvoord, John F. in *Understanding Christian Theology*. p. 1,363.
71. Walvoord, John F. *Major Bible Prophecies*. p. 415.
72. Pentecost. pp. 580-582.

Chapter 8

Biblical Christianity: So What Is Your Decision?

Life is short...compared to eternity. Best-selling author John Ortberg provides some insight into this profound statement with the following story:

> "Grandmother was at her feistiest when it came to Monopoly....She was a gentle and kind soul, but at the Monopoly table she would still take you to the cleaners....
>
> But my grandmother knew how to play the game. She understood that you don't win without risk, and she didn't play for second place. So she would spend every dollar she got. She would buy every piece of property she landed on. She would mortgage every piece of property she owned to the hilt in order to buy everything else.
>
> She understood what I did not—that accumulating is the name of the game, that money is how you keep score, that the race goes to the swift. She played with skill, passion, and reckless abandon. Eventually, inevitably, she would become Master of the Board. When you're the Master of the Board, you own so much property that no one else can hurt you. When you're Master of the Board, you're in control. Other players regard you with fear and envy, shock and awe. From that point on, it's only a matter of time. She would watch me land on Boardwalk one time too many, hand over to her what was left of my money, and put my little race car marker away, all the time wondering why I had lost yet again. "Don't worry about it," she'd say. "One day you'll learn to play the game."

I hated it when she said that.

Then one year when I was 10, I spent a summer playing Monopoly every day with a kid named Steve who lived kitty-corner from me. Gradually it dawned on me that the only way to win this game was to make a total commitment to acquisition. No mercy. No fear. What my grandmother had been showing me for so long finally sank in.

By the fall, when we sat down to play, I was more ruthless than she was. My palms were sweaty. I would play without softness or caution. I was ready to bend the rules if I had to. Slowly, cunningly, I exposed the soft underbelly of my grandmother's vulnerability. Relentlessly, inexorably, I drove her off the board. (The game does strange things to you.)

I can still remember—it happened at Marvin Gardens.

I looked at my grandmother—this was the woman who had taught me how to play. She was an old lady by now. A widow. She had raised my mother. She loved my mother, as she loved me. And I took everything she had. I destroyed her financially and psychologically. I watched her give up her last dollar and quit in utter defeat.

It was the greatest moment of my life.

I had won. I was cleverer, and stronger, and more ruthless than anyone else at the table. I was Master of the Board.

But then my grandmother had one more thing to teach me. The greatest lesson comes at the end of the game. And here it is. In the words of James Dobson, who described this lesson from Monopoly in playing with his family many years ago: "*Now it all goes back in the box.*"

All those houses and hotels. All that property—Boardwalk and Park Place, the railroads and the utility companies. All those thousands of dollars. *When the game is over, it all goes back in the box.*

I didn't want it to go back in the box. I wanted to leave it out as a perpetual memorial to my skill at playing the game—to bronze it, perhaps, so others could admire my tenacity and success. I wanted the sense of power that goes with being Master of the Board to last forever. I wanted the thrill of winning to be my perpetual companion. I was so heady with victory after all these years that for a few moments I lost touch with reality. None of that stuff was mine—not really. Now, for a few moments, it was my turn to play the game. I could get all steamed up about it for a while and act as if the game were going to last forever. But it would not. Not for me. Not for you either...." [1]

King Solomon came to the same conclusion and added a sobering thought—after you die, a fool may gain control over everything that you have worked so hard for:

"As he had come naked from his mother's womb, so will he return as he came. He will take nothing from the fruit of his labor that he can carry in his hand. This also is a grievous evil—exactly as a man is born, thus will he die. So what is the advantage to him who toils for the wind?" Ecclesiastes 5:15-16

"Thus I hated all the fruit of my labor for which I had labored under the sun, for I must leave it to the man who will come after me. And who knows whether he will be a wise man or a fool? Yet he will have control over all the fruit of my labor for which I have labored by acting wisely under the sun. This too is vanity." Ecclesiastes 2:18-19

Whatever you accumulate in this earthly life, you cannot take with you when you die. This is a rather depressing thought, isn't it? Fortunately, though, there is another perspective, one provided by Jesus— you can't take it with you, but you can send it on ahead!

"Do not store up for yourselves treasures on earth, where moth and rust destroy, and where thieves break in and steal. But store up for yourselves treasures in heaven, where neither moth nor rust destroys, and where thieves do not break in or steal; for where your treasure is, there your heart will be also." Matthew 6:19-21

Store up for yourself treasures in heaven. That looks like something worth exploring. But before we do, let's review the key points of the previous chapters:

Chapter 1: You were created by God, in His image, which includes intellect, emotion, and volition. God loves you and wants to have a personal, intimate relationship with you. However, God is Holy and you are not. Your sins separate you from God and one sin—rejecting the gospel of Jesus—is serious enough to separate you eternally from God and from entrance to heaven when you die. However, because God loves you, He sent His Son, Jesus, to earth to live, demonstrate how we should live, and then to die to pay the penalty for all of your sins, including the one that will eternally separate you from God. The gospel is that Jesus lived, died for our sins according to the Scriptures, and rose from the dead according to the Scriptures. When you place your faith, intellectually, emotionally, and volitionally, in the gospel, then God forgives you and welcomes you as an adopted member of His family, where you will remain, now and forever!

Chapter 2: There is sufficient evidence to conclude that the Bible is what it claims to be—the inspired Word of God—and our Bibles today are virtually identical to the earliest manuscripts.

Chapter 3: Jesus demonstrated His humanity and divinity through His words, works, death, and resurrection.

Chapters 4-6: Islam, atheism, and secular socialism are not compatible with biblical Christianity and do not provide the hope and security of the gospel of Jesus Christ, not now and not in eternity.

Chapter 7: With more than 500 prophecies of the Bible literally fulfilled already, it is reasonable to expect that the prophecies concerning the rapture, tribulation, second coming of Jesus, Millennial Kingdom, and Eternal State will be fulfilled literally. Additionally, there are no other events on God's prophetic calendar that must take place before the rapture occurs—It could happen today!

Your Decision

My goal in writing the previous chapters was to provide sufficient objective information so that you can make an informed decision about how you choose to live the rest of your life and where you will reside for eternity. The choice is yours. The decision is yours. There is a heaven, there is a hell, and these will exist forever. You have the freedom to choose where your spirit and resurrected body will reside after you die. God will honor your decision.

Although I have spent the majority of my professional career in medical equipment sales, I know that it is not my responsibility to try to close the sale regarding your eternal destiny. It is my responsibility to share what I know and what I believe to be true. It is the Holy Spirit's responsibility to open your mind and soul to the truth of the gospel. You have the freedom to accept or reject the gospel of Jesus Christ.

If you are ready to place your faith in the gospel of Jesus Christ and accept His gift of eternal salvation, you may do so by praying the following prayer:

"God, I believe that Jesus lived, died to pay the penalty of my sins, and that He rose from the dead, according to the Scriptures. I want to have a personal relationship with you now and forever. I place my faith, my life, and my eternal destiny in Jesus. Thank you, God, for hearing and accepting my prayer. In Jesus' name I pray."

If you sincerely prayed this prayer, then I congratulate you and compliment you on your wise decision! You have changed from being a *creation* of God to being a *child* of God! You have an incredibly exciting future ahead of you!

The rest of this chapter will focus on your relationship with God. You will learn what He has done, is doing, and will do for you. You will also learn you can thank Him for His love and grace. Additionally, you will learn how God will bestow even more blessings on you in the future. The next chapter, Chapter 9, will focus on how you can relate to others in ways that will bestow value and worth on them and bring glory, honor, praise, and worship to God.

If you have not yet placed your faith in the gospel, I encourage you to continue reading. Perhaps the Holy Spirit will communicate clearly your need to do so and you will decide to place your faith in the gospel before you have finished reading this book. This is my prayer for you.

God's Response

When you place your faith in the gospel, you instantly become an adopted member of God's family. You are now a child of God! But there is more good news. You will be amazed to know what God has done to you, in you, and for you, as a result of your accepting His offer of salvation through the gospel of Jesus Christ! These include the following five actions, which God has already done to and in you:

1. Sealed by God with the Holy Spirit;
2. Baptized into the body of believers by the Holy Spirit;
3. Inhabited by the Holy Spirit;
4. Regenerated by the Holy Spirit; and
5. Filling begun by the Holy Spirit.

Because each of these is so important, they will be considered in more detail below.

1. Sealed by God with the Holy Spirit.

The instant that you place your faith in the gospel, God the Father seals you and your decision with the Holy Spirit. In Jesus' time, when a seal was placed on something, it indicated ownership and security. [2] Similarly, God's act of sealing you with the Holy Spirit includes the concepts of ownership, authority, responsibility, and security. The primary concept, however, is security, which is completely ensured by the fact of God's ownership of you, His authority to protect you, and His willingness to accept the responsibility of protecting you. [3, 4] "Sealing guarantees that we shall receive all that God has promised us, some of which awaits our future redemption." [4] Bible verses that confirm this are:

> "In Him, you also, after listening to the message of truth, the gospel of your salvation—having also believed, you were sealed in Him with the Holy Spirit of promise, who is given as a pledge of our inheritance, with a view to the redemption of God's own possession, to the praise of His glory." Ephesians 1:13-14

> "...God, who also sealed us and gave us the Spirit in our hearts as a pledge." 2 Corinthians 1:21b-22

> "Do not grieve the Holy Spirit of God, by whom you were sealed for the day of redemption." Ephesians 4:30

Grudem and Gromacki both indicate that the word translated as "pledge" in two of the verses above was used legally and commercially to refer to an earnest money deposit made by a buyer. This was the first payment guaranteeing that the rest of the price would be paid in the future. [5, 6] So, what does this mean to you? It means that your salvation, eternal destiny, and membership in God's family are secure and cannot be taken from you or lost. Jesus provides further assurance of your eternal security:

> "The Spirit Himself testifies with our spirit that we are children of God." Romans 8:16

> "All that the Father gives Me will come to Me, and the one who comes to Me I will certainly not cast out. For this is the will of My father, that everyone who beholds the Son and believes in Him will have eternal life, and I Myself will raise him up on the last day." John 6:37, 40

> "My sheep hear My voice, and I know them, and they follow Me; and I give eternal life to them, and they will never perish; and no one will snatch them out of My hand. My Father, who has given them to Me, is greater than all; and no one is able to snatch them out of the Father's hand. I and the Father are one." John 10:27-30

So how does it feel to know that your eternal destiny is secured by the creator of the universe, God Himself?

2. Baptized into the body of believers by the Holy Spirit.
On the day that Jesus ascended to heaven, He announced that the believers would be baptized by the Holy Spirit. This occurred 10 days later on the day of Pentecost.

> "for John baptized with water, but you will be baptized with the Holy Spirit not many days from now." Acts 1:5

> "When the day of Pentecost had come, they were all together in one place. And suddenly there came from heaven a noise like a violent rushing wind, and it filled the whole house where they were sitting. And there appeared to them tongues as of fire distributing themselves and they rested on each one of them. And they were all filled with the Holy Spirit and began to speak with other tongues [languages], as the Spirit was giving them utterance." Acts 2:1-4

The day of Pentecost was a transitional event for both the role of the Holy Spirit and the believers. The Holy Spirit began a much more powerful role in the lives of believers than He had in the Old Testament. The more powerful role of the Holy Spirit was manifested on this day in the lives of the early believers through more power and effectiveness in their ministry. [7] Additionally, it had two other effects on the early believers: (1) it identified them with Jesus in His death, burial, and resurrection and (2) it confirmed that each was a member of the body of Christ or His Church. The baptism of the Holy Spirit occurs the instant we place our faith in the gospel and has the same effects upon you today as it had on the early believers. [8, 9]

The benefits of this are that because you are permanently identified with Jesus, God now sees you as He sees Jesus, and you have a specific purpose to serve in the body of believers (i.e., the church). [8] The apostle Paul provides additional insight regarding your identification with Jesus and your membership in the church:

> "I have been crucified with Christ; and it is no longer I who live, but Christ lives in me; and the life which I now live in the flesh I live by faith in the Son of God, who loved me and gave Himself up for me." Galatians 2:20

> "For even as the body is one and yet has many members, and all the members of the body, though they are many, are one body, so also is Christ. For by one Spirit we were all baptized into one body, whether Jews or Greeks, whether slaves or free, and we were all made to drink of one Spirit." 1 Corinthians 12:12-13

Although each believer is an individual and each has a unique function within the church, each is equal in God's sight. Racial, social, and sexual distinctions are irrelevant. [10]

So what do you think about God looking at you and seeing the perfection of Jesus, rather than your sins?

3. *Inhabited by the Holy Spirit.*

At the moment of conversion, the Holy Spirit takes up residence within you and will be with you permanently. [11] This is confirmed by the apostle Paul and John:

> "Or do you not know that your body is a temple of the Holy Spirit who is in you, whom you have from God, and that you are not your own?" 1 Corinthians 6:19

> "...because greater is He who is in you than he who is in the world." 1 John 4:4

Ryrie also comments:

"...whether or not we feel it God the Holy Spirit lives within our beings constantly. This ought to give us (a) a sense of security in our relationship with God, (b) a motivation to practice that presence of God, and (c) a sensitivity to sins against God." [12]

The indwelling of the Holy Spirit is an answer to Jesus' prayer:

> "I will ask the Father, and He will give you another Helper, that He may be with you forever." John 14:16

As a result of the Holy Spirit inhabiting (living within) you, He will minister to you and help you in the following areas:

Purity. The Holy Spirit will guide you to avoid immorality. No believer should be involved in immoral acts of adultery, fornication, or homosexuality (1 Corinthians 6:9-11).

Worship. He will show you how to worship God in spirit and truth (John 4:24).

Assurance. The Holy Spirit will assure you that you belong to God (1 John 4:13).

Service. He will bless you with one or more spiritual gifts specifically for serving the body of Christ (1 Corinthians 12).

Growth. He will help you in your journey from being a spiritual baby to becoming a mature believer (2 Peter 3:18). [13]

Aren't you glad to know that the Holy Spirit will help you in each of these areas of your life?

4. *Regenerated by the Holy Spirit.*

Before you accepted Jesus as your Savior you were separated from God because of your sins. But, more importantly, you were living in a state of sin in that you refused to believe in the gospel of Jesus and refused to accept His pardon. [14] That was the old you. At the moment of conversion, you had a spiritual rebirth, which sometimes is referred to as being born again. [15]

> "Jesus answered and said to him, "Truly, truly, I say to you, unless one is born again he cannot see the kingdom of God." John 3:3

> "Therefore if anyone is in Christ, he is a new creature; the old things passed away; behold, new things have come." 2 Corinthians 5:17

The practical benefit to you for this new birth is that you now have the ability to be lead by and controlled by the Holy Spirit to please God. Certainly, this does not mean that you will now lead a perfect life, but it does mean that you have a Helper who will help you become more Christ-like, if you will let Him! [16]

So, how does it feel to be a new-born babe in Christ?

5. <u>Filling begun by the Holy Spirit.</u>

Filling and inhabiting ministries of the Holy Spirit are related but not the same. A believer is inhabited by the Holy Spirit at the moment of conversion; however, he can only become filled by the Holy Spirit through obedience to God's Word. [17] Grudem provides further explanation:

> "Therefore, it is appropriate to understand filling with the Holy Spirit *not as a one-time event* but *as an event that can occur over and over again* in a Christian's life. It may involve a momentary empowering for a specific ministry (such as apparently happened in Acts 4:8; 7:55), but it may also refer to a long-term characteristic of a person's life (see Acts 6:3; 11:24). In either case such filling can occur many times in a person's life...." [18]

Although filling by the Holy Spirit begins at the moment of conversion, it is not something that continues without your effort. It is, however, something that you are commanded to do.

> "And do not get drunk with wine, for that is dissipation, but be filled with the Spirit." Ephesians 5:18

So, how do you go about getting filled with the Spirit? Gromacki provides guidance on this topic by stating:

1. "Believers can either obey or disobey this command."
2. "We are not commanded to ask or pray for the filling of the Holy Spirit. Rather, we are commanded to be obedient."
3. "Believers do not fill themselves, nor do they actively command the Spirit to fill them....we are acted on by Him."
4. "We must be filled with the Spirit over and over."
5. "We are filled with the Spirit when we are obedient to the Word of God."
6. "We are filled with the Spirit when we are controlled by Him."

"...The Spirit wants to influence us in all areas of our lives: mental, emotional, vocational, sexual, and relational. He wants to control us as we apply the Scriptures to those areas. When we are filled with the Spirit, we will do things that we would not ordinarily do." [19]

As you grow and become more spiritually mature, you will experience the fruit of the spirit.

> "But the fruit of the Spirit is love, joy, peace, patience, kindness, goodness, faithfulness, gentleness, self-control; against such things there is no law. Galatians 5:22-23

So, how does more love, joy, peace, patience, kindness, goodness, faithfulness, gentleness, and self-control in your life sound to you? How can you get these? I am glad you asked because that is what is covered in the next section.

Your Response

To begin this section, take a few moments to reflect on what God has done, is doing, and will do for you. These actions by God are amazing demonstrations of His love for you and His grace! As I mentioned in Chapter 1, God's grace is <u>G</u>od's <u>R</u>iches <u>A</u>t <u>C</u>hrist's <u>E</u>xpense. [20] His grace is unmerited, unearned, and unearnable. [21] It is the gift of God!

> "For by grace you have been saved through faith; and that not of yourselves, it is the gift of God." Ephesians 2:8

So how do you respond to this amazing grace? Perhaps a prayer expressing a sincere and humble "Thank you, God" would be a good starting point. Then, you could ask God to have the Holy Spirit guide you in learning about God and His will for your life, with your ultimate goal of knowing God and living your life in a manner that would be pleasing to Him.

Do you remember Jesus' response to the question, "What is the greatest commandment?" His answer was,

> "And He said to Him, 'YOU SHALL LOVE THE LORD YOUR GOD WITH ALL YOUR HEART, AND WITH ALL YOUR SOUL, AND WITH ALL YOUR MIND.' This is the great and foremost commandment. The second is like it, 'YOU SHALL LOVE YOUR NEIGHBOR AS YOURSELF.' On these two commandments depend the whole Law and the Prophets." Matthew 22:37-40

So, how can you love God? It seems to me that first you need to know who God is and as your knowledge and understanding of God grows, you will be able to more effectively and completely love Him. So, the goals of this section are (1) to provide information about how you can learn who God is so that you can begin to *know* God; and (2) to provide recommendations on how you can demonstrate your love to God. As you grow in your knowledge, understanding, and faith, you will not only know more about God, but, more importantly, you will begin to *know* God, your heavenly Father!

The second part of the greatest commandment is, "You shall love your neighbor as yourself." You already know that Jesus loved you enough to die for you so that He could have an eternal relationship with you.

The same is true of your neighbors. This perspective will motivate you to relate to and serve others in a manner that will be pleasing to God. This will be the focus of Chapter 9.

1. *To Know God:*

What is the purpose of life? According to J.I. Packer, the general editor of the *English Standard Version (ESV) Bible*, it is "to know God." [22] Packer goes on to say, "Once you become aware that the main business that you are here for is to know God, most of life's problems fall into place of their own accord." [23]

To know the God of the Bible is to love Him. But more than that, it is to realize that He is worthy of your reverence, worship, obedience, and service. So, where do you start your journey to know God? I'll recommend the following three things: (a) start with the Bible, (b) then pray, and (c) then become a member of a Bible-teaching, God-honoring church.

(a) Start with the Bible:

> "All Scripture is inspired by God and profitable for teaching, for reproof, for correction, for training in righteousness; so that the man of God may be adequate, equipped for every good work." 2 Timothy 3:16

In Chapter 1, I stated that the Bible is God's Operator's and Service manual for the human race. Realistically, it is that, but it is so much more. Reading, studying, and meditating on the Bible is the best and most reliable place to start to learn more about God and His plan for your life.

If you go shopping for a Bible, you may be overwhelmed by the sheer number of options and different translations of the Bible, all in the English language. In fact, Christianbook.com, the online division of Christian Book Distributors, "the world's largest distributor of Christian products," [24] lists more than 4,000 Bibles in 21 different English language translations of the Bible! Does this seem like it might be a little confusing and difficult to choose the right Bible for you? Perhaps I can help.

The translations of the Bible are based upon the philosophy that guides the translation process from the original languages of the Scriptures, Hebrew and Greek, to English. Simply stated, translation philosophies range from "word-for-word" to "thought-for-thought" translations. The "word-for-word" translations are those that strive to provide a translation that represents the original Hebrew and Greek writings as closely as possible with the equivalent English words. This method produces a more technically correct translation. The "thought-for-thought" translation takes the main point or thought in a passage and translates it into a similar point or thought in today's English. From my perspective, the "thought-for-thought" introduces the possibility of interpreter bias into the translation, which is why I usually avoid these translations.

All of the quotations from the Bible in this book are from the New American Standard Bible, NASB, which is recognized by biblical scholars as one of the most technically accurate translations of the earliest Hebrew (Old Testament) and Greek (New Testament) manuscripts. My preference for the NASB translation is based upon my reverence for the Bible and also upon my linguistic skills.

As I indicated earlier, I have traveled to and done business in more than 40 countries. I have been frequently asked by my professional colleagues how many different languages I speak. I confess that I am indeed multi-lingual. My native language is "Texan" and I am still trying to learn "English"! I decided long ago that I could be most effective and helpful to my international business partners and prospects if I became an expert on the features, benefits, and uses of the medical products I represented rather than trying to learn multiple languages. When required, I relied upon the skills of a translator to help me communicate effectively in foreign languages. Similarly, I do not have a desire to learn Hebrew and Greek languages just to read the Bible in its original languages. However, I do have a tremendous respect for the scholars who have done this and I do want to take advantage of their linguistic expertise, which I do by reading primarily the NASB translation of the Bible. Furthermore, my first choice in a NASB Bible is a "study Bible," which contains notes, comments, and supplemental information to provide additional insight into the books and verses of the Bible. With this said, I would like to make some recommendations to you regarding Bibles and other study aids that I think would be helpful to you as you begin or continue your quest to know God and His will for your life.

Study Bibles:
- *The Zondervan NASB Study Bible*
- *The ESV Study Bible*
- *NIV Life Application Study Bible*
- *The NIV Daily Bible*

Bible Commentary:
* *The Bible Knowledge Commentary*

Bible Study Software:
* Logos Bible Software 4

Reference Books:
* Ryrie, Charles C. *Basic Theology: A Popular Systematic Guide to Understanding Biblical Truth*
* Grudem, Wayne. *Systematic Theology: An Introduction to Biblical Doctrine*
* Packer, J.I. *Knowing God*
* Pentecost, Dwight. *The Words and Works of Jesus Christ*
* Ryrie, Charles C. *The Holy Spirit*

So with this information in mind, where do you start reading and studying the Bible? I recommend starting with *The Gospel According to John*, the fourth book in the New Testament. As stated by John, the purpose of this book was "written so that you may believe that Jesus is the Christ, the Son of God; and that believing you may have life in His name." (John 20:31) This will be a great way to further solidify your faith in Jesus. Then I would suggest you begin reading through the New Testament, beginning with *The Gospel According to Matthew* and progressing through the book of *The Revelation to John*.

(b) Pray:

After getting your Bible and study materials, then pray for the Holy Spirit to guide you in your studies and your new life in Christ. Prayer is direct communication with God. So talk to Him, tell Him what is on your mind. Confess your sins and ask for forgiveness. Ask Him for guidance and protection. Thank Him for His many blessings. In other words, God is your heavenly Father, so talk to Him and you will be surprised how He will communicate to you through the Holy Spirit, the Bible, other believers, and events in your life.

The apostle Paul provides some excellent advice regarding prayer:

"Be anxious for nothing, but in everything by prayer and supplication with thanksgiving let your requests be made known to God. And the peace of God, which surpasses all comprehension, will guard your hearts and your minds in Christ Jesus." Philippians 4:6-7

David provides some words of wisdom that would be appropriate for you to pray:

"Search me, O God, and know my heart; try me and know my anxious thoughts; and see if there be any hurtful way in me, and lead me in the everlasting way." Psalm 139:23-24

"Make me know Your ways, O Lord; Teach me Your paths. Lead me in Your truth and teach me, For You are the God of my salvation; For You I wait all the day." Psalm 25:4-5

(c) Become a member of a Bible-teaching, God-honoring church.

As you continue your spiritual growth and journey, it will be important to regularly join with other believers to learn about God and to worship and praise Him.

""and let us consider how to stimulate one another to love and good deeds, not forsaking our own assembling together, as is the habit of some, but encouraging one another; and all the more, as you see the day drawing near." Hebrews 10:24-25

I encourage you to carefully and prayerfully select the church that you attend. The primary purposes in going to church are to learn about God, worship God, praise God, and to have fellowship with, serve with, and support other believers in Jesus. A simple test to evaluate the focus of a church is to observe the members of a church in the parking lot as they are walking into the church. See how many of them have Bibles with them. If a significant percentage of the attendees take their Bibles with them into the church, then that is a good sign that the church is focused on teaching and preaching from the Bible.

You should also check out the values and mission statements of a church before joining. Some things to look for are statements that they believe that the Bible is inerrant in its original form and that it is God's Word. Additionally, see if the church states that they believe in one God, who exists in three persons, the Father, Son, and Holy Spirit; that Jesus was crucified for our sins, according to the Scriptures, and rose from the dead, according to the Scriptures; and that Jesus will return to the earth as Lord. Although there are other important doctrinal beliefs that can be added to this list, these represent a good start to identify a church that is based upon biblical principles.

Given these factors about how you can begin to know God, let's turn our attention to how you can demonstrate your love to God. If you think about your relationship with your parents, your spouse, and/or your children, you can readily think of ways to demonstrate to them that you love them. No matter what ways come to your mind, most of them demonstrate your love for them through your obedience to them or by doing things that show that you value them. The same is true for God—your obedience and service to Him will demonstrate to Him (and others) your love for Him.

2. To Be Obedient to God

In this subsection, I am going to present some of the verses that have been particularly beneficial to me. These are provided for your consideration and meditation, without comment from me.

> "but sanctify Christ as Lord in your hearts, always being ready to make a defense to everyone who asks you to give an account for the hope that is in you, yet with gentleness and reverence." 1 Peter 3:15

> "He who has My commandments and keeps them, he it is who loves Me; and he who loves Me shall be loved by My Father, and I will love him, and will disclose Myself to him." John 14:21

> "But seek first His kingdom and His righteousness, and all these things will be added to you." Matthew 6:33

> "He has told you, O man, what is good; and what does the Lord require of you but to do justice, to love kindness, and to walk humbly with your God." Micah 6:8

"A new commandment I give to you, that you love one another, even as I have loved you, that you also love one another. By this all men will know that you are My disciples, if you have love for one another." John 13:34-35

"If we confess our sins, he is faithful and righteous to forgive us our sins and to cleanse us from all unrighteousness." 1 John 1:9

"Therefore I urge you, brethren, by the mercies of God, to present your bodies a living and holy sacrifice, acceptable to God, which is your spiritual service of worship. And do not be conformed to this world, but be transformed by the renewing of your mind, so that you may prove what the will of God is, that which is good and acceptable and perfect." Romans 12:1-2

"Flee immorality. Every other sin that a man commits is outside the body, but the immoral man sins against his own body. Or do you not know that your body is a temple of the Holy Spirit who is in you, whom you have from God, and that you are not your own? For you have been bought with a price: therefore glorify God in your body." 1 Corinthians 6:18-20

"Rejoice always; pray without ceasing; in everything give thanks, for this is God's will for you in Christ Jesus." 1 Thessalonians 5:16-18

"The conclusion, when all has been heard, is: fear God and keep His commandments, because this applies to every person." Ecclesiastes 12:13

"so that you will walk in a manner worthy of the Lord, to please Him in all respects, bearing fruit in every good work and increasing in the knowledge of God." Colossians 1:10

Before leaving this subsection on obedience to God, there is one other thing that I would like to share with you. I have found that it is too easy to get caught up in professional, family, and other activities and responsibilities. Sometimes these activities distract me from being focused on and obedient to God and His will for my life. To help ensure that I remain focused I developed a biblically based personal creed. For many years, it has served very well as my spiritual compass and a reminder of the priorities in my life. I'll share it with you to provide some ideas and encouragement for you to develop your own biblically based personal creed.

Rich Trayler's Creed
1. Scripture:

> "all scripture is inspired by God and profitable for teaching, for reproof, for correction, for training in righteousness; that the man of God may be adequate, equipped for every good work." 2 Timothy 3:16-17

I will base my life and my creed on scriptural principles, so that I may be prepared to do the works that God has prepared for me.

> "be diligent to present yourself approved to God as a workman who does not need to be ashamed, handling accurately the word of truth." 2 Timothy 2:15

I will diligently study the Bible and utilize the accepted interpretative tools, so that I can correctly interpret what the writer meant when he wrote it and what it means to me today.

2. Personal

> "so that you may walk in a manner worthy of the Lord, to please Him in all respects, bearing fruit in every good work and increasing in the knowledge of God." Colossians 1:10

I will take specific steps to make sure all aspects of my life (personal, familial, professional, and social) are striving toward a manner pleasing to the Lord.

"And He said to Him, 'YOU SHALL LOVE THE LORD YOUR GOD WITH ALL YOUR HEART, AND WITH ALL YOUR SOUL, AND WITH ALL YOUR MIND.'" Matthew 22:37

On a daily basis I will read the Bible and pray so that I will know more fully God and His will for my life. I will express my love for God by my obedience to His will.

"Be anxious for nothing, but in everything by prayer and supplication with thanksgiving let your requests be made known to God. And the peace of God, which surpasses all comprehension, shall guard your hearts and your minds in Christ Jesus." Philippians 4:6-7

I will acknowledge to God that I know He is in complete control of everything, and, consequently, I don't need to be anxious about anything. I will also thank Him for the opportunities and challenges I face.

"Or do you not know that your body is a temple of the Holy Spirit who is in you, whom you have from God, and that you are not your own? For you have been bought with a price; therefore glorify God in your body." 1 Corinthians 6:19-20

On a daily basis I will take care of my body by trying to get an appropriate amount of sleep, exercise, and nutritious foods.

3. Family

"Husbands, love your wives, just as Christ also loved the church and gave Himself up for her." Ephesians 5:25

I will be more sensitive to my wife's spiritual, emotional, and physical needs and will try to help her daily in each of these areas.

"And, fathers, do not provoke your children to anger; but bring them up in the discipline and instruction of the Lord." Ephesians 6:4

I will continue to love and support my daughter and our nephew (who is handicapped and lives with us) and encourage them to continue growing in their relationship with Jesus.

4. Professional

"Whatever you do, do your work heartily, as for the Lord rather than for men; knowing that from the Lord you will receive the reward of the inheritance. It is the Lord Christ whom you serve." Colossians 3:23-24

I know that I am ultimately accountable to God. Therefore, I will continue to set my professional standards to please and be acceptable to God rather than men.

"Therefore, however you want people to treat you, so treat them, for this is the Law and the Prophets." Matthew 7:12

I will continue to treat my customers, prospects, fellow employees, and the company, as I would want to be treated if the roles were reversed.

Summary

"Teacher, which is the great commandment in the Law? And He said to him, 'YOU SHALL LOVE THE LORD YOUR GOD WITH ALL YOUR HEART, AND WITH ALL YOUR SOUL, AND WITH ALL YOUR MIND. This is the great and foremost commandment. The second is like it, 'YOU SHALL LOVE YOUR NEIGHBOR AS YOURSELF. On these two commandments depend the whole Law and the prophets.'" Matthew 22:36-40

3. *To Serve God*

As with the previous subsection, I will begin this subsection with some key Bible verses that provide some insight into how to serve God.

> "Now Jabez called on the God of Israel, saying, "Oh that You would bless me indeed and enlarge my border, and that Your hand might be with me, and that You would keep me from harm that it may not pain me!" And God granted him what he requested." 1 Chronicles 4:10

> "Be diligent to present yourself approved to God as a workman who does not need to be ashamed, accurately handling the word of truth." 2 Timothy 2:15

> "Whatever you do, do your work heartily, as for the Lord rather than for men, knowing that from the Lord you will receive the reward of the inheritance. It is the Lord Christ whom you serve." Colossians 3:23-24

> "Whether, then, you eat or drink or whatever you do, do all to the glory of God." 1 Corinthians 10:31

> "No one can serve two masters; for either he will hate the one and love the other, or he will be devoted to one and despise the other. You cannot serve God and wealth." Matthew 6:24

> "And He was saying to them, "The harvest is plentiful, but the laborers are few, therefore beseech the Lord of the harvest to send out laborers into His harvest." Luke 10:2

> "Go therefore and make disciples of all the nations, baptizing them in the name of the Father and the Son and the Holy Spirit, teaching them to observe all that I commanded you, and lo, I am with you always, even to the end of the age." Matthew 28:18-20

> "and let us consider how to stimulate one another to love and good deeds, not forsaking our own assembling together, as is

the habit of some, but encouraging one another; and all the more as you see the day drawing near." Hebrews 10:24-25

"So then, while we have opportunity, let us do good to all people, and especially to those who are of the household of faith." Galatians 6:10

These verses clearly communicate that God wants you to actively serve Him in ways that will ultimately bring glory, honor, praise, and worship to Him, as well as benefiting you and others along the way. Let's consider the first and last verses quoted above in a little more detail. The first is called the Prayer of Jabez and was the subject of a best-selling book by the same title. [25] Notice that it is okay to ask for God for blessings, even though you have already been blessed tremendously by God. It is okay to ask God to expand your influence and areas of service. It is okay to ask God to strengthen you so that you may be more effective in your service to Him. It is okay to ask God to protect you from harm. Just as God granted Jabez a positive response to this prayer, He will do so for you also, but on His time frame and in His way.

The last verse encourages us to do good to all people, especially to our Christian brothers and sisters. This is very compatible with the concept presented earlier that you have been adopted into the body of Christ (God's family, the true church) and that you have specific areas of service to perform that will benefit the body of believers (which in turn may benefit non-believers). It should be emphasized that God will not ask you to do anything that you cannot do, through His power. In fact, the Holy Spirit has already equipped you with spiritual gifts to effectively meet the "enlarge my border" request in the Prayer of Jabez and the "do good" command of Galatians 6:10.

One or more spiritual gifts, "a God-given ability for service," [26] are bestowed on each believer by the Holy Spirit. Yes, that includes you! There are three primary passages in the New Testament that provide information about spiritual gifts. These are quoted below.

"For just as we have many members in one body and all the members do not have the same function, so we, who are many, are one body in Christ, and individually members of one another. Since we have gifts that differ according to the grace given to us, <u>each of us</u> is to exercise them accordingly: If ***prophecy***, according to the proportion of his faith; if ***ser-***

vice, in his serving, or he who *teaches*, in his teaching; or he who *exhorts*, in his exhortation; he who *gives*, with liberality; he who *leads*, with diligence; he who shows *mercy*, with cheerfulness." Romans 12:4-8 (emphasis added by me)

"Now concerning spiritual gifts, brethren, I do not want you to be unaware.... Now there are varieties of gifts, but the same Spirit. And there are varieties of ministries, and the same Lord. There are varieties of effects, but the same God who works all things in all persons. But to each one is given the manifestation of the Spirit for the common good. For to one is given the word of *wisdom* through the Spirit, and to another the word of *knowledge* according to the same Spirit; to another *faith* by the same Spirit, and to another gifts of *healing* by the one Spirit, and to another the effecting of *miracles*, and to another *prophecy*, and to another the *distinguishing of spirits*, to another various kinds of *tongues*, and to another the *interpretation of tongues*. But one and the same Spirit works all these things, distributing to each one individually just as He wills....And God has appointed in the church, first *apostles*, second *prophets*, third *teachers*, then *miracles*, then gifts of *healings*, *helps*, *administrations*, various kinds of *tongues*." 1 Corinthians 12:1, 4-11, 28 (emphasis added by me)

"But to each one of us grace was given according to the measure of Christ's gift....And He gave some as *apostles*, and some as *prophets*, and some as *evangelists*, and some as *pastors* and *teachers*, for the equipping of the saints for the work of service, to the building up of the body of Christ; until we all attain to the unity of the faith, and of the knowledge of the Son of God, to a mature man, to the measure of the stature which belongs to the fullness of Christ." Ephesians 4:7, 11-13 (emphasis added by me)

There are some key points to consider from these passages. First, at least one and maybe several spiritual gifts are given to each believer (i.e., biblical Christian). Yes, that includes *you*! These gifts are from God and not for us to choose. Additionally, the purpose of these gifts is to serve the body of believers for the glory of God. Finally, just as in the parable of the talents (Matthew 25:14-29), we are to be faithful servants and use these talents wisely. (1 Peter 4:10) [27]

Rasmussen and Eriksson have categorized, listed, defined, and provided scriptural references for the spiritual gifts, which are shown below in Table 8-1.

Table 8-1. Spiritual Gifts (adapted from Rasmussen and Bubgee) [28, 29]

Gift	Definition	Reference
Leadership/People-intensive Gifts		
Prophecy	The divine enablement to reveal **God's truth about future events**	Romans 12:6; Ephesians 4:11; 1 Corinthians 12:10
Apostleship	"The divine enablement to start and oversee the development of new churches or ministry structures" [29]	1 Corinthians 12:28
Shepherding	The divine enablement to **nurture, lead, and care** for individuals in the body in order to help them **grow** in their faith	Ephesians 4:11
Teaching	"The divine enablement to **understand and communicate clearly** the Word of God to those listening" [28]	Ephesians 4:11; 1 Peter 4:11
Administration	The divine enablement to **organize and plan procedures** to effectively and efficiently accomplish the goals of a ministry	1 Corinthians 12:28
Leadership	"The divine enablement to **attract, lead, and motivate** people in the work of the ministry" [28]	Romans 12:8

Evangelism	The divine enablement to share the gospel with **exceptional clarity and effectiveness**, so that unbelievers place their faith in the gospel of Jesus Christ	Ephesians 4:11
Encouragement	"The divine enablement to present truth so as **to strengthen, comfort, or urge to action** those who are discouraged or wavering in their faith" [29]	Romans 12:8
Wisdom	The divine enablement to **effectively apply biblical truth** to meet a need in a specific situation	1 Corinthians 12:8
Knowledge	The divine enablement to **understand and organize** biblical information effectively; extraordinary insight into truth or a situation	1 Corinthians 12:8
Discernment	"The divine enablement to **distinguish between truth and error**, as well as the **source** of that truth or error" [28]	1 Corinthians 12:10
Creative Communication	"The divine enablement to communicate God's truth through a **variety of art forms**" [28, 29]	1 Chronicles 6:31-32
Support Gifts		
Serving / Helps*	"The divine enablement to **physically support others** in a **wide variety** of areas" [28]	Romans 12:7; 1 Corinthians 12:28
Mercy	The divine enablement to minister with **loving compassion** toward those who are suffering or in need	Romans 12:8

Faith	The divine enablement to **trust God** and act on God's promises with confidence and unwavering belief that He will fulfill His plans regardless of circumstances	Ephesians 4:11
Giving	The divine enablement to impart **material wealth** to support the Lord's ministries, with **liberality, freedom, and joy**	Romans 12:8
Hospitality	The divine enablement to care for others by providing **fellowship, food, and/or shelter** in a way that glorifies God	1 Peter 4:9
Craftsmanship	"The divine enablement to facilitate ministry through the **creative construction of necessary tools** for ministry" [28]	Exodus 31:1-5
Intercession	"The divine enablement to **earnestly and faithfully pray** on **behalf** of others or for a cause, seeing frequent and specific results to those prayers" [28]	Colossians 1:9-12; 4:12-13
Sign Gift Summaries		
Miracles	"The divine enablement to authenticate the ministry and message of God through supernatural interventions that glorify Him" [29]	Romans 12:7; 1 Corinthians 12:28
Healing	"The divine enablement to be God's means for restoring people to wholeness" [29]	1 Corinthians 12:9, 28
Tongues	The divine enablement to **speak languages not otherwise known** to the body of believers	1 Corinthians 12:9, 28

Interpretation	The divine enablement to **make known** to the body of believers the message that is being spoken in tongues	1 Corinthians 12:9

* = Serving is more task-oriented and Helps is more people-oriented.

Here are a few more comments about spiritual gifts for your consideration. These are not aptitudes or abilities to work with a particular age group and are not roles or offices within a church. Additionally, these are not special techniques or natural talents. [30, 31] They are special gifts bestowed by the Holy Spirit to effectively serve the body of believers (the church). In general, leadership gifts enable one to guide and direct others and to prepare other believers for their service. Support gifts help support the structure and facilitate effective function of the church. The spiritual gifts of miracles, healing, tongues, and interpretation were given to authenticate the message of the gospel to unbelievers. There are some who question whether or not these four spiritual gifts are given and are active today. [23] Whether or not they are given today should not be a distraction to you using the spiritual gift(s) given to you for serving God and the church.

So, how do you find out which spiritual gift or gifts have been given to you by the Holy Spirit? There are several ways: praying and asking God to reveal this to you; self-analysis of your desire to serve the church; and asking fellow believers to assess your abilities and tell you how these may relate to your spiritual giftedness. Additionally, there are several online spiritual gift assessment programs that can provide insight into your spiritual giftedness. One of these is Churchgrowth.org and the Spiritual Gifts Inventory (http://store.churchgrowth.org/epages/ChurchGrowth.sf/4c6 9ae9402012cfb2717ac1003570613/Product/View/401S).

I encourage you to identify the spiritual gift or gifts that you have been given and then ask your pastor or other Christian leaders how you can utilize these to most effectively serve the church. I think it is fair to say that the more you use your spiritual gifts the more effective you will become. This will lead you to experience the joy and satisfaction that comes from serving God and the church.

Your Rewards

I hope that when you read the title of this section, "Your Rewards," that you thought, *What do you mean, my rewards? I have already been so blessed by God that I don't need any more rewards!* Well, that is certainly true; however, there are more blessings that God has in mind for you. Recall Jesus' words,

> "...I came that they may have life, and have it abundantly." John 10:10

> "For whoever has, to him more shall be given, and he will have an abundance...." Matthew 13:11

> "But store up for yourselves treasures in heaven...." Matthew 6:20

Yes, God has blessed you richly, but Jesus promised an abundance and encouraged you to store up treasures for yourself in heaven. Regarding abundance, this may or may not mean additional material blessings while you are on earth. However, the Bible is very clear that when you appear before Jesus at the Bema Judgment, you will be rewarded for the good works that you do in this life (2 Corinthians 5:10).

So, what do you think about purposely doing things so that you will receive a reward at the Bema Judgment? Realistically, regardless of your motivation, the things that bring reward at the Bema Judgment are things that please and bring glory to God.

Consider the encouragement by the apostle Paul, a man who totally devoted his life to serving God:

> "Do you not know that those who run in a race all run, but only one receives the prize? Run in such a way that you may win." 1 Corinthians 9:24

> "I press on toward the goal for the prize of the upward call of God in Christ Jesus." Philippians 3:14

> "Also if anyone competes as an athlete, he does not win the prize unless he competes according to the rules." 2 Timothy 2:5

So, according to Paul, it is okay to be motivated to win the Bema Judgment prizes. Before discussing the prizes, let's first consider the rules or the divine principles that Jesus will follow in the Bema Judgment. Joe Wall, in his book, *Going for the Gold*, provides a very good explanation of the "doctrine of rewards" as they relate to the Bema Judgment. [33] In it he provides 12 principles that apply to the Bema Judgment rewards, as well as 10 principles for wise spiritual investment for us to follow in this life. These are summarized below in Tables 8-2 and 8-3.

Table 8-2. Principles for Divine Reward. [34]

#	Principle	Reference
1	Jesus will judge our deeds, our words, our thoughts, and our motives	Rom. 2:5-6; Matt. 12:36-37; Luke 12:3; Heb. 4:12-13; 1 Cor. 4:5
2	Only what Christ through the Holy Spirit produces in our lives has any value at the Bema	John 15:5
3	Jesus will reward us according to our preserving faith in God and His promises	Hebrews 6:12, 10:35-36
4	Jesus will reward us in proportion to our faithful and wise stewardship	Matthew 25:14-30; Luke 19:11-27
5	Jesus will take into account how we responded to the Word of God	Psalm 19
6	Jesus will be concerned with the purity of our lives	1 Corinthians 9:27; 2 Timothy 2:15-23; 1 John 2:27—3:3
7	Jesus will take into account how long we have been saved	Matthew 20:1-16
8	Jesus will reward us according to our secondary involvement in the ministry of others	Matthew 10:40-42
9	If we judge others, Jesus will apply our standards when He judges us	Matthew 7:1-2
10	Jesus will reward us for the results of our ministry in the lives of others	1 Thessalonians 2:19-20

| 11 | Teachers will receive stricter judgment | James 3:1 |
| 12 | Not only production but contribution to production will receive reward | 1 Corinthians 3:6-8 |

Table 8-3. "Principles of Wise Spiritual Investment." [35]

#	Principle	Reference
1	Invest in the lives of those who minister the Word	Galatians 6:6-7
2	Minister to those in need	Matthew 10:42
3	Sacrifice to follow Christ	Matthew 19:27-29
4	Give without fanfare	Matthew 6:1-4
5	Accept abuse for the sake of Christ	Matthew 5:11-12
6	Pray in secret	Matthew 6:5-6
7	Engage in spiritual activity without fanfare	Matthew 6:16-18
8	Love your enemies by being willing to help them	Luke 6:35
9	Give hearty service to the Lord and not just to please men	Colossians 3:23-24
10	Entertain those who cannot repay you	Luke 14:12-14

Wow! What incredible insight is contained in these two sets of principles. As a matter of fact, there is so much information that someone could write a book to explain these in more detail! However, there is no need for me to do so or to comment further, because Joe Wall has already done so, exceptionally well, in his book, *Going for the Gold*! [33] I highly recommend it to you.

So, if you utilize your spiritual gifts effectively and invest your life wisely for Jesus, what are the rewards that you will receive? There are several types, one of which is crowns, which could be thought of as somewhat equivalent to Olympic Gold Medals. However, these crowns will last for eternity. [36] For the sake of brevity, these will be summarized in the table below:

Table 8-4. Crowns Awarded at the Bema Judgment [37]

Crown of	Rewarded for	Reference
Righteousness	Finishing life with our eyes on Jesus (i.e., our faith in Jesus)	2 Timothy 4:7-8
Life	Persevering under trial and/or martyrdom	James 1:12; Revelation 2:10; Matthew 5:11-12
Joy	Leading people to Christ	1 Thessalonians 2:19-20; Philippians 4:1
Glory	Serving as an elder in a church	1 Peter 5:2-4

Wall concludes by stating:

"We do not know for certain if there are crowns other than the four mentioned in Scripture. But we do know that those four are the ones the Lord wanted us to know about in order to understand what in our lives is really important to God. The crown of righteousness focuses our attention on the importance of carrying out the ministry God has designed for us, persevering righteously to the end of our course. The crown of life reminds us of the importance of always entrusting ourselves to the arms of our beloved Lord as we endure suffering. The crown of joy emphasizes the great need to minister the gospel to others. And the crown of glory in an encouragement to accept and carry out the leadership responsibilities we have been given in the life of the church." [37]

So what do you think? Does this look like a good "benefits package"? As remarkable as this is, there is more! However, before providing information on additional rewards, some background information will be helpful.

The Bible guarantees eternal life to all who place their faith in Jesus (John 3:16). Consequently, all believers will enter heaven and reside there for eternity. However, the Bible also indicates that it is possible for some believers to receive an "inheritance" in the kingdom of God (Ephesians 1:11, 14; Colossians 1:12, 3:24; Hebrews 6:12, 9:15; 1 Peter 1:4, 3:9; Revelation 21:7). This inheritance is in addition to the crown awards listed above and is awarded to some, but not all believers. [38] For example, consider the Apostle Paul's warning:

"Or do you not know that the unrighteous will not inherit the kingdom of God? Do not be deceived; neither fornicators, nor idolaters, nor adulterers, nor effeminate, nor homosexuals, nor thieves, nor the covetous, nor drunkards, nor revilers, nor swindlers, will inherit the kingdom of God." 1 Corinthians 6:9-10

Paul is very clear that the unrighteous will not inherit the kingdom of God. If prior to placing your faith in the Gospel, you were or if you now are a fornicator, idolater, adulterer, effeminate, homosexual, thief, coveter, drunkard, reviler, swindler you will be allowed to enter heaven (assuming that you have placed your faith in the Gospel of Jesus Christ); but you will not be able receive the greater blessing of inheriting the kingdom of God.

The good news, however, is that if you repent, which means to recognize that these actions are sins and that you confess your sins, and turn from them, then God will forgive you.

"If we confess our sins, He is faithful and righteous to forgive our sins and to cleanse us from all unrighteousness." 1 John 1:9

"The LORD is compassionate and gracious, slow to anger and abounding in lovingkindness. For as high as the heavens are above the earth, so great is His loving kindness toward those who fear Him. As far as the east is from the west, so far has He removed our transgressions from us." Psalm 103:8,11-12

These are comforting and reassuring words, whether or not you are guilty of the sins listed above. So, if you are guilty of the sins listed above, confess them and turn from them, so that you might live a righteous life that is pleasing to God, which is the key to receiving an inheritance in the kingdom of God.

With this background information in mind, let's now turn our attention back to the topic of more rewards and the inheritance. The book of Revelation provides insight into other rewards that will be awarded to those who faithfully serve Jesus in this life. In the book of Revelation, Jesus states eight times that someone who "overcomes" will receive specific blessings. Seven of these occurred in two chapters. Do you think

Jesus was stuttering or that He wants us to know that being an overcomer is very important to Him, and consequently to us? The rewards and the references to one who overcomes are summarized in Table 8-5 below.

Table 8-5. Rewards Given to Overcomers.

#	Reward	Reference
1	The right to eat of the tree of life that is in the Paradise of God	Rev. 2:7
2	Be unhurt by the second death	Rev. 2:11
3	Hidden manna, a white stone, and a (secret) new name written on the stone	Rev. 2:17
4	Authority over nations	Rev. 2:26
5	Clothing of white garments, his name will not be erased from the book of life, and Jesus will announce his name before God and angels	Rev. 3:5
6	Become a pillar in the temple of God, reside in the temple, and Jesus will write on him God's name, Jerusalem's name, and Jesus' name (indicating special honor)	Rev. 3:12
7	Sit with Jesus on His throne	Rev. 3:21
8	Inherit these things, Jesus will be his God, and he will be Jesus' son	Rev. 21:7

So what defines one who overcomes? Dillow, in his comprehensive text, *The Reign of the Servant Kings: A Study of the Eternal Security and the Final Significance of Man*, [39] provides a detailed study of an "overcomer." The Greek word that is translated as "overcomer" was used to describe one who was victorious in both military and legal combat. [40] As it is used in Revelation, it refers to one who victoriously perseveres through the trials of life and faithfully serves Jesus during this life on earth. [41] Now with this in mind, take time to reconsider the blessings promised to the one who overcomes. Note in particular, that he/she will have authority over nations, will sit on Jesus throne with Him (and co-reign), and inherit these things. Can you grasp the magnitude of these promises?

Dillow presents a very compelling case that the final significance of man is to co-rule the universe with Jesus.

"Instead of merely being destined to rule a small planet, mankind has been chosen to subdue something far greater, the vast cosmos itself. No challenge could be greater than to be placed over all the works of God's hands!" [42]

Dillow also provides a very good perspective on the doctrine of rewards and our potential future reign with Christ:

"Whatever our role in that great future is, it will be magnificent. Because we love Him we want to earn the right to rule with Him. So it is our love for Him and the joy set before us that motivates. We are not saying that the desire for future reward is to replace altruism as a motivator, only that it enhances it.

It is impossible to separate the motivation of love and the motivation derived from reward. They are, in the Bible at least, inextricably interrelated. This is so because to strive for the biblical inheritance requires that one strive "according to the rules." This means that he must strive (1) with a heart motive that what he does is for Christ's sake and in response to Christ's love; and (2) with a realization that, once he has done all he can do, he still has only done his duty (Luke 17:10); and (3) with an understanding that there is no strict contractual correspondence between a certain amount of work resulting in a certain amount of reward (Matt. 20:1-16). Since he has only done his duty, he understands that God rewards him not out of debt but out of grace. His work has not obligated God or placed God in his debt, but God in His grace has freely chosen to reward him even though there is no obligation placed upon Him to do so." [43]

Perhaps the words of the apostle Paul will be an appropriate way to end this chapter:

"...run in such a way that you may win." 1 Corinthians 9:24b

References:

1. Ortberg, John. *When the Game Is Over IT ALL GOES BACK IN THE BOX*. Grand Rapids, MI: Zondervan, 2007, pp. 13-14.
2. Radmacher, Earl D. "Salvation: A Necessary Work of God" in Swindoll, Charles R. and Roy B. Zuck (general editors). *Understanding Christian Theology*. Nashville, TN: Thomas Nelson Publishers, 2003, p. 915.
3. Ryrie, Charles C. *The Holy Spirit*. Chicago, IL: Moody Press, 1965, pp. 80-82.

4. Ryrie, Charles C. *Basic Theology*. Wheaton, IL: Victor Books, 5th printing, 1988, pp. 359-361.
5. Grudem, Wayne. *Systematic Theology: An Introduction to Bible Doctrine*. (Electronic version, Copyright 1997, 2004 Wayne Grudem and John Hughes; published by Bits & Bytes, Inc., Whitefish, MT. Print version: Leicester, Great Britain: Inter-Varsity Press and Grand Rapids, MI: Zondervan Publishing House, 1994, p. 790.
6. Gromacki, Robert G. "The Holy Spirit: Who He is, What He Does" in Swindoll, Charles. R. and Roy B. Zuck. *Understanding Christian Theology*. Nashville, TN: Thomas Nelson, Inc., 2003, p. 423.
7. Grudem, Wayne. *Systematic Theology*. pp. 770-771.
8. Gromacki, Robert G. "The Holy Spirit: …" in *Understanding Christian Theology*. p. 481.
9. Grudem, Wayne. *Systematic Theology*. p. 772.
10. Gromacki, Robert G. "The Holy Spirit: …" in *Understanding Christian Theology*. p. 492.
11. Ryrie, Charles C. *The Holy Spirit*. p. 73.
12. Ryrie, Charles C. *Basic Theology*. p. 358.
13. Gromacki, Robert G. "The Holy Spirit: …" in *Understanding Christian Theology*. pp. 499-500.
14. Ryrie, Charles C. *The Holy Spirit*. p. 58.
15. Ryrie, Charles C. *The Holy Spirit*. pp. 64-65.
16. _____. p. 66.
17. Gromacki, Robert G. "The Holy Spirit: …" in *Understanding Christian Theology*. p. 498.
18. Grudem, Wayne. *Systematic Theology*. p. 782.
19. Gromacki, Robert G. "The Holy Spirit: …" in *Understanding Christian Theology*. pp. 501-502.
20. Packer, J.I. *Knowing God*. Downers Grove, IL: InterVarsity Press, 1993, p. 128.
21. Ryrie, Charles C. *So Great Salvation*. Wheaton, IL: Victor Books, 1989, p. 17.
22. Packer, J.I. *Knowing God*. p. 33.
23. _____. p. 34.
24. Christianbook.com website. http://www.christianbook.com/Christian/Books/cms_content?page=128863&sp=104857&event=FAQ|12882.
25. Wilkinson, Bruce. *The Prayer of Jabez: Breaking Through to the Blessed Life*. Sisters, OR: Multnomah Publishers, 2000.
26. Ryrie, Charles C. *The Holy Spirit*. p. 83.
27. Rasmussen, Jamie with Steve Eriksson. *Discovery: Finding Your Gifts and Passions*. Scottsdale, AZ: Scottsdale Bible Church, 2010, pp. 6-7.
28. _____. pp. 15-16, 21, 23.
29. Bugbee, Bruce. *Discover Your Spiritual Gifts the Network Way*. Grand Rapids, MI: Zondervan, 2005, pp. 59-61.
30. Ryrie, Charles C. *Basic Theology*. pp. 367-368.
31. Rasmussen, Jamie with Steve Eriksson. *Discovery*. p. 4.

32. Ryrie, Charles C. *Basic Theology*. pp. 372-373.
33. Wall, Joe L. *Going for the Gold: Reward and Loss at the Judgment of Believers*. Chicago, IL: Moody Press, 1991.
34. _____. pp. 91-103.
35. _____. pp. 107-110.
36. _____. pp. 125-127.
37. _____. pp. 127-130.
38. Dillow, Joseph C. *The Reign of the Servant Kings: A Study of Eternal Security and the Final Significance of Man*. Miami Springs, FL: Schoettle Publishing Co. 1992, p. 62.
39. Dillow, Joseph C. *The Reign of the Servant Kings: A Study of Eternal Security and the Final Significance of Man*. Miami Springs, FL: Schoettle Publishing Co. 1992.
40. _____. p. 469.
41. _____. pp. 82, 105, 470.
42. _____. p. 563.
43. _____. p. 592.

Chapter 9

Your Faith: How Can You Share It?

W hen you go to a new restaurant and have an exceptionally good meal, outstanding service, with an enjoyable ambiance, at an extremely good price, do you tell your friends and neighbors about it or do you keep it as your secret? Most people can't wait to tell others about their new favorite restaurant. They want to share this new information with everyone they know. Why should it be any different with the gospel?

Bill Bright, the founder of Campus Crusade for Christ, exclaims and then explains,

> *"We Christians have in our possession the greatest gift available to mankind—the greatest news ever announced.*
>
> Christ is risen! We serve a living Savior who not only lives within us in all His resurrection power but has assured us of eternal life. He died on the cross in our place for our sin, then rose from the dead. We have direct fellowship with God through Jesus Christ. And this fellowship, this peace, this gift of eternal life, is available to all who receive Him." [1]

You, along with every Christian in the world, have the privilege, as well as the responsibility, to tell everyone about the good news of the gospel of Jesus Christ! (Mark 16:15) To help prepare you to do this "heartily, as for the Lord" (Colossians 3:23), this chapter will focus on five topics: your lifestyle, your creed, your testimony, how to share the gospel, and how to fulfill Jesus' command to make disciples.

Your Lifestyle: Actions Speak Louder Than Words

As I traveled internationally, I realized that I was not only a representative of the company, but also a representative of America and, more importantly, an ambassador for Jesus Christ. As such, I wanted to represent my company in a positive and professional manner; as an American, in a respectful and courteous manner; and as a Christian, as one who recognized and valued the inherent worth of all the people who Jesus loved enough to die for.

Because of severe legal restrictions regarding sharing one's faith within a business environment with fellow workers, as well as standards of "acceptable business practices," I could not speak openly and freely about my faith, unless and until someone asked me directly about my faith. The greatest compliment I could and did receive on several occasions was when someone would say something to the effect, "There is something different about you. What is it? I want to know why you conduct yourself in the manner in which you do."

Do you realize that you are now an ambassador for Jesus Christ? You are the only "Bible" that some people will ever read. Will they get an accurate picture of biblical Christianity by observing you and examining how you treat other people, conduct your business affairs, and live your life?

Jesus encourages you with the following words,

> "You are the light of the world. A city set on a hill cannot be hidden; nor does anyone light a lamp and put it under a basket, but on the lampstand, and it gives light to all who are in the house. Let your light shine before men in such a way that they may see your good works, and glorify your Father who is in heaven." Matthew 5:14-16

Similarly, the apostle Paul stated:

> "so that you will prove yourselves to be blameless and innocent, children of God above reproach in the midst of a crooked and perverse generation, among whom you appear as lights in the world, holding fast the word of life...."
> Philippians 2:15-16

Bible Study. So, how do you become a brighter light in the world and more effectively allow the light of Christ to shine through you? The best source of information on this topic is the Bible.

If you followed my recommendation in the previous chapter and bought one of the study Bibles, then you have taken a great next step in your new spiritual journey. Now I have another recommendation for you: learn from one of the masters about how to study your Bible and apply it to your life. For more than 50 years, Dr. Howard Hendricks taught courses at Dallas Theological Seminary on how to study the Bible and how the seminary students could apply the teachings of the Bible to their lives. One of his former students, Dr. Charles Swindoll, a well-respected pastor, author, and radio Bible teacher, shares a story about how Dr. Hendricks' Bible study course impacted his life and ministry:

> "In early 1960, as I was finishing my first year at Dallas Theological Seminary; I took a course from Dr. Howard Hendricks that would mark my life and ministry forever. Day after day I listened to his presentation, then I would rush back to our little campus apartment stimulated with fresh excitement and plunge into the homework he assigned. As weeks turned into months, the fog that had surrounded the Scripture slowly began to lift. Those puzzling passages no longer seemed so intimidating. As bigger pieces fell into place, I felt increasingly more comfortable with the Word of God. I realize now that it was becoming a "lamp to my feet, and a light to my path" (Psalm 119:105).
>
> In today's terms, the Bible became "user friendly," thanks to this course that was destined to change my life. Dr. Hendricks convinced us that the Bible could be understood. Unfortunately, it often seems intimidating to the average person; it is a long book with lots of fine print and very little visual interest. He gave his students techniques that, when perfected by practice, opened up the Bible to us. Before that year had passed, the mystery dissolved into meaningful and reasonable truths. I soon discovered that my wife, Cynthia, and I were not merely talking about God's Book, we had started living by the Book." [2]

That is a powerful testimony from a godly man, who credits Dr. Hendricks' course for enriching his life and his ministry and starting his life on the path of living by the Bible. Dr. Hendricks and his son have now written a book entitled, *Living by the Book*, and produced a DVD training series and workbooks by the same title. [3] The DVD training series is an exceptional treasure:

"Join Dr. Howard G. Hendricks live as he shows you how to understand and apply God's Word for yourself. Millions around the world have been captivated by this brilliant teacher's highly energetic style, friendly manner, unforgettable illustrations, and laugh-out-loud humor. In these series of 25-minute sessions, Dr. Hendricks will walk you step-by-step through his signature model for self-study: Observation, Interpretation, Application. Your experience in Scripture will never be the same. And your life will be transformed as you begin Living by the Book!" [3]

I believe that you deserve the best teaching available on establishing good Bible study techniques. Dr. Hendricks' book and DVD series are the best I know. I believe that after you read *Living by the Book* and watch the DVD series that you will come to the same conclusion that I have: the money spent for the book and DVD series was a wise investment.

Dr. Hendricks provides an overview of the three-step approach that he has developed and used for decades:

"1. Observation. In this step, you ask and answer the question, *What do I see?* The moment you come to the Scriptures you ask, What are the facts? You assume the role of a biblical detective, looking for clues. No detail is trivial. That leads to the second step.

2. Interpretation. Here you ask and answer the question, *What does it mean?* Your quest is for meaning. Unfortunately, too much Bible study begins with interpretation, and furthermore, it usually ends there. But I'm going to show you that it does not begin there. Before you understand, you have to learn to see. Nor does it end there, because the third step is...

3. Application. Here you ask and answer the question, *How does it work?* Not, Does it work? People say they're going to make the Bible "relevant." But if the Bible is not already relevant, nothing you or I do will help. The Bible is relevant because it is revealed. It's always a return to reality. And for those who read it and heed it, it changes their lives." [4]

To expand on the steps in this method, Hendrickson explains that in the **observation step**, you first need to pay attention to the **terms** or words, especially those that are repeated in a passage, chapter, or book. He uses the example of the word *believe*, which is in 85 verses in the book of John. Obviously, this is an important word and deserves further investigation and study. Then consider the sentence **structure** of a passage. Consider the grammatical structure of a sentence, then the literary structure—is the sentence a statement or a question, does it provide background information or the main point?

In the observation phase it is also important to recognize the **literary form**. Is the passage a letter, poem, parable, allegory, or prophecy? To fully appreciate and understand a passage, specific rules or guidelines must be used for each type of literary form. The **atmosphere** surrounding the passage is important to consider. Placing yourself in the author's shoes in his environment will add richness and depth to your understanding of a passage.

In the **interpretation step**, ask and answer questions. For example, when you see the word *therefore* ask and answer the question, what is it "there for"? The more questions you ask about a passage the more digging you will have to do to answer them and gain valuable insight into what the author meant when he wrote it. Hendricks provides an interesting perspective on the answers to the questions you ask about a passage:

> "The answers to your questions will come directly from the observation process. That is why I say, the more time you spend in Observation, the less time you will need to spend in Interpretation and the more accurate will be your results. The less time you spend in Observation, the more time you will need to spend in Interpretation, and the less accurate will be your results." [5]

He then points out that after you have asked and answered your questions, then you need to put the passage back together—to integrate it back into the chapter or book. How does it fit with the rest and what does it add to the whole?

In the **application step**, the goal is to determine how does the passage and message work for you and how does it work for others. Of these two, the more important is to ask yourself, "what does this passage say to me?" How could or should it apply in my life? After answering these personal application questions, then you can consider how it may apply and benefit others. [6]

I believe the more you study the Bible, the more respect that you will have for it. It is the inspired Word of God. So, immerse yourself in Bible study and take advantage of the opportunity to have Dr. Howard Hendricks, as well as other godly biblical scholars, and most importantly, the Holy Spirit, help you get the most out of your study.

I view Bible study as a goal-oriented process. The goal is to increase my knowledge, understanding, and application of a specific passage, chapter, or book of the Bible. This is an extremely important part of spiritual growth. I like to start each day with a Bible study, during which I pray, read a portion of the Bible, think about and meditate on the passage, consult some trusted commentaries (e.g., *Bible Knowledge Commentary*) and compare my thoughts about the passage with scholars who have devoted their professional lives to the study of God's Word, and consider how the passage relates to me and my plans and activities for the day. As I pray, I typically ask the Holy Spirit to guide me in understanding, applying, and sharing God's Word. Being a goal-oriented person, the discipline required for my daily Bible study comes naturally for me.

Now I will introduce you to a use of the Bible that doesn't come as easily for me: daily devotionals. These are times that are less structured and less goal-oriented, but often still focus on the use of the Bible to facilitate spiritual growth. There are many passages in the Bible that can guide your thoughts, meditations, and prayers to God. With these it is important that you patiently wait and listen for His reply.

As you begin your daily devotionals, you may find that the book of Psalms is an excellent place to begin. Consider the following passages from Psalms and see if you agree that they will help focus your thoughts on God and how His Word can positively impact your life.

"How blessed is the man who does not walk in the counsel of the wicked, nor stand in the path of sinners, nor sit in the seat of scoffers! But his delight is in the law of the LORD, and in His law he meditates day and night. He will be like a tree firmly planted by the streams of water, which yields its fruit in its season and its leaf does not wither; and in whatever he does, he prospers." Psalm 1:1

"The LORD is my shepherd, I shall not want. He makes me lie down in green pastures; He leads me beside quiet waters. He restores my soul; He guides me in the paths of righteousness For His name's sake. Even though I walk through the valley of the shadow of death, I fear no evil, for You are with me; Your rod and Your staff, they comfort me. You prepare a table before me in the presence of my enemies; You have anointed my head with oil; My cup overflows. Surely goodness and lovingkindness will follow me all the days of my

life, And I will dwell in the house of the LORD forever."
Psalm 23:1-6

"This is the day which the LORD has made; Let us rejoice
and be glad in it." Psalm 118:24

What wonderful thoughts these are. Can you see how starting each day with thoughts such as these will help you put things that happen to you during the day in the proper perspective and enable you to rejoice in the fact that ultimately God is completely in control of everything? Along with this thought, add the words of the apostle Paul:

"And we know that God causes all things to work together for good to those who love God, to those who are called according to His purpose....For I am convinced that neither death, nor life, nor angels, nor principalities, nor things present, nor things to come, nor powers, nor height, nor depth, nor any other created thing, will be able to separate us from the love of God, which is in Christ Jesus our Lord."
Romans 8:28, 38-39

These are profound thoughts, which will have a tremendously positive effect on your life, if you will let them. Think about these and meditate on these during your daily devotionals.

Prayer. In regards to public prayers, this is an area in which I confess that it will be better for you to "do as I say, and not as I do." I am an introvert by nature and do not consider myself to be particularly verbally adept. I could go for days without talking to anyone. You may find it hard to believe that I have had a very successful sales career and do not like to talk. How could that be? Well, I am a very good listener, I have a tremendous respect for the power of questions in a sales presentation, and I have been blessed with a very good analytical mind so that I can analyze what a prospect says and usually reply in an appropriate, compelling manner. But these skills do not enable me to give the kind of impromptu, articulate public prayers that would glorify God in the manner in which I would like. So, I don't like to pray in public. However, I have been able to develop an effective private prayer life and communicate with God in ways that are very meaningful, to me at least.

Something that has helped me grow in my prayer life is to recognize and use different types of prayers. These are: Adoration, Confession, Thanksgiving, and Supplication, which can be represented by the acronym, "ACTS." [7]

Adoration is to worship or honor God.

> "... Let the name of God be blessed forever and ever, For wisdom and power belong to Him. It is He who changes the times and the epochs; He removes kings and establishes kings; He gives wisdom to wise men and knowledge to men of understanding. It is He who reveals the profound and hidden things; He knows what is in the darkness, and the light dwells with him. To You, O God of my fathers, I give thanks and praise...." Daniel 2:20-23

Other verses that express adoration for God include Psalm 19:1-3; 62:5-7; 100; 139:1-17, and Isaiah 40:12-14, 21-26. [7]

Confession is to admit that something that you have thought, said, and/or done is contrary to God's Word. Although it is certainly important to admit to your sins, it is even more important that you repent and turn from these sins.

> "If we say that we have no sin, we are deceiving ourselves and the truth is not in us. If we confess our sins, He is faithful and righteous to forgive us our sins and to cleanse us from all unrighteousness. If we say that we have not sinned, we make Him a liar and His word is not in us." 1 John 1:8-10

Other verses on the topic of confession include Psalm 32; 51; 139:23-24; Proverbs 28:13; and Luke 15:17-21. [8]

Thanksgiving is to express your thanks or gratitude to God.

"Rejoice always; pray without ceasing; in everything give thanks; for this is God's will for you in Christ Jesus." 1 Thessalonians 5:15

Additional verses that provide examples of prayers of thanksgiving include Daniel 6:10; Psalm 105:1; Ephesians 1:15-16; and Colossians 3:10. [8]

Supplication is to humbly and earnestly submit your requests to God.

"Be anxious for nothing, but in everything by prayer and supplication with thanksgiving let your requests be made known to God. And the peace of God, which surpasses all comprehension, will guard your hearts and your minds in Christ Jesus." Philippians 4:6-7

"Now Jabez called on the God of Israel, saying, "Oh that You would bless me indeed and enlarge my border, and that Your hand might be with me, and that You would keep me from harm that it may not pain me!" And God granted him what he requested." 1 Chronicles 4:10

The following verses are also examples of prayers of supplication: Genesis 18:23-32; Psalm 143:8-10; John 16:24; and 1 John 5:14-15. [8]

I will share one other comment about prayer. I constantly look for "TYL" moments. To me, TYL stands for "Thank You, Lord!" Whenever I see something magnificent, like a beautiful mountain scene, sunrise, or sunset, or have something happen that I think reflects God's grace, my prayer is simply, "Thank You, Lord!"

So, if you study the Bible and apply it to your life, have devotionals in which you meditate on God and His plan for your life, and develop a healthy prayer life, will these things change your life? Will others recognize changes and see that these are consistent with being a Christian? Yes, they will!

Jesus summarizes the distinctive of a Christian by saying,

"By this all men will know that you are My disciples, if you have love for one another." John 13:35

The apostle Paul added that Christians differ from non-Christians by faith, hope, and love. Petersen explains:

"**Faith**. The New Testament states again and again that the foundation of our faith is in the (person), Jesus Christ. "Let us fix our eyes on Jesus, the author and perfecter of our faith" (Hebrews 12:2) We "live by faith in the Son of God" (Galatians 2:20). Our faith is based on the conviction that Jesus is what He said He was, and that He will keep His promises.

Hope. Our hope is rooted in three facts about Jesus Christ. First there is the fact that *He was resurrected from the dead*. God "has given us new birth into a living hope through the resurrection of Jesus Christ from the dead" (1 Peter 1:3). Second, there is the fact that *He ascended* to the Father where He constantly defends our case. "We who have fled to take hold of the hope offered to us may be greatly encouraged. We have this hope as an anchor for the soul, firm and secure. It enters the inner sanctuary...where Jesus, who went before us, has entered on our behalf" (Hebrews 6:18-20). Third, there is the hope that *He will return*. We wait for the blessed hope—the glorious appearing of our great God and Savior, Jesus Christ" (Titus 2:13).

Love. "This is how we know what love is: Jesus Christ laid down his life for us" (1 John 3:16). "This is love: not that we loved God, but that he loved us and sent His Son as an atoning sacrifice" (1 John 4:10). Hence, Christian love has the death of Jesus Christ as its source." [9]

So, what else can you do to ensure that your light is shining before men in a way that brings glory to God? You can develop your creed and testimony.

Your Creed

In the previous chapter, I shared my personal creed with you and encouraged you to develop your own creed. I again encourage you to do so. This can help ensure that you have a biblically based compass to alert you when you may be getting too distracted by the distractions of this life. As you prepare to read and study the Bible, ask the Holy Spirit to point out verses that He wants to have special significance to you. I think you will be surprised and pleased how some of the verses become "highlighted" for you.

In your creed, select verses that will guide you in your relationship with God, your family, friends, and neighbors. Also, include verses that will guide you in your professional conduct and spiritual growth and obedience. Write these verses on a piece of paper and then state how each verse applies to you. Read and memorize these verses and you will be amazed at how these will begin to guide you in your daily life.

In addition to the verses I used in my creed, I have listed some additional verses, in no particular order, that have been meaningful to me over the years and perhaps some of these may be appropriate for you to include in your creed.

"Therefore if anyone is in Christ, he is a new creature; the old things passed away; behold, new things have come." 2 Corinthians 5:17

"Do you know not that you are a temple of God and that the Spirit of God dwells in you?" 1 Corinthians 3:16

"For we are His workmanship, created in Christ Jesus for good works, which God prepared beforehand so that we would walk in them." Ephesians 2:10

"But seek first His kingdom and His righteousness, and all these things will be added to you." Matthew 6:33

"Do not store up for yourselves treasures on earth, where moth and rust destroy, and where thieves break in and steal. But store up for yourselves treasures in heaven, where neither moth nor rust destroys, and where thieves do not break in or steal; for where your treasure is, there your heart will be also." Matthew 6:19-21

"For you formed my inward parts; You wove me in my mother's womb. I will give thanks to You, for I am fearfully and wonderfully made; Wonderful are Your works, and my soul knows it very well." Psalm 139:13-14

"Your eyes have seen my unformed substance; and in Your book were written the days that were ordained for me, when as yet there was not one of them." Psalm 139:16

"Make me know Your ways, O Lord; Teach me Your paths. Lead me in Your truth and teach me, For You are the God of my salvation; For You I wait all the day." Psalm 25:4-5

"He has told you, O man, what is good; and what does the Lord require of you but to do justice, to love kindness, and to walk humbly with your God." Micah 6:8

"so that you will walk in a manner worthy of the Lord, to please Him in all respects, bearing fruit in every good work and increasing in the knowledge of God." Colossians 1:10

"He who has My commandments and keeps them, he it is who loves Me; and he who loves Me shall be loved by My Father, and I will love him, and will disclose Myself to him." John 14:21

"Whether, then, you eat or drink or whatever you do, do all to the glory of God." 1 Corinthians 10:31

"Treat others the same way you want them to treat you." Luke 6:31

"Enjoy life with the woman whom you love all the days of your fleeting life which He has given to you under the sun; for this is your reward in life and in your toil in which you have labored under the sun." Ecclesiastes 9:9

"Instruct those who are rich in this present world not to be conceited or to fix their hope on the uncertainty of riches, but on God, who richly supplies us with all things to enjoy. Instruct them to do good, to be rich in good works, to be generous and ready to share, storing up for themselves the treasure of a good foundation for the future, so that they may take hold of that which is life indeed." 1 Timothy 6:17-19

"A new commandment I give to you, that you love one another, even as I have loved you, that you also love one another. By this all men will know that you are My disciples, if you have love for one another." John 13:34-35

"And He was saying to them, "The harvest in plentiful, but the laborers are few, therefore beseech the Lord of the harvest to send out laborers into His harvest." Luke 10:2

"No temptation has overtaken you but such is common to man; and God is faithful, who will not allow you to be tempted beyond what you are able, but with the temptation will provide the way of escape also, so that you will be able to endure it." 1 Corinthians 10:13

Your Testimony

As you grow in your faith and your relationship with God, Jesus, and the Holy Spirit, your life will change, for the better. People will notice and they will want to know what caused the changes—and you will want to share with them the Good News. As you are sharing with them, you may find that they do not want to believe in God or Jesus, and may argue and try to discredit the Bible. However, what they cannot discount is your own personal experience, so be ready and willing to share that with them.

To get started in preparing your testimony, consider the following recommendation:

"Take several moments to reflect on what your relationship with Jesus Christ means to you. Complete the statement, "Because Christ rose from the dead and lives in me, I...." Isn't this truly the greatest, most joyful news you could ever share with another person?" [10]

Now expand on these thoughts and think about what your life was like before you placed your faith in the gospel. Recall the circumstances that surrounded your decision. Finally, think about the changes that have taken place in your life since you accepted Jesus as your Savior. Now, put these thoughts in writing. Then read the draft of your testimony to your-self and time it. Ideally, it would be between two to four minutes. Now edit and refine the draft to ensure that it is accurate and concise.

Some recommendations on things to avoid in your testimony:

"1. Exaggeration.
2. Glittering generalities ("My life is wonderful now, totally full of joy and peace, and all my problems are gone").
3. Talking negatively about any particular church or denomination.
4. Religious lingo ("I was immediately born again and transformed into a new creation by exercising faith in the substitutionary atonement of Christ").
5. Too much detail.
6. Irrelevant material." [11]

Here are some things that would be good to consider including in your testimony:

"1. The three divisions: Before, How, After.
2. Exactly how he [you] received Christ, so that when he [you] finishes sharing, the listener will have a good idea of how he [or she] too, can receive Christ.
3. A Bible verse or two." [11]

The apostle Paul shares his testimony in Acts 22:3-21 and 26:4-23. As he was traveling from Jerusalem to Damascus a bright light appeared from heaven and he fell to the ground, heard Jesus talk directly to him, and was blinded for three days. He received his sight back when Jesus sent a believer to him to restore his sight and tell Paul that Jesus had chosen him to share the gospel with Gentiles (Acts 9:1-19). Now, that testimony has an incredible "wow" factor. When people hear about Paul's conversion, they are impressed.

If you think about assigning "wow" factors to testimonies, with Paul's at the extreme end of the scale in one direction, my testimony is at the extreme end of the scale in the opposite direction. Here is my testimony:

> "So how and when did I accept Jesus as my Savior? My experience was not like the apostle Paul, who saw a flash of light from heaven and heard Jesus speak to him. I did not see a flash of light or hear the voice of Jesus. In fact, I do not even remember the day or any events surrounding the time when I first placed my faith in Jesus.

What I do remember, however, is that at a very young age, I understood that I was adopted as an infant by Bill and Mildred Trayler, because they wanted me as their son. Even as a child, I clearly understood that they loved me unconditionally and often sacrificially, even though I did not know what the terms unconditional and sacrificial love meant.

I remember seeing how Dad loved and cared for Mom and our family and how Mom loved and respected Dad and our family. I remember that we went to church almost every Sunday and worshiped God.

Although Dad and Mom did not discuss religion or read the Bible routinely, I do remember when I was a child that they read John 3:16 to me, which says, "For God so loved the world, that He gave His only begotten Son, that whoever believes in Him shall not perish, but have eternal life." I had no trouble understanding that in addition to me being adopted into the Trayler family because Dad and Mom loved me, God loved me, too, and I was part of His heavenly family.

As I grew up, I wanted to express my love for Dad, Mom, and God by my obedience to them and my commitment to excellence. Consequently, I have earned many academic, athletic, and professional honors as a result. Certainly, there have been times when I have been disobedient and have not fully lived up to their expectations or my desire to be obedient to them. However, I have never seriously questioned or doubted Dad's, Mom's, or God's love for me. In fact, the more I have studied the Bible, the more I believe that God loves me. Furthermore, I know that when I die, I will spend eternity in heaven because Jesus loved me enough to die and pay the penalty of my sins and that He rose from the dead, according to the Scriptures. I also believe that God loves you and wants to have a personal, intimate relationship with you. May I share this good news with you?

So, now you can understand why I say that my testimony is at the opposite end of the spectrum from Paul's. As I have thought about my life and testimony over the years, I have often thought it would have been good to be able to say something like, "I was a scoundrel until I saw the flash of light from heaven and then everything in my life changed in an instant!" Well, that is just not the way it was for me. I have also even said "the sinner's prayer" just to make sure that I was a Christian and do you know what happened after I said the prayer? Absolutely nothing!

The more I have thought my life's experience, the more thankful I am that God blessed me with an adopted Dad and Mom who not only loved me, unconditionally and sacrificially, but demonstrated how I could live a life that would be pleasing to God. In fact, I think this is the model that God has in mind for you and me as parents. In the 62 years that Dad and Mom were married, I don't ever remember seeing or hearing them argue. I don't remember seeing Dad or Mom smoke or drink alcohol, although my sister told me that they did, before I came along.

Very rarely do I remember Dad saying anything bad about anyone else. I do remember Dad and Mom spending countless hours volunteering at church and in other organizations and activities to help others, often those who were less fortunate than us. Shortly after Dad died, I told a colleague about Dad and how much I respected him and how much I wish more people could have known him. She gave me a tremendous compliment by saying that "the apple does not fall far from the tree." It is still my desire to conduct my life in a manner that will be pleasing to both my earthly and my heavenly Father. Although I do not know your earthly father, I do know your heavenly Father, and I encourage you to live your life so that it will bring glory, honor, praise, and worship to Him!

I'll close this section with the following verse that relates to your testimony,

> "Who is there to harm you if you prove zealous for what is good? But even if you should suffer for the sake of righteousness, you are blessed. AND DO NOT FEAR THEIR INTIMIDATION, AND DO NOT BE TROUBLED, but sanctify Christ as Lord in your hearts, always being ready to make a defense to everyone who asks you to give an account for the hope that is in you, yet with gentleness and reverence." 1 Peter 3:15

Sharing the Gospel

Jesus commanded us to share the gospel:

> "And He said to them, "Go into all the world and preach the gospel to all creation." Mark 16:15

> "Seeing the people, He felt compassion for them, because they were distressed and dispirited like sheep without a

shepherd. Then He said to His disciples, "The harvest is plentiful, but the workers are few. Therefore beseech the Lord of the harvest to send out workers into His harvest." Matthew 9:36-38

Fortunately, Jesus doesn't command or "expect eloquence, just obedience" as we preach the gospel to all creation. [12]

Think about this: you know that God created all people in His image, He loves each person, and He wants to have a personal relationship with each person even though everyone is a sinner. He willingly sacrificed His own Son to pay the penalty of each person's sins and whenever anyone places their faith in the gospel, God does amazing things for them now and forever. Why not share this Good News with everyone you know?

Billy Graham, one of the most well-known Christian evangelists of our time, summarizes the reasons that we don't share the good news of the gospel at every opportunity by saying that "fear and lack of know-how" prevent most Christians from sharing their faith. [13] If either of these factors is preventing you from sharing your faith, you will be happy to know that Bill Bright, another famous evangelist, wrote about ways to overcome fear and lack of know-how in the book entitled *Witnessing Without Fear: How to Share Your Faith With Confidence.* Regarding this book, Billy Graham wrote,

> "In *Witnessing Without Fear*, Bill Bright effectively addresses both [fear and lack of know-how], and shows how you can overcome fear to share your faith with confidence." [13]

Bill Bright's book *Witnessing Without Fear: How to Share Your Faith With Confidence* (as well as his many other publications), is an exceptionally valuable book that shares his insight and experience that have helped him and thousands of others lead millions of people to faith in Jesus Christ. For example, how do you respond when someone tells you that religion is a personal and private matter? Here is how Bill handled this objection with a U.S. Senator:

> "My religion is personal and private, and I don't want to talk about it."
>
> He was one of America's great statesmen—a Christian—and I had just shared with him a plan for world evangelism. As we talked about involving a thousand key Christian leaders in the effort, his statement startled me.

"You're a Christian, aren't you?" I asked him.

"Yes, I am," he replied. "But I'm not a religious fanatic."

I've heard this logic several times, and it grieves me every time I hear it. It grieved me that day as I heard this fine gentleman rationalize his passive faith.

I prodded gently: "Did it ever occur to you that it cost Jesus Christ His life so that you could say you're a Christian?"

He thought a moment, but didn't respond.

"And it cost the disciples their lives," I continued. "Millions of Christians throughout the centuries have suffered and many have died as martyrs to get the message of love and forgiveness to you. Now do you really believe that your faith in Christ is personal and private and that you shouldn't talk about it?"

"No, sir," the man sighed. "I'm wrong. Tell me what I can do about it."

Without even realizing it, this Christian leader had fallen for one of Satan's favorite lines: that one's faith should be a very private thing, something you just don't talk about. As a result, his witness for Christ was next to nil. He had held in his possession the greatest news ever announced, but up to that point he had refused to share it." [14]

Powerful stories like this and personal experience gained through decades of sharing the gospel fill the pages of this book. I highly recommend that you add this book (as well as other books by Bill Bright and other materials developed by Campus Crusade for Christ International (http://www.ccci.org/) to your personal library and learn from him how to more effectively share the Good News.

In his book, Bright highlights "five compelling reasons why Christians should witness as a way of life." [15] These are:

"1. Christ has given a clear command to every Christian."

> "And He said to them, "Go into all the world and preach the gospel to all creation." Mark 16:15

"2. Men and women are lost without Jesus Christ."

"Jesus said to him, "I am the way, the truth, and the life; no one comes to the Father but through Me." John 14:6

"And there is salvation in no one else; for there is no other name under heaven that has been given among men by which we must be saved." Acts 4:12

"3. Rather than being 'not interested,' the people of the world are truly hungry for the gospel."

"Do not say, 'There are yet four months, and then comes the harvest'? Behold, I say to you, lift up your eyes and look on the fields, that they are white for harvest." John 4:35-38

"4. We Christians have in our possession the greatest gift available to mankind: the greatest news ever announced."

"Christ is risen! We serve a living Savior, who not only lives within us in all His resurrection power but has assured us of eternal life. He died on the cross in our place for our sin, then rose from the dead. We have direct fellowship with God through Jesus Christ. And this fellowship, this peace, this gift of eternal life, is available to all who receive Him." [16]

"But as many as received Him, to them He gave the right to become children of God, even to those who believe in His name." John 1:12

"For God so loved the world, that He gave His only begotten Son, that whoever believes in Him shall not perish, but have eternal life." John 3:16

"For He rescued us from the domain of darkness, and transferred us to the kingdom of His beloved Son." Colossians 1:13-14

"5. The love of Jesus Christ for us, and our love for Him, compels us to share Him with others." [15]

"He who has My commandments and keeps them is the one who loves Me; and he who loves Me will be loved by My Father, and I will love him and will disclose Myself to him." John 14:21

As a side note, the mark of personal integrity is when one's speech and actions are consistent. Bill Bright died in 2003 but left behind an incredible legacy that attests to his integrity. His passion was to share the love and claims of Jesus Christ with every person on earth. In 1951, he and his wife founded Campus Crusade for Christ, which became the world's largest Christian ministry. It serves people in more than 190 countries, with a staff of more than 26,000 people and more than 225,00 trained volunteers.

From the initial focus on college students, the ministry has grown to include more than 60 niche ministries. He wrote a booklet entitled *The Four Spiritual Laws* in 1956, which has since been printed in more than 200 languages and distributed to more than 2.5 billion people. In 1979, he commissioned the *Jesus* film that documents the life of Jesus Christ. It has been translated into more than 786 languages, shown in more than 234 countries, and viewed by more than 5.1 billion people! Bill Bright was a man of integrity who joyfully and obediently served our Lord Jesus Christ! [17]

Now that you have a better understanding of Bill Bright's commitment to evangelism and know about Jesus' commandment for you to share the gospel, where and how do you start? You probably have many questions, some of which will not be answered in this section or in this book. So, let's just focus on the basics. In Chapter I, I provided 10 verses as Rules for the Game and God's plan for your salvation. Although I believe that these 10 verses can be used very effectively by the Holy Spirit in bringing someone to salvation (i.e., placing their faith in the gospel), there are other very effective, proven approaches. As indicated above, the most widely used of these is *The Four Spiritual Laws,* developed and used extensively by Bill Bright and the Campus Crusade for Christ team. These spiritual laws and their supporting verses are provided below for your consideration:

Law 1. "GOD **LOVES** YOU, AND OFFERS A WONDERFUL **PLAN** FOR YOUR LIFE." Just as there are physical laws that govern the physical universe, so are there spiritual laws which govern your relationship with God.

God's Love: "For God so loved the world, that He gave His only begotten Son, that whoever believes in Him should not perish, but have eternal life." John 3:16

God's Plan: "I came that they might have life, and might have it abundantly." (that it might be full and meaningful) John 10:10

"Why is it that most people are not experiencing the abundant life? Because...

Law 2. "MAN IS **SINFUL** AND **SEPARATED** FROM GOD. THEREFORE, HE CANNOT KNOW AND EXPERIENCE GOD'S LOVE AND PLAN FOR HIS LIFE."

Man Is Sinful: "For all have sinned and fall short of the glory of God." Romans 3:23

Man Is Separated: "For the wages of sin is death" (spiritual separation from God) Romans 6:23

"... God is holy and man is sinful. A great gulf separates the two....man is continually trying to reach God and the abundant life through his own efforts, such as a good life, philosophy, or religion.

The third law explains the only way to bridge this gulf...

Law 3. "JESUS CHRIST IS GOD'S **ONLY** PROVISION FOR MAN'S SIN. THROUGH HIM YOU CAN KNOW AND EXPERIENCE GOD'S LOVE AND PLAN FOR YOUR LIFE."

He Died in Our Place: "But God demonstrates His own love toward us, in that while we were yet sinners, Christ died for us." Romans 5:8

He Rose From the Dead: "Christ died for our sins...He was buried...He was raised on the third day, according to the Scriptures...He appeared to Peter, then to the twelve. After that He appeared to more than five hundred..." 1 Corinthians 15:3-6

He is the Only Way to God: "Jesus said to him, 'I am the way, and the truth, and the life; no one comes to the Father but through Me.'" John 14:6

"...God has bridged the gulf which separates us from Him by sending His Son, Jesus Christ, to die on the cross in our place to pay the penalty of our sins."

"It is not enough just to know these three laws..."

Law 4. WE MUST INDIVIDUALLY RECEIVE JESUS CHRIST AS SAVIOR AND LORD; THEN WE CAN KNOW AND EXPEIRIENCE GOD'S LOVE AND PLAN FOR OUR LIVES.

We Must Receive Christ: "But as many as received Him, to them He gave the right to become children of God, even to those who believe in His name." John 1:12

We Receive Christ Through Faith: "For by grace you have been saved through faith; and that not of yourselves, it is the gift of God; not as a result of works, that on one should boast." Ephesians 2:8-9

When We Receive Christ, We Experience a New Birth: "Now there was a man of the Pharisees, named Nicodemus, a ruler of the Jews; this man came to Jesus by night and said to Him, "Rabbi, we know that You have come from God as a teacher; for no one can do these signs that You do unless God is with him." Jesus answered and said to him, "Truly, truly, I say to you, unless one is born again he cannot see the kingdom of God." Nicodemus said to Him, "How can a man be born when he is old? He cannot enter a second time into his mother's womb and be born, can he?" Jesus answered, "Truly, truly, I say to you, unless one is born of water and the Spirit he cannot enter into the kingdom of God. That which is born of the flesh is flesh, and that which is born of the Spirit is spirit. Do not be alarmed that I said to you, 'You must be born again.' The wind blows where it wishes and you hear the sound of it, but do not know where it comes from and where it is going; so is everyone who is born of the Spirit." John 3:1-8

We Receive Christ by Personal Invitation: (Christ is speaking): "Behold, I stand at the door and knock; if any one hears My voice and opens the door, I will come in to him." Revelation 3:20

"Receiving Christ involves turning to God from self (repentance) and trusting Christ to come into our lives to forgive our sins and to make us the kind of people He wants us to be. Just to agree intellectually that Jesus Christ is the Son of God and that He died on the cross for our sins is not enough. Nor is it enough to have an emotional experience. We receive Jesus Christ by faith, as an act of the will....The following explains how you can receive Christ:

YOU CAN RECEIVE CHRIST RIGHT NOW BY FAITH THROUGH PRAYER
(Prayer is talking with God)

God knows your heart and is not so concerned with your words as He is with the attitude of your heart. The following is a suggested prayer:

'Lord Jesus, I need You. Thank you for dying on the cross for my sins. I open the door of my life and receive You as my Savior and Lord. Thank You for forgiving my sins and giving me eternal life. Take control of the throne of my life. Make me the kind of person You want me to be.'

Does this prayer express the desire of your heart?

If it does, pray this prayer right now, and Christ will come into your life, as He promised." [18]

I have a couple of comments for your consideration. First, notice that the prayer indicates the person receives Jesus as Savior *and* Lord. I have presented a different perspective on this, which is supported by biblical scholars, who like Bill Bright have devoted their lives to sharing the gospel. I believe and have indicated in this book that salvation comes when a person places their faith in the gospel and accepts Jesus as their Savior. Ideally, and subsequently, through the guidance of the Holy Spirit the person grows spiritually and then comes to the point of asking Jesus to become the Lord of his or her life. In other words, I believe that salvation is a "point-in-time" event that occurs when one places their faith in the gospel and that asking Jesus to be Lord of a person's life (lordship) is part of the spiritual growth and maturing process. This view is different than that expressed in the prayer above which indicates that salvation and lordship both occur at the moment of conversion. Ask God to provide His guidance to you on this topic.

The second point is that I completely agree with the statement that, "God knows your heart and is not so concerned with your words as He is with the attitude of your heart." This will remove some pressure from you thinking that there is a magical prayer that must be prayed and if any words are left out then the prayer does not result in salvation. This is not true. The most important factor is that the person places their intellectual, emotional, and volitional faith in the gospel of Jesus Christ. [19, 20]

Also, to help put sharing the gospel in proper perspective, consider these words by Bill Bright and Dawson Trotman, founders of Campus Crusade for Christ and The Navigators, respectively. These men and the members of their respective organizations have led literally millions of people to salvation. So, when they speak, listen:

"Success in witnessing is simply taking the initiative to share Christ in the power of the Holy Spirit, and leaving the results to God." [21]

"Dawson Trotman, founder of The Navigators, used to pray that God would use him in the life of every person he met. That is a good request to emulate. If coming to Christ is a process, why not help every person we meet to move just one step closer to Christ? Some people are only a step away and it would be our joy to assist in the birth. Others are farther out, but the step we help them take would be just as significant." [22]

It is not up to you to close the sale of salvation. It is your job to share what you know to be true-the gospel—and what you believe to be true—how placing your faith in the gospel has changed your life. So, God's plan for your involvement in a person's life may be to help him or her take another step closer to placing their faith in the gospel. Examples of steps that a person may take, suggesting that he or she is moving in the right direction, include:

If the God of the Bible exists, the Bible says He loves me. That would be incredible! I wonder if it is really true?

The logic and order of the universe and of living beings does suggest intelligent design, maybe God does exist.

The prophetic accuracy of the Bible cannot be explained by chance. Fulfilled prophecy certainly supports the assertion that the Bible is divinely inspired.

The historical evidence does indicate that Jesus lived, died, and rose from the dead. The Bible says that He died to pay the penalty for my sin.

I will admit that I have committed sins and that these probably separate me from God.

I know that someday I will die and that if there is a heaven and a hell
I would prefer to spend eternity in heaven.

Jesus said He provides the only way for me to spend eternity in
heaven. I believe Him and am ready to place my faith and eternal
destiny in Him.

The Old Testament prophet Isaiah puts this in this process perspective,

> "For as the rain and the snow come down from heaven, and
> do not return there without watering the earth and making it
> bear and sprout, and furnishing seed to the sower and bread
> to the eater; So will My word be which goes forth from
> My mouth; It will not return to Me empty, without accom-
> plishing what I desire, and without succeeding in the matter
> for which I sent it." Isaiah 55:10-11

The New Testament apostle (and evangelist) Paul also commented on
the evangelism process by stating,

> "I planted, Apollos watered, but God was causing the
> growth." 1 Corinthians 3:2

Just remember, when the time is right, the Holy Spirit will take care
of the conviction, closing the sale, and conversion. When that happens,
then join the angels in heaven rejoicing that another person has accepted
God's gift of salvation and will spend eternity in heaven!

For more information about how to effectively share the gospel, the
following three organizations are ones which I have personally benefitted
from and consequently highly recommend:

Campus Crusade for Christ Started by Bill and Vonette Bright on the
campus of UCLA in 1951. It now has ministries in more than 190
countries, with more than 25,000 staff members. [24] Ministry
areas of focus include high school, college, grad students and fac-

ulty, family, sports, and marketplace. The website is http://www. ccci.org/

The Navigators Founded in 1933 by Dawson Trotman when he began sharing the gospel with sailors in the U.S. Navy. It now has ministries in more than 100 countries and more than 4,000 staff members. [25] The Navigators focus on "small group studies and one-to-one relationships focused on discipleship." [26] The website is http://www.navigators.org/portal/page/portal/publicbuild.

Ravi Zacharias International Ministries (RZIM) Founded in 1984 by Ravi Zacharias. The RZIM Team focuses on four areas of ministry: evangelism, apologetics, spiritual disciplines, and training. [27] The website is http://www.rzim.org/default.aspx.

As you are fulfilling Jesus' command to "preach the gospel to all creation," be sure to share the love of God with everyone you meet and when necessary, use words! In other words, live your life so that people will see the love of God for them manifested through your life and will be drawn to God.

Making Disciples

Jesus also commanded us to make disciples, who are committed followers of Jesus.

> "Go therefore and make disciples of all the nations, baptizing them in the name of the Father and the Son and the Holy Spirit, teaching them to observe all that I commanded you; and lo, I am with you always, even to the end of the age." Matthew 28:19-20

I want to strongly emphasize *if you recently accepted Jesus as your Savior, you are not ready or prepared to make disciples.* Regardless of your chronological age, you are a spiritual babe. You have a lot of growing to do before you can effectively disciple others. Ideally, you will identify a mature Christian (of your same gender) who will come alongside you and help you grow and mature spiritually. This could be someone at the church you attend or someone involved in ministries such as Campus Crusade for Christ, The Navigators, RZIM, or other biblically based organizations.

If you are not fortunate enough to find someone to serve as your mentor or disciple maker, then buy, read, study, and apply the lessons of Christopher Adsit's book, *Personal Disciple-Making: A Step-by-Step Guide for Leading a Christian From New Birth to Maturity*. In fact, this book is so good that even if you do have a mentor disciple maker, get the book anyway and use it as a guide. As Dr. Howard Hendricks stated, Adsit's book is "The most comprehensive, practical approach to disciplemaking I've seen." [28]

Adsit defines a disciple and disciplemaking as

"A disciple is a person-in-process who is eager to learn and apply the truths that Jesus Christ teaches him, which will result in ever-deepening commitments to a Christ-like lifestyle." [29]

"Disciplemaking is seeking to fulfill the imperative of the Great Commission by making a conscientious effort to help people move toward spiritual maturity—drawing on the power and direction of the Holy Spirit, utilizing the resources of the local church, and fully employing the gifts, talents, and skills acquired over the years." [30]

The apostle John indicated that there are four levels of spiritual growth in Christians: infants, children, adolescents, and adults.

Infants: "I am writing to you, little children, because your sins have been forgiven you for His name's sake." 1 John 2:12

Children: "I have written to you, children, because you know the Father." 1 John 2:13

Adolescents: "I am writing to you, young men, because you have overcome the evil one....I have written to you, young men, because you are strong, and the word of God abides in you, and you have overcome the evil one." 1 John 2:13b-14b

Adults: "I am writing to you, fathers, because you know Him who has been from the beginning." 1 John 2:13a

Adsit summarizes some of the scriptural references to each of these levels of spiritual maturity:

Infants:
> "They are helpless, and need much care and protection (Luke 2:12, 16; Acts 7:19)
>
> They crave spiritual nourishment (1 Peter 2:2)
>
> But they are not yet able to handle meat and solid food (1 Corinthians 3:1-3; Hebrews 5:11-14)"

Children:
> [They are] "relatively helpless and in need of parents' protection (Matthew 2:13-16)
>
> [They are] sometimes capable of making strategic contributions (John 6:90)
>
> [They are] still deficient in spiritual understanding (1 Corinthians 14:20)"

Adolescents:
> "They are urged to maintain humility and proper respect for their elders (1 Peter 5:5-6)
>
> They are urged to keep their lusts and passions in check (2 Timothy 2:22, Titus 2:4-6)
>
> They are gaining strength and experiencing spiritual victory (1 John 2:14)"

Adults:
> Spiritually mature (Ephesians 4:13-14)
>
> Trainer (Ephesians 6:4; 1 Corinthians 4:14-15)
>
> Encourager (2 Corinthians 1:3-7, 7:4; Ephesians 4:29; 1 Thessalonians 2:11-12) [31]

Just as these Christians in these four phases of spiritual growth have different characteristics, they have different needs and motivators, which require different roles for disciple makers. These are summarized below in Table 9-1.

Table 9-1. Growth Stages and Needs of Christians (adapted from Adsit) [32]

Factors	Baby	Child	Adolescent	Adult
Main Need	Protection, love, basic knowledge	Consistent, strong guidance	Strength, experience, responsibility	Leadership ability, consistent self-discipline
Key Motivator	His spiritual vacuum	His disciple	Himself	God and the ministry
Disciple Maker's Role	"Mother" to nourish and cherish	Teacher to equip for service	Coach to help him develop strength and responsibility	Peer to motivate for the long haul

Adsit also provides an overview of spiritual growth principles. These are summarized below, along with an abbreviated listing of Scripture references:

"1. We grow as we give Christ top priority in our lives. (Matthew 6:33; John 15:5-7; Galatians 2:20)
2. We grow as we feed upon God's Word. (Joshua 1:8; Matthew 4:4; 2 Timothy 3:16-17)
3. We grow as we pray. (Matthew 7:7-8; John 14:13-14; Hebrews 4:16)
4. We grow as we fellowship. (Hebrews 10:24,25; John 17:21; 1 John 4:7)
5. We grow as we witness. (Proverbs 11:30; Matthew 5:16; 1 Peter 3:15)
6. Growth takes time. (Luke 3:23; Acts 7:23-34; Galatians 1:15-2:1)
7. Adversity facilitates growth. (Psalm 119:71; Romans 5:3-5; James 1:2-4)
8. God sovereignly oversees our growth. (Psalm 119:75; Romans 8:28; 1 Corinthians 10:13) [33]

So you can see, you have a lot of growing to do. So grow and then come alongside new believers to help them grow in their obedience and service to Jesus. You have an exciting spiritual journey ahead of you as you strive to become conformed to the image of Jesus Christ (Romans 8:29). To put your exciting journey in proper perspective, in addition to the opportunity that you have to serve Jesus and become more like Him in this life, recall God's prophetic promises for the future.

Think about your role in the rapture, the Bema Judgment and rewards you can receive, the possibility of co-reigning with Jesus in the Millennial

Kingdom, and entering the Eternal State and having intimate fellowship with God, Jesus, and the Holy Spirit FOREVER! With this perspective, you can more fully appreciate and look forward to your EXCITING SPIRITUAL JOURNEY, because God loves you and He is in control!

> "For God so loved the world, that He gave His only begotten Son, that whoever believes in Him shall not perish, but have eternal life." John 3:16

References:

1. Bright, Bill. *Witnessing Without Fear: How to Share Your Faith With Confidence*. San Bernardino, CA: Here's Life Publishers, 1987, p. 45.
2. Swindoll, Charles R. "Foreword" in Hendricks, Howard G and William D Hendricks. *Living by the Book*. Chicago, IL: Moody Press, 1991, p. 5.
3. Living By The Book website. http://www.livingbythebook.net/.
4. Hendricks, Howard G and William D Hendricks. *Living by the Book*. Chicago, IL: Moody Press, 1991,pp. 35-36.
5. _____. p. 39.
6. _____. pp. 36-42
7. Adsit, Christopher B. *Personal Disciple-Making: A Step-by-Step Guide for Leading a Christian From New Birth to Maturity*. San Bernardino, CA: Here's Life Publishers, 1988, p. 252.
8. _____. p. 253.
9. Petersen, Jim. *Living Proof: Sharing the Gospel Naturally*. Colorado Springs, CO, 3rd Printing, 1990, pp. 94-95.
10. Bright, Bill. *Witnessing Without Fear*. p. 51.
11. Adsit, Christopher B. *Personal Disciple-Making*. p. 281.
12. Bright, Bill. *Witnessing Without Fear*. p. 44.
13. Graham, Billy. "Foreword" in Bright, Bill. *Witnessing Without Fear*. p. 7.
14. Bright, Bill. *Witnessing Without Fear*. pp. 53-54.
15. _____. pp. 37-51.
16. _____. p. 45.
17. Bill Bright Memorial website: http://billbright.ccci.org/public/
18. Bright, Bill. *Witnessing Without Fear*. pp. 122-130.
19. Petersen, Jim. *Living Proof*. p. 202.
20. Bright, Bill. *Witnessing Without Fear*. p. 82.
21. _____. p. 67.
22. Petersen, Jim. *Living Proof*. p. 149.
23. _____. p. 154.
24. Campus Crusade for Christ website. http://www.ccci.org/about-us/index.htm.

25. The Navigators website. http://www.navigators.org/us/aboutus.
26. _____. http://www.navigators.org/us/.
27. Ravi Zacharias International Ministries website. http://www.rzim.org/aboutus.aspx.
28. Hendricks, Howard. Cover of Adsit, Christopher B. Christopher B. *Personal Disciple-Making*. Front and back cover of book.
29. Adsit, Christopher B. *Personal Disciple-Making*. p. 35.
30. _____. p. 40.
31. _____. pp. 62-70.
32. _____. pp. 73-75.
33. _____. pp. 196-198.

Epilogue

Those Who Have Never
Heard the Gospel

As you grow and mature in your faith in Jesus and as you share your faith with others, questions will arise for which you don't have the answers. So, where do you go to get the answers? The ultimate source of authority for a Christian must be the Bible. It provides answers to and/or sufficient insight into the answers to the vast majority of life's questions. Having said that, however, there are some questions that the Bible does not address directly or provide sufficient insight into so that we confidently know God's thoughts on some topics.

The subject of this epilogue: "What about those who have never heard the gospel?" is an example of this. Sooner or later you and some of those you share the gospel with will ask about the eternal destiny of unborn children who have been aborted or miscarried, of children who die before they can understand the gospel, and of adults living in remote parts of the earth who have never heard of Jesus or the gospel. So, let's examine these questions in more detail and look to the Bible for answers, or at least insight into the answers.

Let's first review related topics in which biblical teaching is very clear:

Sinfulness of man:

> "Therefore, just as through one man [Adam] sin entered into this world, and death through sin, and so death spread to all men, because all sinned." Romans 5:12

"Behold, I was brought forth in iniquity, and in sin my mother conceived me." Psalm 51:5

"for all have sinned and fall short of the glory of God." Romans 3:23

Penalty of man's sinfulness is death (separation from God), but Jesus paid this debt:

"For the wages of sin is death, but the free gift of God is eternal life in Christ Jesus our Lord." Romans 6:21

"So then as through one transgression there resulted in condemnation to all men, even so through one act of righteousness there resulted justification of life to all men." Romans 5:18

Faith in Jesus is required to obtain eternal life:

"Jesus said to him, "I am the way, and the truth, and the life; no one comes to the Father but through Me." John 14:6

"And there is salvation in no one else; for there is no other name under heaven that has been given among men by which we must be saved." Acts 4:12

"For by grace you have been saved through faith; and that not of yourselves, it is the gift of God." Ephesians 2:8

These are clear and direct biblical teachings, which are part of what I referred to in Chapter 1 as the Rules of the Game of life. Assuming that you have read the rest of this book, you understand that God has the right to establish the rules of the game and that these rules are fair and just. However, it is legitimate to ask, "What about those who are not yet old enough (the unborn and young children) to understand the rules so that they can "play" in the game of life?" Similarly, it is fair to ask, "What about those who are playing their game of life on another field, such as in the jungle of Africa, where no one has told them about these rules of the game of life?" Does God still hold these people accountable to the same rules as He does for us?

These are very good questions that are not directly answered in the Bible. Nevertheless, they deserve our most diligent efforts to answer them in a manner that is consistent with biblical principles and teaching. However, before proceeding, it is very important to heed the warnings given by two highly respected biblical scholars, Charles Ryrie and Wayne Grudem. Ryrie warns about extending our theological system (i.e., our understanding of God as provided by the Bible) into areas in which the Bible does not directly address:

> "In a word, the limitations of a theological system must coincide with the limitations of biblical revelation. In an effort to present a complete system, theologians are often tempted to fill in the gaps in the biblical evidence with logic or implications that may not be warranted.

> Logic and implications do have their appropriate place. God's revelation is orderly and rational, so logic has a proper place in the scientific investigation of that revelation. When words are put together in sentences, those sentences take on implications that the theologian must try to understand.

> However, when logic is used to create truth, as it were, then the theologian will be guilty of pushing his system beyond the limitations of biblical truth. Sometimes this is motivated by the desire to answer questions that the Scripture does not answer. In such cases (and there are a number of crucial ones in the Bible) the best answer is silence, not clever logic, or almost invisible implications, or wishful sentimentality. Examples of particularly tempting areas include sovereignty and responsibility, the extent of the atonement, and the salvation of infants who die." [1]

Grudem reinforces Ryrie's warning by concisely stating,

> "Where Scripture is silent, it is unwise for us to make definitive pronouncements." [2]

The Unborn

The Bible does indicate that an unborn child is known and loved by God.

"For You formed my inward parts; You wove me in my mother's womb. I will give thanks to You, for I am fearfully and wonderfully made; Wonderful are Your works, And my soul knows it very well.... Your eyes have seen my unformed substance; And in Your book were all written The days that were ordained for me, When as yet there was not one of them." Psalm 139:13-14, 16

The life of an unborn child has the same value to God as that of the mother and the taking of the life of an unborn child is considered murder by God. Under the Old Testament's Levitical Law, the death penalty was given to one guilty of causing an unborn child to die.

"If men struggle with each other and strike a woman with child so that she gives birth prematurely, yet there is no injury, he shall surely be fined as the woman's husband may demand of him, and he shall pay as the judges decide. But if there is any further injury, then you shall appoint as a penalty life for life." Exodus 21:22-23

Commenting on these verses, *The Bible Knowledge Commentary* adds additional insight into the biblical view of the "humanness" of an unborn child.

"If...a pregnant woman delivered her child prematurely as a result of a blow, but both were otherwise uninjured, the guilty party was to pay compensation determined by the woman's husband and the court. However, if there was injury to the expectant mother or her child, then the assailant was to be penalized in proportion to the nature of severity of the injury. While unintentional life-taking was usually not a capital offense (cf. vv 12-13), here it clearly was. Also the unborn child is viewed in this passage as just as much a human being as its mother; the abortion of a fetus [unborn child] was considered murder." [3]

Shannon cites additional verses to further substantiate the fact that God regards conception as the moment that a human life ("personhood") begins (Job 10:8-12; 31:15 and Psalm 139:13-16. Additionally, several verses indicate that God has a plan for the life of the child, even before it is born (Genesis 25:23; Isaiah 49:1-5; Jeremiah 1:4-5; and Galatians 1:15-16) Finally, several verses indicate that the child has emotions (Luke 1:41-45; Genesis 25:22; and Hosea 12.3). [4] He concludes, and I agree,

> "The Bible overwhelmingly argues for the personhood of the prenatal child, while denouncing the horrible murder of unborn humans (cf. Exodus 21:22-23). When all the facts are in, abortion may have been legalized by the Supreme Court, but it cannot be viewed as anything less than a direct assault on the moral law of God." [5]

Related to the idea that God has a plan for each unborn child, Grudem highlights an interesting point on how God acted in an unusual way in the life of John the Baptist while he was still in his mother's womb:

> "Yet it is certainly possible for God to bring regeneration (that is, new spiritual life) to an infant even before he or she is born. This was true of John the Baptist, for the angel Gabriel, before John was born, said, "He will be filled with the Holy Spirit, *even from his mother's womb*" (Luke 1:15). We might say that John the Baptist was "born again" before he was born! There is a similar example in Psalm 22:10: David says, "Since my mother bore me you have been my God." It is clear, therefore, that God is able to save infants in an unusual way, apart from their hearing and understanding the gospel, by bringing regeneration to them very early, sometimes even before birth. This regeneration is probably also followed at once by a nascent, intuitive awareness of God and trust in him at an extremely early age, but this is something we simply cannot understand.

> We must, however, affirm very clearly that this is not the usual way for God to save people. Salvation usually occurs when someone hears and understands the gospel and then places trust in Christ. But in unusual cases like John the Baptist, God brought salvation before this understanding. And this leads us to conclude that it certainly is possible that God would also do this where he knows the infant will die before hearing the gospel." [2]

In spite of the two examples cited above in the "pre-birth" lives of John the Baptist and David, the Bible does not address the eternal destiny of unborn children who die as a result of miscarriage or abortion, either directly or indirectly, in sufficient detail to confidently know their eternal destiny. Consequently, I will rely on God's wisdom, mercy, grace, and justice to righteously determine the eternal destiny of these unborn humans. I encourage you to do the same.

Children

What about children who die before they are old enough to understand the gospel and make a decision on whether or not to place their faith in Christ? This is sometimes referred to as reaching the "age of accountability." [6] The Bible does provide some insight into the possibility that children of believing parents will go to heaven when they die.

The best support of this conclusion is found in Second Samuel 2. David, the king of Israel, had an adulterous relationship with Bathsheba that resulted in a son being born to them. God told David, through the prophet Nathan, that as a result of his sin the baby would die. David repented of his sin and asked God to spare the life of his son. God forgave David's sin but told him that his infant son would die. The infant died one week after his birth.

> "Then it happened on the seventh day that the child died. And the servants of David were afraid to tell him that the child was dead, for they said, "Behold while the child was still alive, we spoke to him and he did not listen to our voice. How then can we tell him that the child is dead, since he might do himself harm! But when David saw that his servants were whispering together, David perceived that the child was dead; so David said to his servants, "Is the child dead?" And they said, "He is dead." So David arose from the ground, washed, anointed himself, and changed his clothes; and he came into the house of the LORD and worshiped. Then he came to his own house, and when he requested, they set food before him and he ate. Then his servants said to him, "What is this thing that you have done? While the child was alive, you fasted and wept; but when the child died, you arose and ate food." He said, "While the child was still alive, I fasted and wept; for I said 'Who knows, the LORD may be gracious to me, that the child may live.' "But now he has died; why should I fast? Can I bring him back again? **I will go to him**, but he will not return to me." 2 Samuel 12:18-23 [emphasis added by me]

Most biblical scholars agree that the phrase, "I will go to him," indicated that David had faith that his son was in heaven and that he would join his son in heaven when he died. [2, 6, 7, 8]

In addition to the example of David's infant son, Grudem provides several examples of God acting in unusual ways to protect children of believers. He cites the following passages: Gen. 7:1; cf. Heb. 11:7; Josh. 2:18; Ps. 103:17; John 4:53; Acts 2:39; 11:14; 16:31; 18:8; 1 Cor. 1:16; 7:14; Titus 1:6; cf. Matt. 18:10, 14 and states,

> "These passages do not show that God automatically saves the children of all believers (for we all know of children of godly parents who have grown up and rejected the Lord, and Scripture also gives such examples as Esau and Absalom), but they do indicate that God's ordinary pattern, the "normal" or expected way in which he acts, is to bring the children of believers to himself. With regard to believers' children who die very young, we have no reason to think that it would be otherwise." [2]

Grudem concludes:

> "[David] had confidence that he would see his infant son again when he died. This can only imply that he would be with his son in the presence of the Lord forever. This passage, together with the others mentioned above, should be of similar assurance to all believers who have lost children in their infancy, that they will one day see them again in the glory of the heavenly kingdom.
>
> Regarding the children of **unbelievers** who die at a very early age Scripture is silent. We simply must leave that matter in the hands of God and trust Him to be both just and merciful. If they are saved, it will not be on the basis of any merit of their own or any innocence that we might presume that they have. If they are saved, it will be on the basis of Christ's redeeming work; and their regeneration, like that of John the Baptist before he was born, will be by God's mercy and grace. Salvation is always because of His mercy, not because of our merits (see Rom. 9:14-18). Scripture does not allow us to say more than that." [2]

Adults Living in Primitive Societies or Where the Gospel Is Not Taught

The term *heathen* is frequently used to refer to those people living in primitive societies in which the gospel has never been taught. [9] In this section, the term *heathen* will be used to refer to those who have never heard the gospel of Jesus Christ, regardless of whether they live in a primitive or non-primitive society.

It is estimated that by the end of the 20th century, approximately half of the world's 5 billion people had never heard the gospel. [9] So what is their eternal destiny? Some Christians propose that if the heathen respond to God's general revelation and place their faith in God, as they know Him through His creation, that they will be saved and spend eternity in heaven. [9] I do not find either the arguments used or the Scriptures used to support this view to be convincing.

I am convinced, however, that if someone is drawn to God through general revelation (Psalm 19:1, 50:6; Romans 1:20), that God will reward those who seek Him (Jeremiah 29:13; Hebrews 11:6). [10] Evans points out that God could do this by (a) sending an evangelist to preach the gospel to him, (b) supernaturally appearing to him and preaching the gospel directly to him, or (c) applying another dispensation to him. [11]

The last comment regarding applying another dispensation to the heathen deserves more consideration. Do you remember that I indicated my views on biblical prophecy could be described as "dispensational, pre-tribulational, and premillennial"? To refresh your memory, a dispensation is God's way of dealing with certain people at a certain time in history that brings a different responsibility to man in dealing with or relating to God. For example, in the Old Testament times, since Jesus had not lived, died, and risen from the dead, salvation was obtained through faith in God, not in the gospel. However, after Jesus' death and resurrection, God implemented a new dispensation (the church age) in which faith in the gospel is required for salvation.

Although we currently live under the church age dispensation, it is possible (but certainly not required) that God could also have a different dispensation operational for heathens, who have never heard the gospel. If so, such a dispensation could require a heathen to place his/her faith in God, just as the Old Testament believers did. Furthermore, it is possible that God may have different dispensations active today for the unborn and children of believers and unbelievers who die before the age of accountability. Different dispensations simultaneously operational would be consistent with several different passages that indicate that God does not want any to perish

> "The Lord is not slow about His promise, as some count slowness, but is patient toward you, not wishing for any to perish but for all to come to repentance." 2 Peter 3:9

"For I have no pleasure in the death of anyone who dies," declares the Lord GOD. "Therefore, repent and live." Ezekiel 18:32

Our Responsibility
To the Unborn:

Consider what the world would be like if all people followed biblical principles. Among the positive changes, there would be no rape, no incest, no adultery, and no fornication (sexual relations outside of the marital relationship). The only time abortion would be considered would be in the very rare instances in which the life of the mother was threatened by the pregnancy. In these cases, then the expectant mother and the father, along with their pastor, would seek God's guidance through the Holy Spirit in each individual case. This is a wonderful example of "God knows best" and if we would follow His guidance, most of today's problems would disappear or resolve themselves!

Unfortunately, that is not the world that we live in today. So, what should we do to address the eternal destiny of the unborn? Here are my recommendations for your consideration:

1. We should recognize the sanctity of all human life, especially the unborn and know that it is God's *desired will* that an unborn child not be aborted.
2. Pray that God would lead us in ways to educate those around us about the sanctity of human life.
3. Follow up on God's direction and lovingly communicate God's truth to the people in such a way that it would bring glory to God and hopefully change our societal and cultural views and practices. After all, "on demand" abortion is really not about choice or reproductive rights; it is about personal responsibility, accountability, and protecting the life of the unborn.
4. Share the gospel with those who have not accepted Jesus as their Savior so that we can help individuals and our society turn to God and live godly lives.
5. Support (through our prayers, our finances, and our volunteer work) agencies and organizations that provide education about God's Word, abstinence programs to the unwed, crisis pregnancy intervention, pre-natal health care, foster care, and adoption services.

6. Use all legislative and legal means to end "on demand" abortion. [12]
7. If you know someone who has an abortion, try to share with them God's perspective on abortion and if they are receptive, reassure them of God's love for them and His willingness to forgive their sin of ending the life of their unborn baby. The following verses may be appropriate:

"The LORD is compassionate and gracious, Slow to anger and abounding in lovingkindness. He will not always strive with us, Nor will He keep His anger forever. He has not dealt with us according to our sins, Nor rewarded us according to our iniquities. For as high as the heavens are above the earth, So great is His lovingkindness toward those who fear Him. As far as the east is from the west, So far has He removed our transgressions from us." Psalm 103:8-12

"If we confess our sins, He is faithful and righteous to forgive us our sins and to cleanse us from all unrighteousness." 1 John 1:9

To Children:

What can you do to help ensure that children will go to heaven if they die at a young age? There are many things that you can do and some of these are listed below:

1. Personally sharing the gospel with newlyweds, expectant parents, and the parents of small children. Then help them to teach their children about Jesus and the gospel. Can you imagine what it would be like to know that you were involved in leading a child to Jesus who would become the next great evangelist of our time?
2. Actively support the children's ministries of your church with your prayers, finances, and volunteer efforts.
3. Actively support the evangelistic and discipling ministries of organizations that specialize in Christian educational materials for children.
4. Actively support foster care agencies and orphanages through your prayer, finances, and volunteer efforts.

5. Support the outreach ministries at your church that focus on children, both in the U.S. and other countries.

To Adults Who Have Not Heard the Gospel:

Based upon the biblical knowledge that we have, the only certain way that someone can be assured of eternal life is by placing their faith in the gospel of Jesus Christ. Consequently, our goal should be to be obedient in every way that we can to fulfill Jesus' command to preach the gospel to all people (Mark 16:14). This includes:

1. Personally sharing the gospel with those you come in contact with. You may find out that you are the next "Bill Bright" or the next "Billy Graham" or maybe one of the people you lead to Christ will be the next great evangelist of our time.
2. Actively support the missions outreach ministries of your church with your prayers, finances, and volunteer efforts.
3. Actively support the evangelistic and discipling ministries of organizations such as Campus Crusade for Christ, The Navigators, and RZIM with your prayers, finances, and volunteer efforts.

And He said to them, "Go into all the world and preach the gospel to all creation." Mark 16:14

My prayer is that this book will be a blessing to you so that you may be a blessing to others and bring glory, honor, praise, and worship to God!

References:

1. Ryrie, Charles. C. *Basic Theology: A Popular Systematic Guide to Understanding Biblical Truth*. Chicago, Ill.: Moody Press, 1999, p. 18.
2. Grudem, Wayne. *Systematic Theology: An Introduction to Bible Doctrine*. (Electronic version, Copyright 1997, 2004 Wayne Grudem and John Hughes; published by Bits & Bytes, Inc., Whitefish, MT. Print version: Leicester, Great Britain: Inter-Varsity Press and Grand Rapids, MI: Zondervan Publishing House, 1994, p. 499.
3. Walvoord, J. F., Zuck, R. B., & Dallas Theological Seminary. (1983-c1985). *The Bible Knowledge Commentary: An Exposition of the Scriptures* (2:202). Wheaton, IL: Victor, 1985. p. 1,141.
4. Shannon, Bill. "When Life is Reduced to a Choice: Opposing Abortion While Reaching Out to Hurting Women." in MacArthur, John. *Right Thinking in a*

World Gone Wrong: A Biblical Response to Today's Most Controversial Issues. Eugene, Oregon: Harvest House Publishers, 2009, p. 81.

5. _____. p. 82.

6. Geisler, Norman L. *Baker Encyclopedia of Christian Apologetics*. Grand Rapids, MI: Baker Book House, 1999, p. 362.

7. Evans, Tony. *Totally Saved: Understanding, Experiencing and Enjoying the Greatness of Your Salvation*. Chicago, IL: Moody Press, 2002, p. 362.

8. Ryrie, C. C. *Ryrie Study Bible: New American Standard Bible, 1995 update*. Chicago: Moody Press, 1994, p. 496.

9. Geisler, Norman L. *Baker Encyclopedia of Christian Apologetics*. p. 301.

10. Evans, Tony. *Totally Saved*. P. 359.

11. _____. pp. 359-360.

12. Shannon, Bill. "When Life is Reduced to a Choice: Opposing Abortion While Reaching Out to Hurting Women." in MacArthur, John. *Right Thinking in a World Gone Wrong*. p. 85.

Subject Index

Gingrich, Newt. *To Save America*. "From the book *To Save America* by Newt Gingrich. Copyright©2010. Published by Regnery Publishing, Inc. All rights reserved. Reprinted by special permission of Regnery Publishing Inc., Washinton, D.C."

Grudem, Wayne. *Systematic Theology*: "Taken from Systematic Theology by WAYNE A. GRUDEM. Copyright © 1994 by Wayne Grudem. Used by permission of Zondervan. WWW.ZONDERVAN.COM.)

Grudem, Wayne. *Systematic Theology: An Introduction to Bible Doctrine*. (Electronic version, Copyright 1997, 2004 Wayne Grudem and John Hughes; published by Bits & Bytes, Inc., Whitefish, MT. Print version: Leicester, Great Britain: Inter-Varsity Press and Grand Rapids, MI: Zondervan Publishing House, 1994. Used by permission.

Jacob, Stanley W. and Clarice Ashworth Francone. Structure and Function in Man. Jacob and Francone "This illustration was published in *Structure and Function in Man.*, Jacob, Stanley W. and Clarice Ashworth Francone, Page 19, Copyright W.B. Saunders Company, (1970)" Used by permission.

Muncaster, Ralph O. *Examine the Evidence*: "Permission to use copyrighted material granted by Dr. Ralph O. Muncaster."

O'Reilly, Bill. *Culture Warrior*. "From CULTURE WARRIOR by Bill O'Reilly, copyright © 2006 by Bill O'Reilly. Used by permission of Broadway Books, a division of Random House, Inc."

Ortberg, John. *When the Game Is Over*: "Taken from When the Game Is Over, It all Goes Back in the Box by JOHN ORTBERG. Copyright © 2007 by John Ortberg. Used by permission of Zondervan. WWW. ZONDERVAN.COM."

Petersen, Jim. Living Proof. *"Living Proof*, by Jim Petersen, copyright 1988. Used by permission of NavPress, all rights reserved. www.navpress.com"

Philips, J.B. Map of the Roman Empire. http://www.ccel.org/bible/phillips/JBPlillips.htm. Used by permission.

Ryrie, Charles C. *Basic Theology*. Wheaton, IL: Victor Books, 1988. Used by permission.

Ryrie, Charles C. *Basic Theology: A Popular Systematic Guide to Understanding Biblical Truth*. Chicago, IL: Moody Press, 1999.

Wall, Joe L. *Going for the Gold: Reward and Loss at the Judgment of Believers*. Chicago, IL: Moody Press, 1991.

Walvoord, John. *The Prophecy Knowledge Handbook*. "©1990 John Walvoord. *The Prophecy Knowledge Handbook* (now titled *Every*

Prophecy of the Bible) published by David C. Cook. Publisher permission required to reproduce. All rights reserved."

About the Author

Richard Trayler earned a magna cum laude Bachelor of Science Degree from Texas A & M University, a Master of Science Degree from the University of Washington, and a Master of Christian Leadership Degree from Western Conservative Baptist Seminary (at the Phoenix, Arizona campus, then named Western Seminary, Phoenix, now named Phoenix Seminary). His early professional career focused on the clinical practice of exercise physiology in cardiology and cardiac rehabilitation settings. For the past 29 years he has enjoyed a very successful career focusing on sales of medical equipment as a representative, manager, and executive.

While serving as chief operating officer and subsequently as vice president of international operations and new market development for CardioDynamics, he traveled extensively in the U.S. and in more than 40 countries. During his travels, he saw thousands of people who do not know about biblical Christianity or Jesus. His goal in writing this book is to share what he knows to be true and what he believes to be true about biblical Christianity and the gospel of Jesus Christ so that more people may do as he has done and place their faith and eternal destiny in the gospel of Jesus Christ.

Subject Index